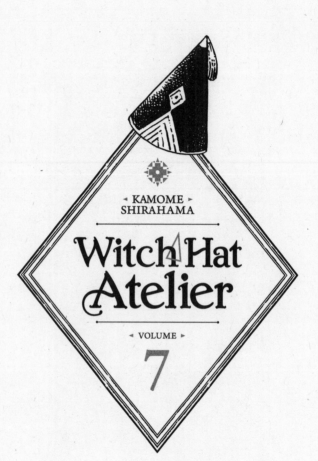

KAMOME
SHIRAHAMA

Witch Hat
Atelier

VOLUME

7

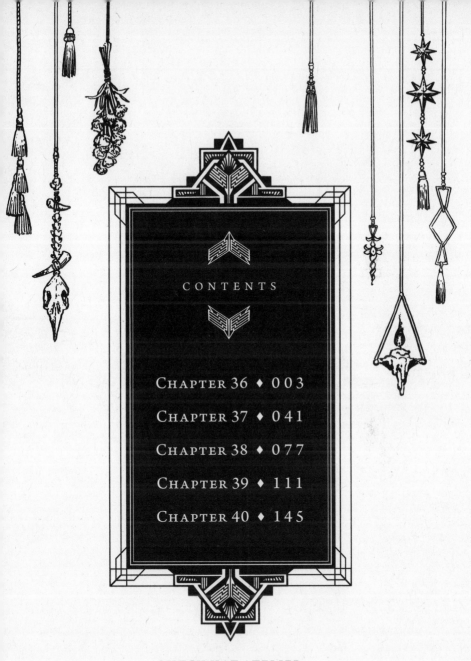

CONTENTS

CHAPTER 36 ♦ 003

CHAPTER 37 ♦ 041

CHAPTER 38 ♦ 077

CHAPTER 39 ♦ 111

CHAPTER 40 ♦ 145

WITCH HAT ATELIER

♦

KAMOME
SHIRAHAMA

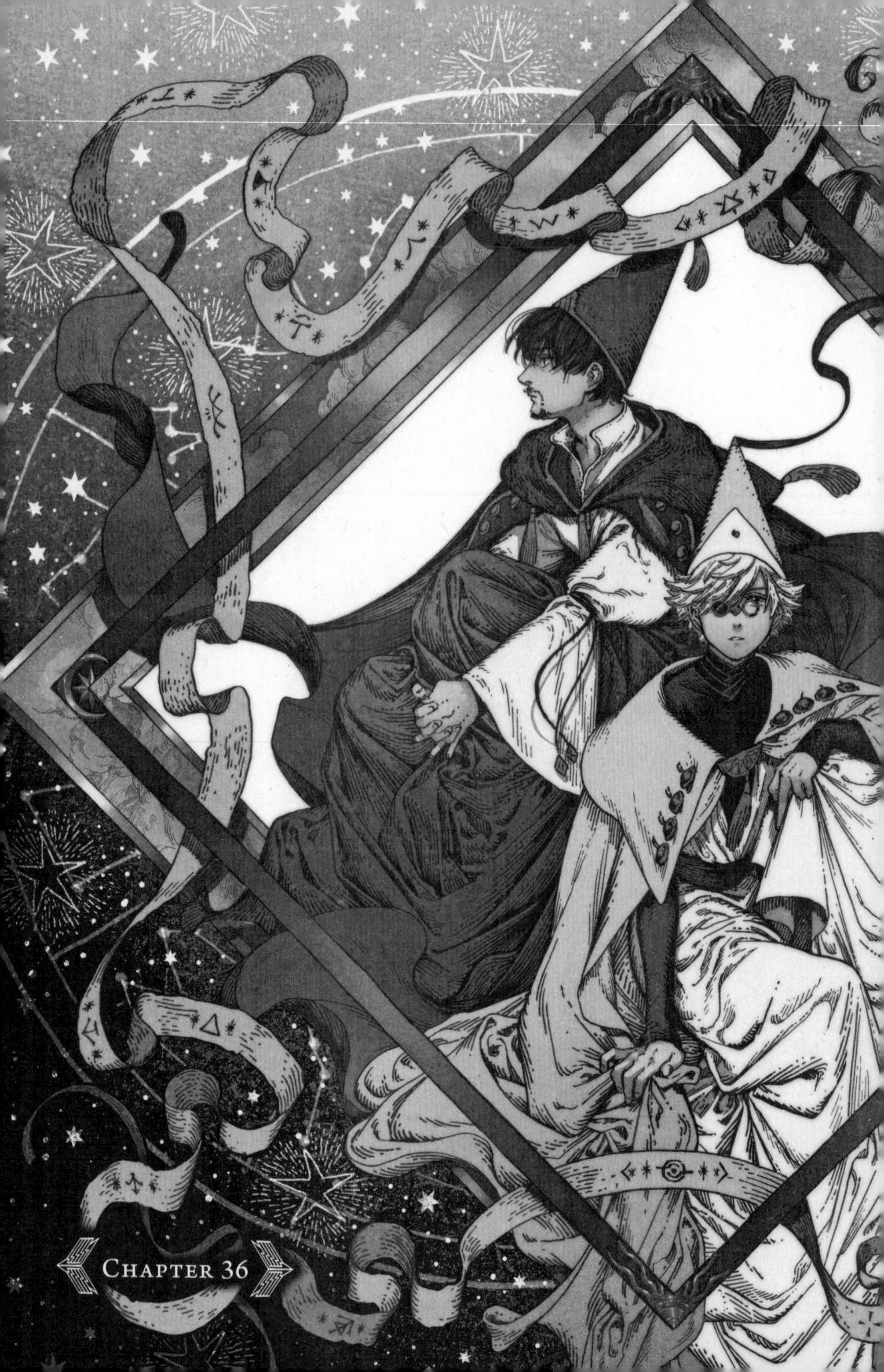
Chapter 36

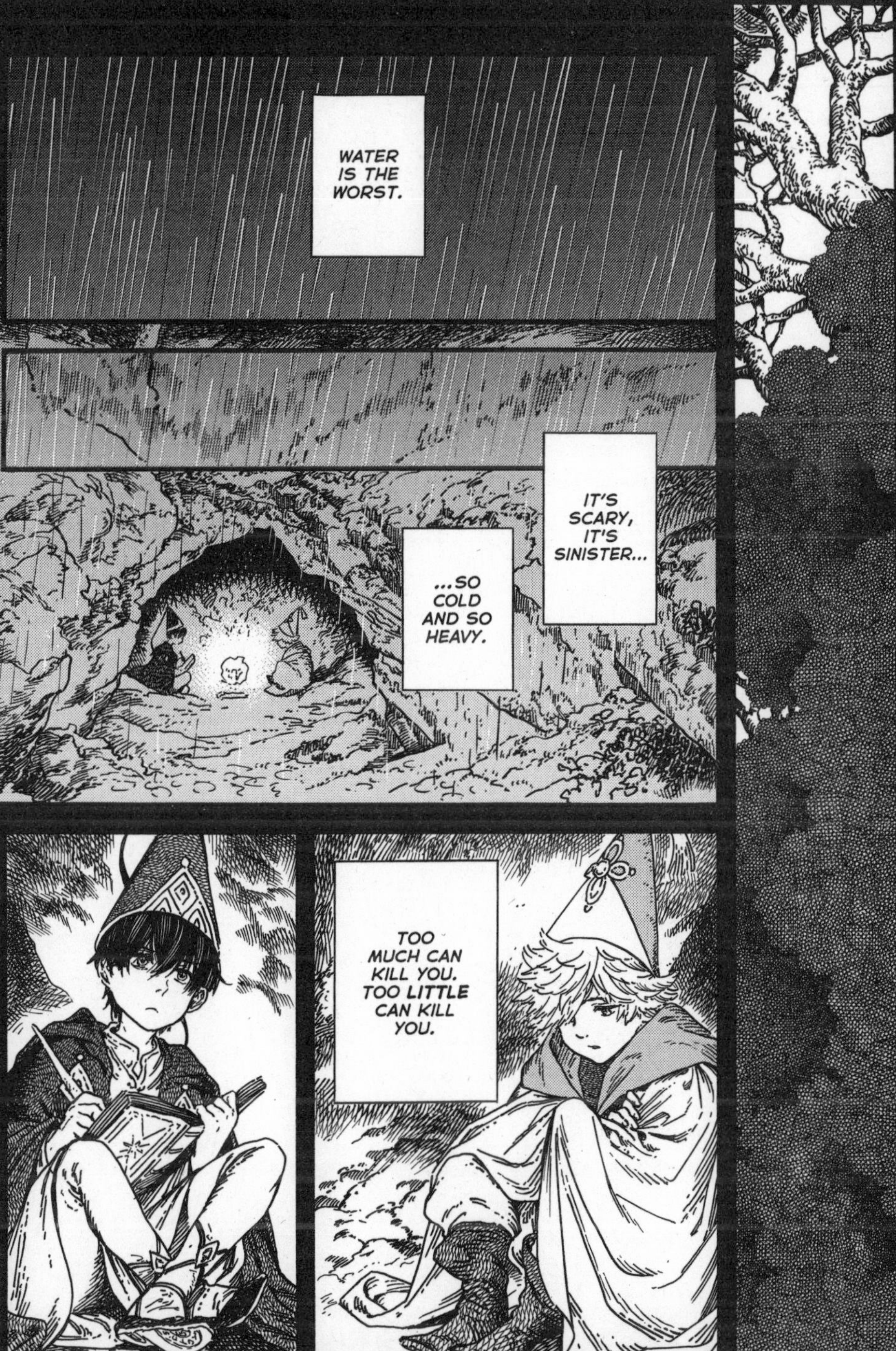
WATER IS THE WORST.
IT'S SCARY, IT'S SINISTER...
...SO COLD AND SO HEAVY.
TOO MUCH CAN KILL YOU. TOO **LITTLE** CAN KILL YOU.

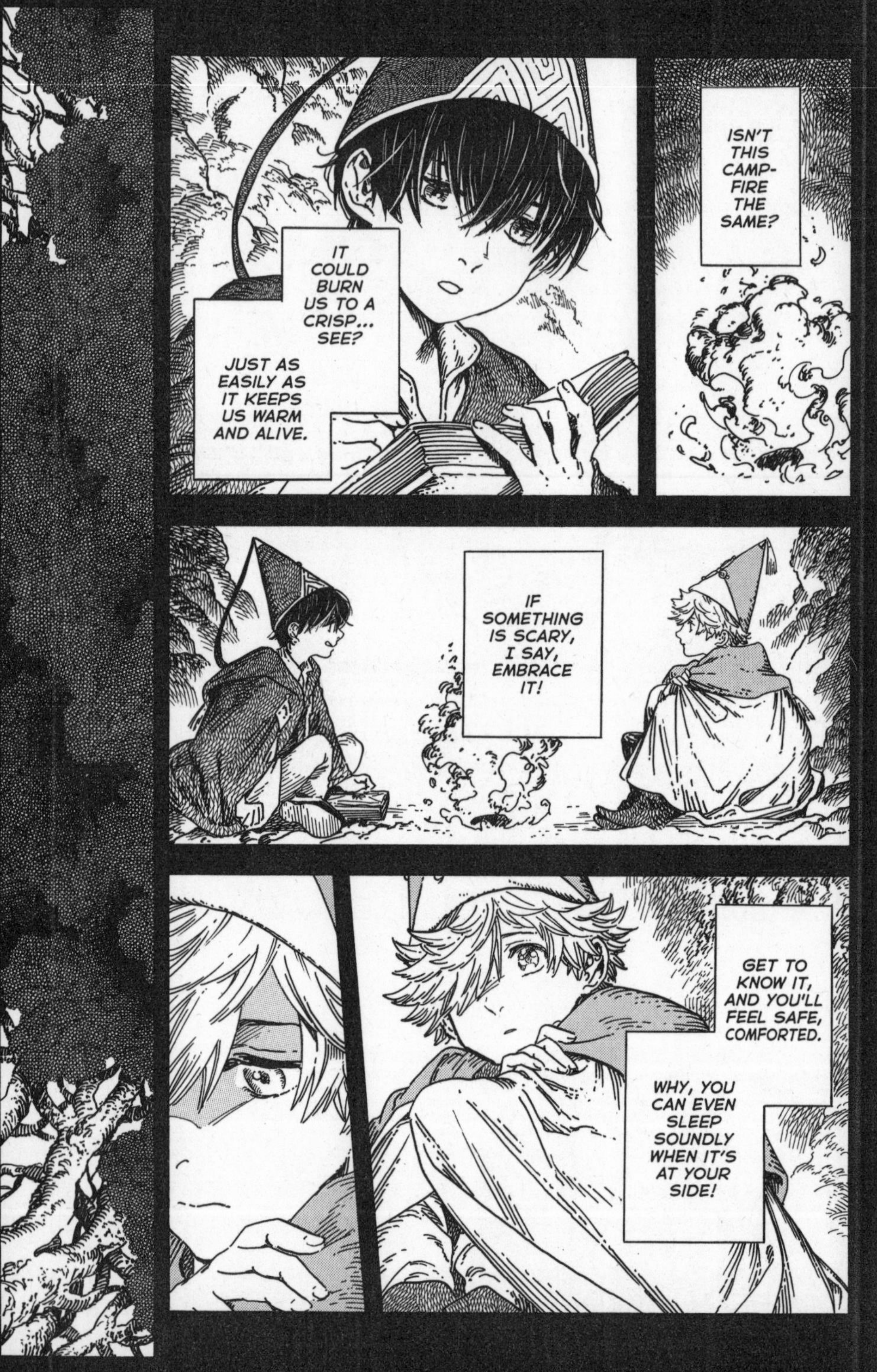
ISN'T THIS CAMP-FIRE THE SAME?
IT COULD BURN US TO A CRISP... SEE?
JUST AS EASILY AS IT KEEPS US WARM AND ALIVE.
IF SOMETHING IS SCARY, I SAY, EMBRACE IT!
GET TO KNOW IT, AND YOU'LL FEEL SAFE, COMFORTED.
WHY, YOU CAN EVEN SLEEP SOUNDLY WHEN IT'S AT YOUR SIDE!

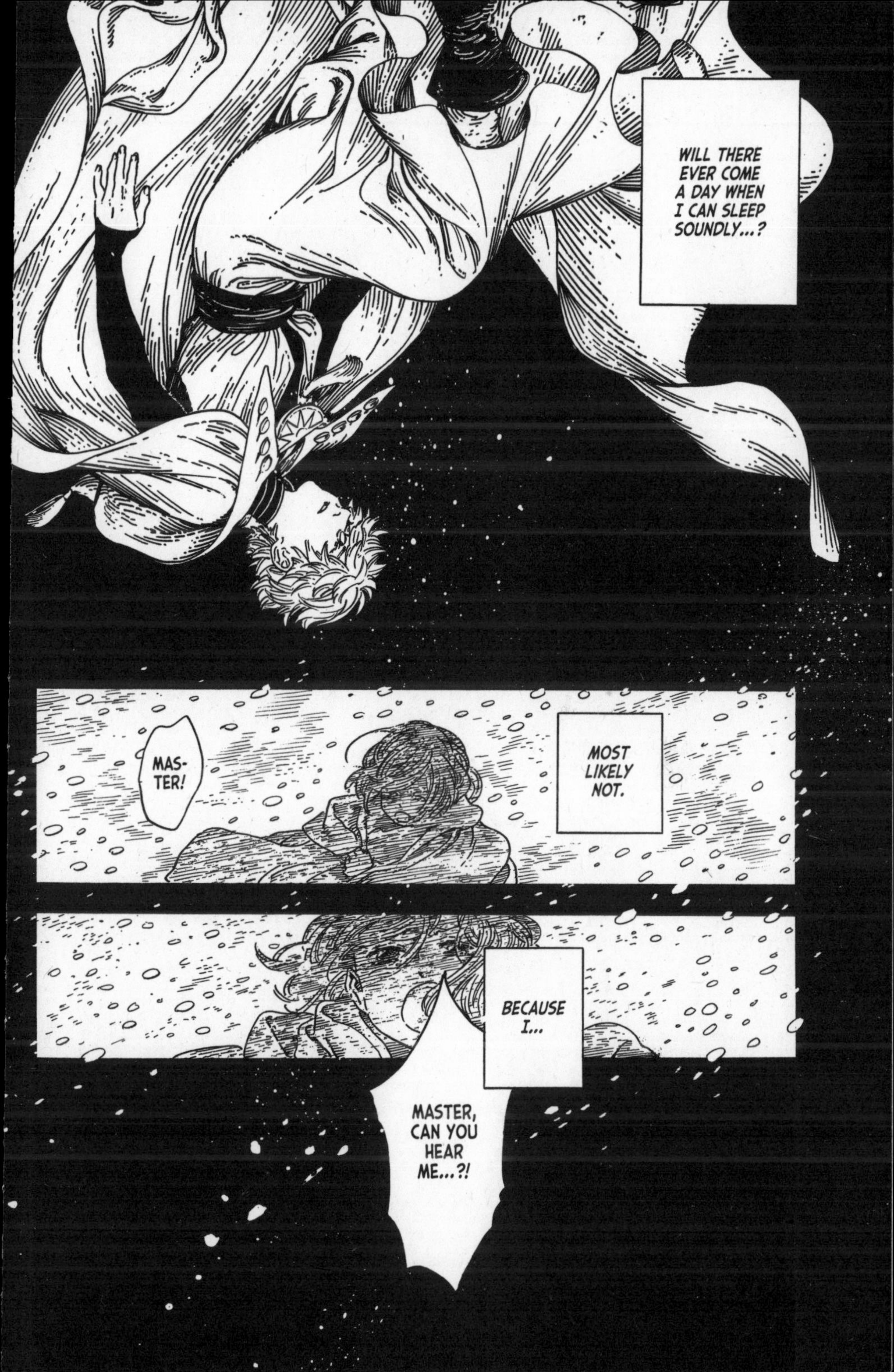
WILL THERE EVER COME A DAY WHEN I CAN SLEEP SOUNDLY...?
MOST LIKELY NOT.
MAS-TER!
BECAUSE I...
MASTER, CAN YOU HEAR ME...?!

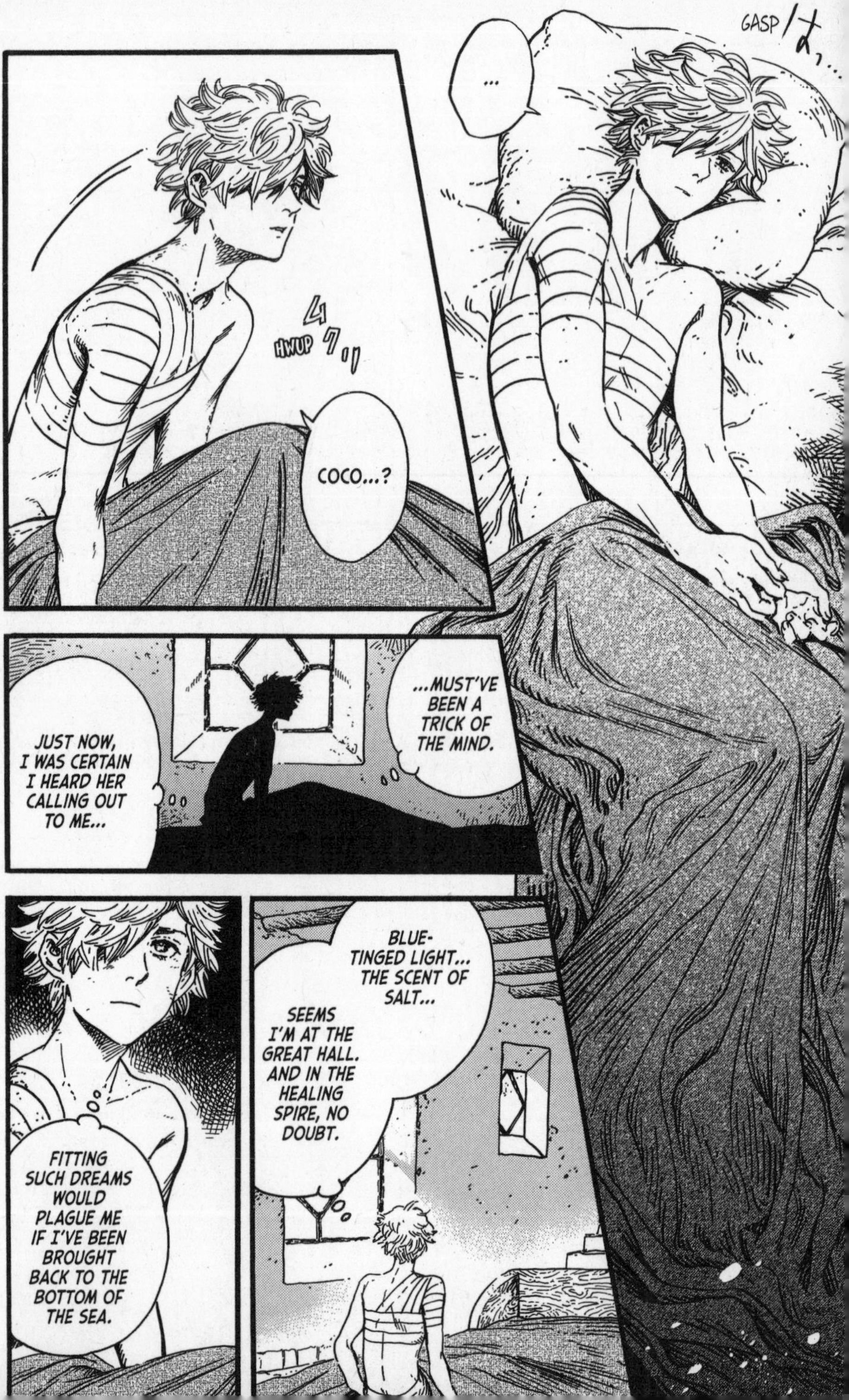
GASP
...
HWUP
COCO...?
...MUST'VE BEEN A TRICK OF THE MIND.
JUST NOW, I WAS CERTAIN I HEARD HER CALLING OUT TO ME...
BLUE-TINGED LIGHT... THE SCENT OF SALT...
SEEMS I'M AT THE GREAT HALL. AND IN THE HEALING SPIRE, NO DOUBT.
FITTING SUCH DREAMS WOULD PLAGUE ME IF I'VE BEEN BROUGHT BACK TO THE BOTTOM OF THE SEA.

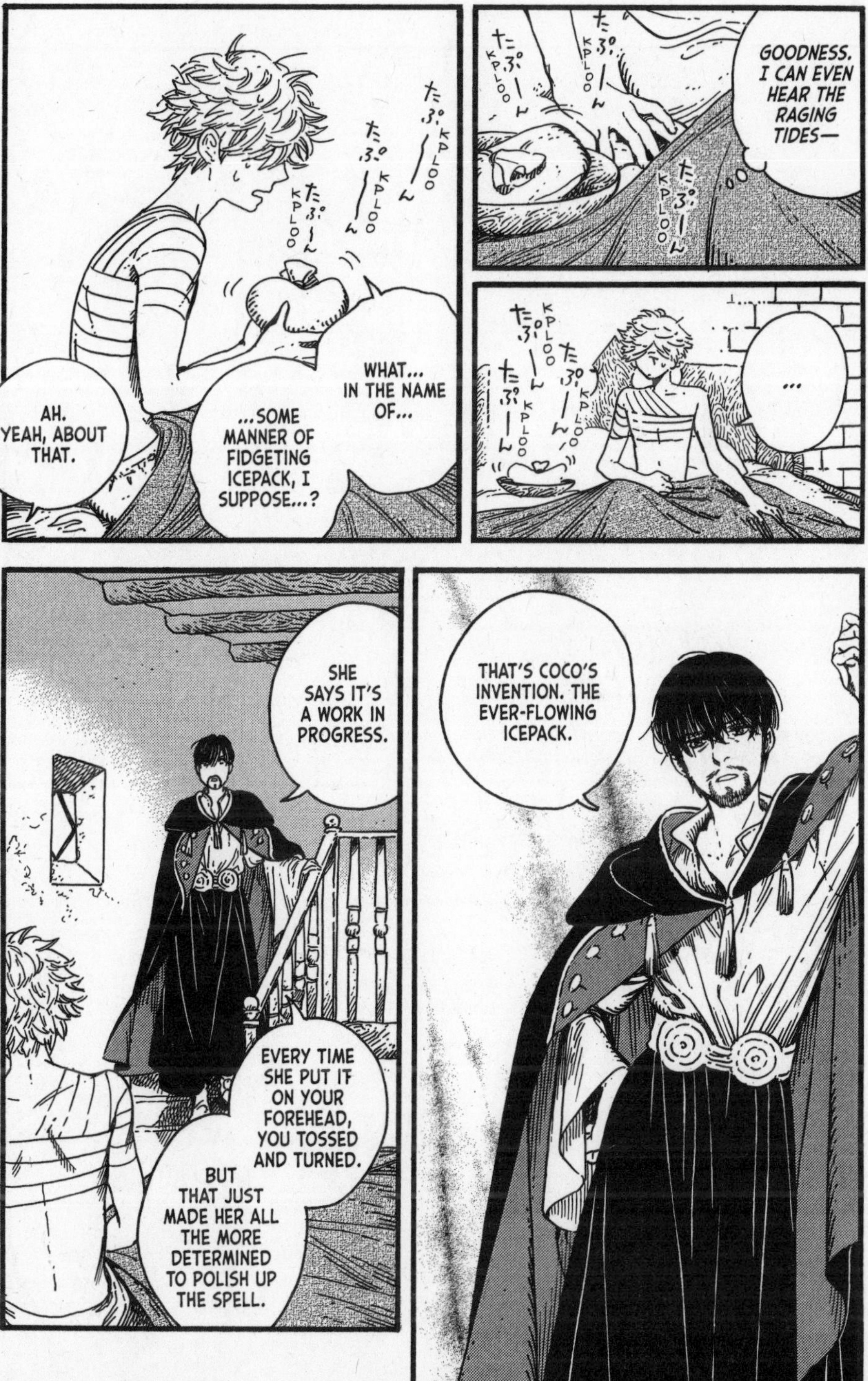
たぷーん KPLOO
たぷーん KPLOO
GOODNESS. I CAN EVEN HEAR THE RAGING TIDES—
たぷーん KPLOO
たぷーん KPLOO
たぷーん KPLOO
たぷーん KPLOO
...
たぷーん KPLOO
たぷーん KPLOO
たぷーん KPLOO
WHAT... IN THE NAME OF...
...SOME MANNER OF FIDGETING ICEPACK, I SUPPOSE...?
AH. YEAH, ABOUT THAT.
THAT'S COCO'S INVENTION. THE EVER-FLOWING ICEPACK.
SHE SAYS IT'S A WORK IN PROGRESS.
EVERY TIME SHE PUT IT ON YOUR FOREHEAD, YOU TOSSED AND TURNED.
BUT THAT JUST MADE HER ALL THE MORE DETERMINED TO POLISH UP THE SPELL.

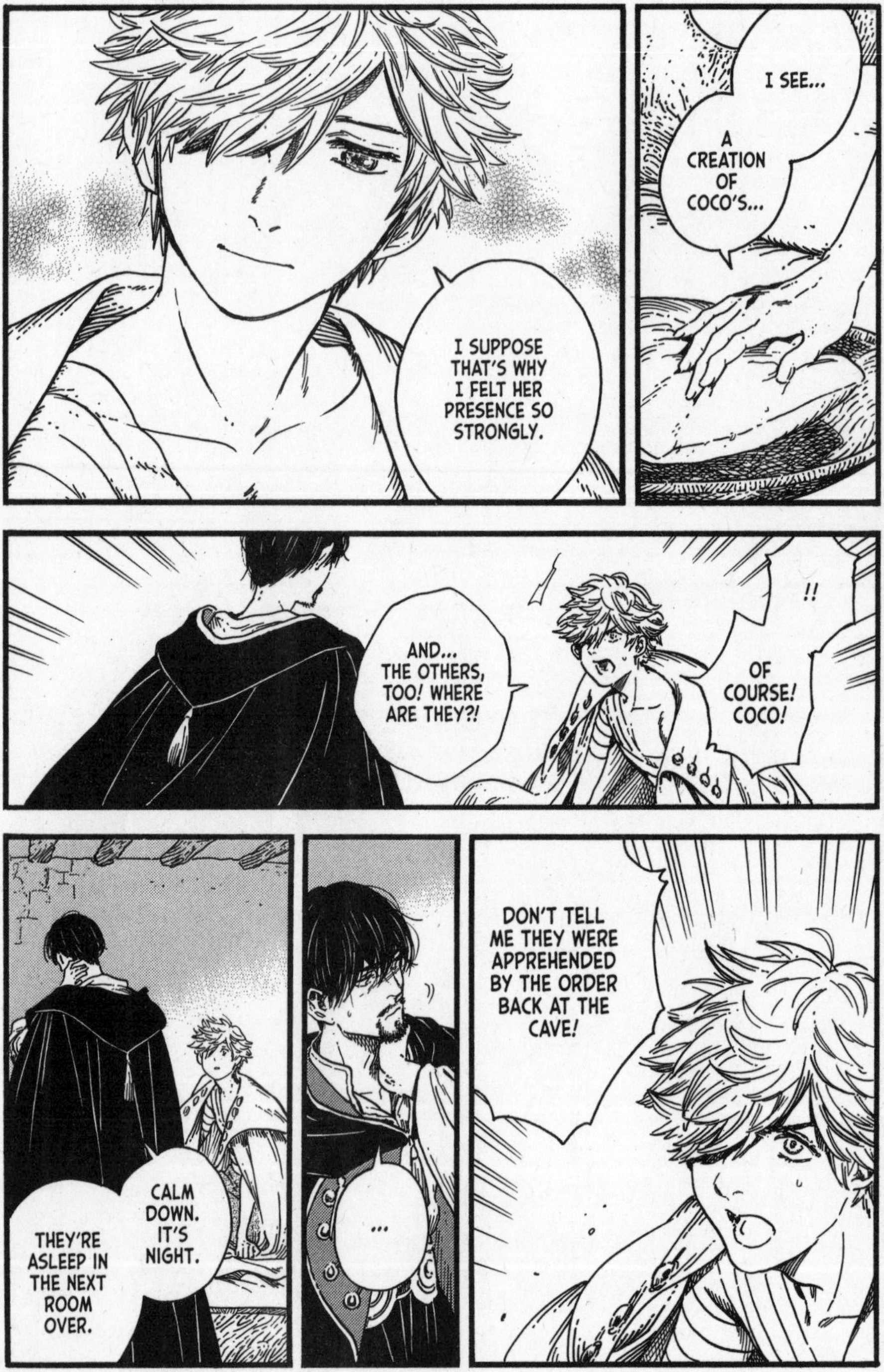
I SEE...
A CREATION OF COCO'S...
I SUPPOSE THAT'S WHY I FELT HER PRESENCE SO STRONGLY.
!!
OF COURSE! COCO!
AND... THE OTHERS, TOO! WHERE ARE THEY?!
DON'T TELL ME THEY WERE APPREHENDED BY THE ORDER BACK AT THE CAVE!
...
CALM DOWN. IT'S NIGHT.
THEY'RE ASLEEP IN THE NEXT ROOM OVER.

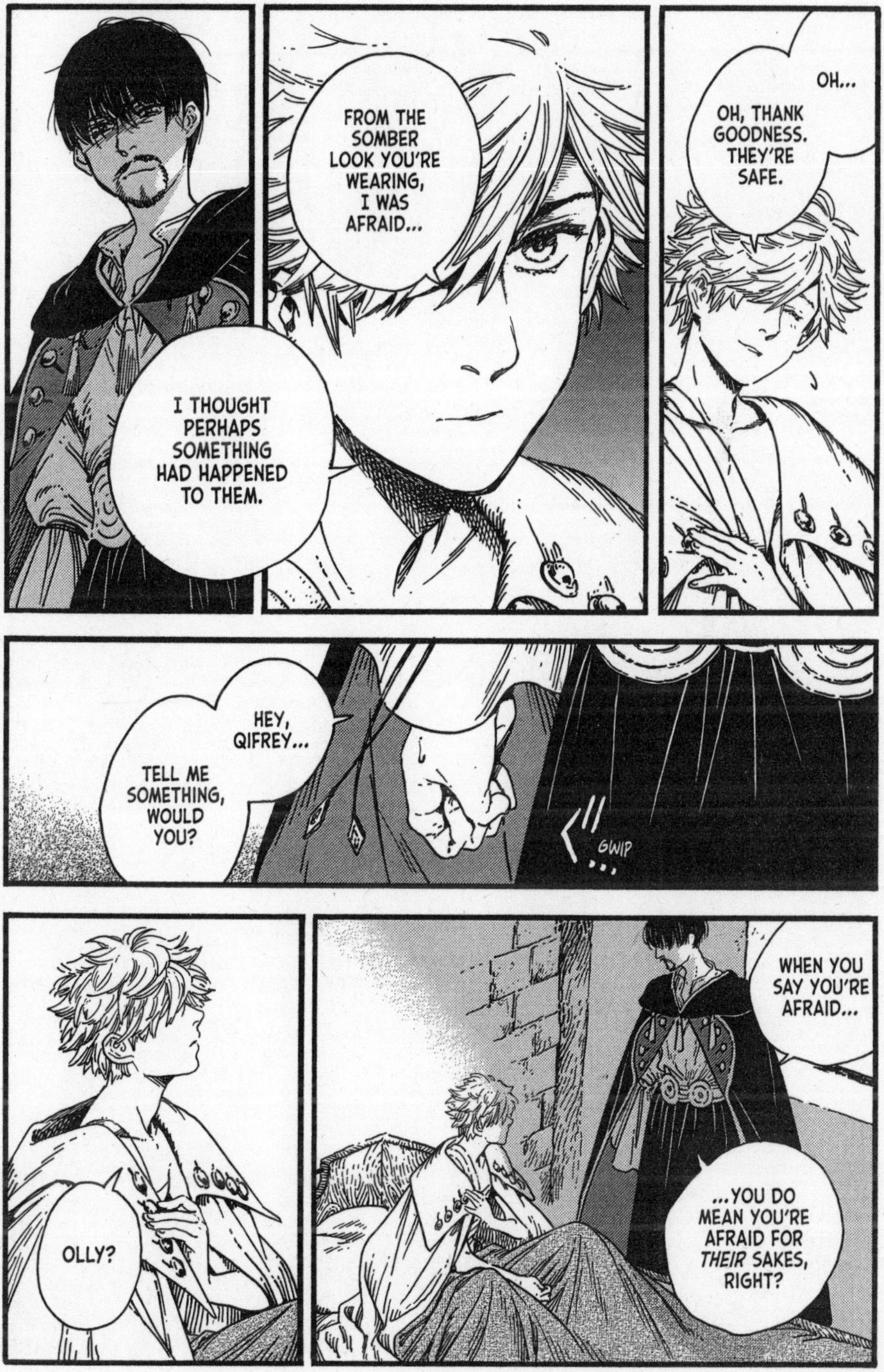
OH...
OH, THANK GOODNESS. THEY'RE SAFE.
FROM THE SOMBER LOOK YOU'RE WEARING, I WAS AFRAID...
I THOUGHT PERHAPS SOMETHING HAD HAPPENED TO THEM.
HEY, QIFREY...
TELL ME SOMETHING, WOULD YOU?
GWIP
WHEN YOU SAY YOU'RE AFRAID...
...YOU DO MEAN YOU'RE AFRAID FOR *THEIR* SAKES, RIGHT?
OLLY?

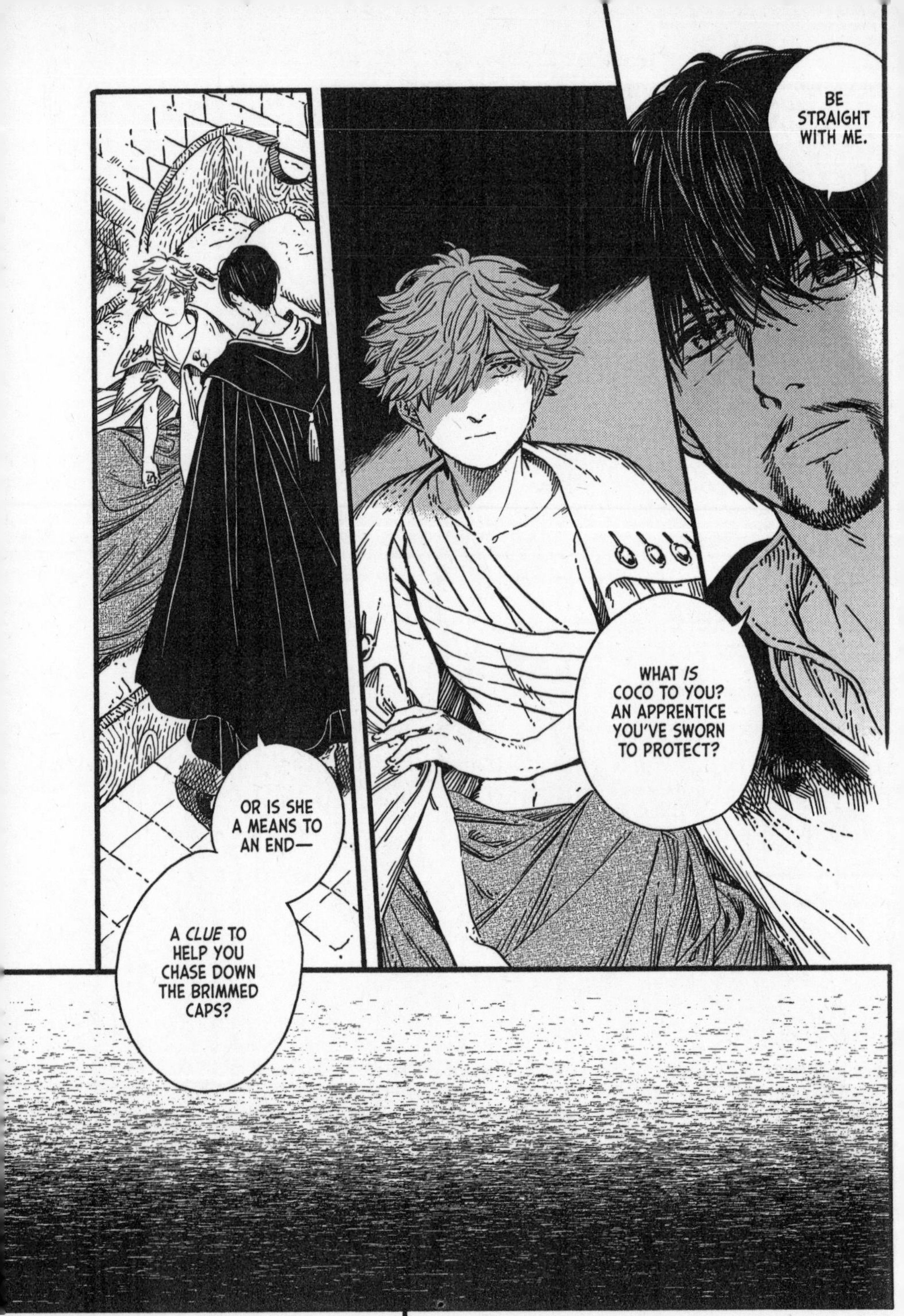
BE STRAIGHT WITH ME.
WHAT *IS* COCO TO YOU? AN APPRENTICE YOU'VE SWORN TO PROTECT?
OR IS SHE A MEANS TO AN END—
A *CLUE* TO HELP YOU CHASE DOWN THE BRIMMED CAPS?

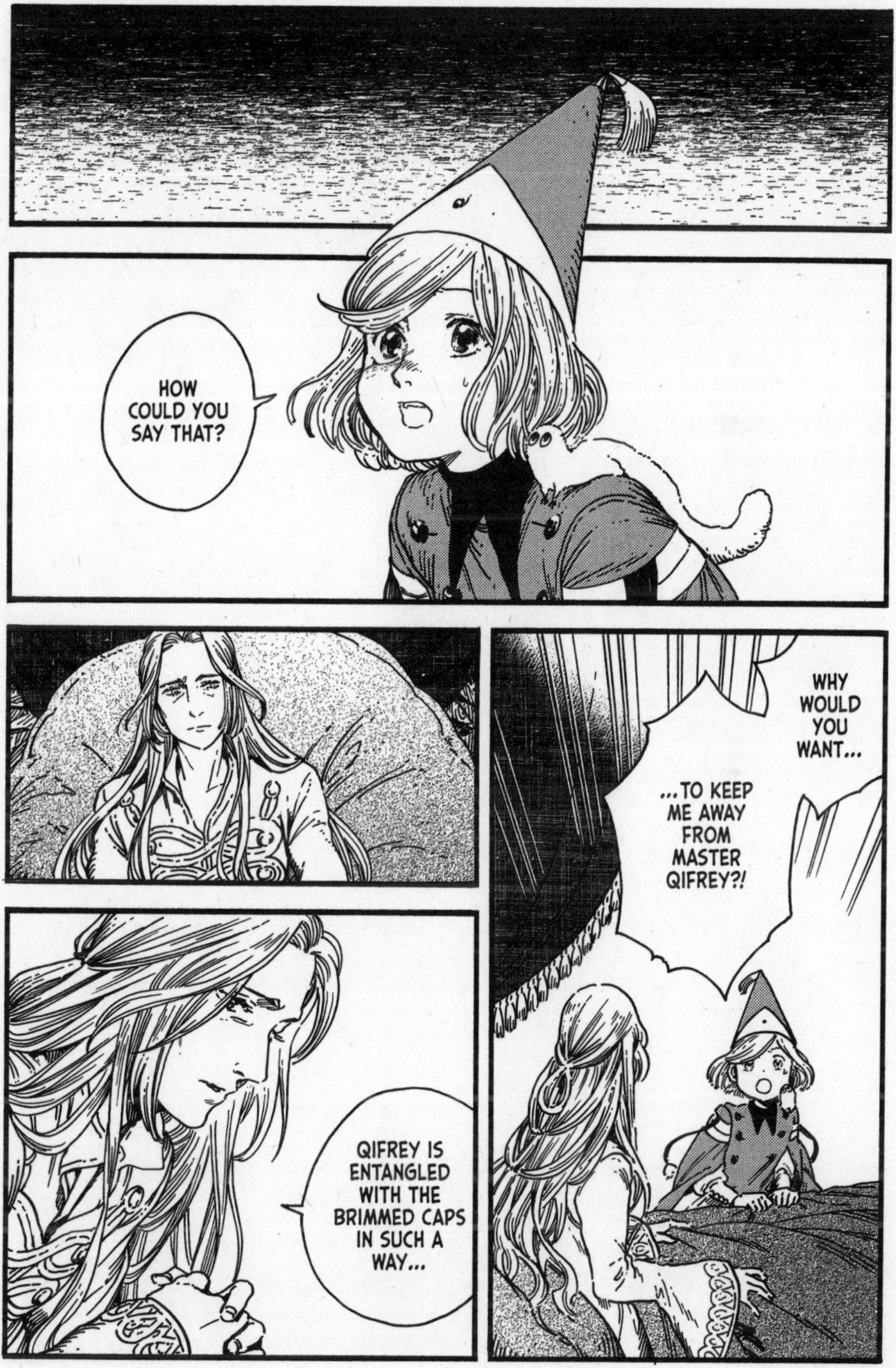
HOW COULD YOU SAY THAT?
WHY WOULD YOU WANT...
...TO KEEP ME AWAY FROM MASTER QIFREY?!
QIFREY IS ENTANGLED WITH THE BRIMMED CAPS IN SUCH A WAY...

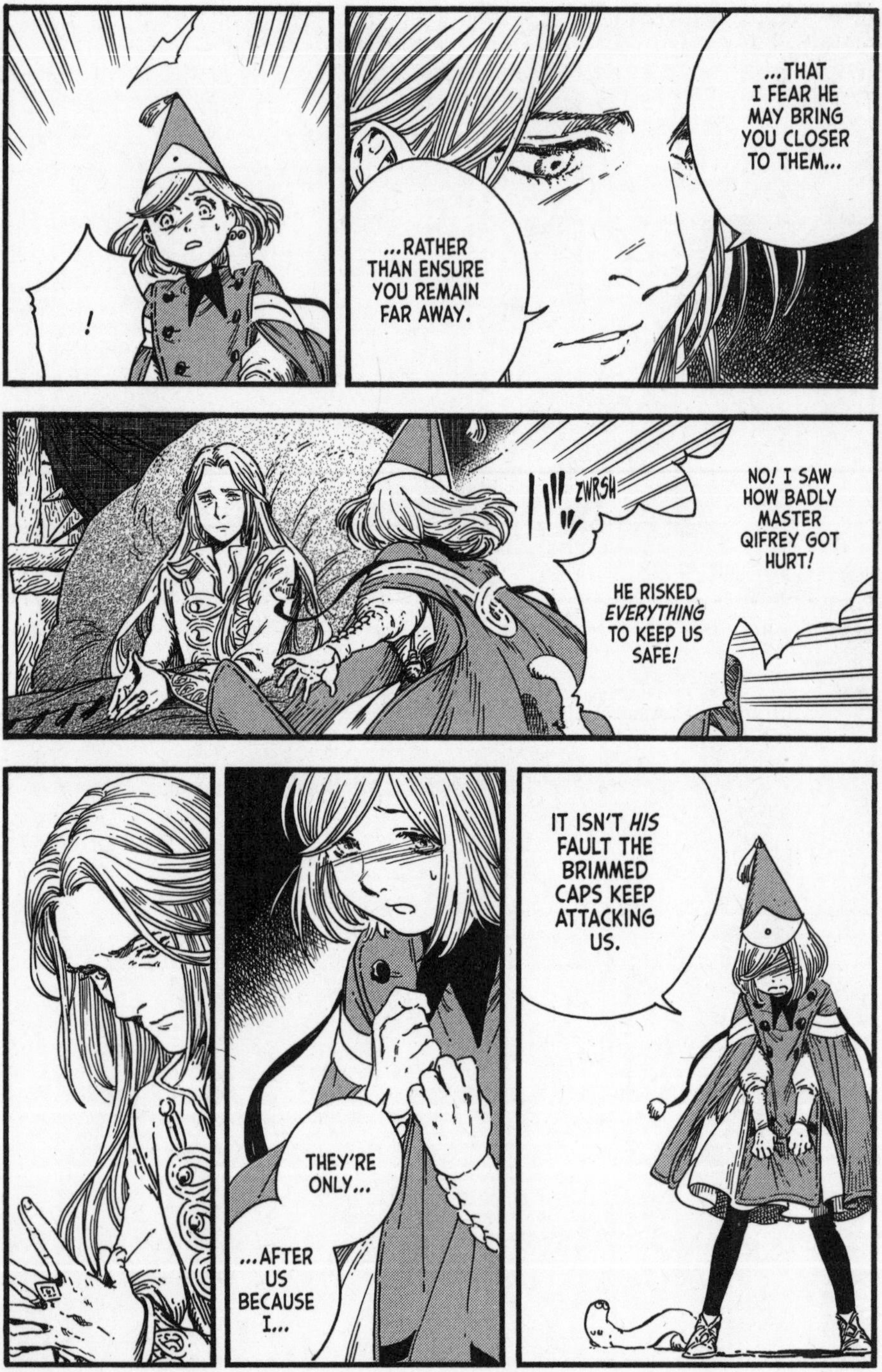
...THAT I FEAR HE MAY BRING YOU CLOSER TO THEM...
...RATHER THAN ENSURE YOU REMAIN FAR AWAY.
!
NO! I SAW HOW BADLY MASTER QIFREY GOT HURT!
HE RISKED EVERYTHING TO KEEP US SAFE!
ZWRSH
IT ISN'T HIS FAULT THE BRIMMED CAPS KEEP ATTACKING US.
THEY'RE ONLY...
...AFTER US BECAUSE I...

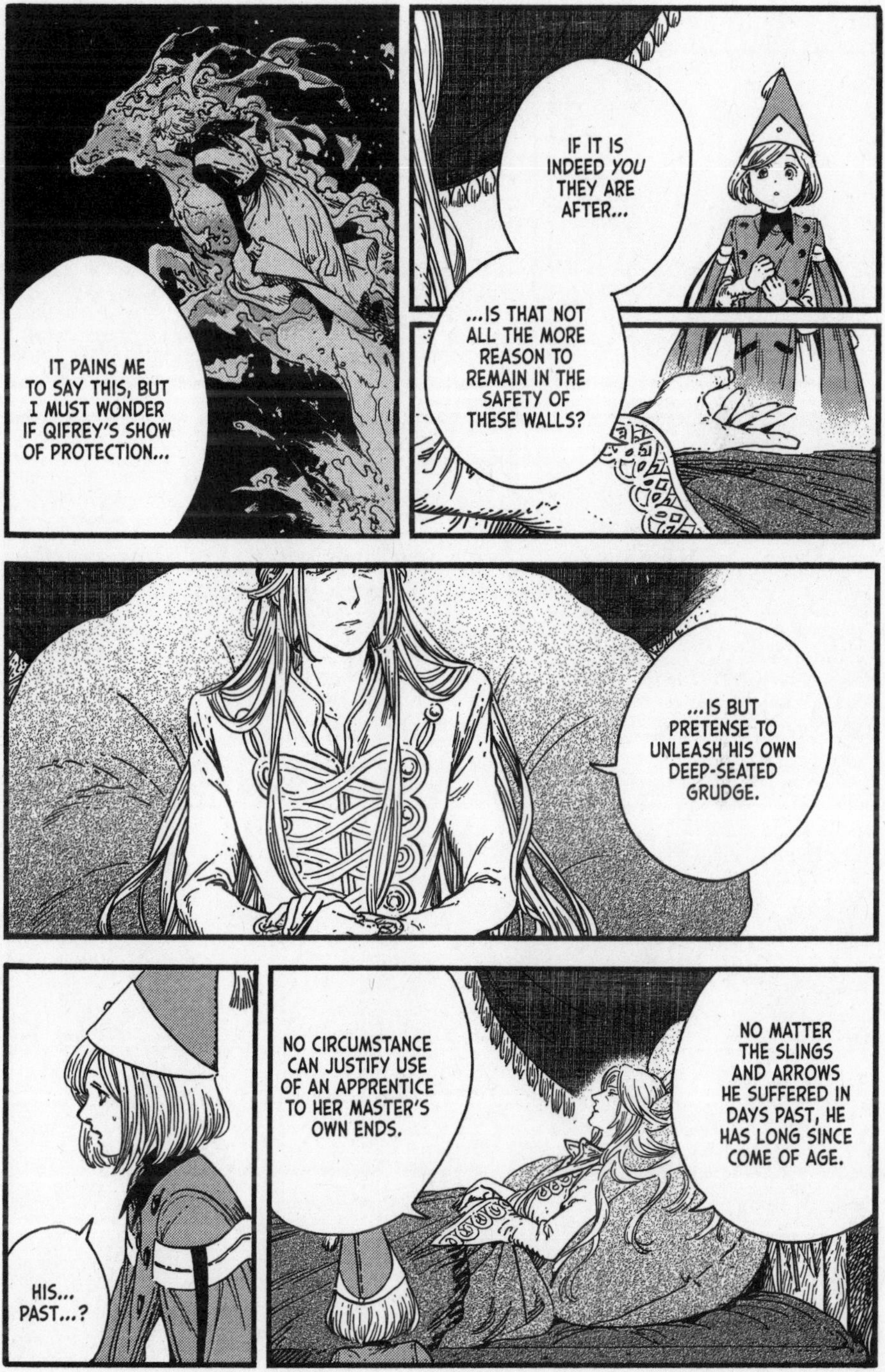
IF IT IS INDEED *YOU* THEY ARE AFTER...
...IS THAT NOT ALL THE MORE REASON TO REMAIN IN THE SAFETY OF THESE WALLS?
IT PAINS ME TO SAY THIS, BUT I MUST WONDER IF QIFREY'S SHOW OF PROTECTION...
...IS BUT PRETENSE TO UNLEASH HIS OWN DEEP-SEATED GRUDGE.
NO MATTER THE SLINGS AND ARROWS HE SUFFERED IN DAYS PAST, HE HAS LONG SINCE COME OF AGE.
NO CIRCUMSTANCE CAN JUSTIFY USE OF AN APPRENTICE TO HER MASTER'S OWN ENDS.
HIS... PAST...?

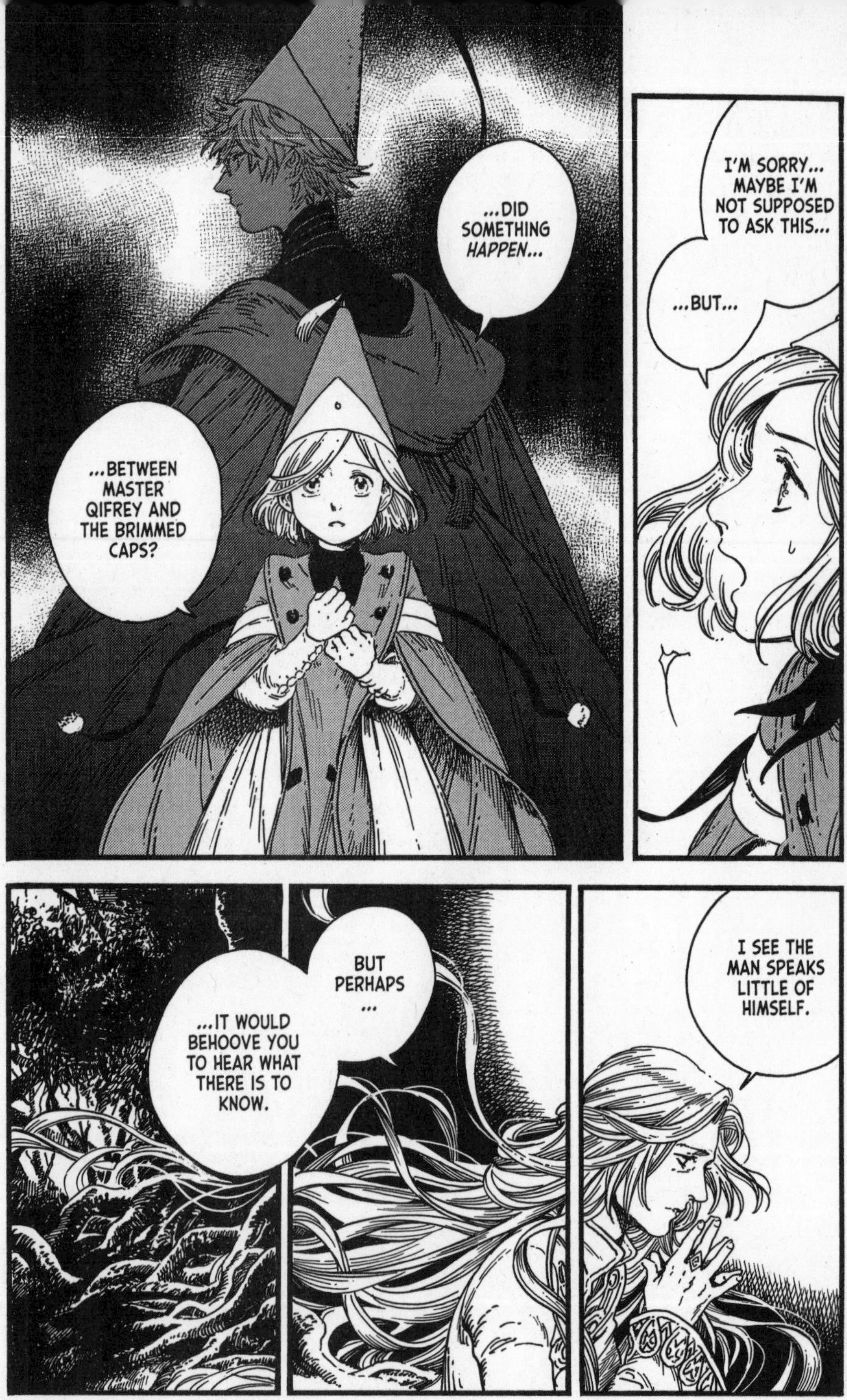
I'M SORRY... MAYBE I'M NOT SUPPOSED TO ASK THIS...
...BUT...
...DID SOMETHING *HAPPEN*...
...BETWEEN MASTER QIFREY AND THE BRIMMED CAPS?
I SEE THE MAN SPEAKS LITTLE OF HIMSELF.
BUT PERHAPS...
...IT WOULD BEHOOVE YOU TO HEAR WHAT THERE IS TO KNOW.

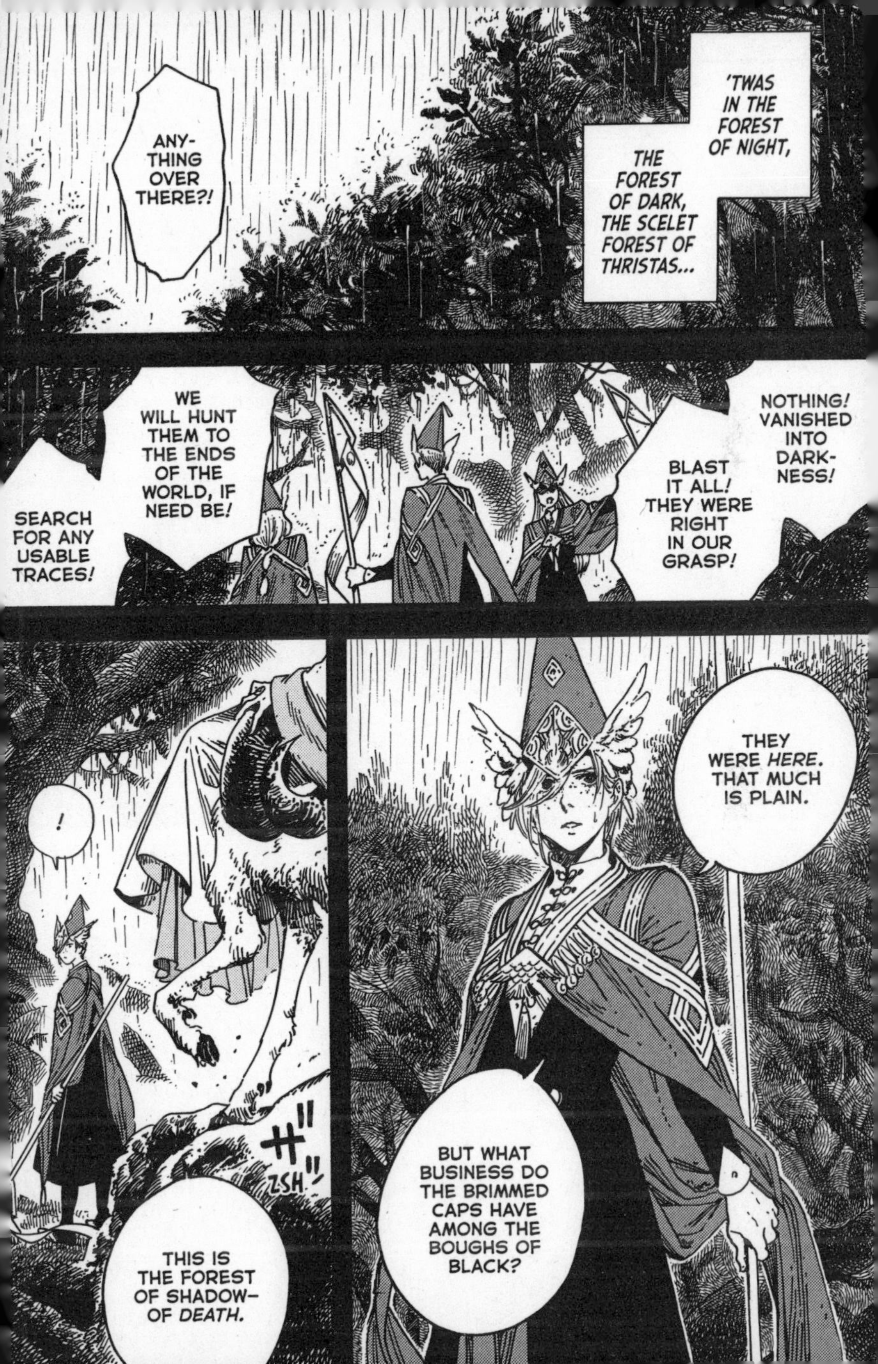
'TWAS IN THE FOREST OF NIGHT,
THE FOREST OF DARK, THE SCELET FOREST OF THRISTAS...
ANY-THING OVER THERE?!
NOTHING! VANISHED INTO DARK-NESS!
BLAST IT ALL! THEY WERE RIGHT IN OUR GRASP!
WE WILL HUNT THEM TO THE ENDS OF THE WORLD, IF NEED BE!
SEARCH FOR ANY USABLE TRACES!
THEY WERE *HERE*. THAT MUCH IS PLAIN.
BUT WHAT BUSINESS DO THE BRIMMED CAPS HAVE AMONG THE BOUGHS OF BLACK?
!
ZSH
THIS IS THE FOREST OF SHADOW— OF *DEATH*.

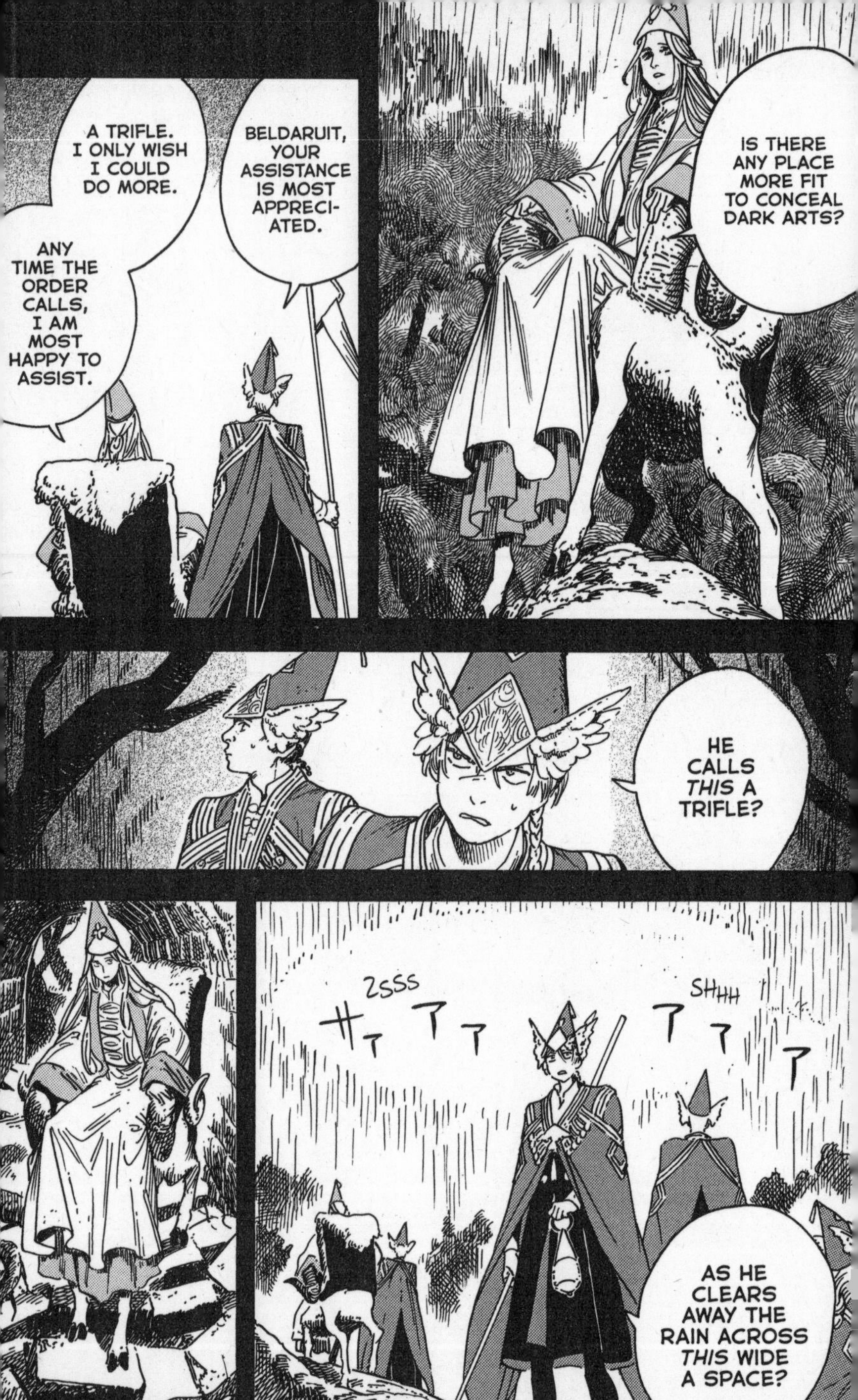
IS THERE ANY PLACE MORE FIT TO CONCEAL DARK ARTS?
BELDARUIT, YOUR ASSISTANCE IS MOST APPRECIATED.
A TRIFLE. I ONLY WISH I COULD DO MORE.
ANY TIME THE ORDER CALLS, I AM MOST HAPPY TO ASSIST.
HE CALLS *THIS* A TRIFLE?
ZSSS
サァアア
SHHH
アアア
AS HE CLEARS AWAY THE RAIN ACROSS *THIS* WIDE A SPACE?

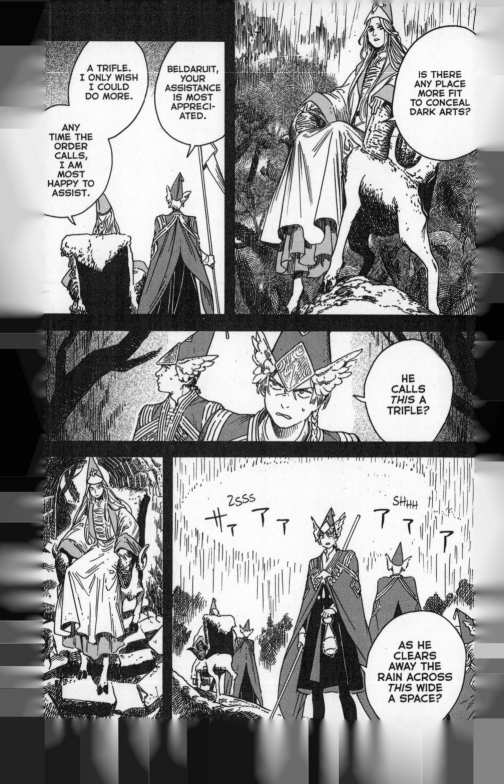

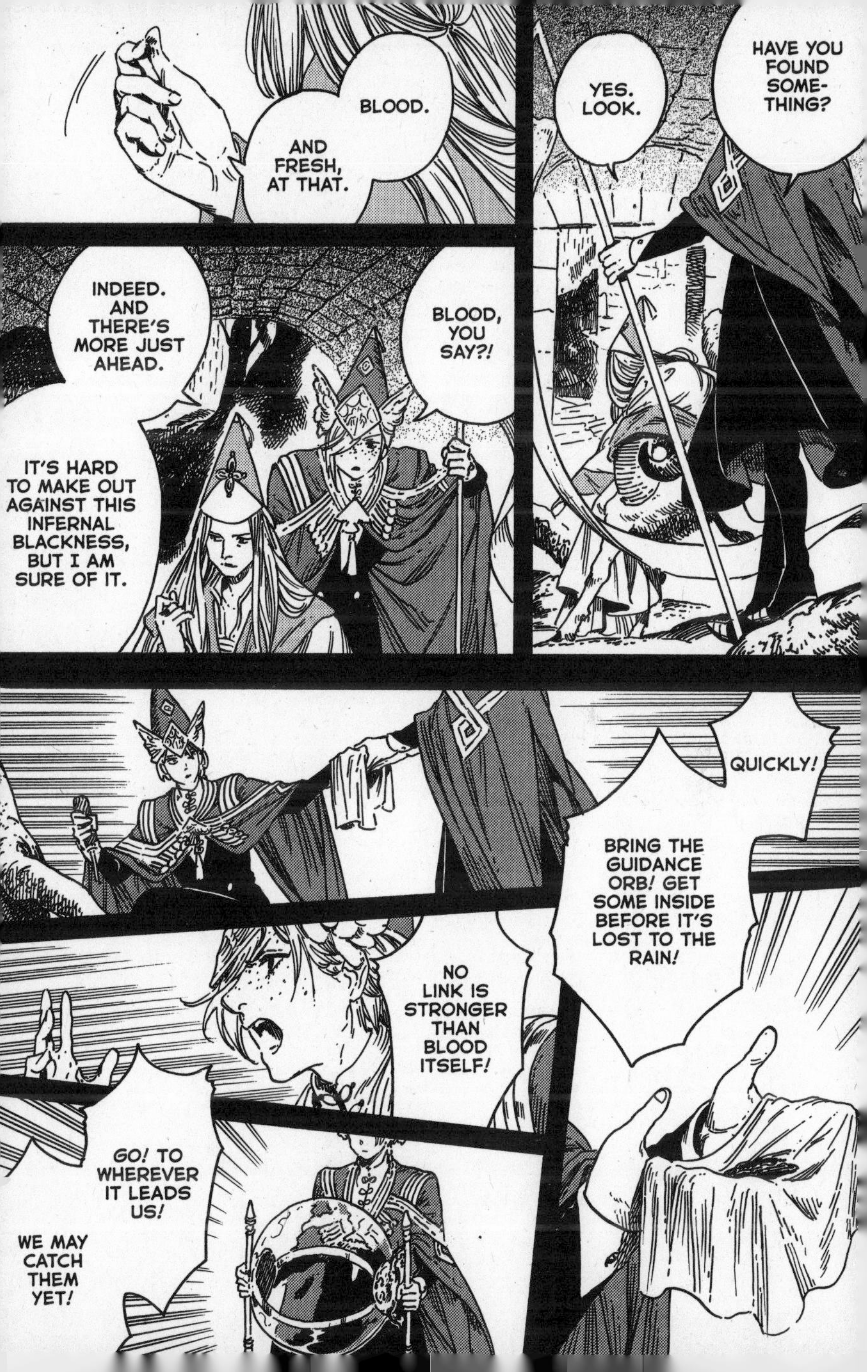
HAVE YOU FOUND SOME-THING?
YES. LOOK.
BLOOD.
AND FRESH, AT THAT.
BLOOD, YOU SAY?!
INDEED. AND THERE'S MORE JUST AHEAD.
IT'S HARD TO MAKE OUT AGAINST THIS INFERNAL BLACKNESS, BUT I AM SURE OF IT.
QUICKLY!
BRING THE GUIDANCE ORB! GET SOME INSIDE BEFORE IT'S LOST TO THE RAIN!
NO LINK IS STRONGER THAN BLOOD ITSELF!
GO! TO WHEREVER IT LEADS US!
WE MAY CATCH THEM YET!

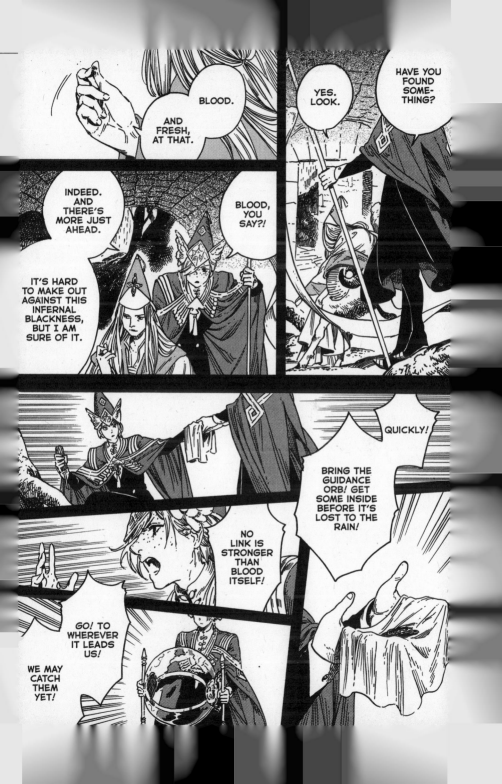

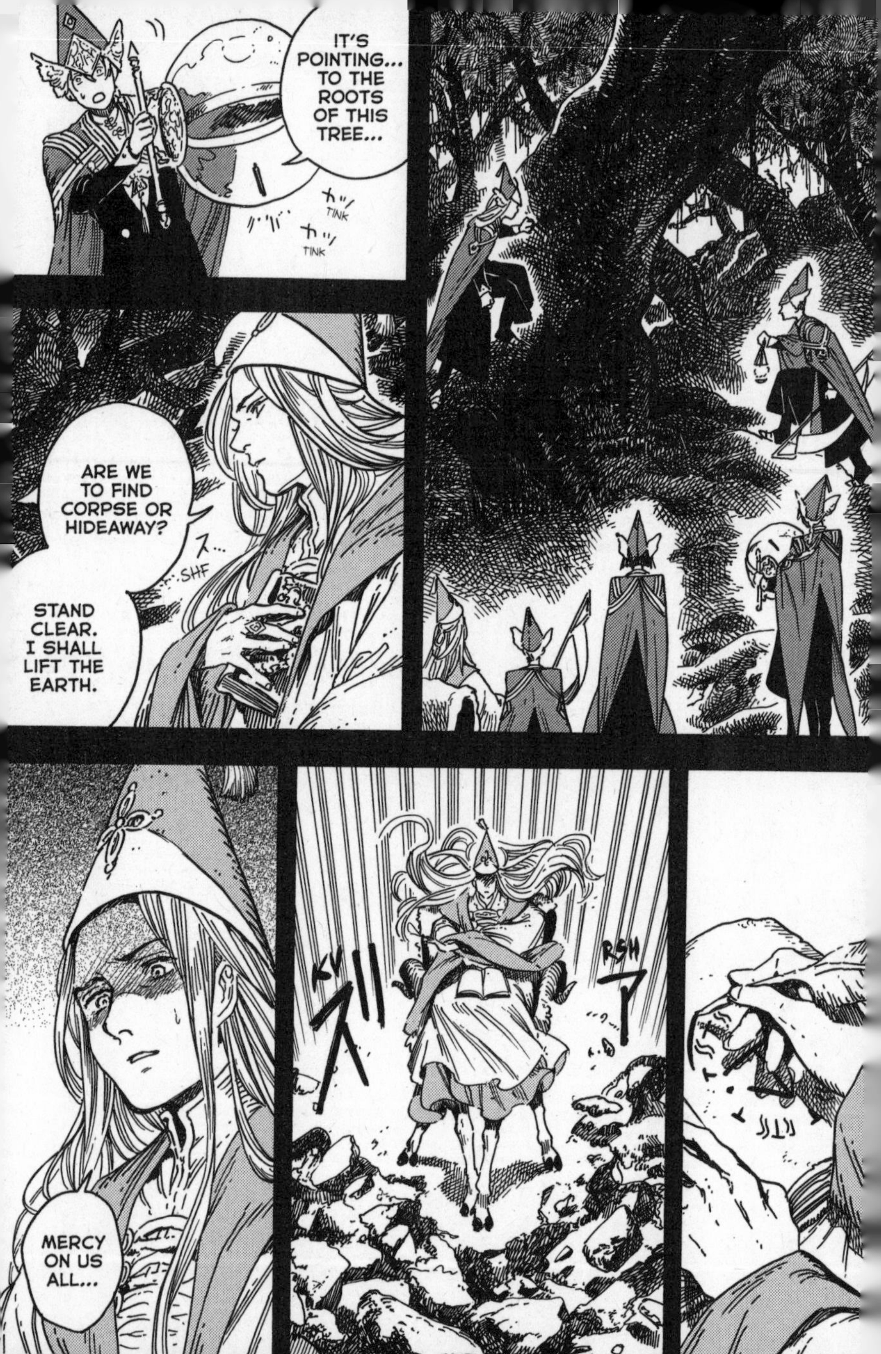

IT'S POINTING... TO THE ROOTS OF THIS TREE...
TINK
TINK
ARE WE TO FIND CORPSE OR HIDEAWAY?
SHF
STAND CLEAR. I SHALL LIFT THE EARTH.
RSH
KU
MERCY ON US ALL...

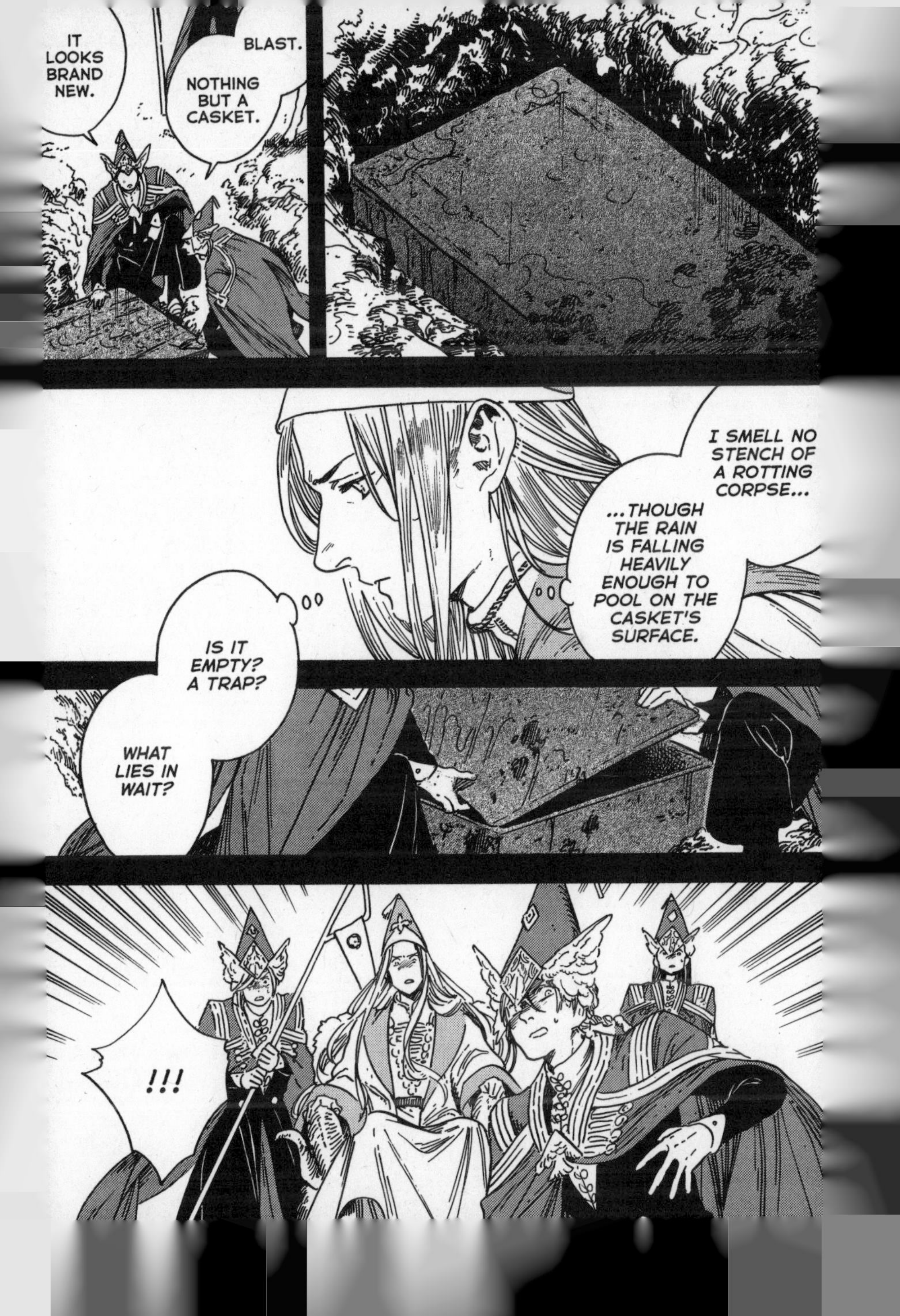
BLAST.
NOTHING BUT A CASKET.
IT LOOKS BRAND NEW.
I SMELL NO STENCH OF A ROTTING CORPSE...
...THOUGH THE RAIN IS FALLING HEAVILY ENOUGH TO POOL ON THE CASKET'S SURFACE.
IS IT EMPTY? A TRAP?
WHAT LIES IN WAIT?
!!!

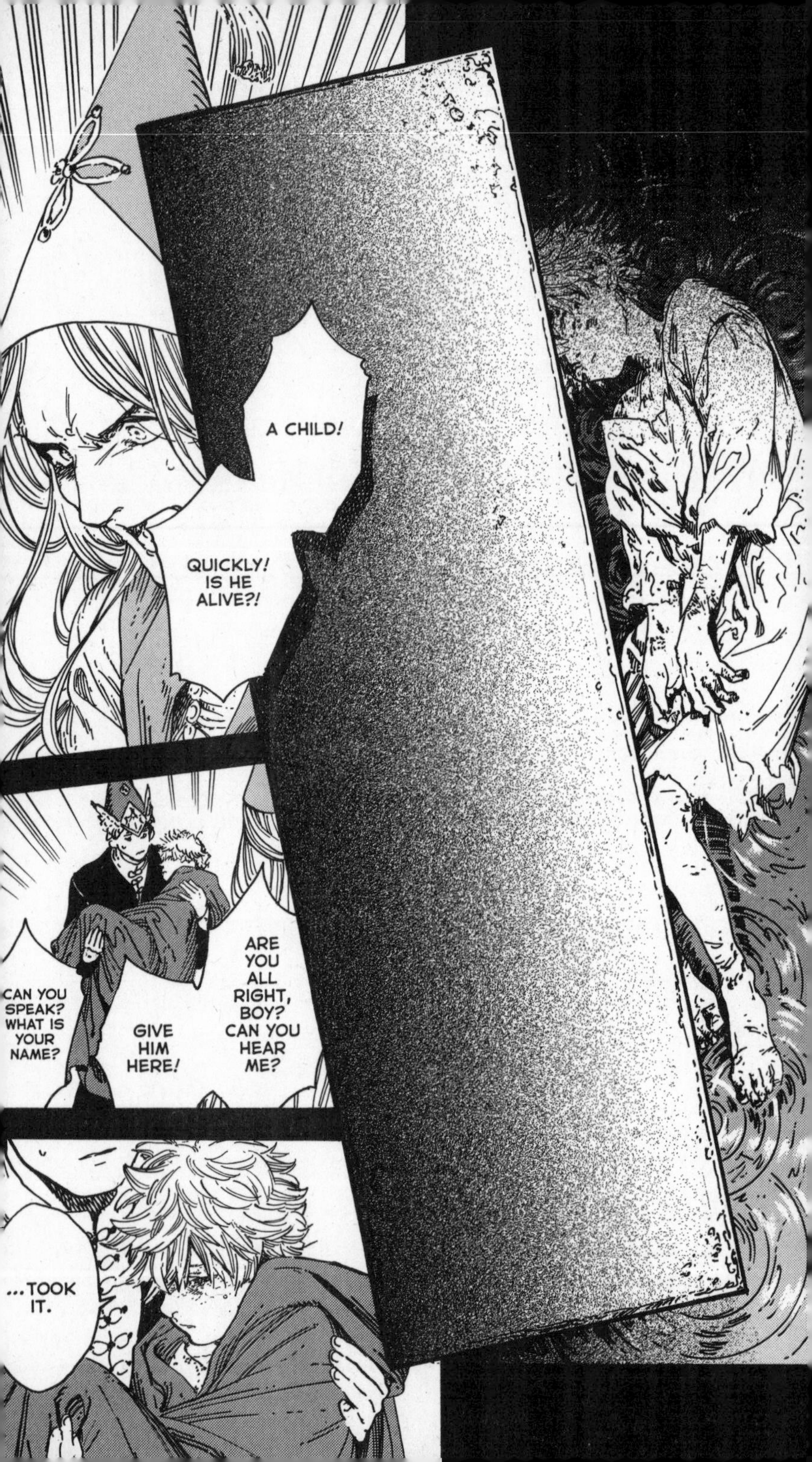
A CHILD!
QUICKLY! IS HE ALIVE?!
ARE YOU ALL RIGHT, BOY? CAN YOU HEAR ME?
GIVE HIM HERE!
CAN YOU SPEAK? WHAT IS YOUR NAME?
...TOOK IT.

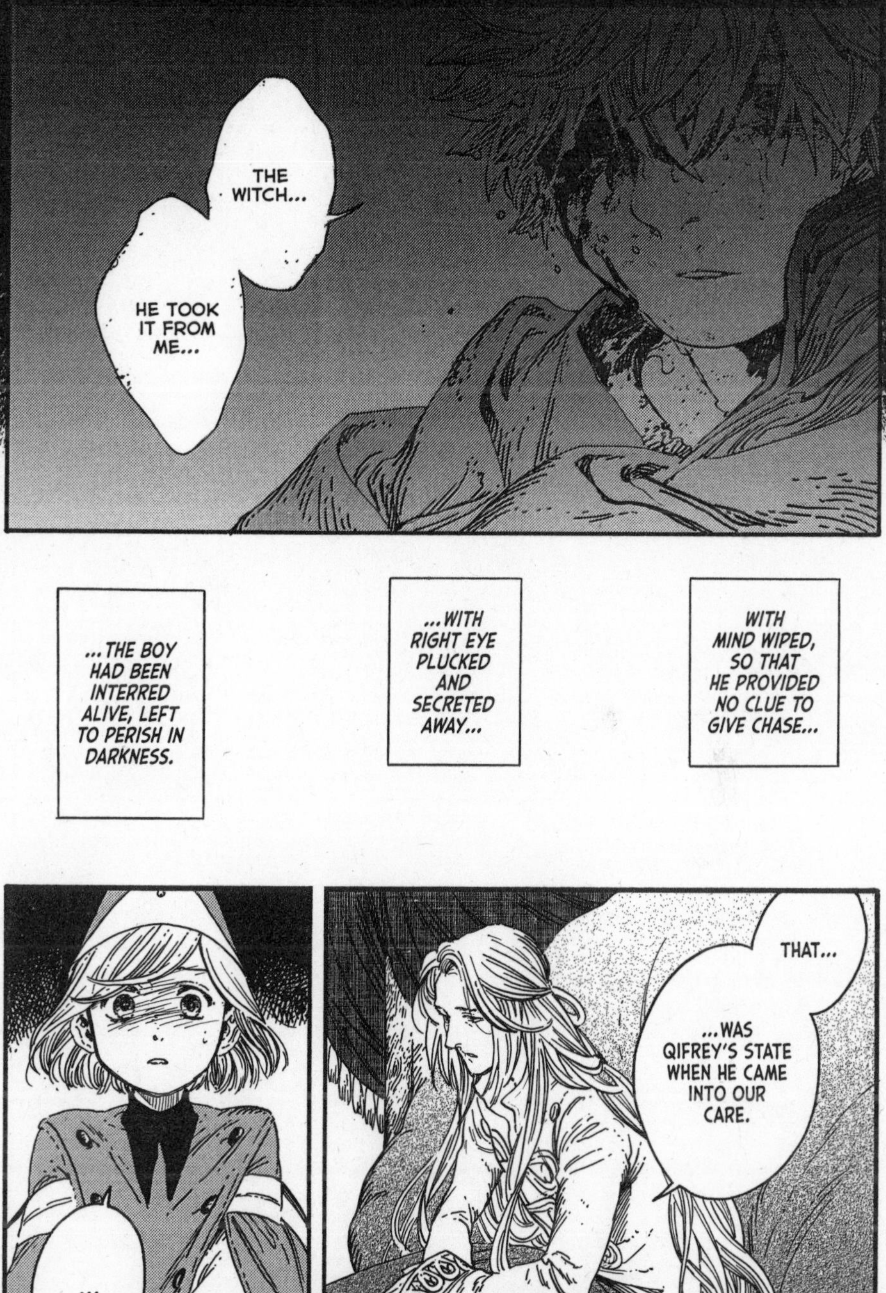
THE WITCH...
HE TOOK IT FROM ME...
WITH MIND WIPED, SO THAT HE PROVIDED NO CLUE TO GIVE CHASE...
...WITH RIGHT EYE PLUCKED AND SECRETED AWAY...
...THE BOY HAD BEEN INTERRED ALIVE, LEFT TO PERISH IN DARKNESS.
THAT...
...WAS QIFREY'S STATE WHEN HE CAME INTO OUR CARE.
...

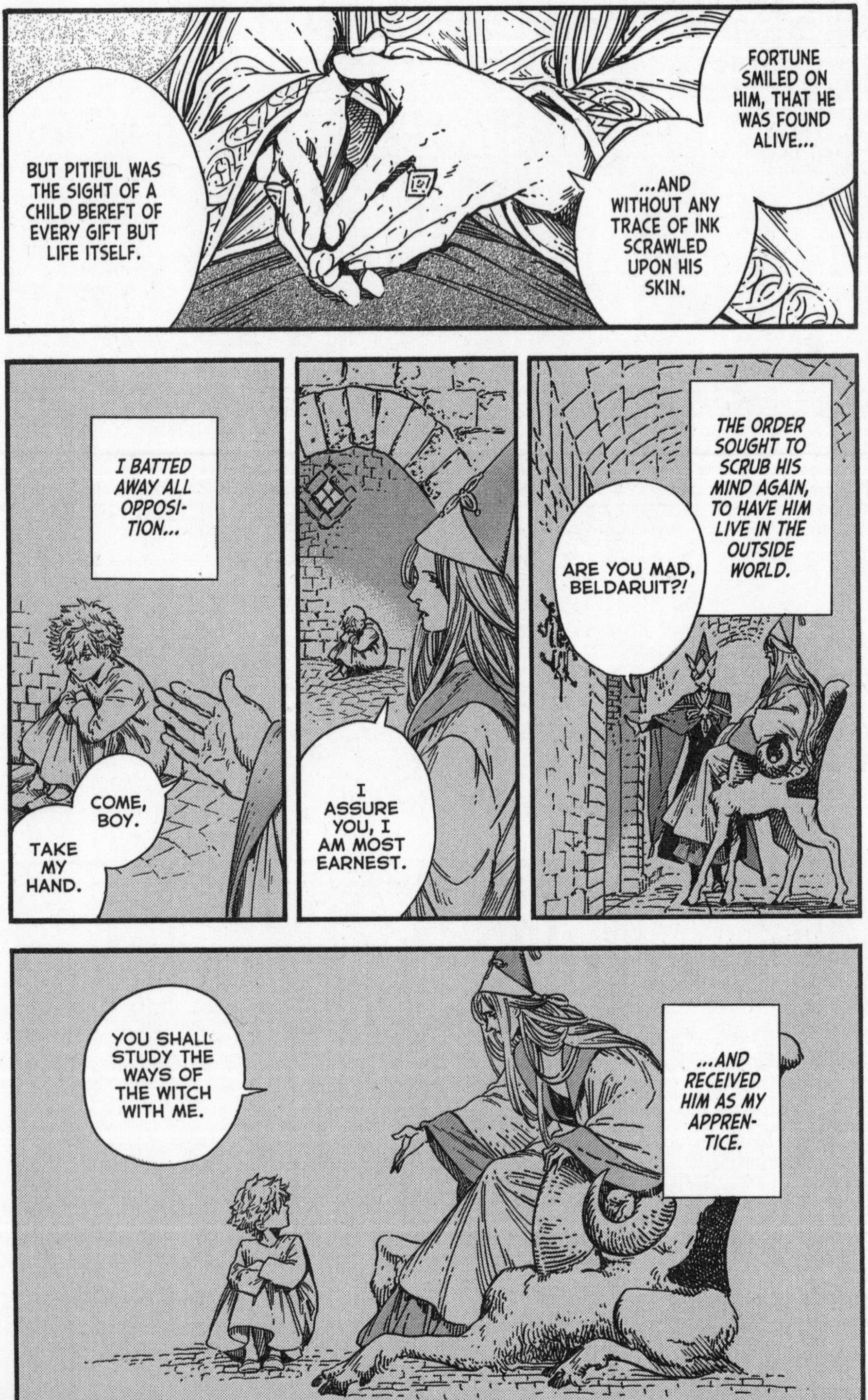
FORTUNE SMILED ON HIM, THAT HE WAS FOUND ALIVE...
...AND WITHOUT ANY TRACE OF INK SCRAWLED UPON HIS SKIN.
BUT PITIFUL WAS THE SIGHT OF A CHILD BEREFT OF EVERY GIFT BUT LIFE ITSELF.
THE ORDER SOUGHT TO SCRUB HIS MIND AGAIN, TO HAVE HIM LIVE IN THE OUTSIDE WORLD.
ARE YOU MAD, BELDARUIT?!
I ASSURE YOU, I AM MOST EARNEST.
I BATTED AWAY ALL OPPOSITION...
COME, BOY.
TAKE MY HAND.
...AND RECEIVED HIM AS MY APPRENTICE.
YOU SHALL STUDY THE WAYS OF THE WITCH WITH ME.

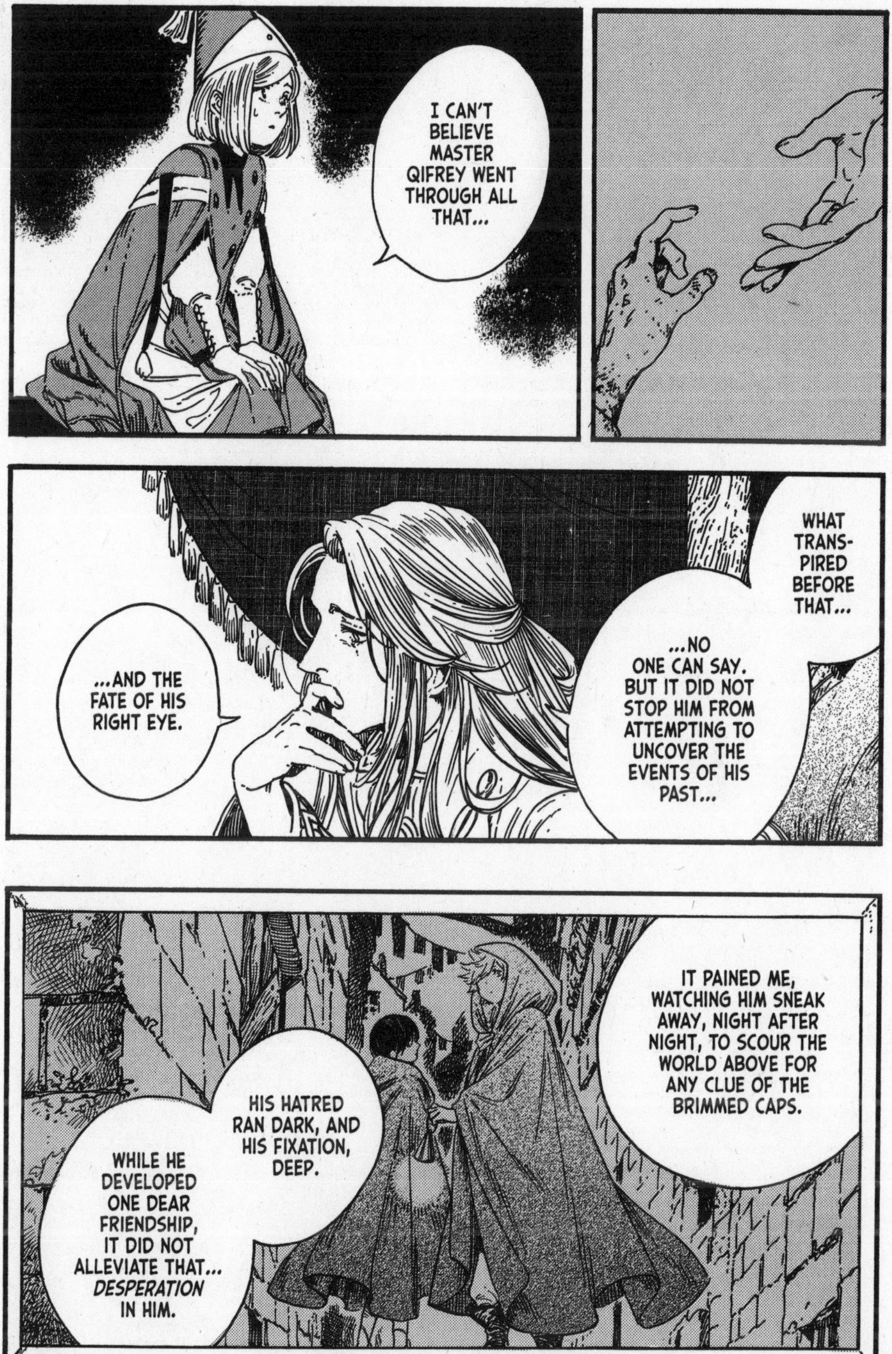
I CAN'T BELIEVE MASTER QIFREY WENT THROUGH ALL THAT...
WHAT TRANS-PIRED BEFORE THAT...
...NO ONE CAN SAY. BUT IT DID NOT STOP HIM FROM ATTEMPTING TO UNCOVER THE EVENTS OF HIS PAST...
...AND THE FATE OF HIS RIGHT EYE.
IT PAINED ME, WATCHING HIM SNEAK AWAY, NIGHT AFTER NIGHT, TO SCOUR THE WORLD ABOVE FOR ANY CLUE OF THE BRIMMED CAPS.
HIS HATRED RAN DARK, AND HIS FIXATION, DEEP.
WHILE HE DEVELOPED ONE DEAR FRIENDSHIP, IT DID NOT ALLEVIATE THAT... *DESPERATION* IN HIM.

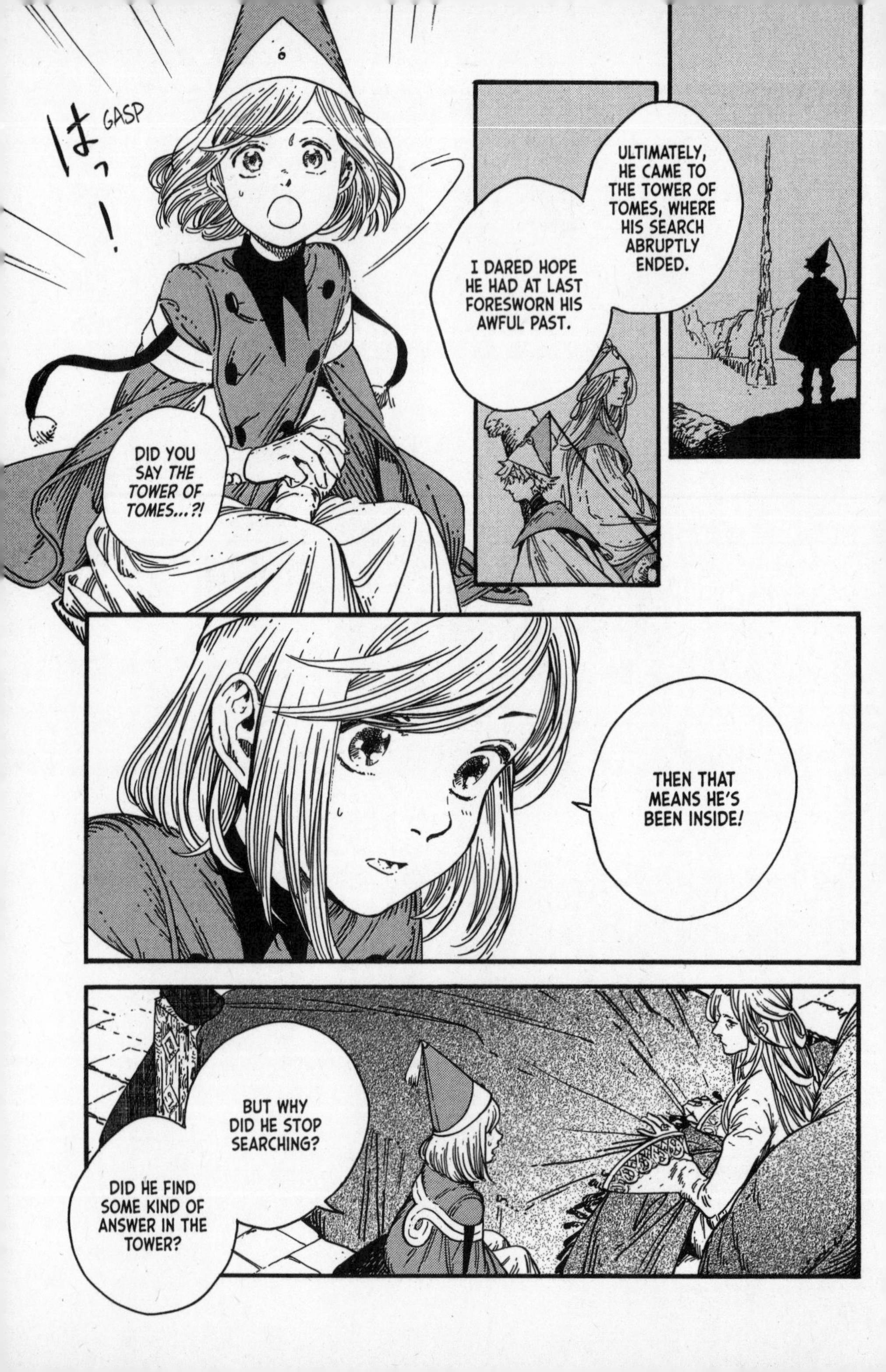

ULTIMATELY, HE CAME TO THE TOWER OF TOMES, WHERE HIS SEARCH ABRUPTLY ENDED.
I DARED HOPE HE HAD AT LAST FORESWORN HIS AWFUL PAST.
はっ!
GASP
DID YOU SAY *THE TOWER OF TOMES...?!*
THEN THAT MEANS HE'S BEEN INSIDE!
BUT WHY DID HE STOP SEARCHING?
DID HE FIND SOME KIND OF ANSWER IN THE TOWER?

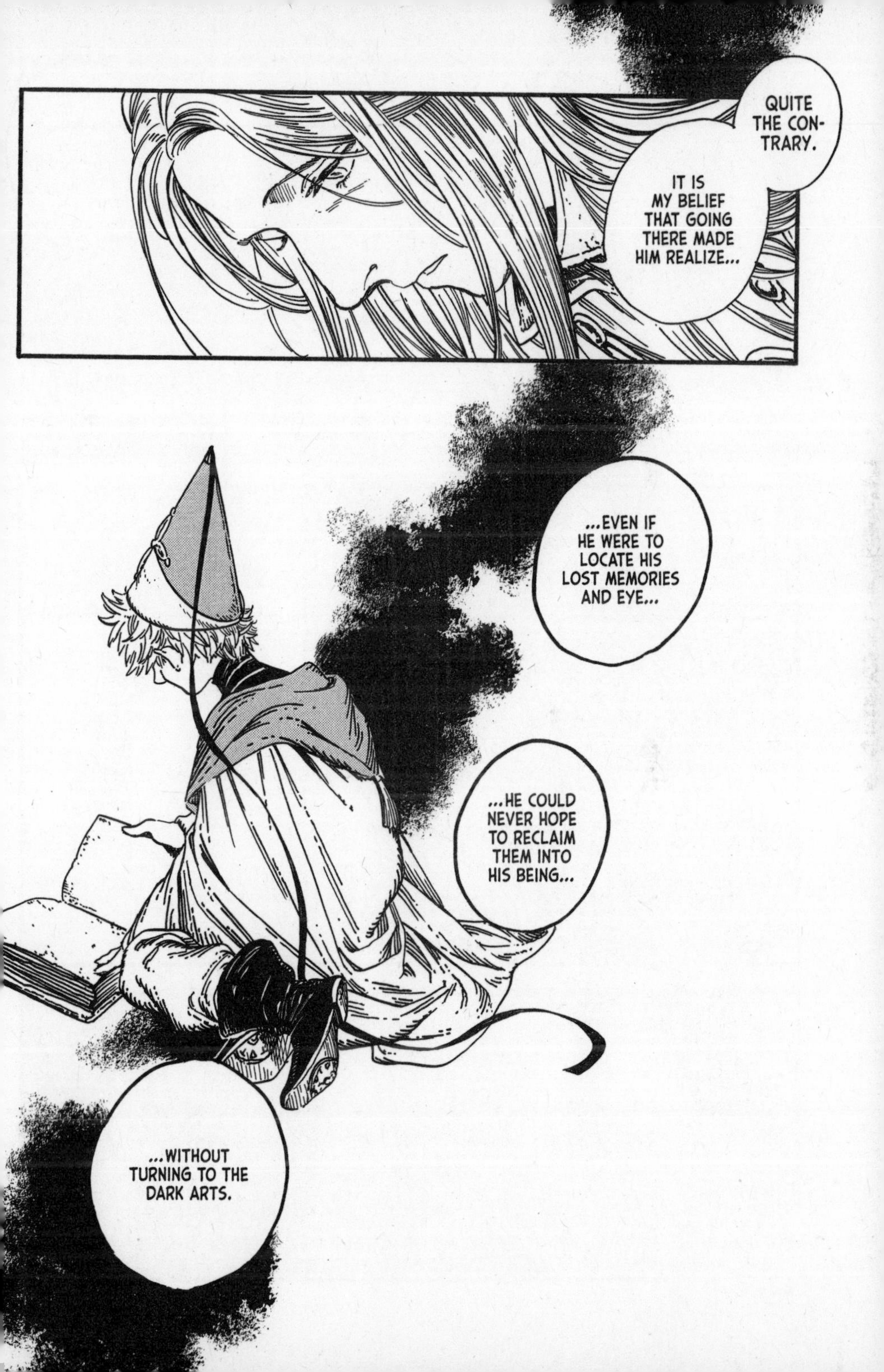
QUITE THE CONTRARY.
IT IS MY BELIEF THAT GOING THERE MADE HIM REALIZE...
...EVEN IF HE WERE TO LOCATE HIS LOST MEMORIES AND EYE...
...HE COULD NEVER HOPE TO RECLAIM THEM INTO HIS BEING...
...WITHOUT TURNING TO THE DARK ARTS.

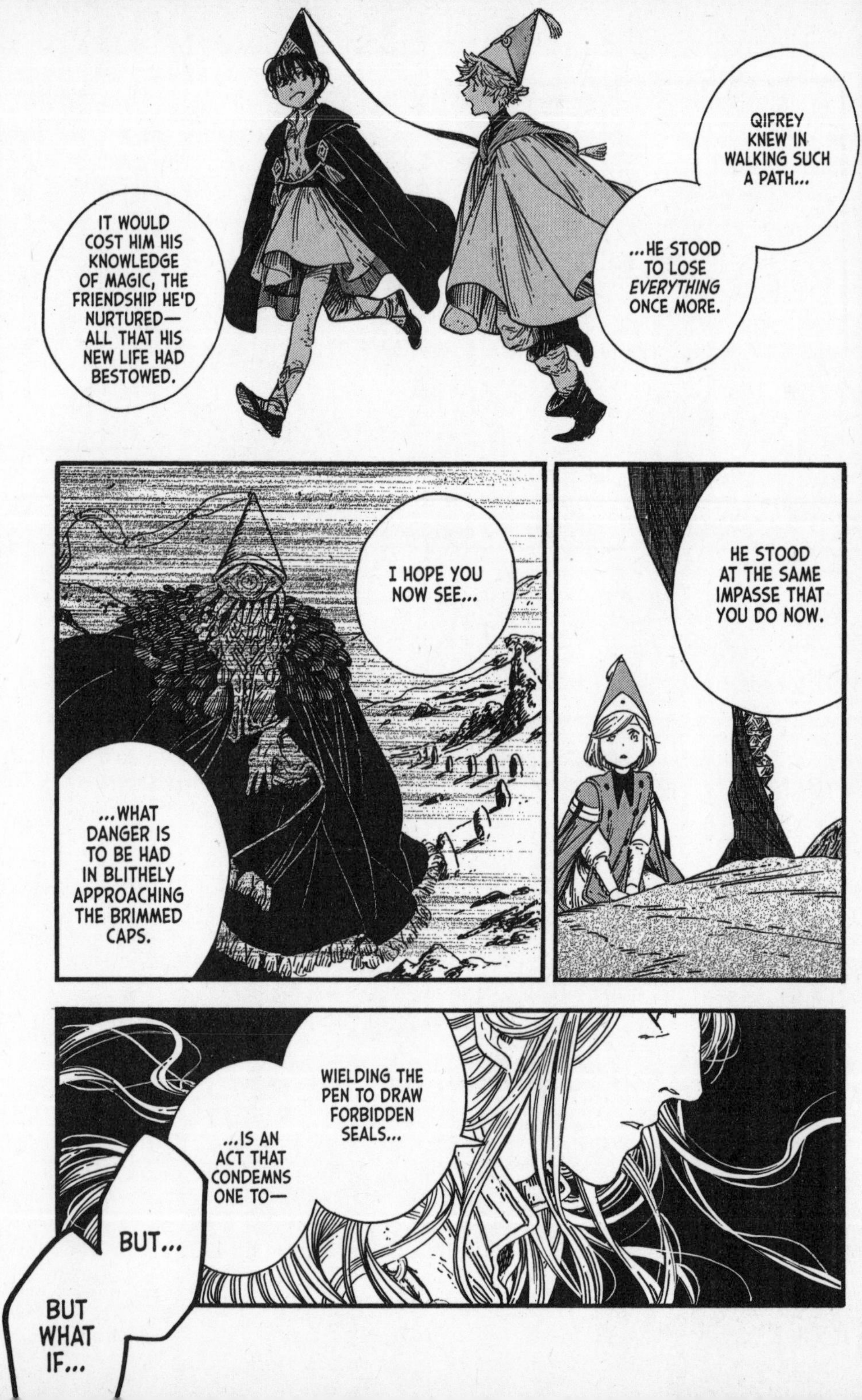
QIFREY KNEW IN WALKING SUCH A PATH...
...HE STOOD TO LOSE *EVERYTHING* ONCE MORE.
IT WOULD COST HIM HIS KNOWLEDGE OF MAGIC, THE FRIENDSHIP HE'D NURTURED—ALL THAT HIS NEW LIFE HAD BESTOWED.
HE STOOD AT THE SAME IMPASSE THAT YOU DO NOW.
I HOPE YOU NOW SEE...
...WHAT DANGER IS TO BE HAD IN BLITHELY APPROACHING THE BRIMMED CAPS.
WIELDING THE PEN TO DRAW FORBIDDEN SEALS...
...IS AN ACT THAT CONDEMNS ONE TO—
BUT...
BUT WHAT IF...

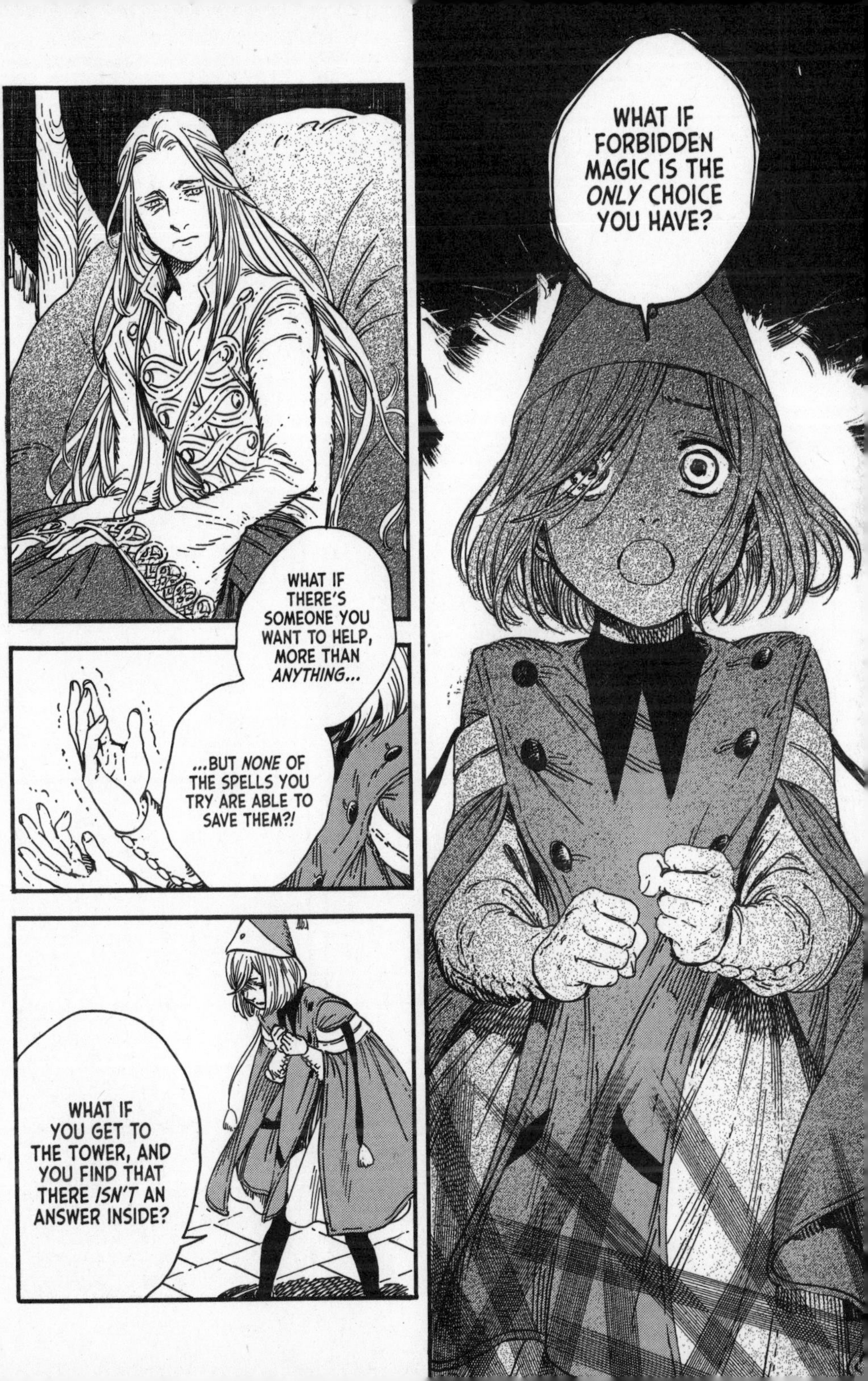
WHAT IF FORBIDDEN MAGIC IS THE *ONLY* CHOICE YOU HAVE?
WHAT IF THERE'S SOMEONE YOU WANT TO HELP, MORE THAN *ANYTHING*...
...BUT *NONE* OF THE SPELLS YOU TRY ARE ABLE TO SAVE THEM?!
WHAT IF YOU GET TO THE TOWER, AND YOU FIND THAT THERE *ISN'T* AN ANSWER INSIDE?

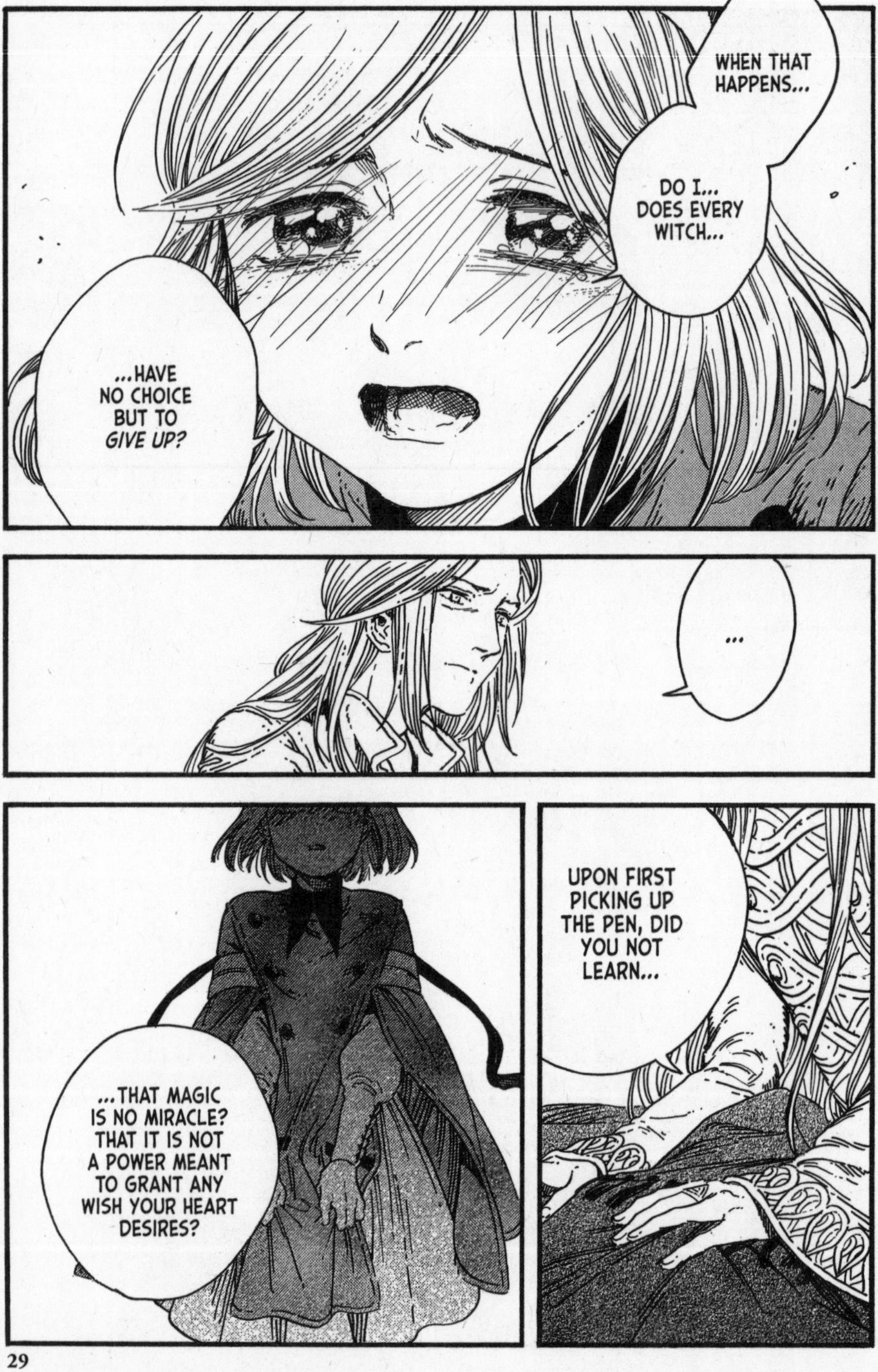
WHEN THAT HAPPENS...
DO I... DOES EVERY WITCH...
...HAVE NO CHOICE BUT TO *GIVE UP?*
...
UPON FIRST PICKING UP THE PEN, DID YOU NOT LEARN...
...THAT MAGIC IS NO MIRACLE? THAT IT IS NOT A POWER MEANT TO GRANT ANY WISH YOUR HEART DESIRES?

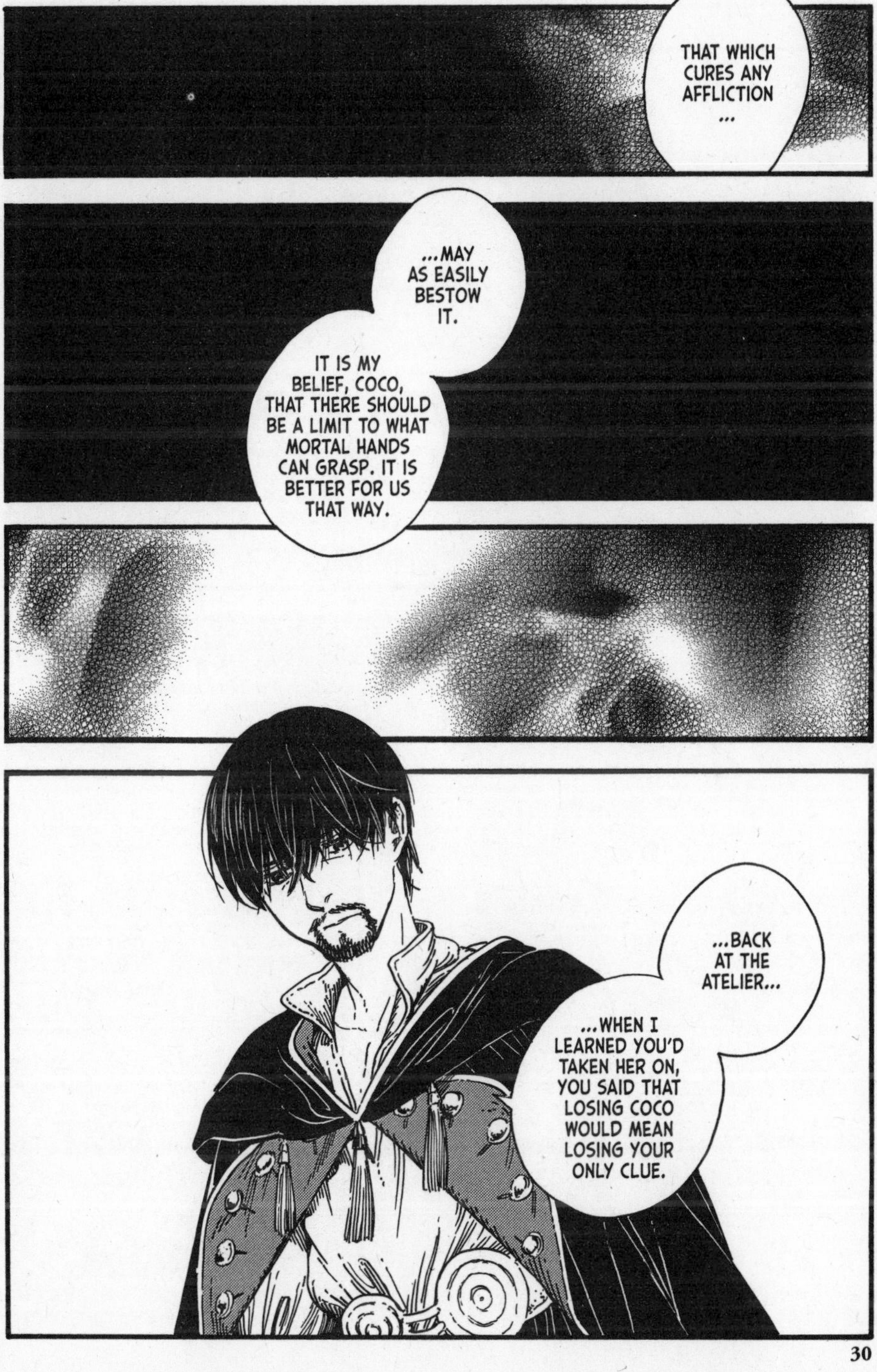
THAT WHICH CURES ANY AFFLICTION ...
...MAY AS EASILY BESTOW IT.
IT IS MY BELIEF, COCO, THAT THERE SHOULD BE A LIMIT TO WHAT MORTAL HANDS CAN GRASP. IT IS BETTER FOR US THAT WAY.
...BACK AT THE ATELIER...
...WHEN I LEARNED YOU'D TAKEN HER ON, YOU SAID THAT LOSING COCO WOULD MEAN LOSING YOUR ONLY CLUE.

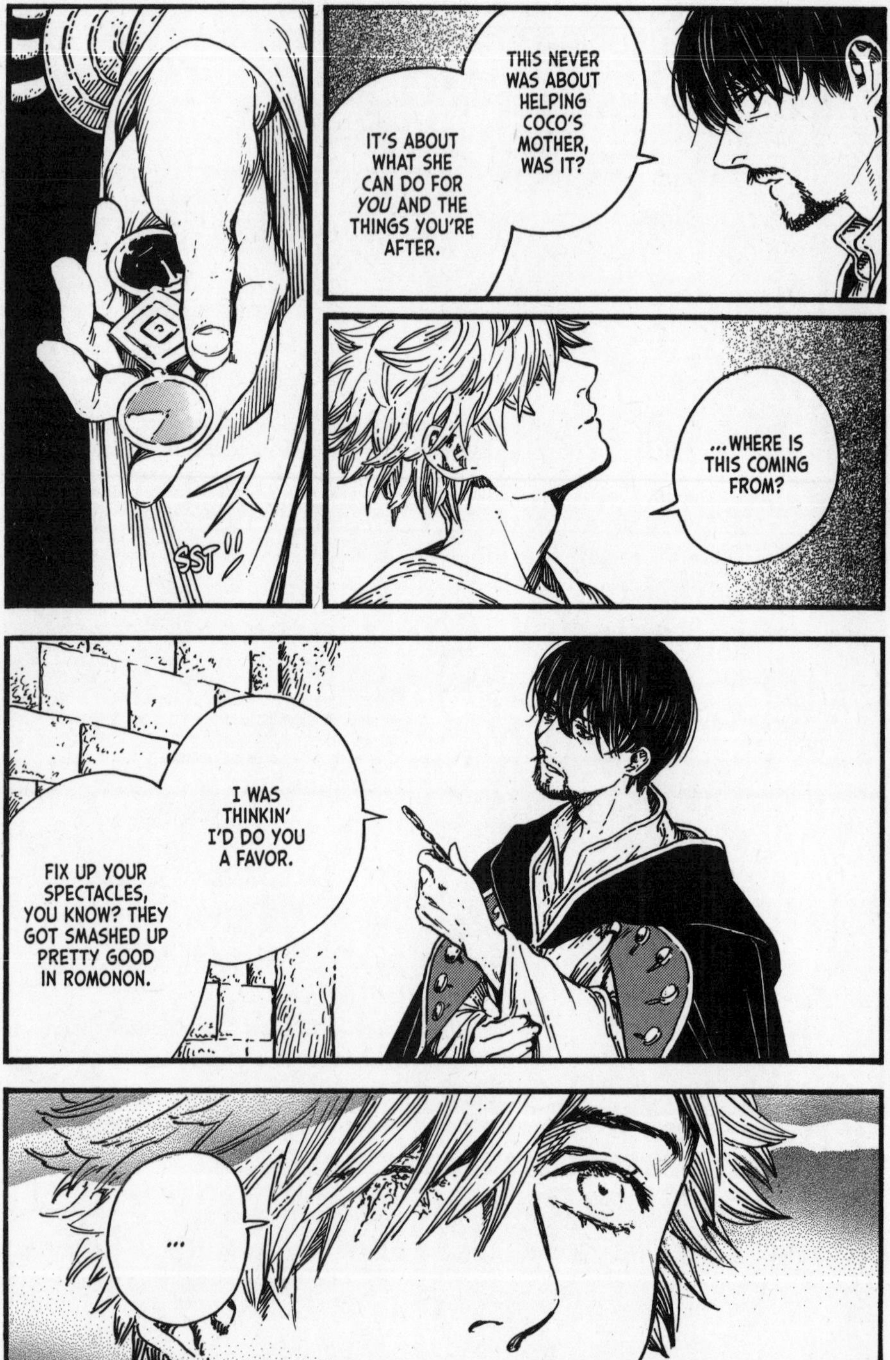
THIS NEVER WAS ABOUT HELPING COCO'S MOTHER, WAS IT?
IT'S ABOUT WHAT SHE CAN DO FOR *YOU* AND THE THINGS YOU'RE AFTER.
...WHERE IS THIS COMING FROM?
SST
I WAS THINKIN' I'D DO YOU A FAVOR.
FIX UP YOUR SPECTACLES, YOU KNOW? THEY GOT SMASHED UP PRETTY GOOD IN ROMONON.
...

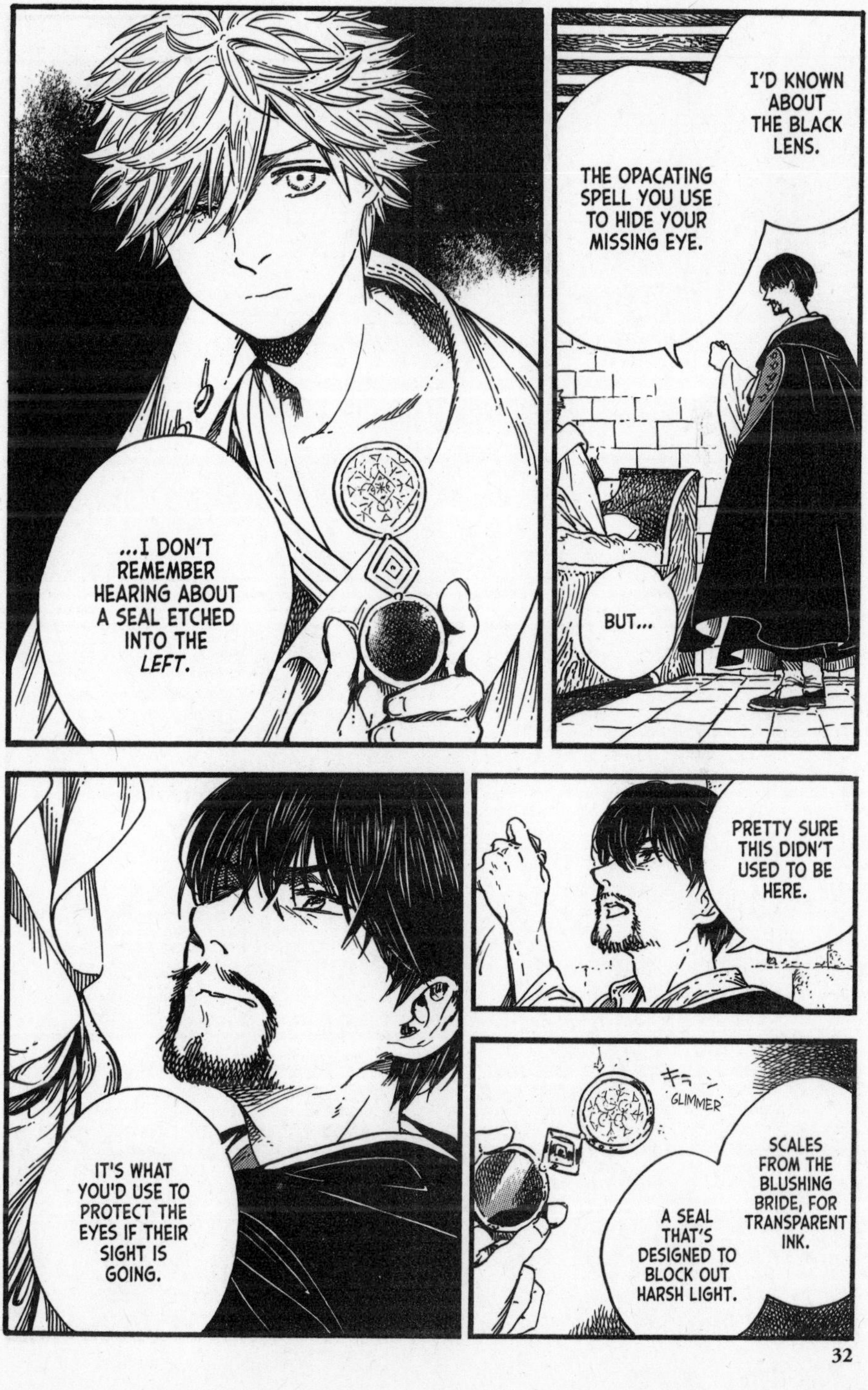
I'D KNOWN ABOUT THE BLACK LENS.
THE OPACATING SPELL YOU USE TO HIDE YOUR MISSING EYE.
BUT...
...I DON'T REMEMBER HEARING ABOUT A SEAL ETCHED INTO THE *LEFT*.
PRETTY SURE THIS DIDN'T USED TO BE HERE.
キラン
GLIMMER
SCALES FROM THE BLUSHING BRIDE, FOR TRANSPARENT INK.
A SEAL THAT'S DESIGNED TO BLOCK OUT HARSH LIGHT.
IT'S WHAT YOU'D USE TO PROTECT THE EYES IF THEIR SIGHT IS GOING.

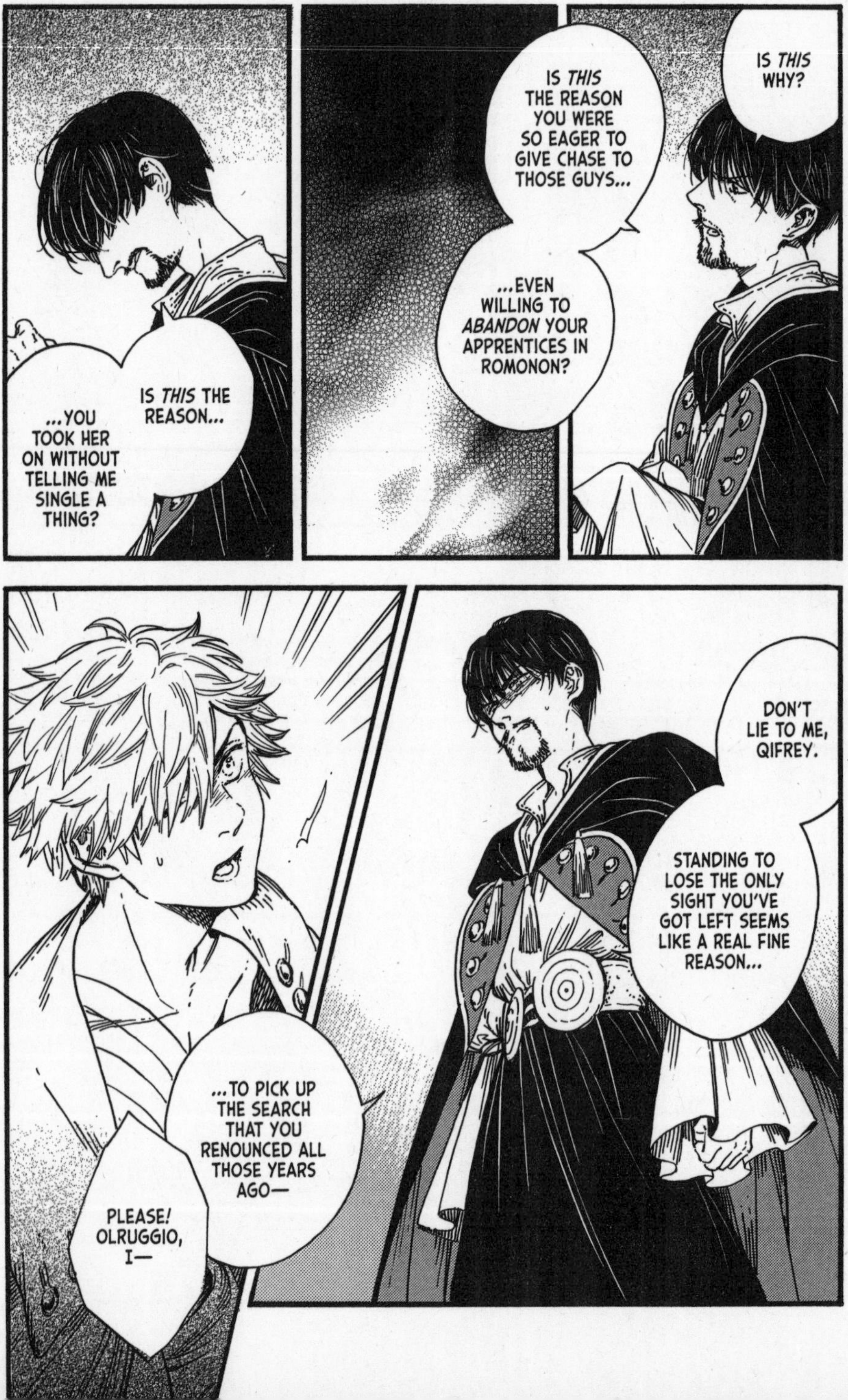
IS *THIS* WHY?
IS *THIS* THE REASON YOU WERE SO EAGER TO GIVE CHASE TO THOSE GUYS...
...EVEN WILLING TO *ABANDON* YOUR APPRENTICES IN ROMONON?
IS *THIS* THE REASON...
...YOU TOOK HER ON WITHOUT TELLING ME SINGLE A THING?
DON'T LIE TO ME, QIFREY.
STANDING TO LOSE THE ONLY SIGHT YOU'VE GOT LEFT SEEMS LIKE A REAL FINE REASON...
...TO PICK UP THE SEARCH THAT YOU RENOUNCED ALL THOSE YEARS AGO—
PLEASE! OLRUGGIO, I—

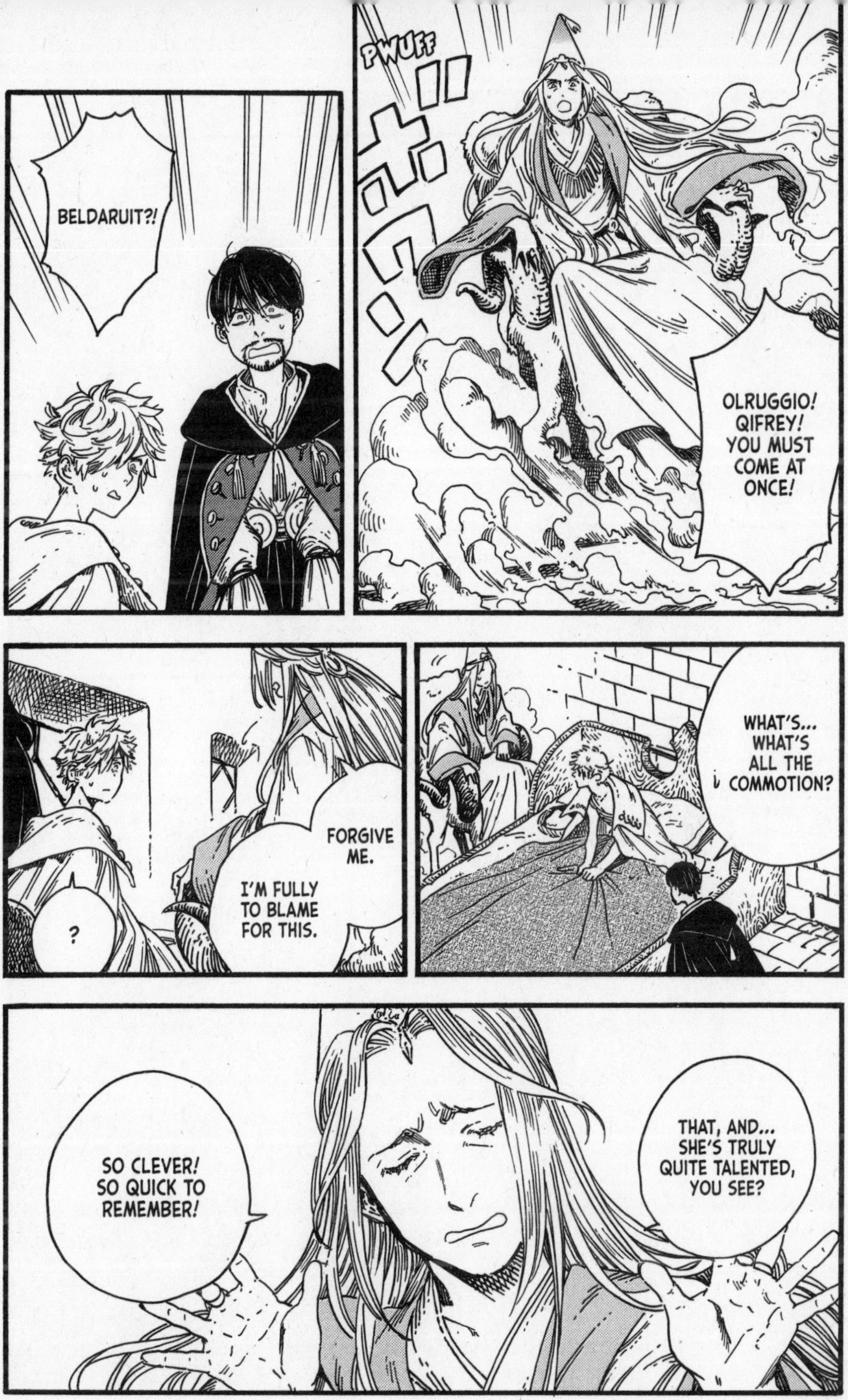
PWUFF
OLRUGGIO! QIFREY! YOU MUST COME AT ONCE!
BELDARUIT?!
WHAT'S... WHAT'S ALL THE COMMOTION?
FORGIVE ME.
I'M FULLY TO BLAME FOR THIS.
?
THAT, AND... SHE'S TRULY QUITE TALENTED, YOU SEE?
SO CLEVER! SO QUICK TO REMEMBER!

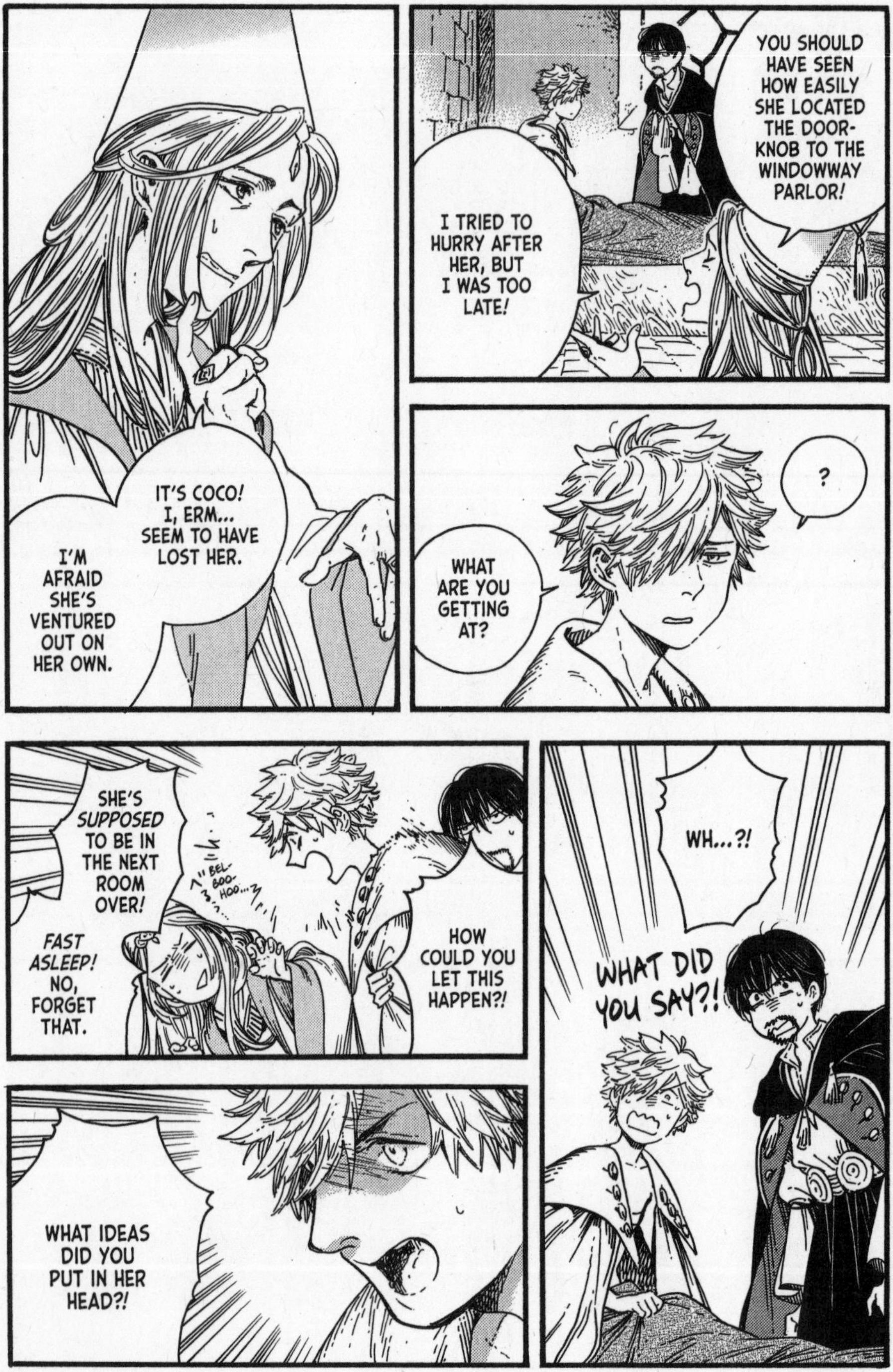
YOU SHOULD HAVE SEEN HOW EASILY SHE LOCATED THE DOOR-KNOB TO THE WINDOWWAY PARLOR!
I TRIED TO HURRY AFTER HER, BUT I WAS TOO LATE!
?
WHAT ARE YOU GETTING AT?
IT'S COCO! I, ERM... SEEM TO HAVE LOST HER.
I'M AFRAID SHE'S VENTURED OUT ON HER OWN.
WH...?!
WHAT DID YOU SAY?!
HOW COULD YOU LET THIS HAPPEN?!
BEL- BOO- HOO...
SHE'S *SUPPOSED* TO BE IN THE NEXT ROOM OVER!
FAST ASLEEP! NO, FORGET THAT.
WHAT IDEAS DID YOU PUT IN HER HEAD?!

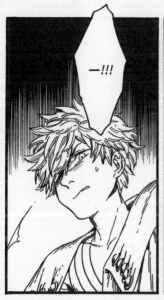

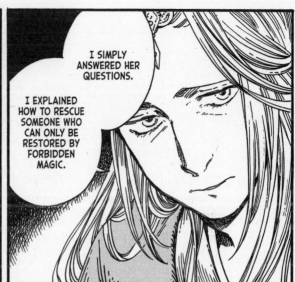

I SIMPLY ANSWERED HER QUESTIONS.
I EXPLAINED HOW TO RESCUE SOMEONE WHO CAN ONLY BE RESTORED BY FORBIDDEN MAGIC.
—!!!
FWSH
WELL IT DOESN'T TAKE MUCH...
...TO GUESS ALL THAT YOU TOLD HER!
EASY THERE!
I HAVE TO GO AFTER HER.
I HAVE TO BRING HER BACK...

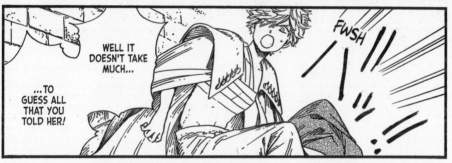

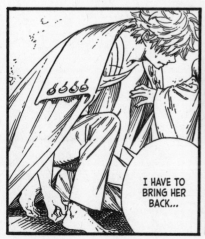

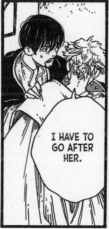

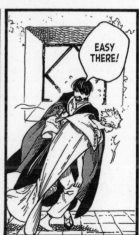

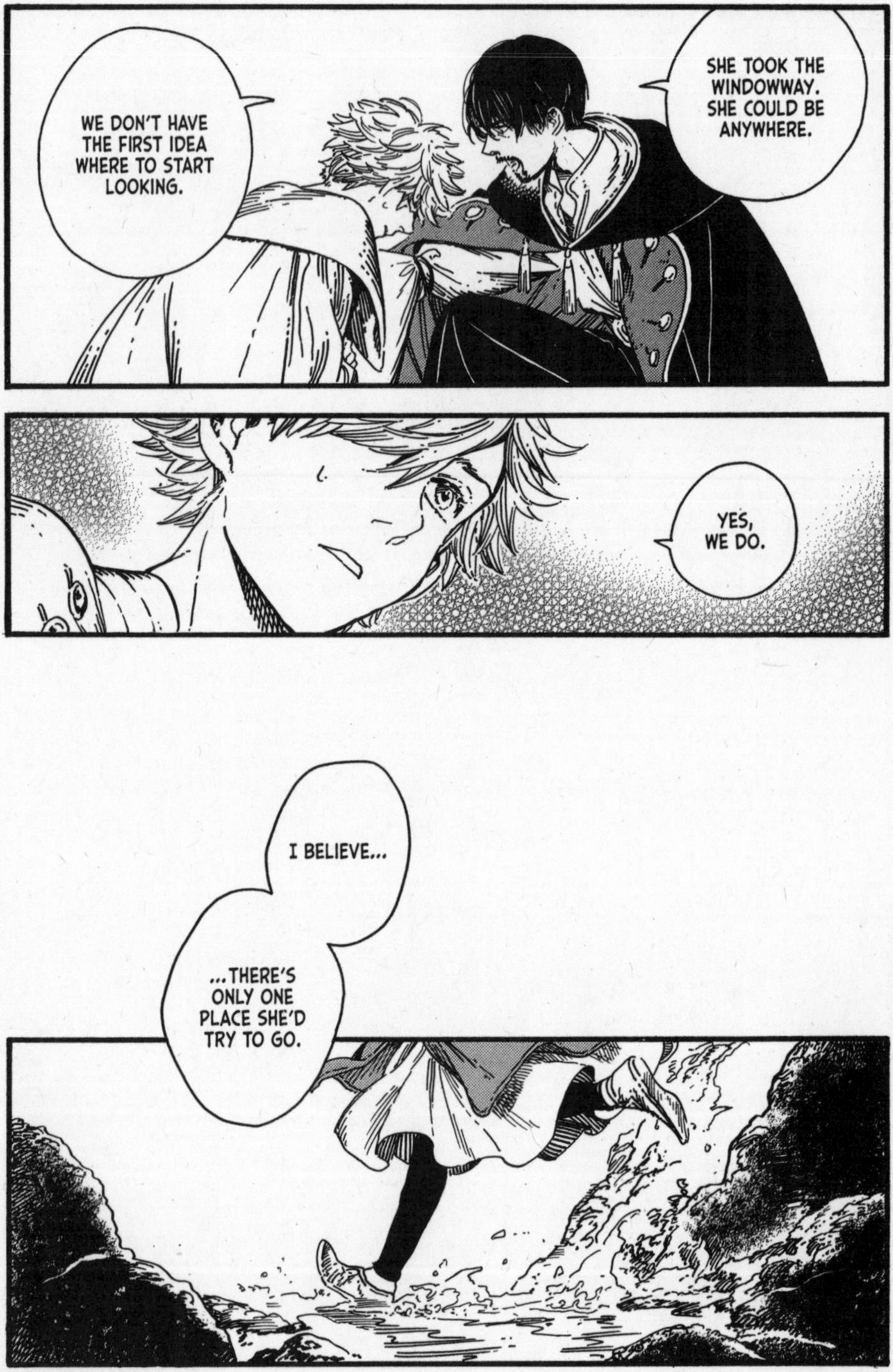
SHE TOOK THE WINDOWWAY. SHE COULD BE ANYWHERE.
WE DON'T HAVE THE FIRST IDEA WHERE TO START LOOKING.
YES, WE DO.
I BELIEVE...
...THERE'S ONLY ONE PLACE SHE'D TRY TO GO.

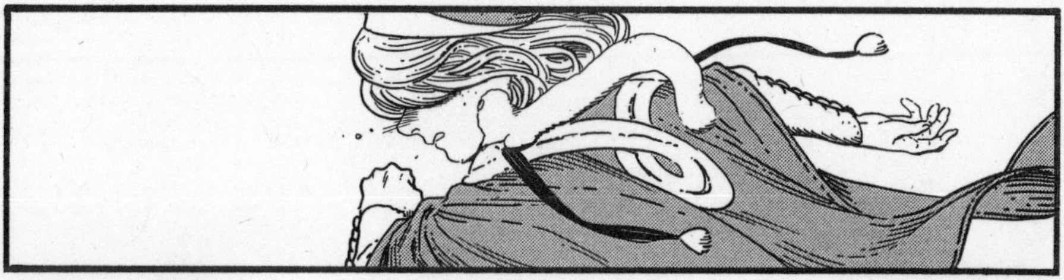

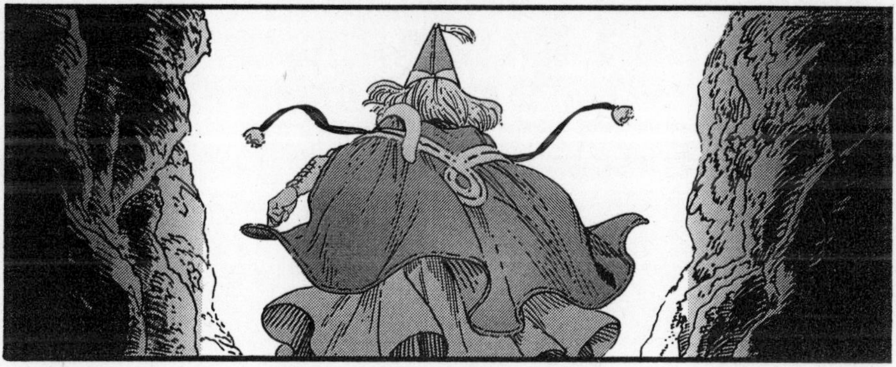

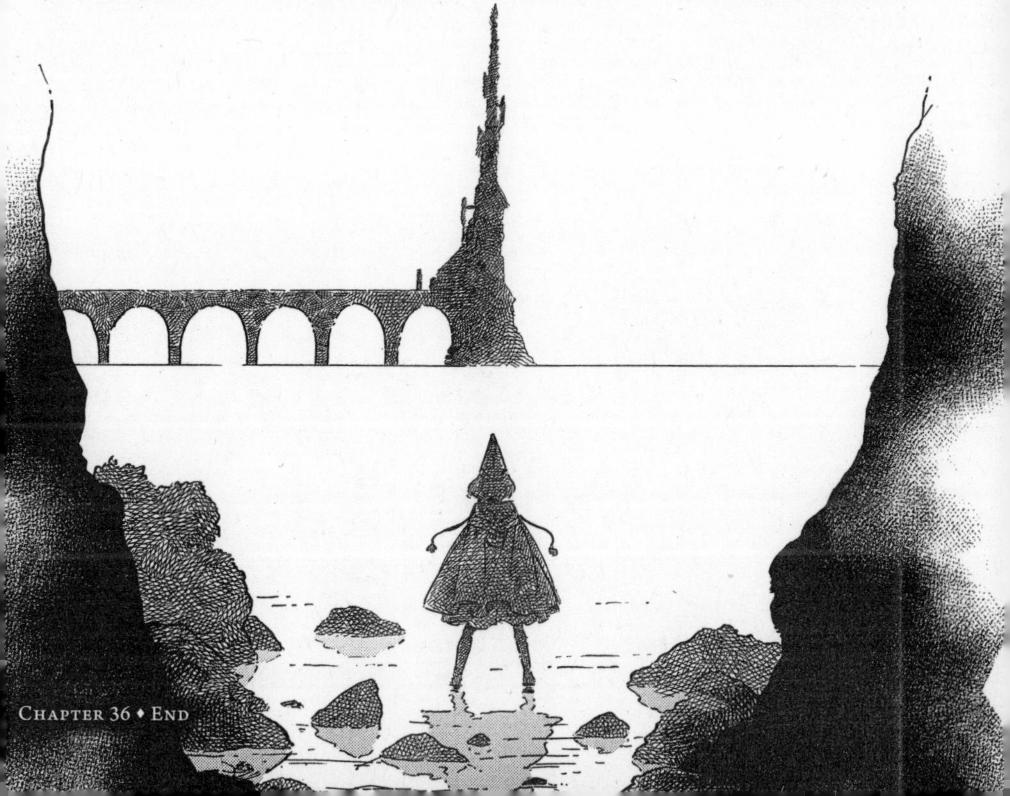
Chapter 36 ♦ End

Witch Hat Atelier

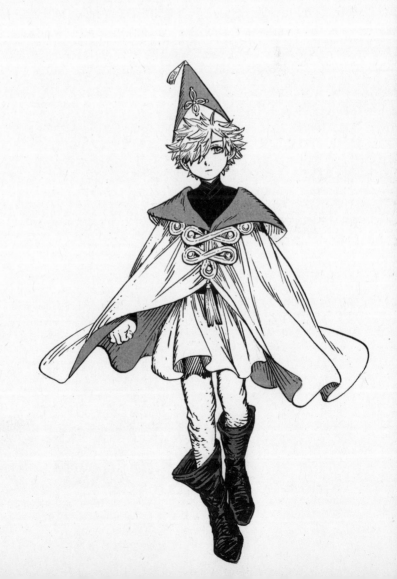

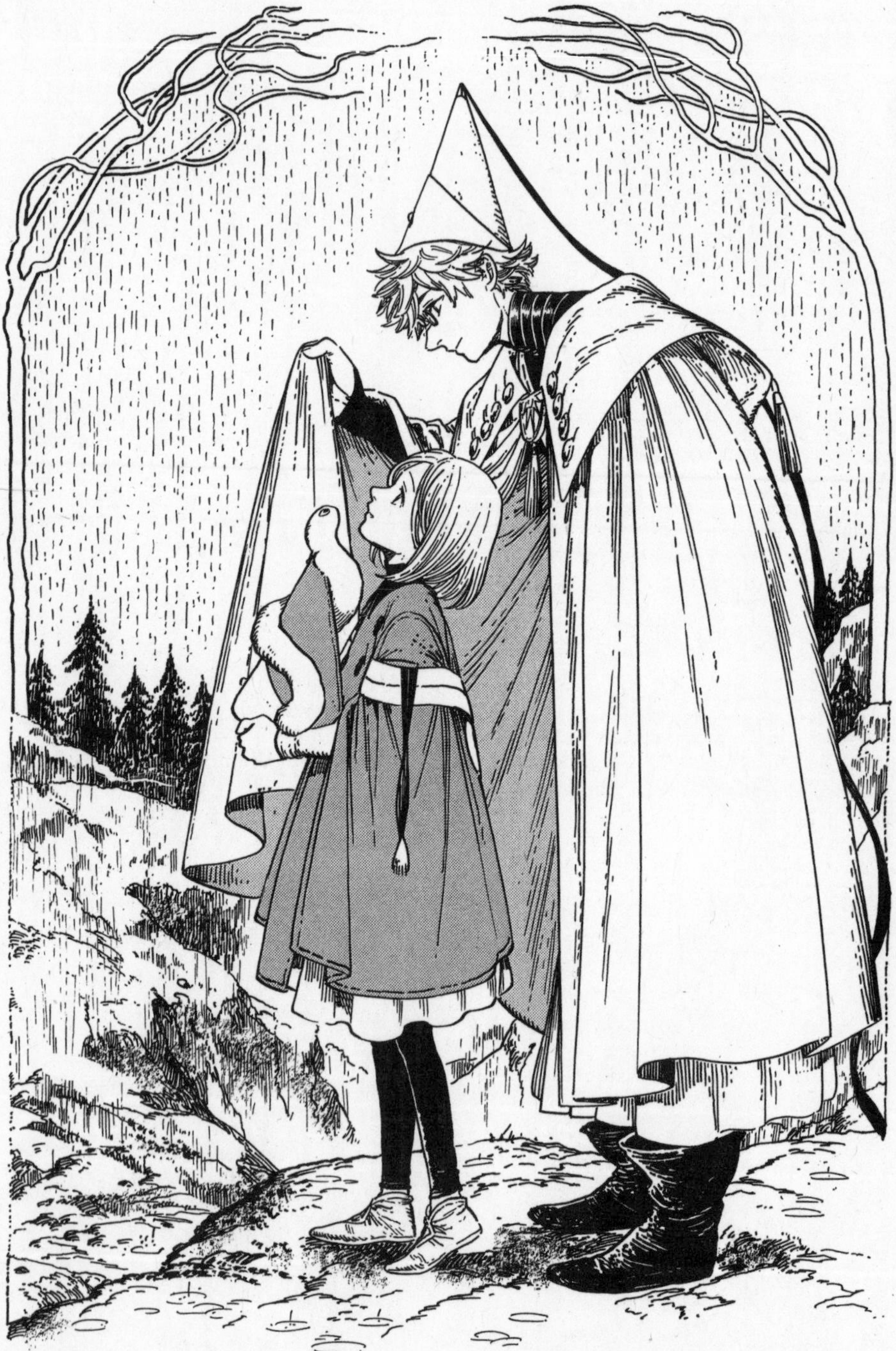

CHAPTER 37

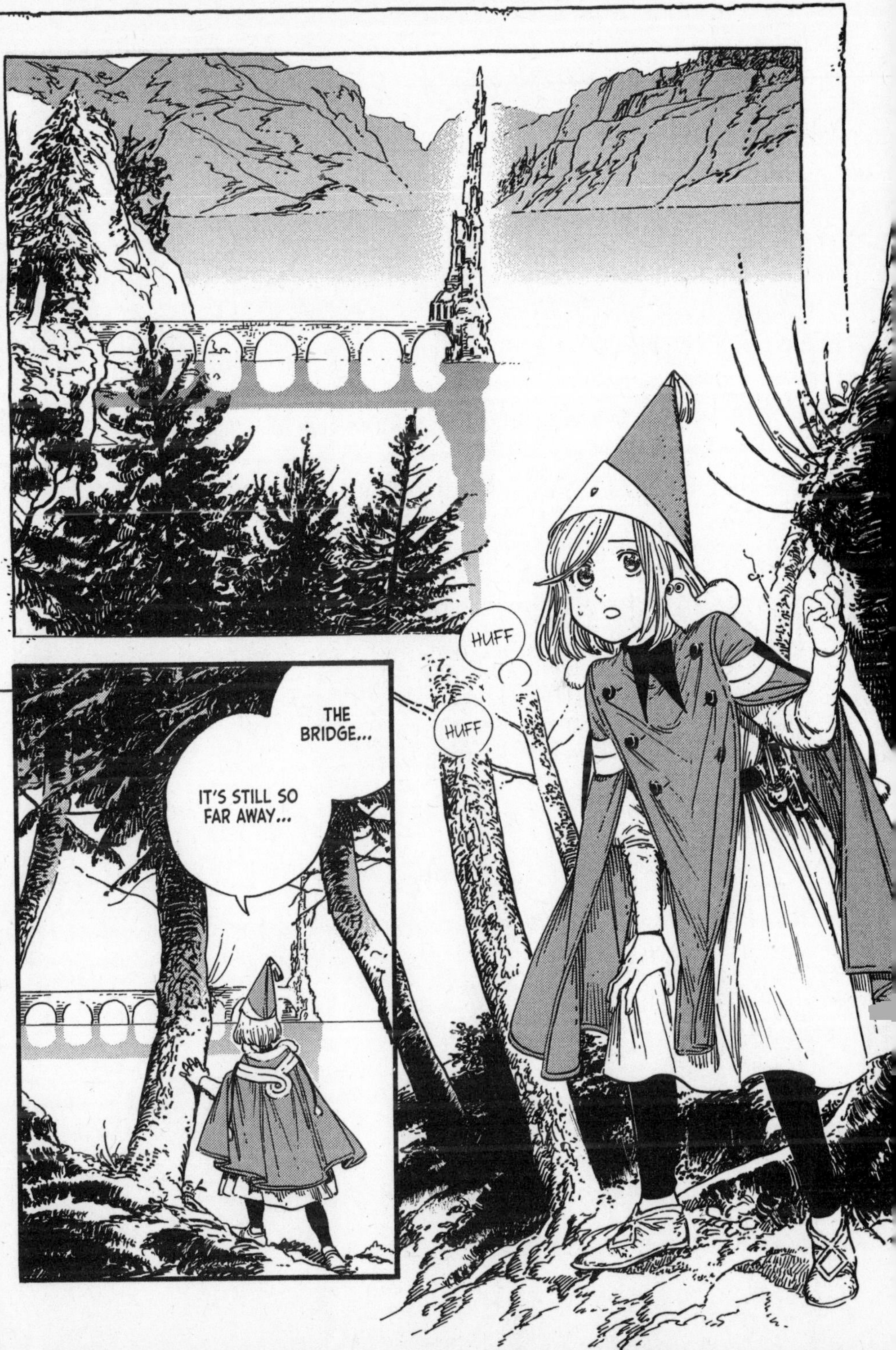
HUFF
HUFF
THE BRIDGE...
IT'S STILL SO FAR AWAY...

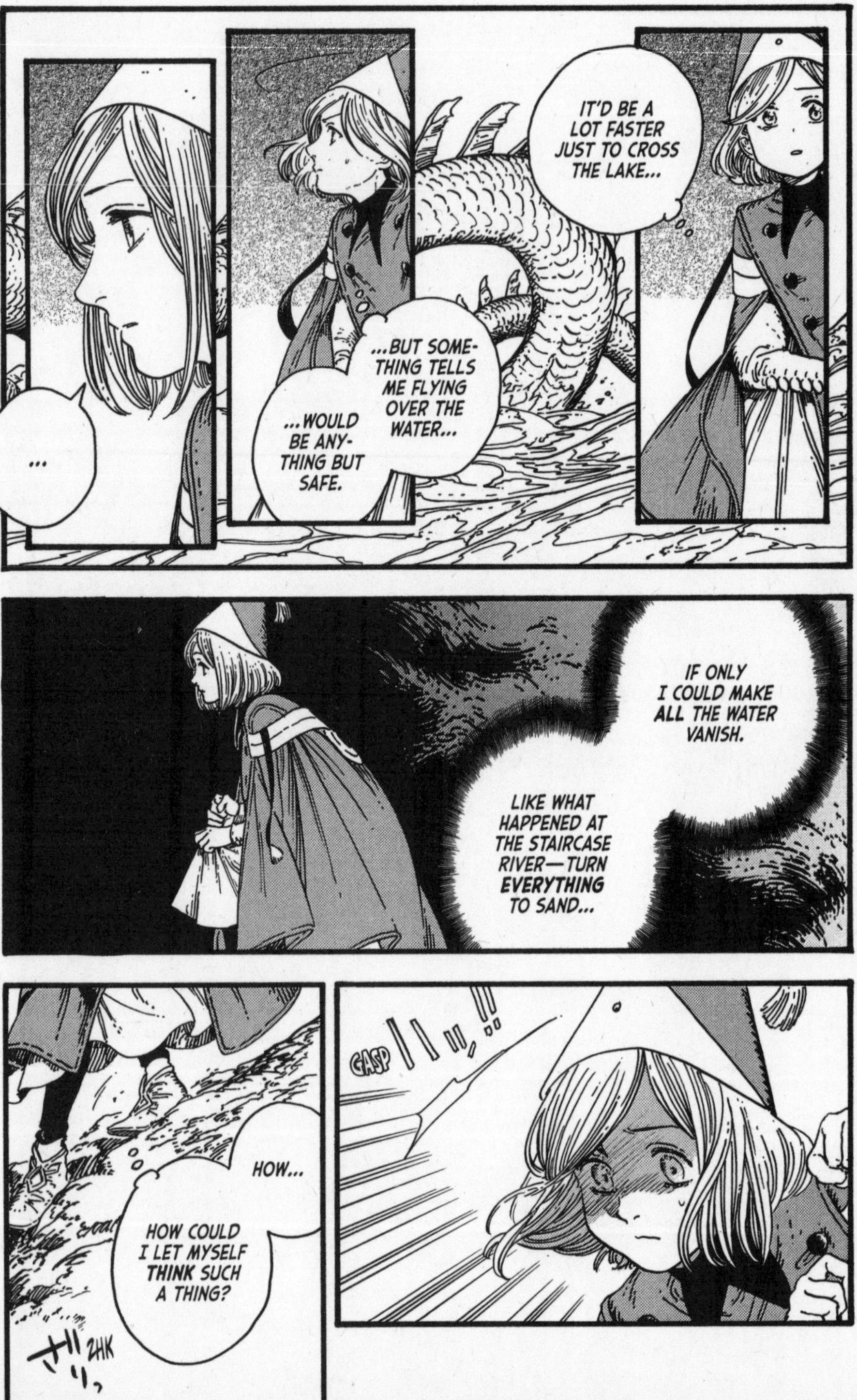
IT'D BE A LOT FASTER JUST TO CROSS THE LAKE...
...BUT SOMETHING TELLS ME FLYING OVER THE WATER...
...WOULD BE ANYTHING BUT SAFE.
...
IF ONLY I COULD MAKE ALL THE WATER VANISH.
LIKE WHAT HAPPENED AT THE STAIRCASE RIVER—TURN EVERYTHING TO SAND...
GASP
HOW...
HOW COULD I LET MYSELF THINK SUCH A THING?
ZHK

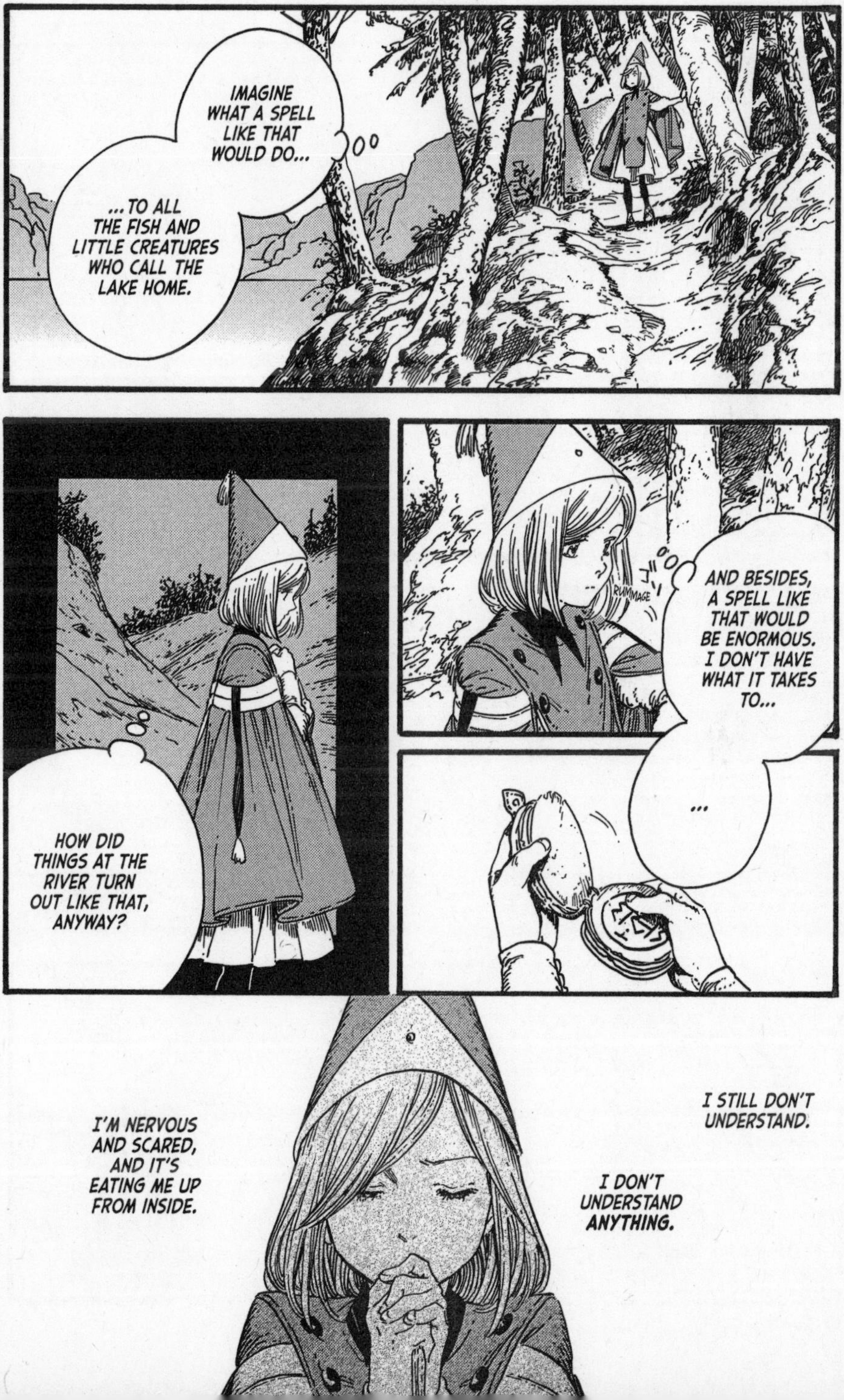
IMAGINE WHAT A SPELL LIKE THAT WOULD DO...
...TO ALL THE FISH AND LITTLE CREATURES WHO CALL THE LAKE HOME.
RUMMAGE
AND BESIDES, A SPELL LIKE THAT WOULD BE ENORMOUS. I DON'T HAVE WHAT IT TAKES TO...
...
HOW DID THINGS AT THE RIVER TURN OUT LIKE THAT, ANYWAY?
I STILL DON'T UNDERSTAND.
I DON'T UNDERSTAND ANYTHING.
I'M NERVOUS AND SCARED, AND IT'S EATING ME UP FROM INSIDE.

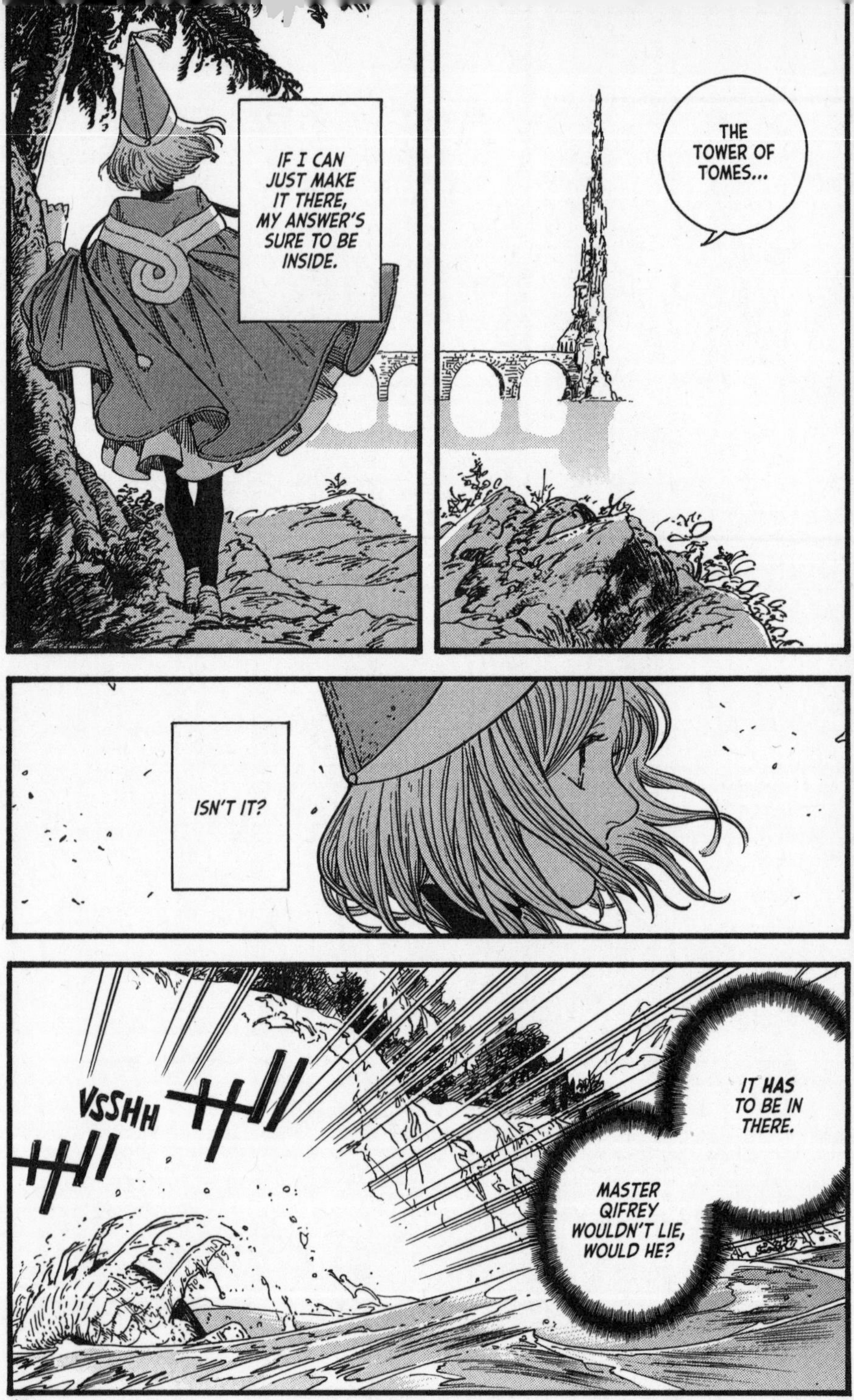
THE TOWER OF TOMES...
IF I CAN JUST MAKE IT THERE, MY ANSWER'S SURE TO BE INSIDE.
ISN'T IT?
IT HAS TO BE IN THERE.
MASTER QIFREY WOULDN'T LIE, WOULD HE?
VSSHH

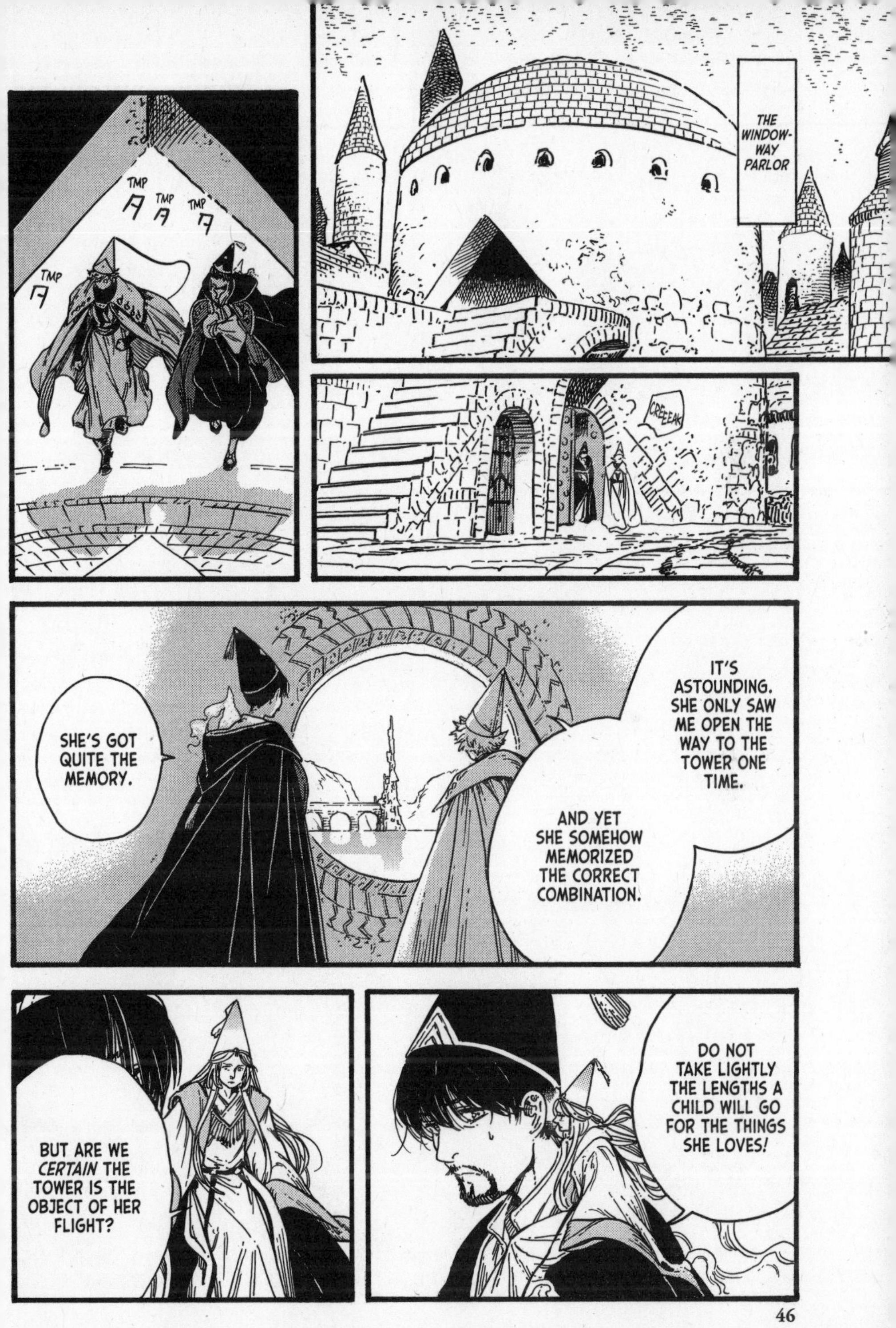
THE WINDOW-WAY PARLOR
CREEEAK
TMP TMP TMP
TMP
IT'S ASTOUNDING. SHE ONLY SAW ME OPEN THE WAY TO THE TOWER ONE TIME.
AND YET SHE SOMEHOW MEMORIZED THE CORRECT COMBINATION.
SHE'S GOT QUITE THE MEMORY.
DO NOT TAKE LIGHTLY THE LENGTHS A CHILD WILL GO FOR THE THINGS SHE LOVES!
BUT ARE WE *CERTAIN* THE TOWER IS THE OBJECT OF HER FLIGHT?

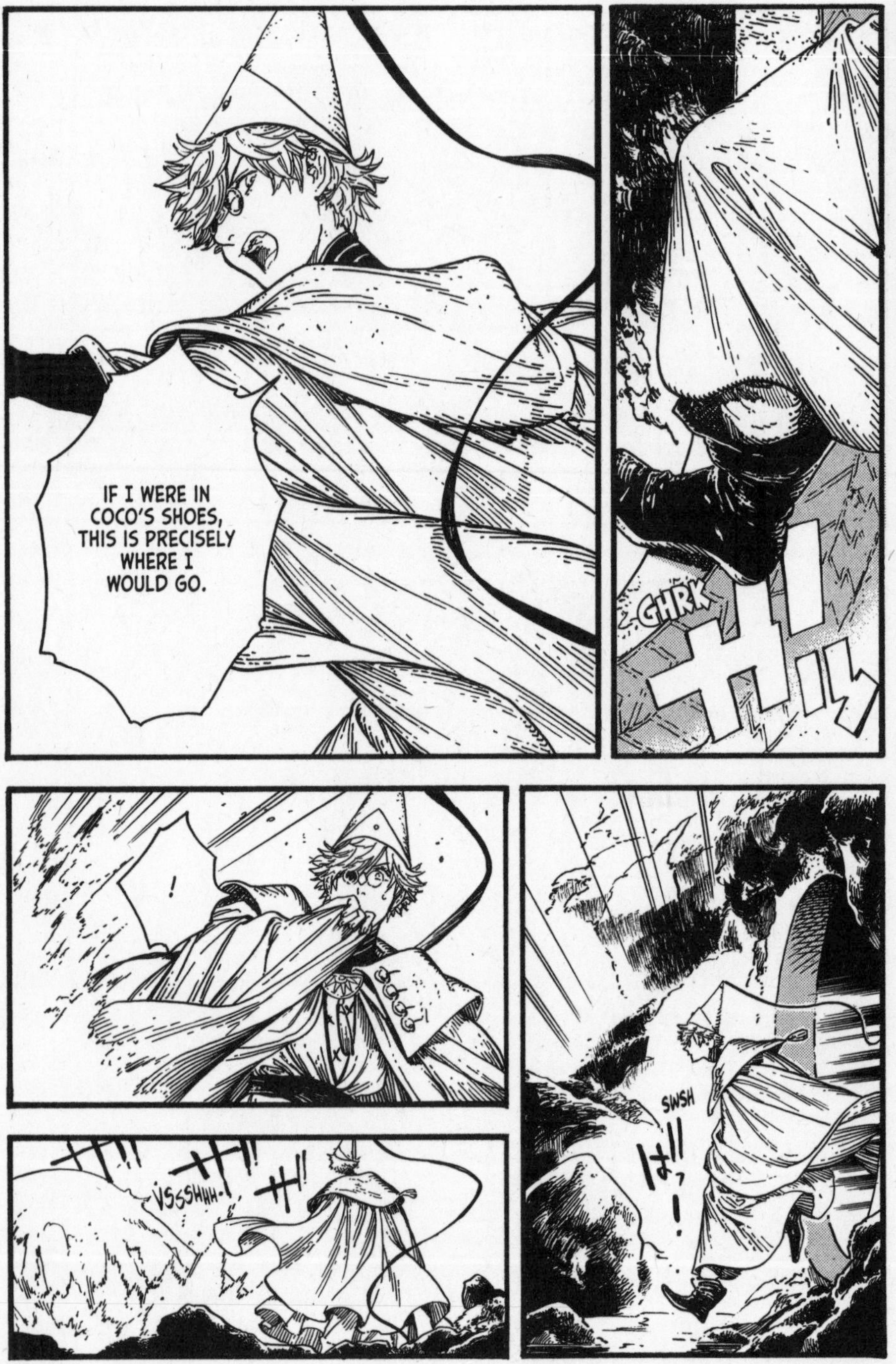
GHRK
IF I WERE IN COCO'S SHOES, THIS IS PRECISELY WHERE I WOULD GO.
SWSH
はっ!
!
VSSSHHH
ザ!!
ザ!
ザ!

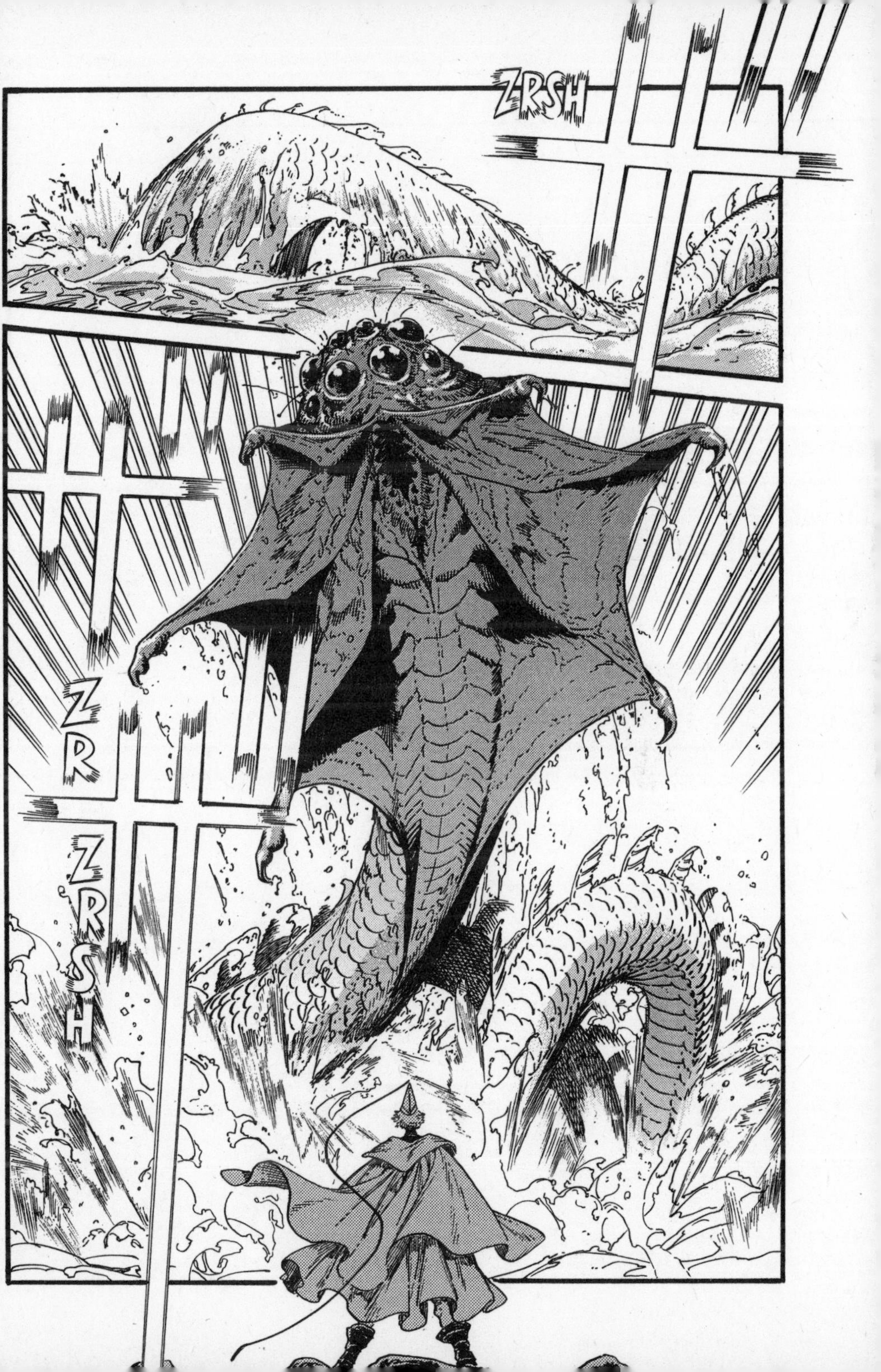
ZRSH
ZR
ZRSH

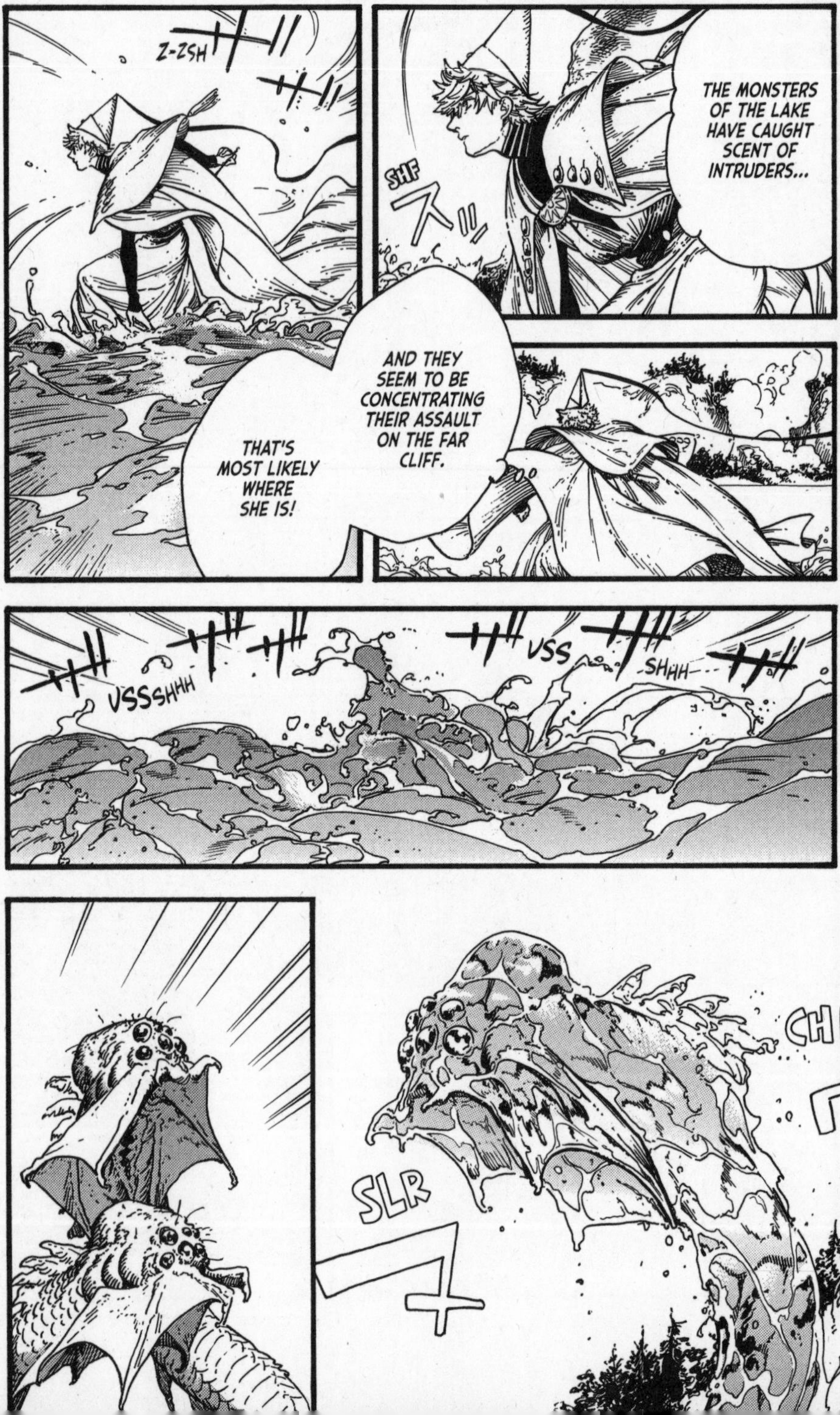
SHF
THE MONSTERS OF THE LAKE HAVE CAUGHT SCENT OF INTRUDERS...
AND THEY SEEM TO BE CONCENTRATING THEIR ASSAULT ON THE FAR CLIFF.
Z-ZSH
THAT'S MOST LIKELY WHERE SHE IS!
SHHH
VSS
VSSSHHH
CH
SLR

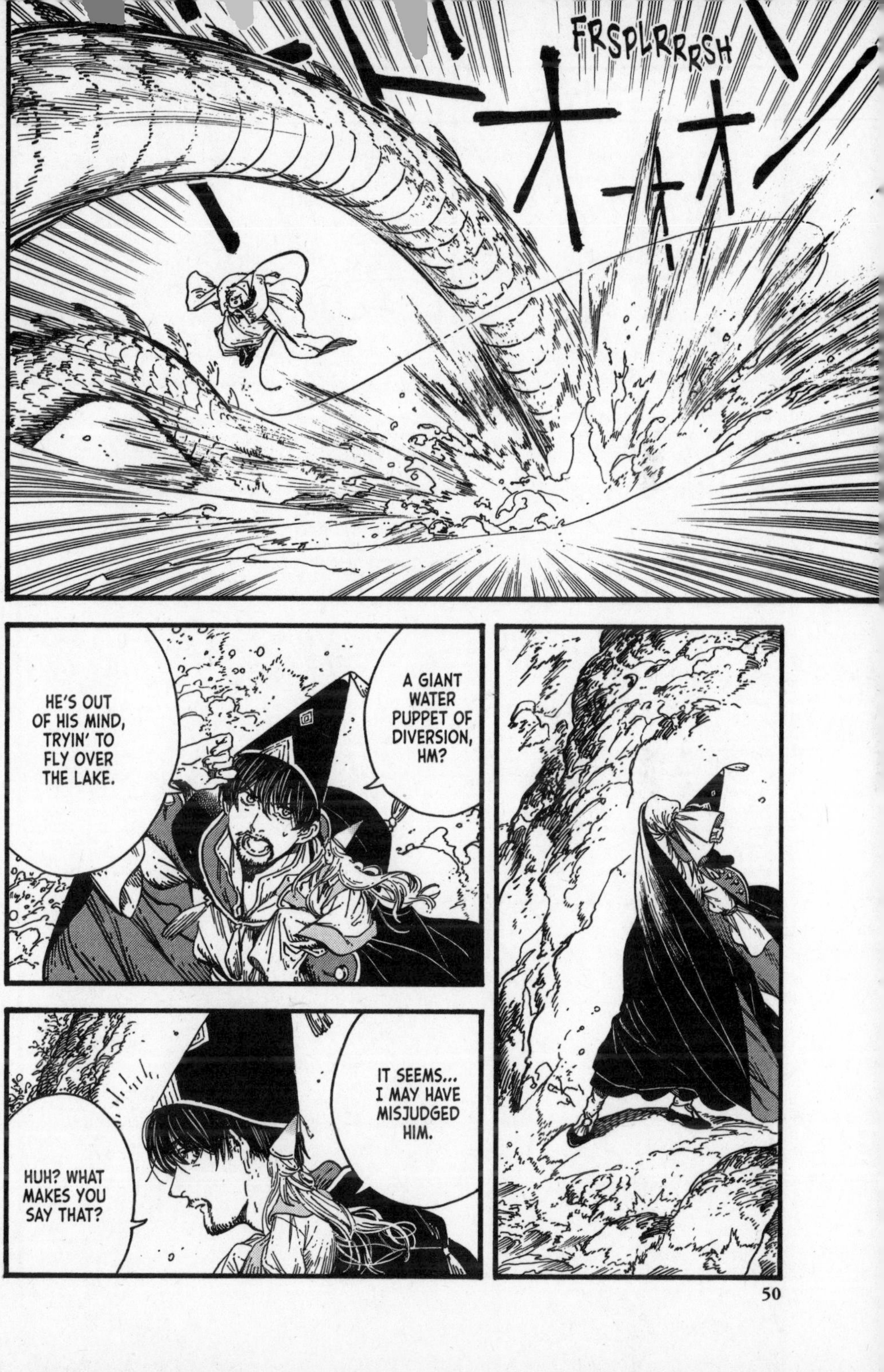
FRSPLRRRSH
A GIANT WATER PUPPET OF DIVERSION, HM?
HE'S OUT OF HIS MIND, TRYIN' TO FLY OVER THE LAKE.
IT SEEMS... I MAY HAVE MISJUDGED HIM.
HUH? WHAT MAKES YOU SAY THAT?

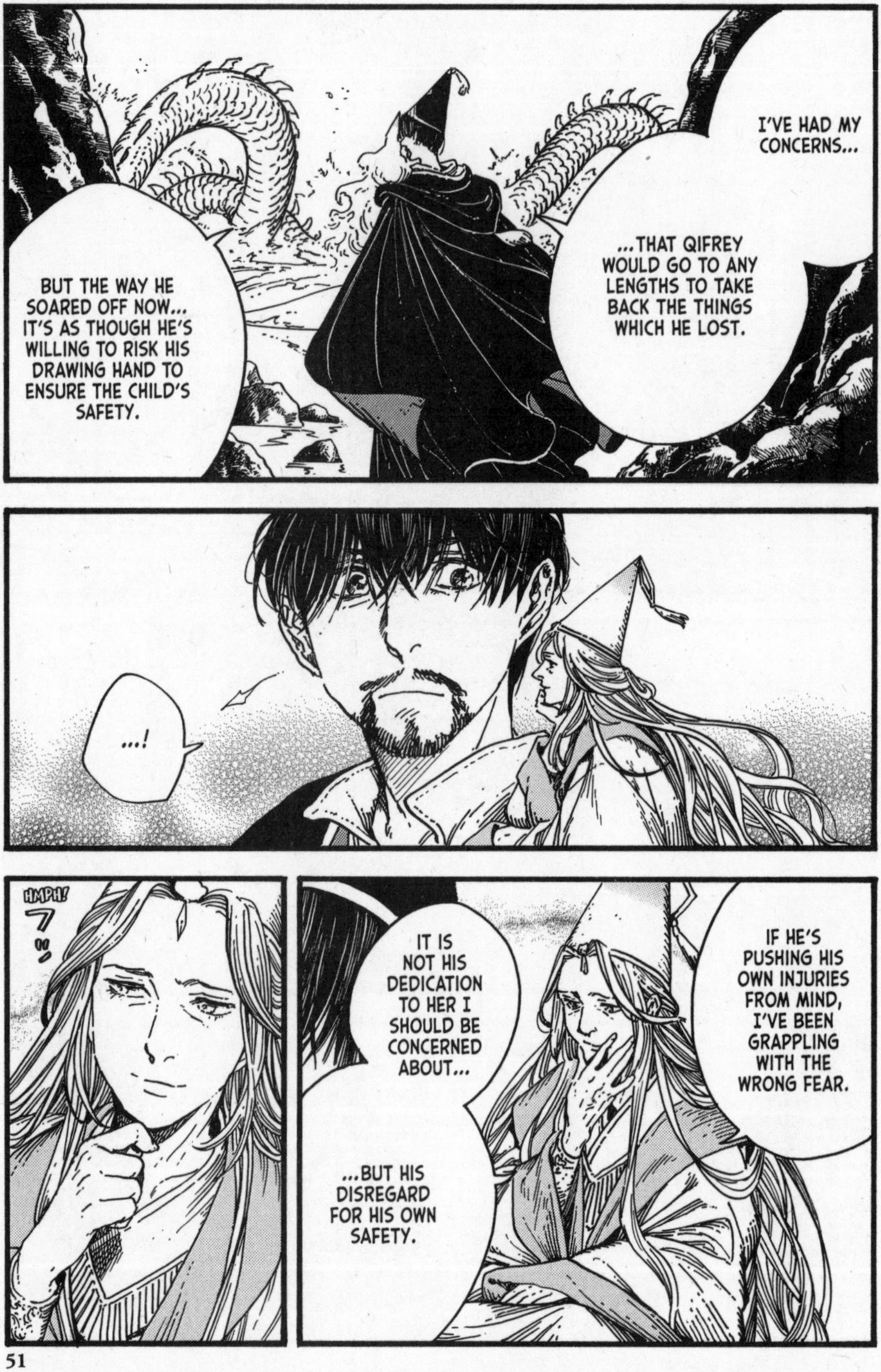
I'VE HAD MY CONCERNS...
...THAT QIFREY WOULD GO TO ANY LENGTHS TO TAKE BACK THE THINGS WHICH HE LOST.
BUT THE WAY HE SOARED OFF NOW... IT'S AS THOUGH HE'S WILLING TO RISK HIS DRAWING HAND TO ENSURE THE CHILD'S SAFETY.
...!
IF HE'S PUSHING HIS OWN INJURIES FROM MIND, I'VE BEEN GRAPPLING WITH THE WRONG FEAR.
IT IS NOT HIS DEDICATION TO HER I SHOULD BE CONCERNED ABOUT...
...BUT HIS DISREGARD FOR HIS OWN SAFETY.
HMPH!

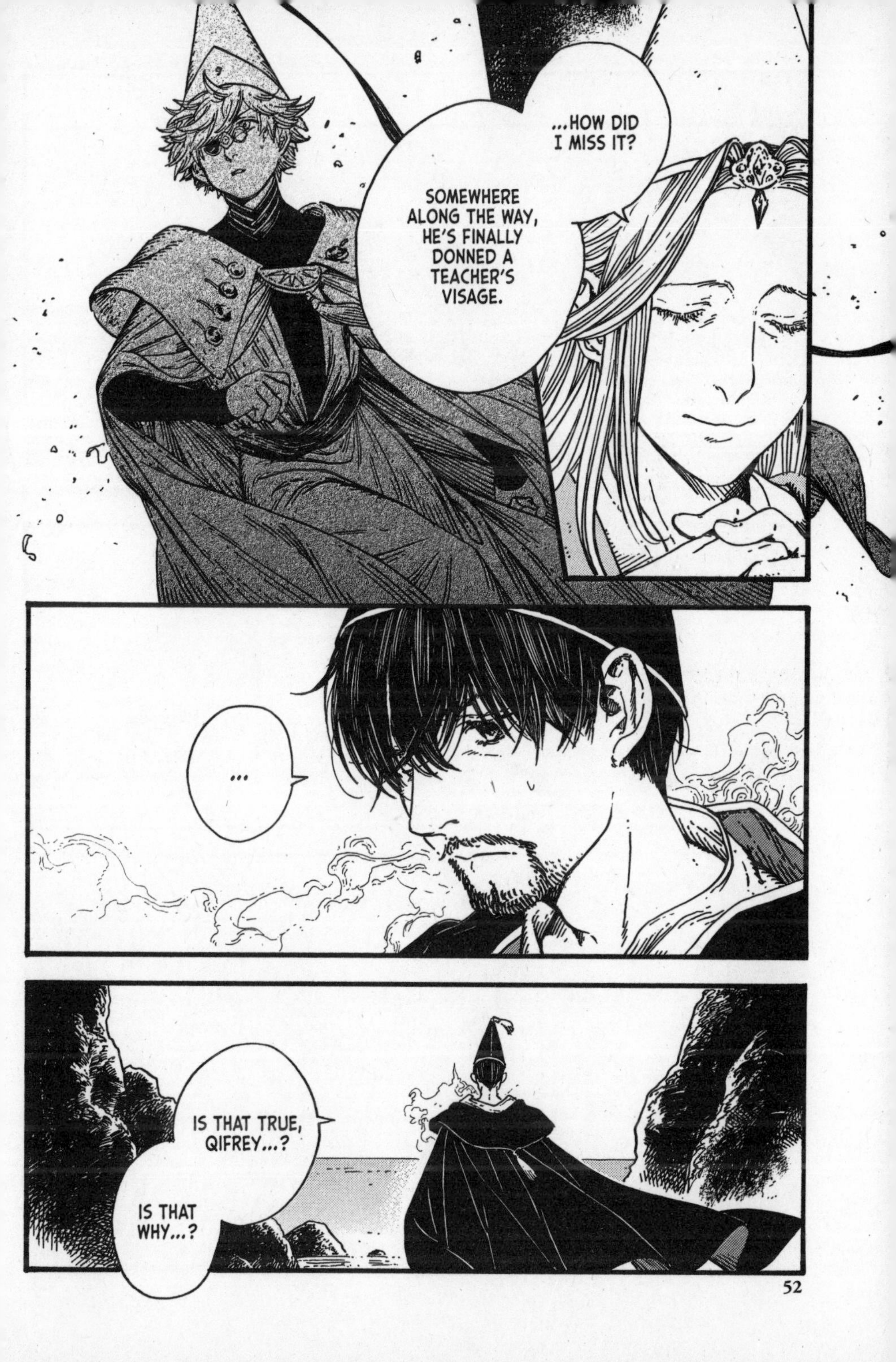
...HOW DID I MISS IT?
SOMEWHERE ALONG THE WAY, HE'S FINALLY DONNED A TEACHER'S VISAGE.
...
IS THAT TRUE, QIFREY...?
IS THAT WHY...?

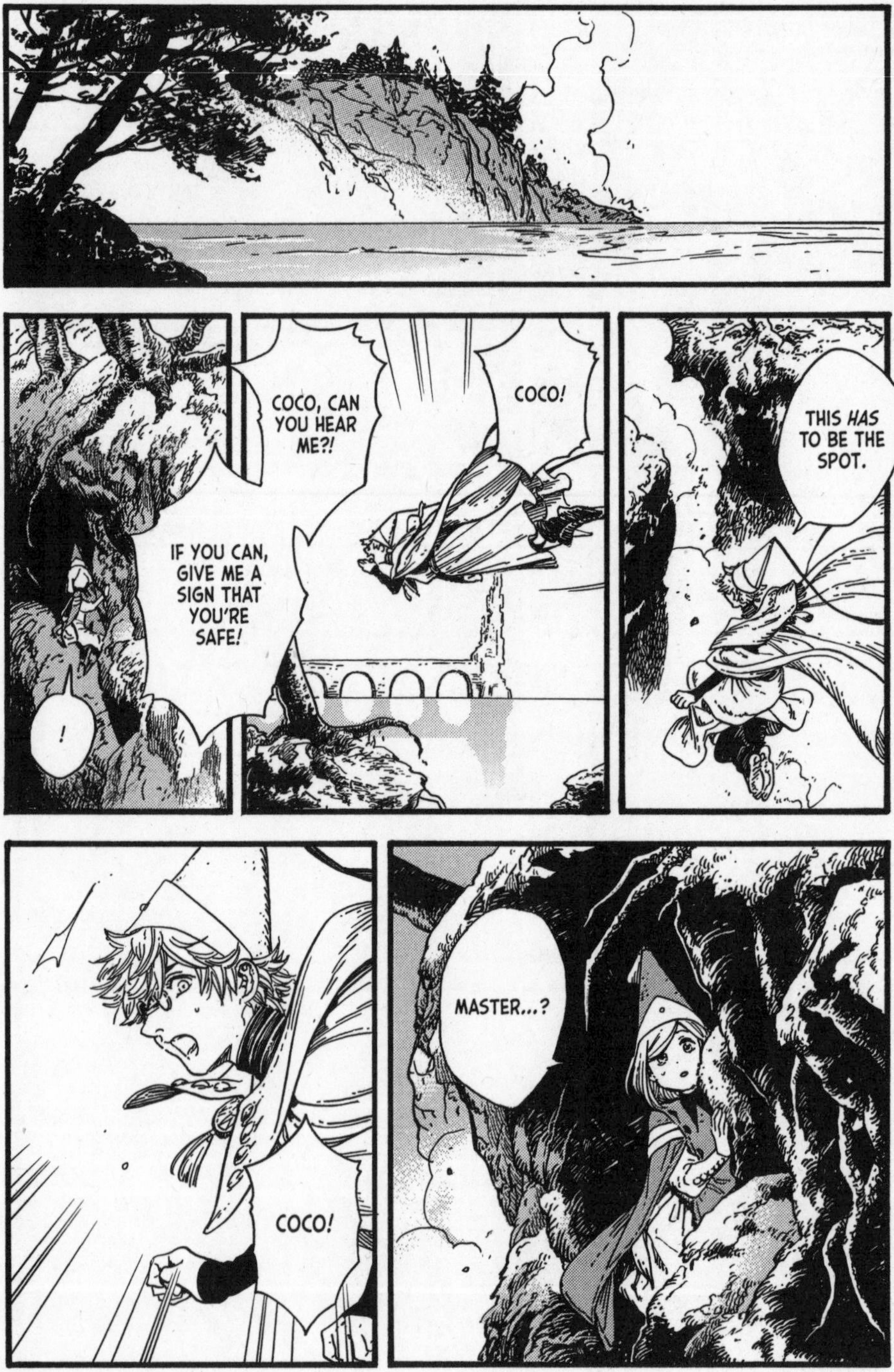
THIS *HAS* TO BE THE SPOT.
COCO!
COCO, CAN YOU HEAR ME?!
IF YOU CAN, GIVE ME A SIGN THAT YOU'RE SAFE!
!
MASTER...?
COCO!

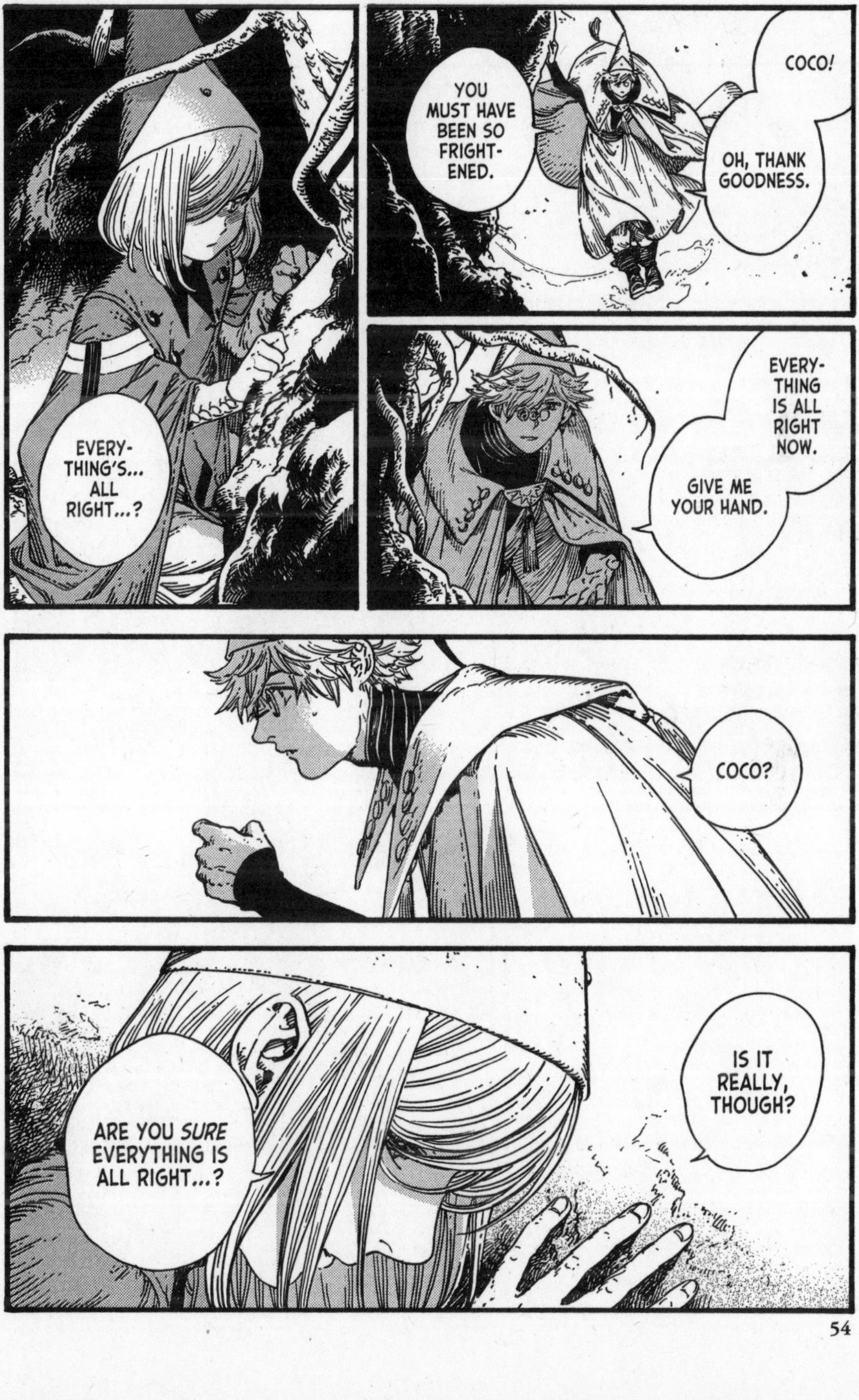
COCO!
OH, THANK GOODNESS.
YOU MUST HAVE BEEN SO FRIGHTENED.
EVERYTHING IS ALL RIGHT NOW.
GIVE ME YOUR HAND.
EVERYTHING'S... ALL RIGHT...?
COCO?
IS IT REALLY, THOUGH?
ARE YOU *SURE* EVERYTHING IS ALL RIGHT...?

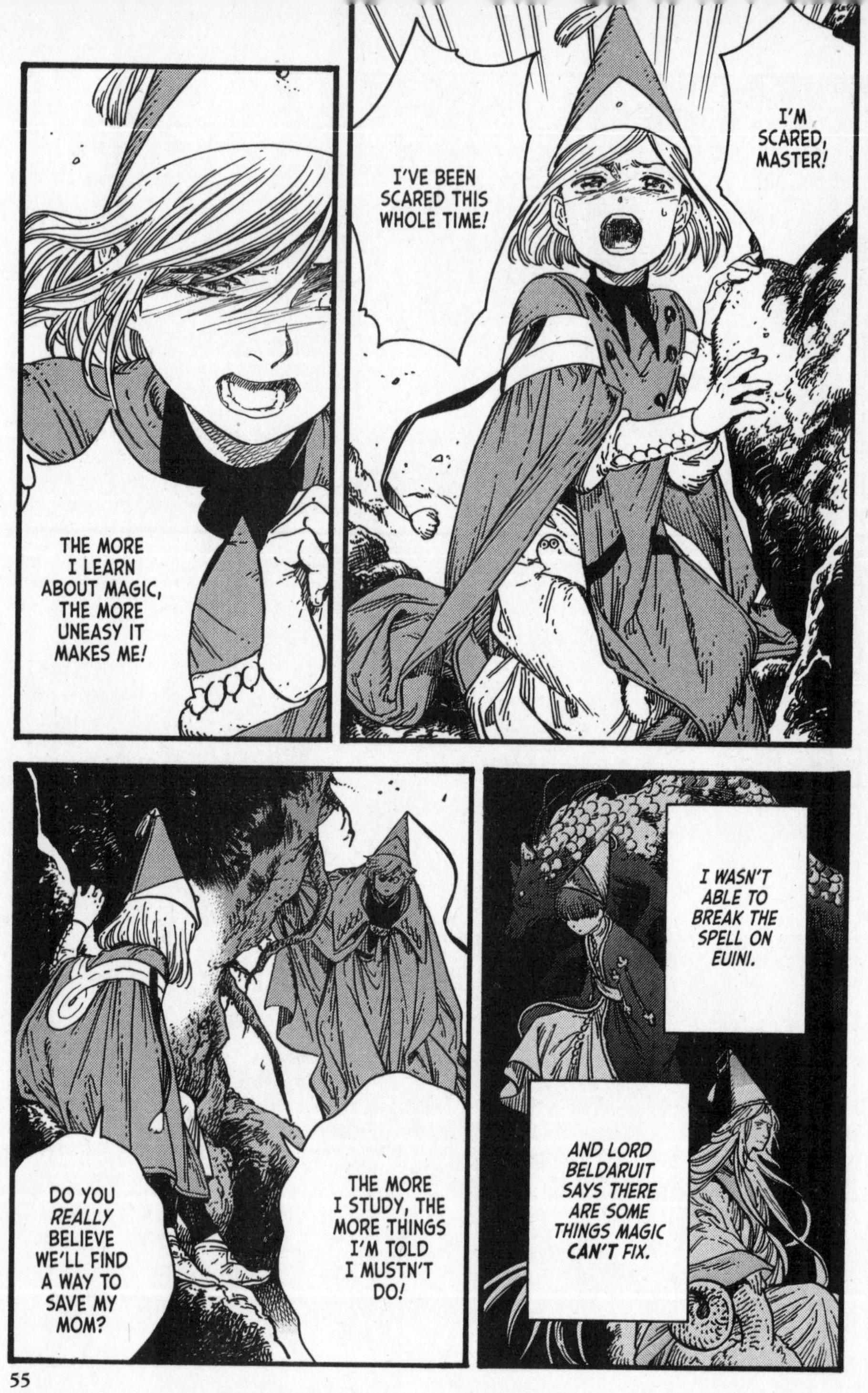
I'M SCARED, MASTER!
I'VE BEEN SCARED THIS WHOLE TIME!
THE MORE I LEARN ABOUT MAGIC, THE MORE UNEASY IT MAKES ME!
I WASN'T ABLE TO BREAK THE SPELL ON EUINI.
AND LORD BELDARUIT SAYS THERE ARE SOME THINGS MAGIC *CAN'T* FIX.
THE MORE I STUDY, THE MORE THINGS I'M TOLD I MUSTN'T DO!
DO YOU *REALLY* BELIEVE WE'LL FIND A WAY TO SAVE MY MOM?

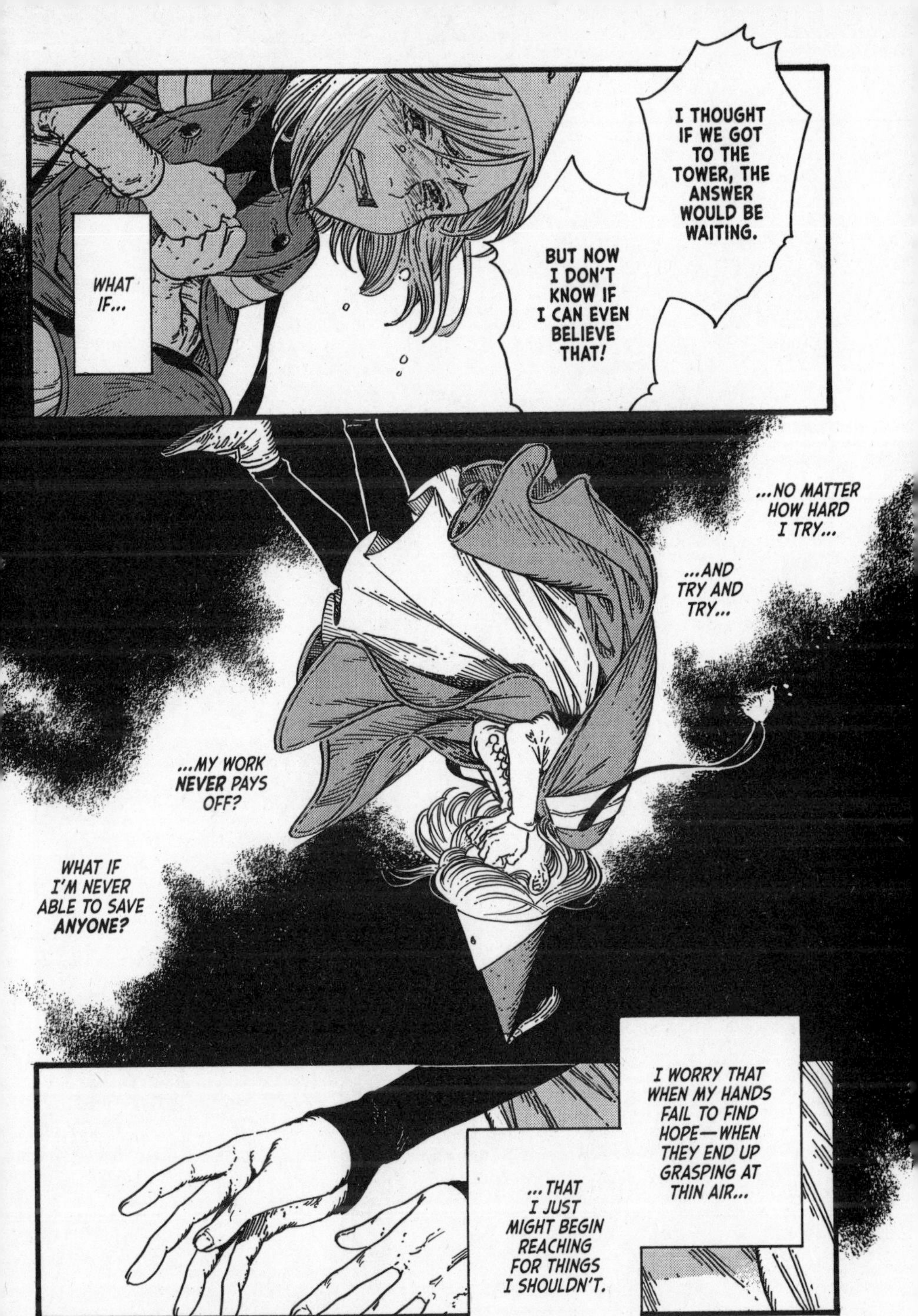
I THOUGHT IF WE GOT TO THE TOWER, THE ANSWER WOULD BE WAITING.
BUT NOW I DON'T KNOW IF I CAN EVEN BELIEVE THAT!
WHAT IF...
...NO MATTER HOW HARD I TRY...
...AND TRY AND TRY...
...MY WORK NEVER PAYS OFF?
WHAT IF I'M NEVER ABLE TO SAVE ANYONE?
I WORRY THAT WHEN MY HANDS FAIL TO FIND HOPE—WHEN THEY END UP GRASPING AT THIN AIR...
...THAT I JUST MIGHT BEGIN REACHING FOR THINGS I SHOULDN'T.

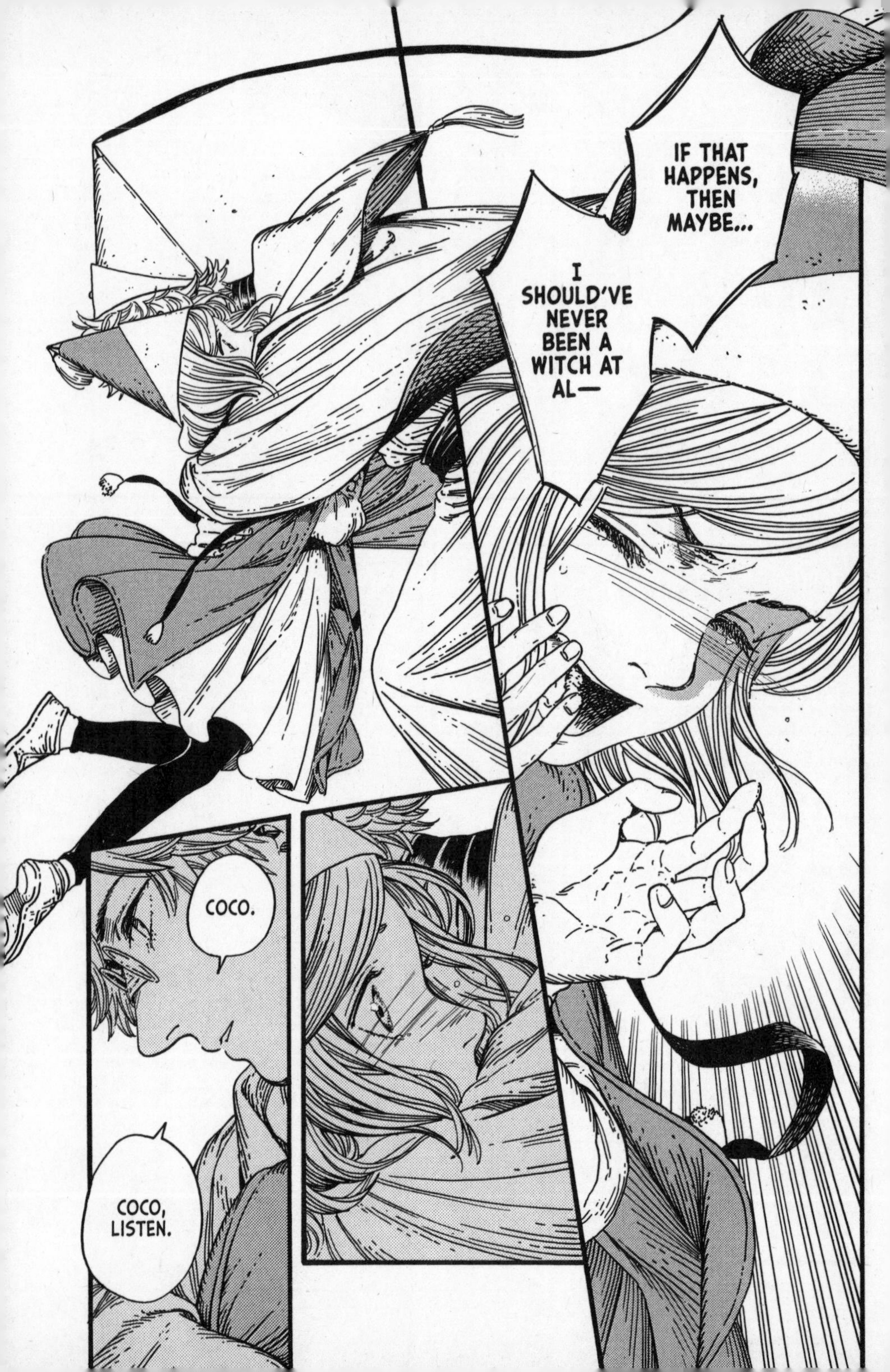
IF THAT HAPPENS, THEN MAYBE...
I SHOULD'VE NEVER BEEN A WITCH AT AL—
COCO.
COCO, LISTEN.

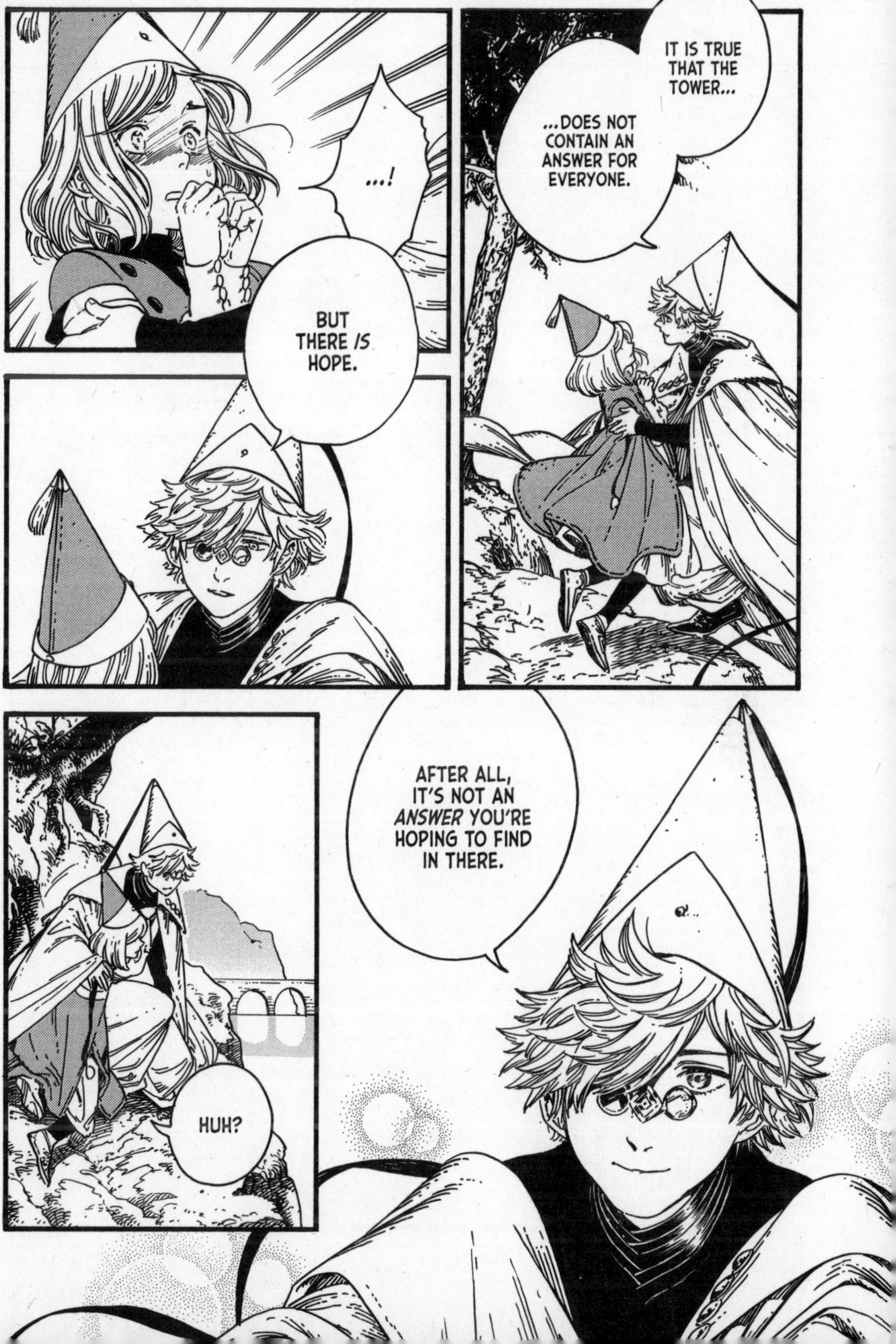
IT IS TRUE THAT THE TOWER...
...DOES NOT CONTAIN AN ANSWER FOR EVERYONE.
...!
BUT THERE *IS* HOPE.
AFTER ALL, IT'S NOT AN *ANSWER* YOU'RE HOPING TO FIND IN THERE.
HUH?

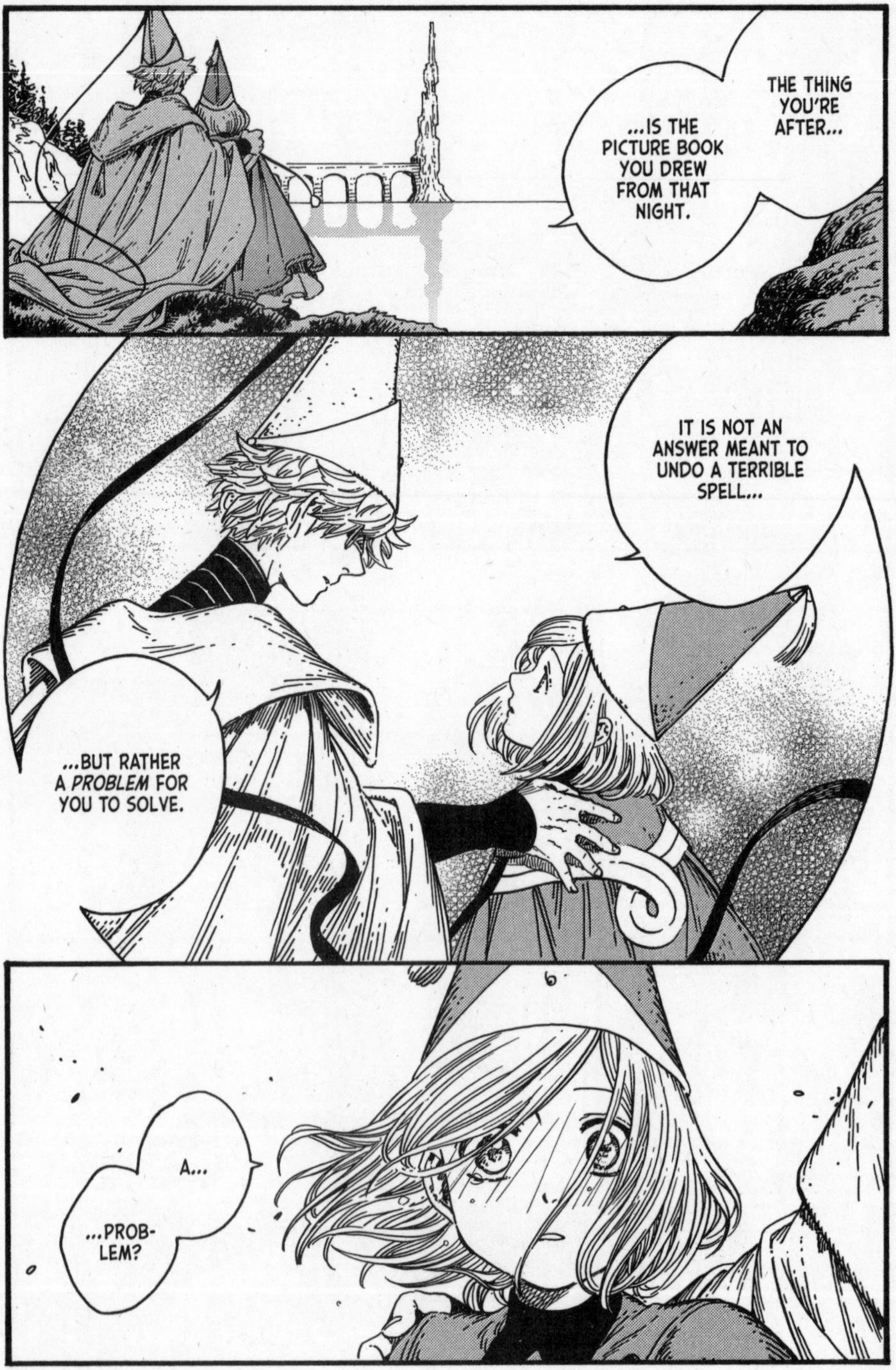
THE THING YOU'RE AFTER...
...IS THE PICTURE BOOK YOU DREW FROM THAT NIGHT.
IT IS NOT AN ANSWER MEANT TO UNDO A TERRIBLE SPELL...
...BUT RATHER A *PROBLEM* FOR YOU TO SOLVE.
A... ...PROB-LEM?

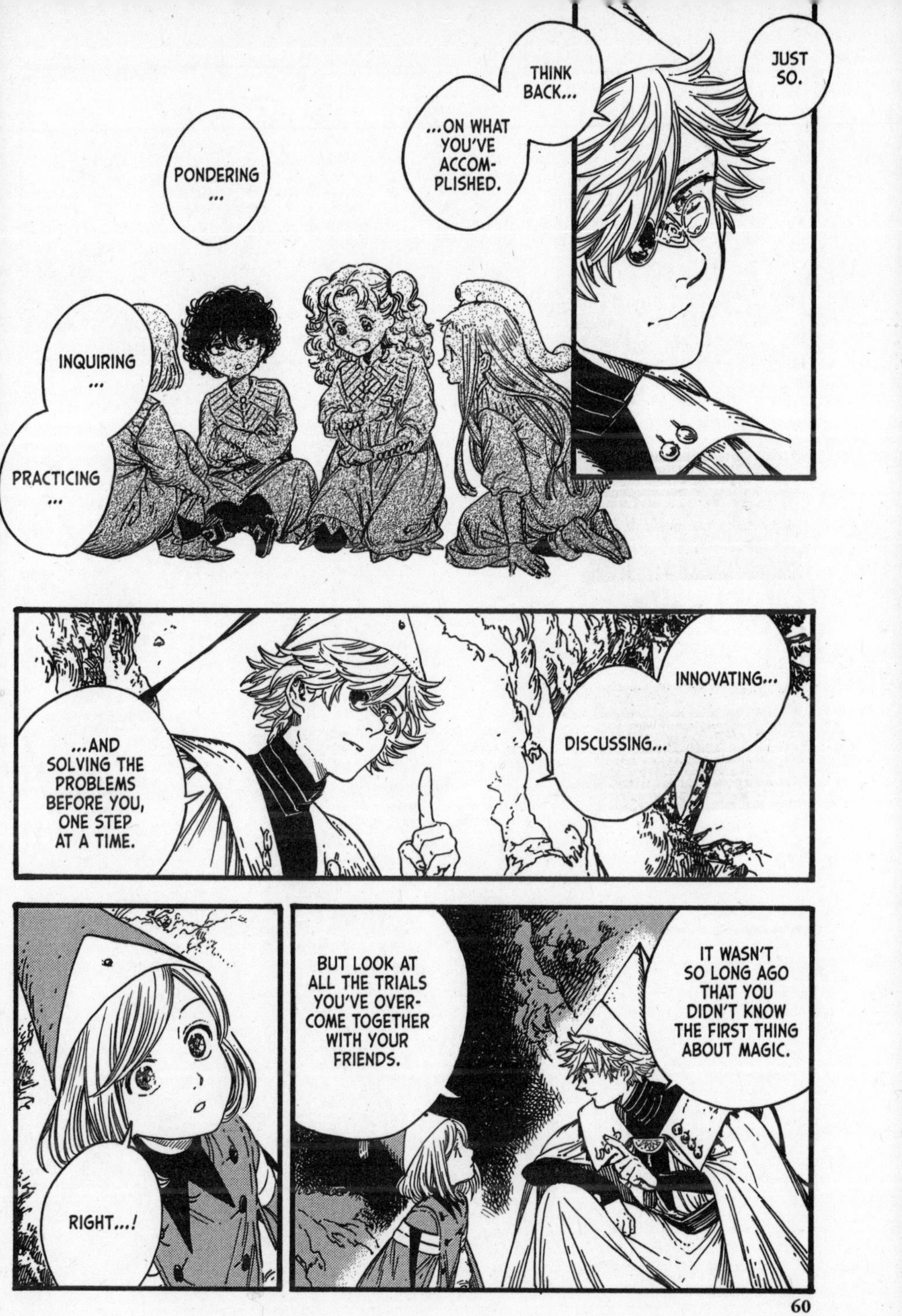
JUST SO.
THINK BACK...
...ON WHAT YOU'VE ACCOMPLISHED.
PONDERING...
INQUIRING...
PRACTICING...
INNOVATING...
DISCUSSING...
...AND SOLVING THE PROBLEMS BEFORE YOU, ONE STEP AT A TIME.
IT WASN'T SO LONG AGO THAT YOU DIDN'T KNOW THE FIRST THING ABOUT MAGIC.
BUT LOOK AT ALL THE TRIALS YOU'VE OVERCOME TOGETHER WITH YOUR FRIENDS.
RIGHT...!

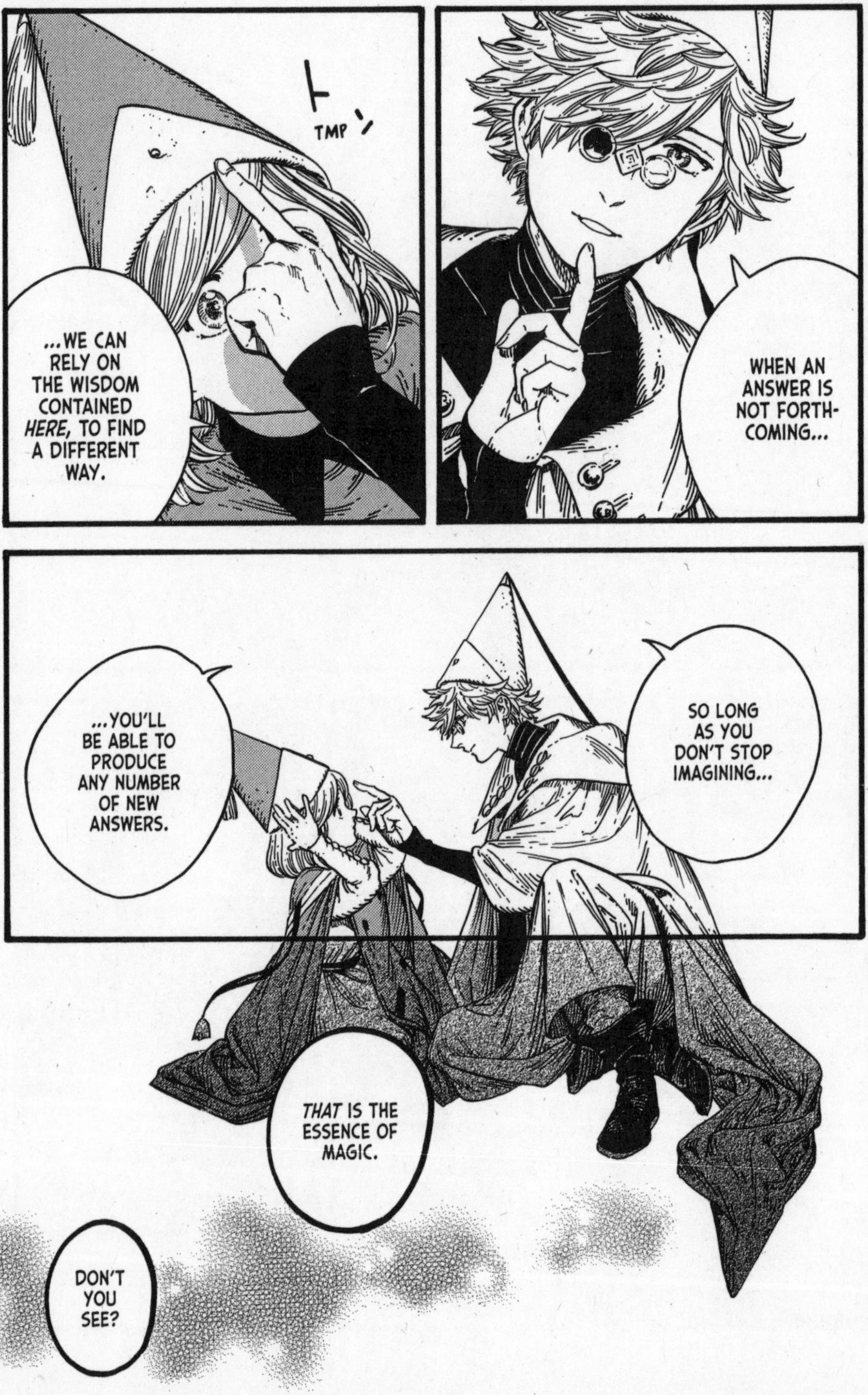
WHEN AN ANSWER IS NOT FORTH-COMING...
TMP
...WE CAN RELY ON THE WISDOM CONTAINED *HERE*, TO FIND A DIFFERENT WAY.
SO LONG AS YOU DON'T STOP IMAGINING...
...YOU'LL BE ABLE TO PRODUCE ANY NUMBER OF NEW ANSWERS.
THAT IS THE ESSENCE OF MAGIC.
DON'T YOU SEE?

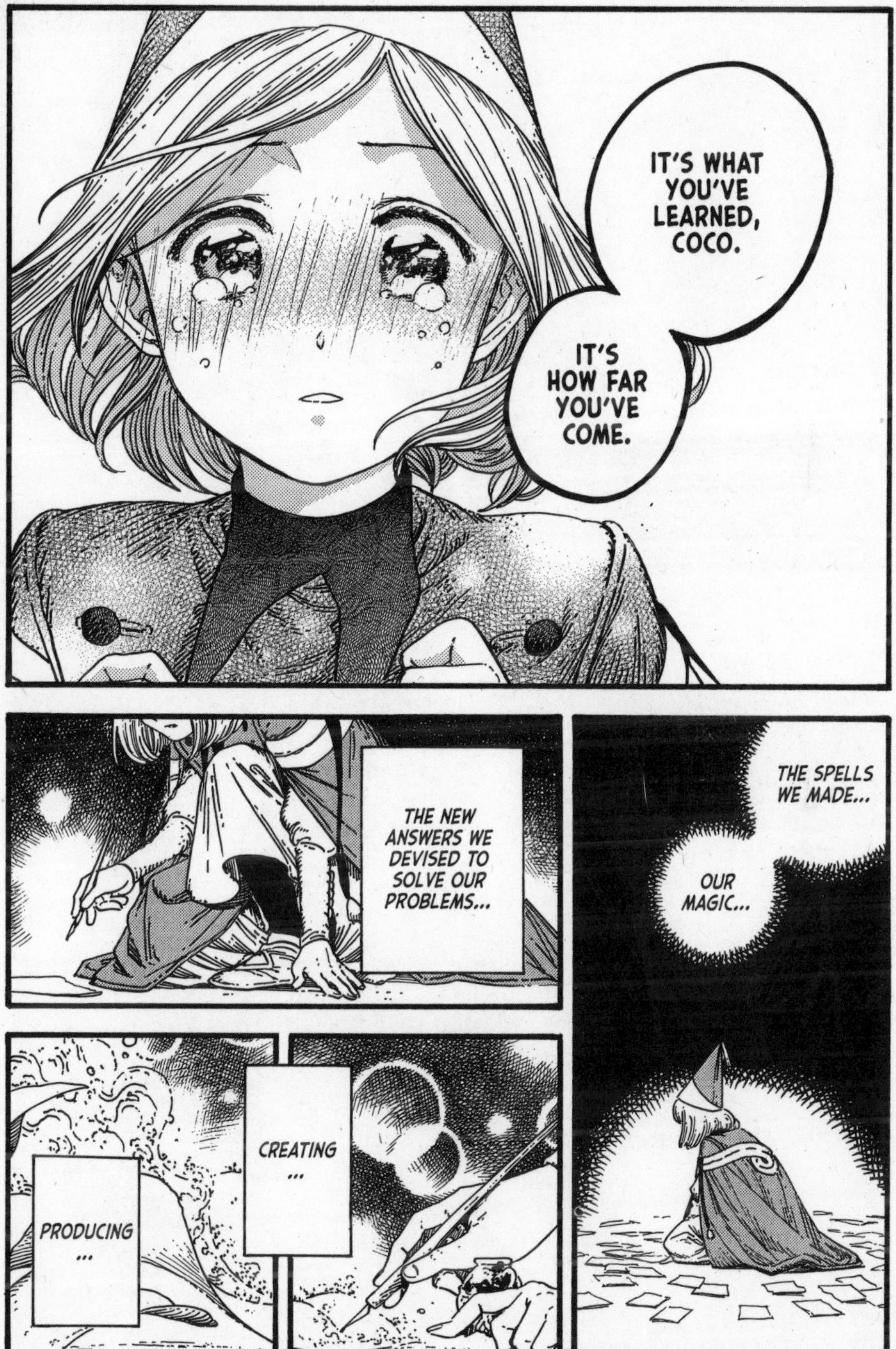
IT'S WHAT YOU'VE LEARNED, COCO.
IT'S HOW FAR YOU'VE COME.
THE SPELLS WE MADE...
OUR MAGIC...
THE NEW ANSWERS WE DEVISED TO SOLVE OUR PROBLEMS...
CREATING ...
PRODUCING ...

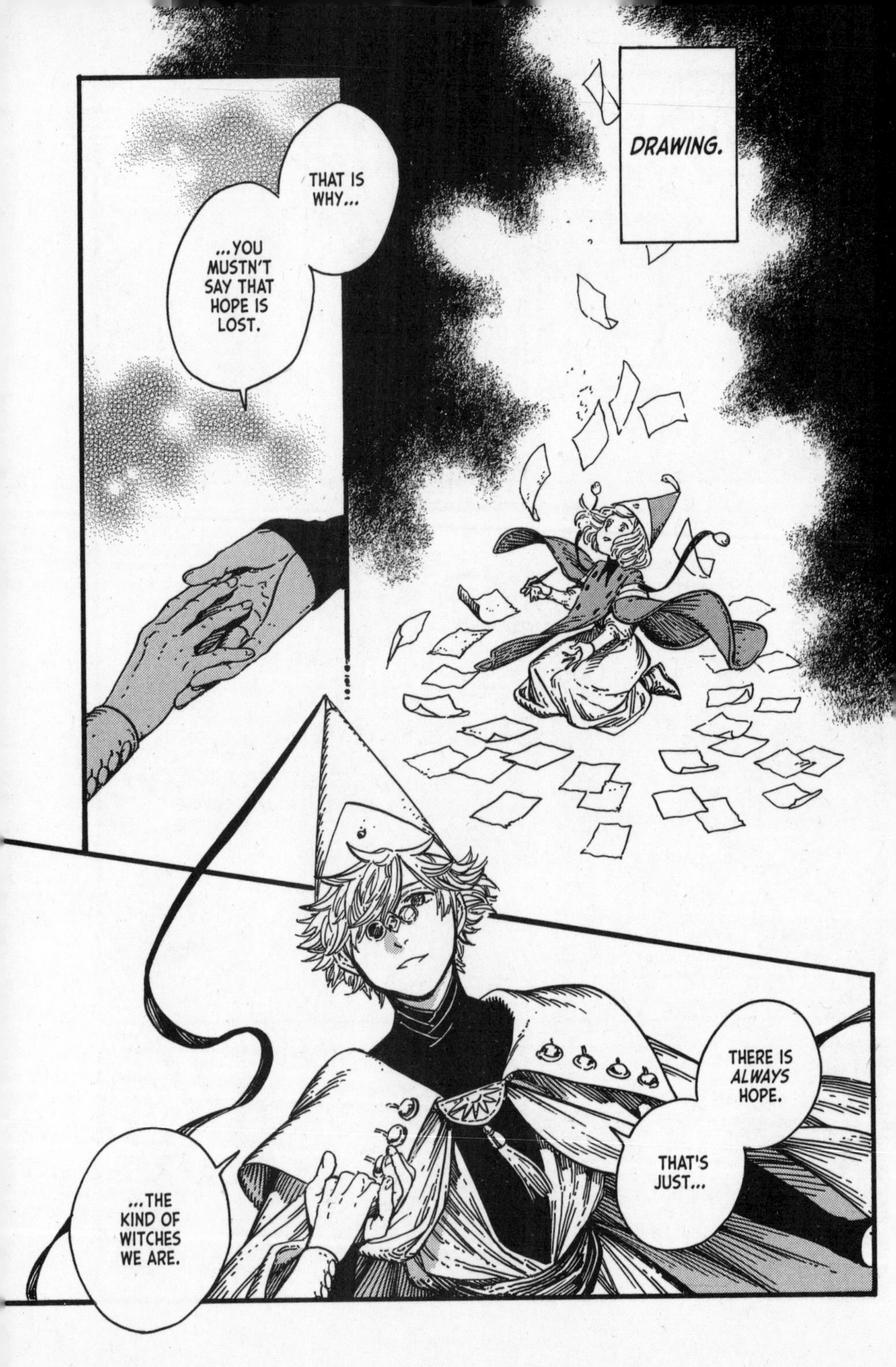
DRAWING.
THAT IS WHY...
...YOU MUSTN'T SAY THAT HOPE IS LOST.
THERE IS *ALWAYS* HOPE.
THAT'S JUST...
...THE KIND OF WITCHES WE ARE.

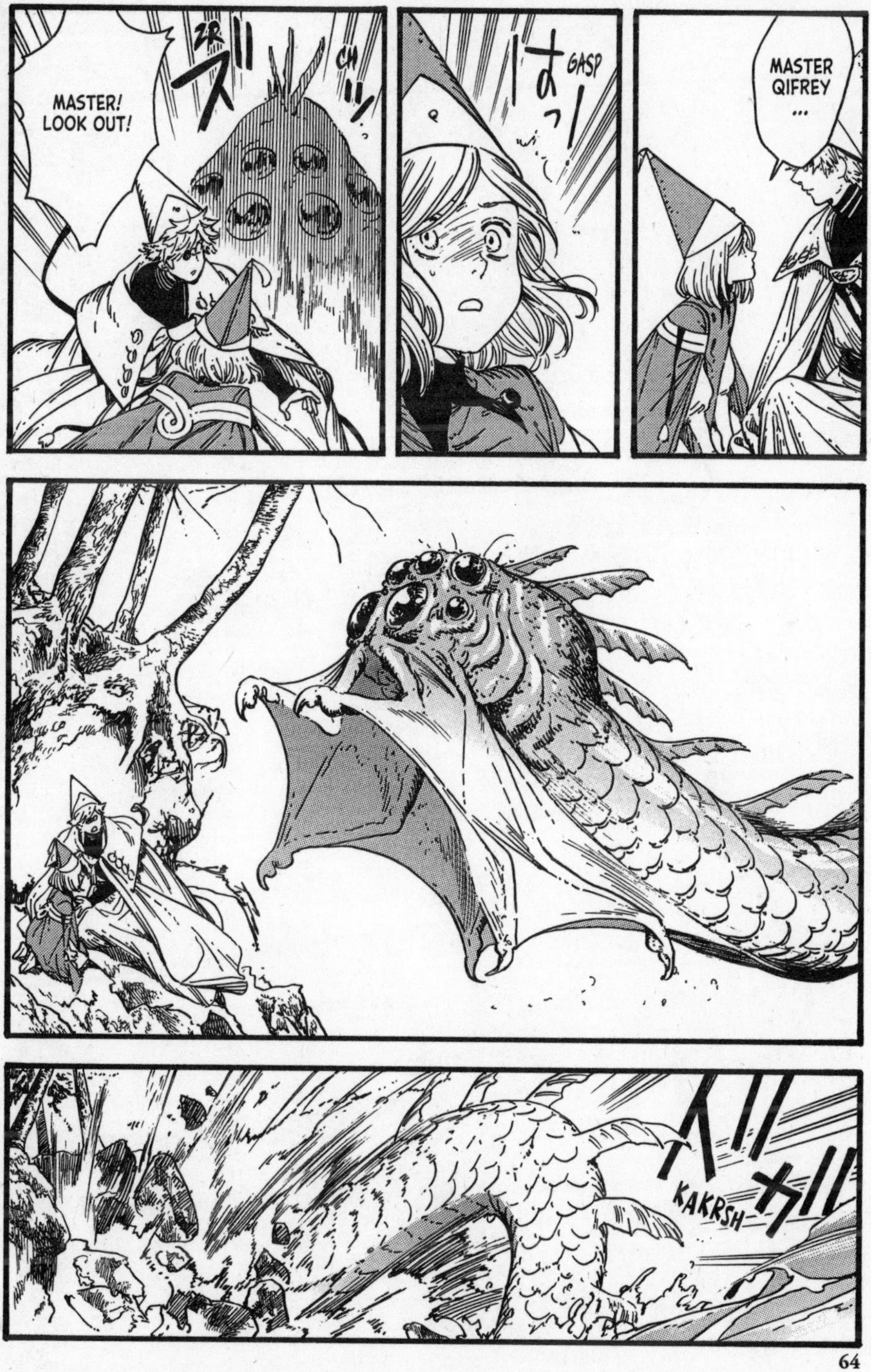
MASTER QIFREY ...
はっ
GASP
CH
ZR
MASTER! LOOK OUT!
KAKRSH

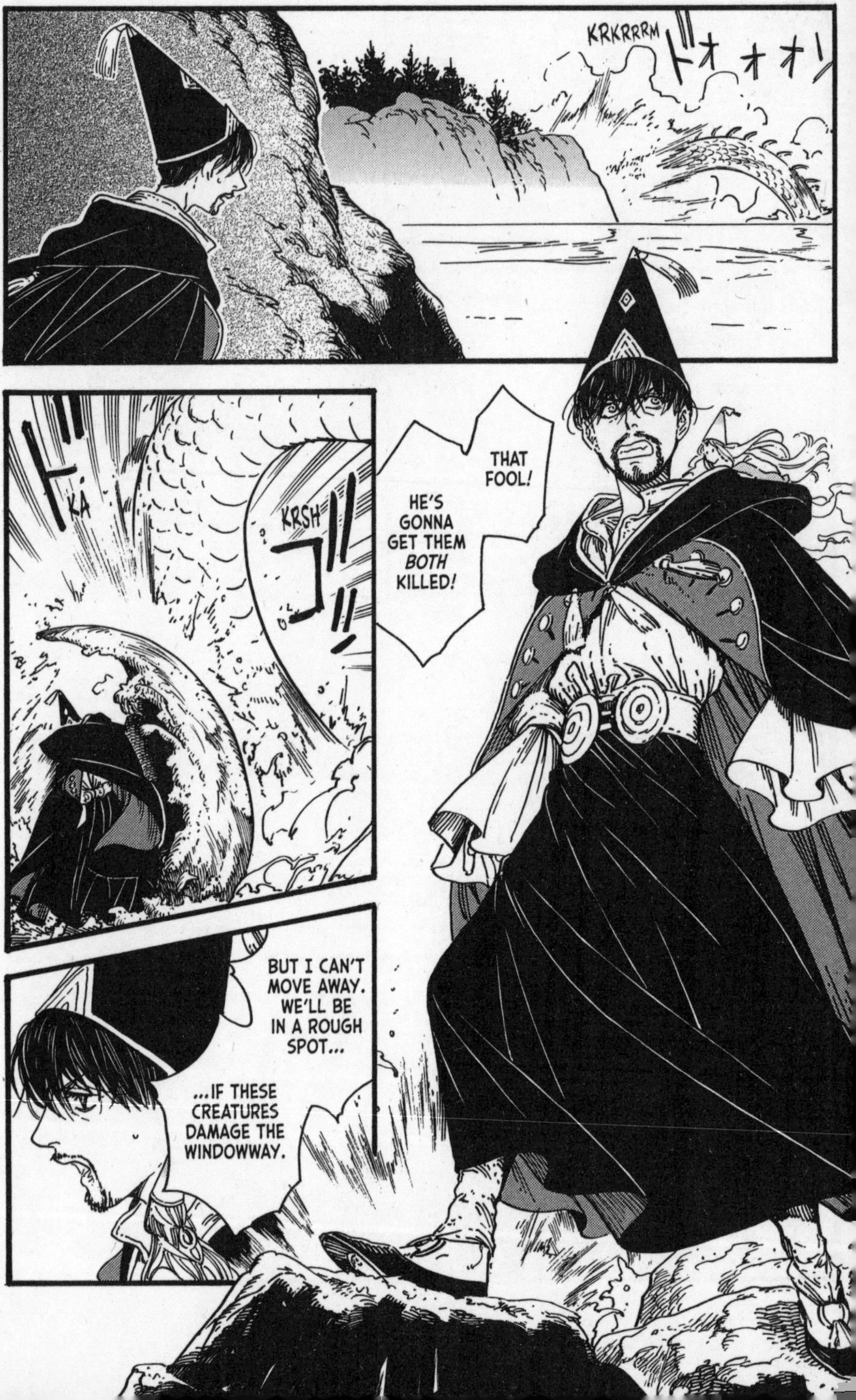
KRKRRRM
ドオオオン
THAT FOOL!
HE'S GONNA GET THEM BOTH KILLED!
KRSH
ゴ
ド
KA
BUT I CAN'T MOVE AWAY. WE'LL BE IN A ROUGH SPOT...
...IF THESE CREATURES DAMAGE THE WINDOWWAY.

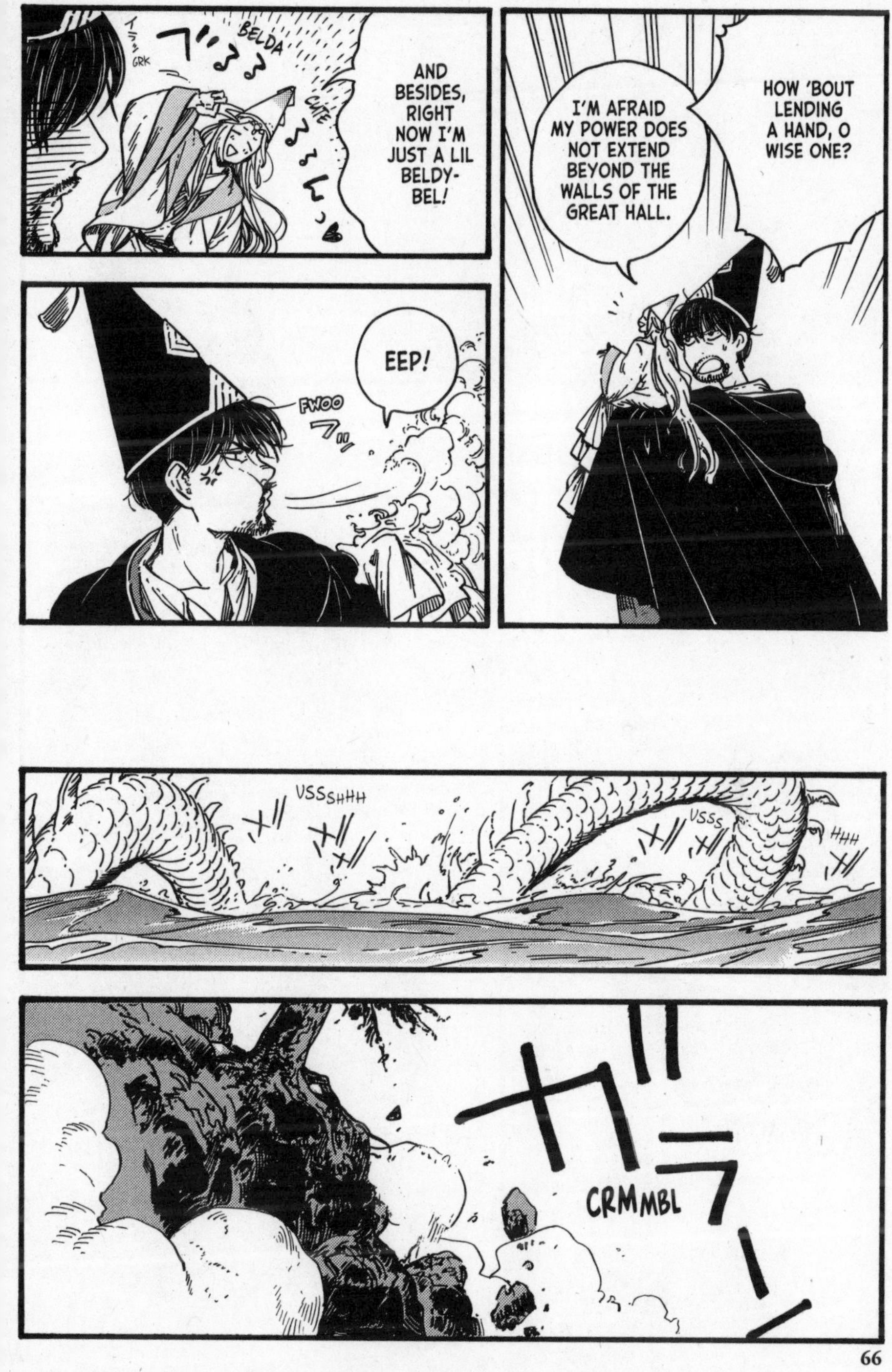
HOW 'BOUT LENDING A HAND, O WISE ONE?
I'M AFRAID MY POWER DOES NOT EXTEND BEYOND THE WALLS OF THE GREAT HALL.
AND BESIDES, RIGHT NOW I'M JUST A LIL BELDY-BEL!
BELDA
CUTE
GRK
EEP!
FWOO
VSSSHHH
VSSS
HHH
CRMMBL

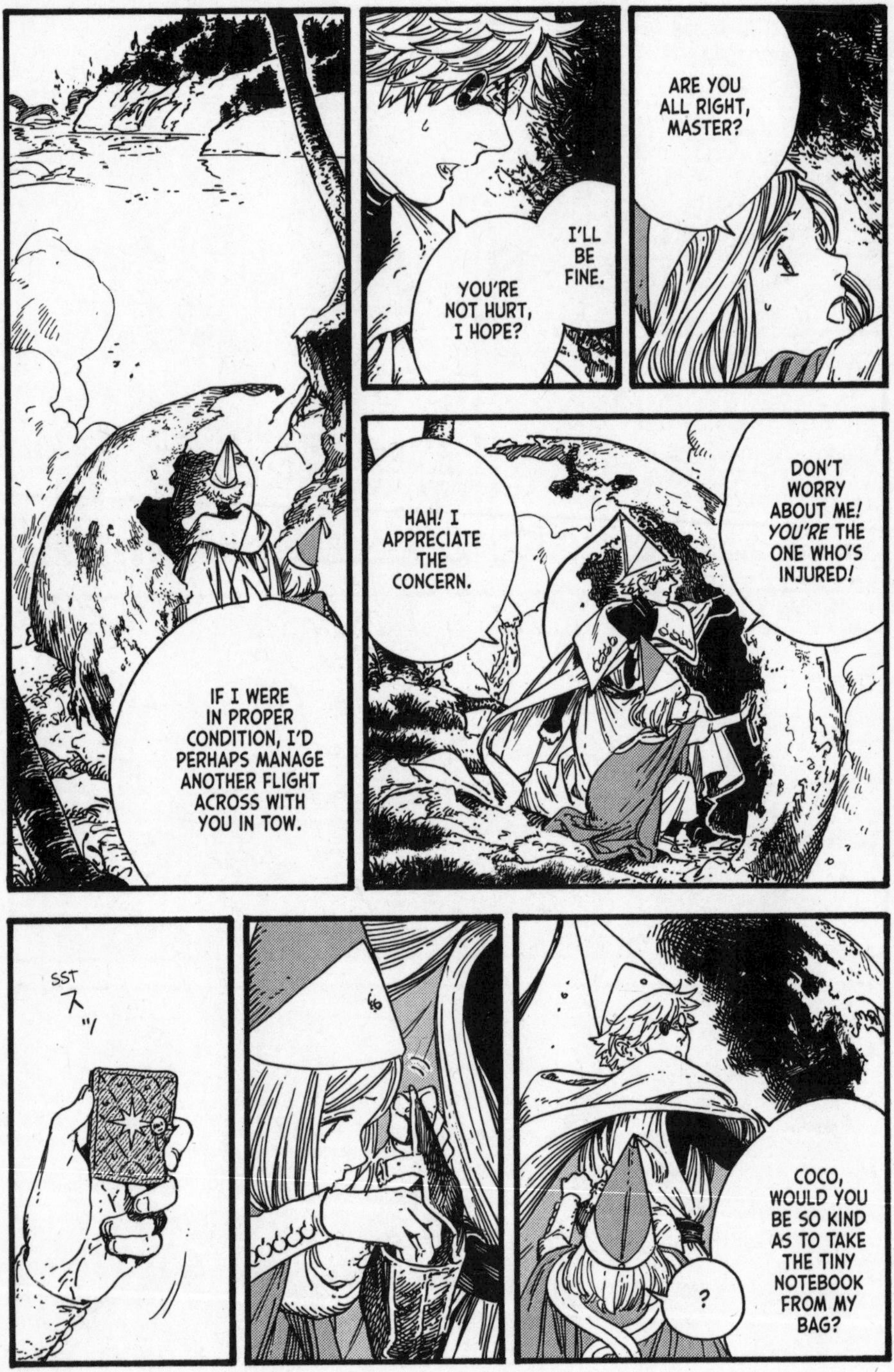
ARE YOU ALL RIGHT, MASTER?
I'LL BE FINE.
YOU'RE NOT HURT, I HOPE?
DON'T WORRY ABOUT ME! *YOU'RE* THE ONE WHO'S INJURED!
HAH! I APPRECIATE THE CONCERN.
IF I WERE IN PROPER CONDITION, I'D PERHAPS MANAGE ANOTHER FLIGHT ACROSS WITH YOU IN TOW.
COCO, WOULD YOU BE SO KIND AS TO TAKE THE TINY NOTEBOOK FROM MY BAG?
?
SST
スッ

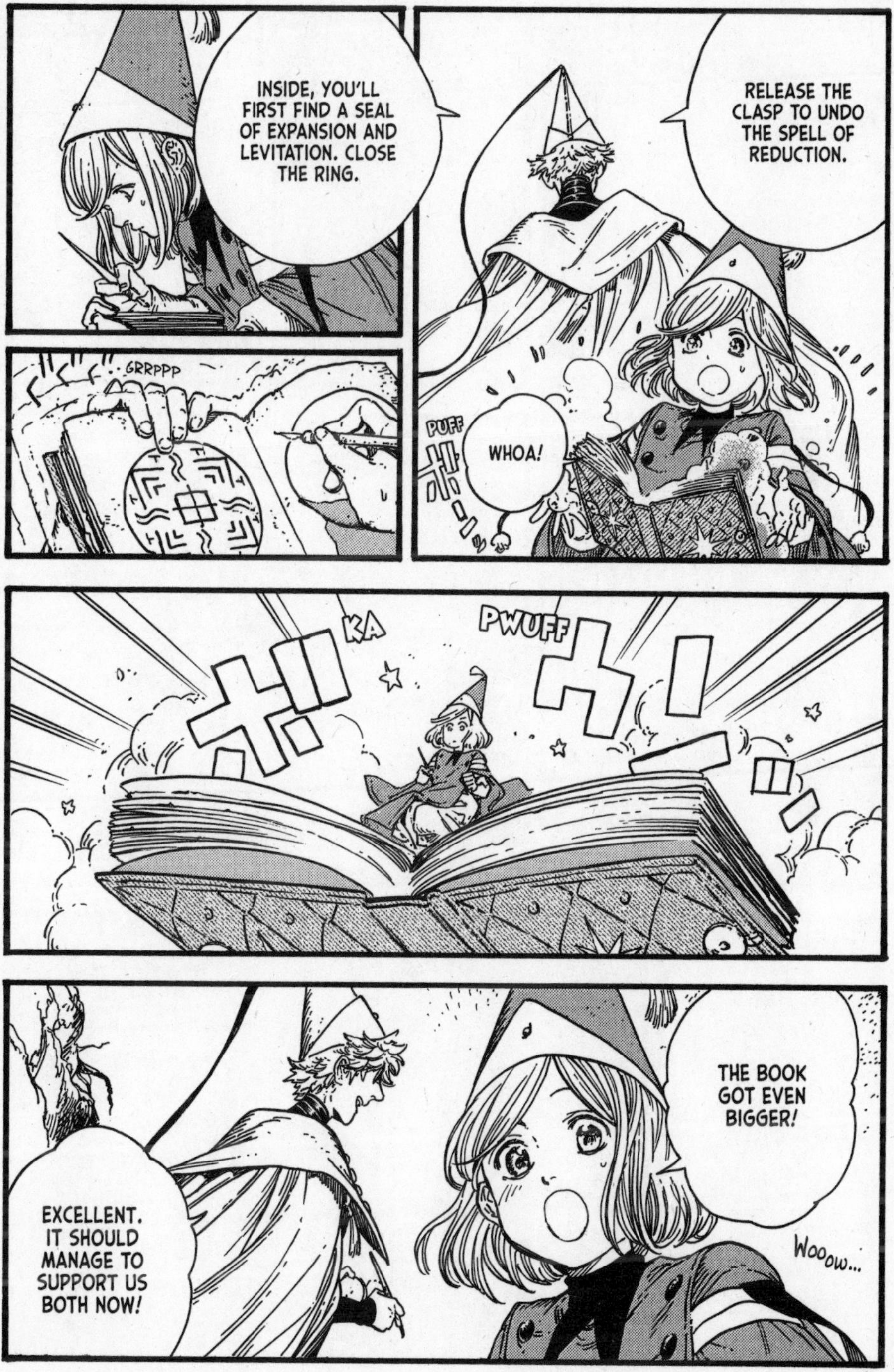
RELEASE THE CLASP TO UNDO THE SPELL OF REDUCTION.
PUFF
WHOA!
INSIDE, YOU'LL FIRST FIND A SEAL OF EXPANSION AND LEVITATION. CLOSE THE RING.
GRRPPP
KA
PWUFF
THE BOOK GOT EVEN BIGGER!
Wooow...
EXCELLENT. IT SHOULD MANAGE TO SUPPORT US BOTH NOW!

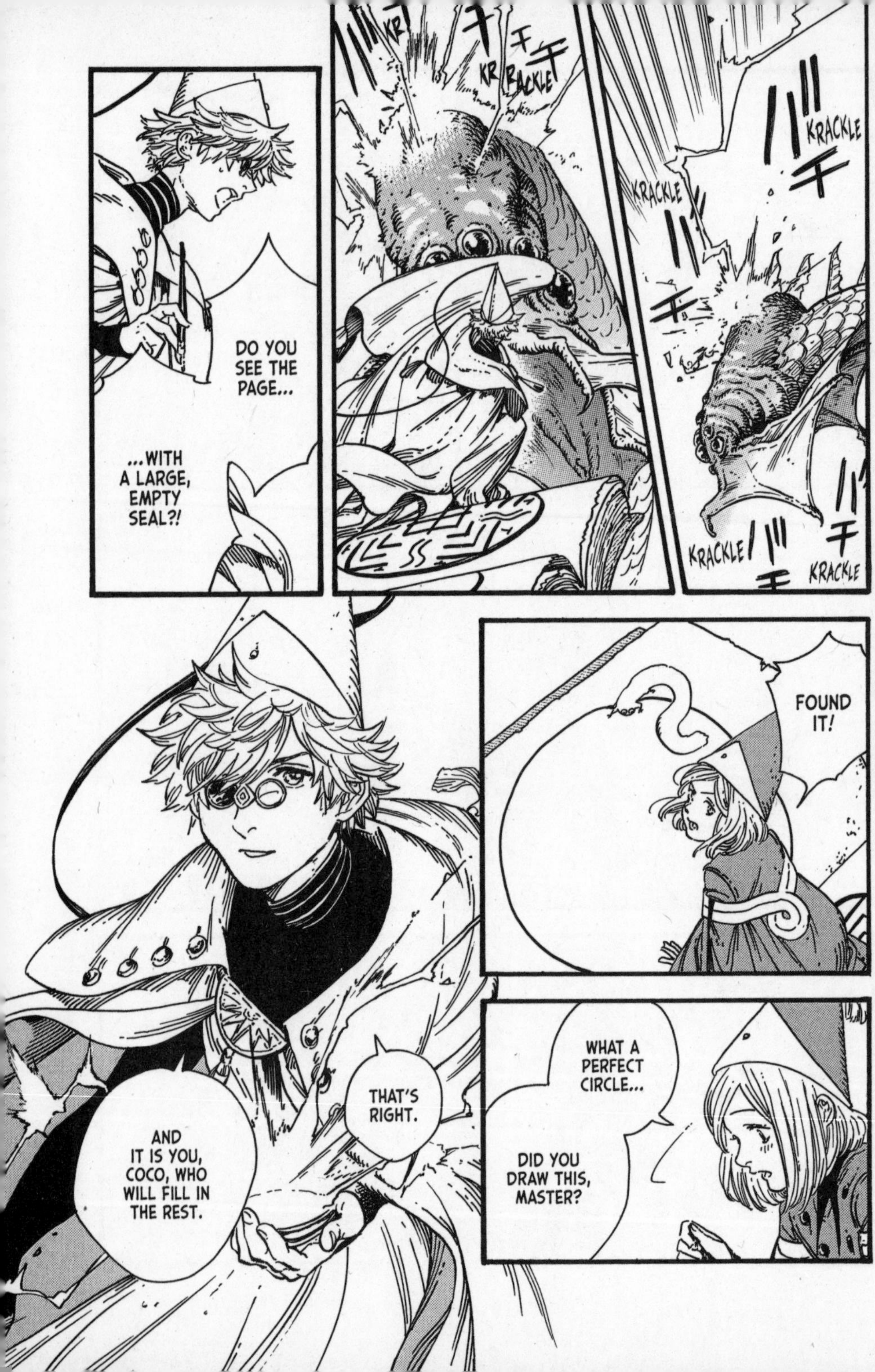
KRACKLE
KRACKLE
KRACKLE
KRACKLE
KR
KR
KRACKLE
DO YOU SEE THE PAGE...
...WITH A LARGE, EMPTY SEAL?!
FOUND IT!
WHAT A PERFECT CIRCLE...
DID YOU DRAW THIS, MASTER?
THAT'S RIGHT.
AND IT IS YOU, COCO, WHO WILL FILL IN THE REST.

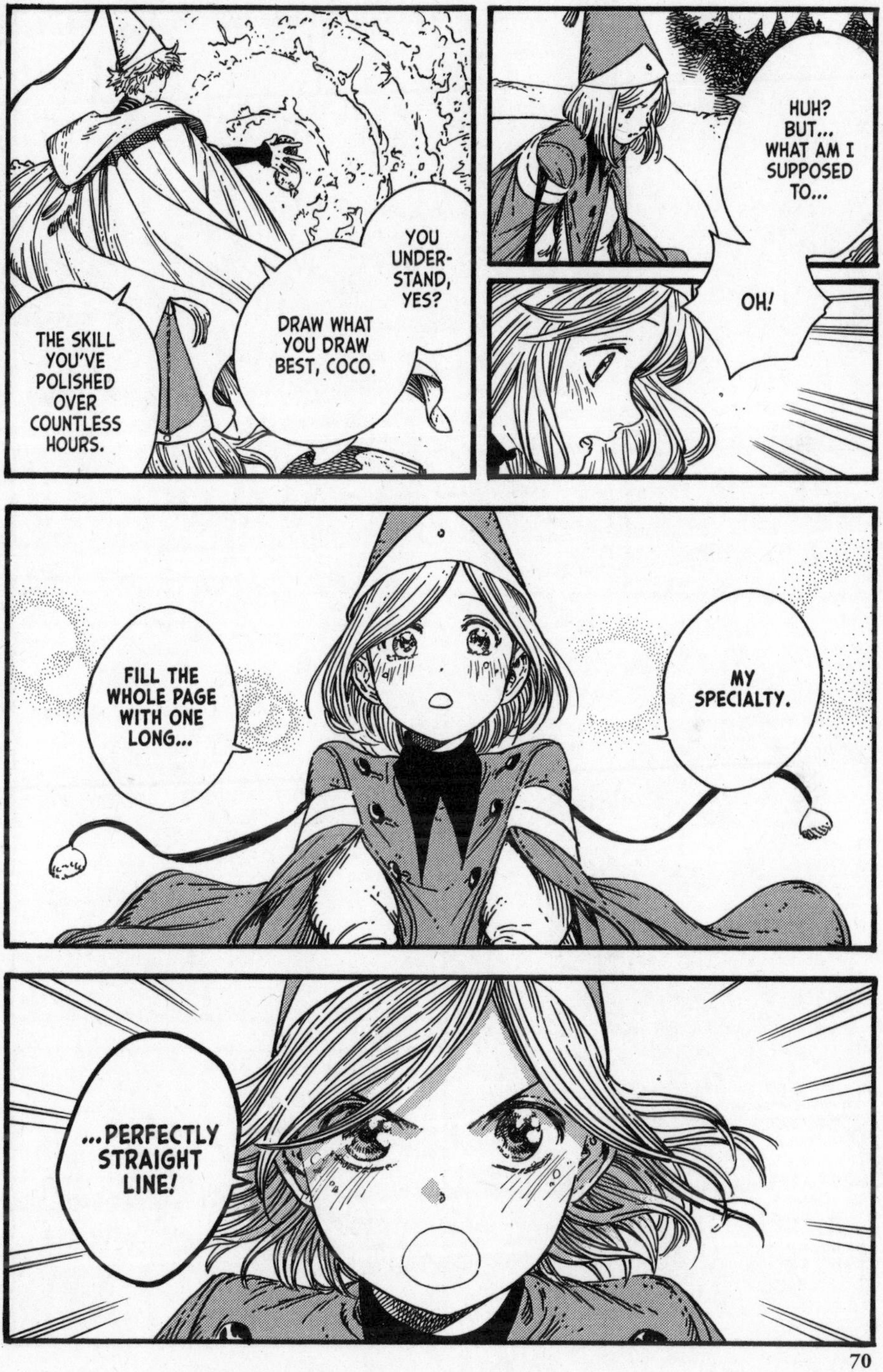
HUH? BUT... WHAT AM I SUPPOSED TO...
OH!
YOU UNDER-STAND, YES?
DRAW WHAT YOU DRAW BEST, COCO.
THE SKILL YOU'VE POLISHED OVER COUNTLESS HOURS.
MY SPECIALTY.
FILL THE WHOLE PAGE WITH ONE LONG...
...PERFECTLY STRAIGHT LINE!

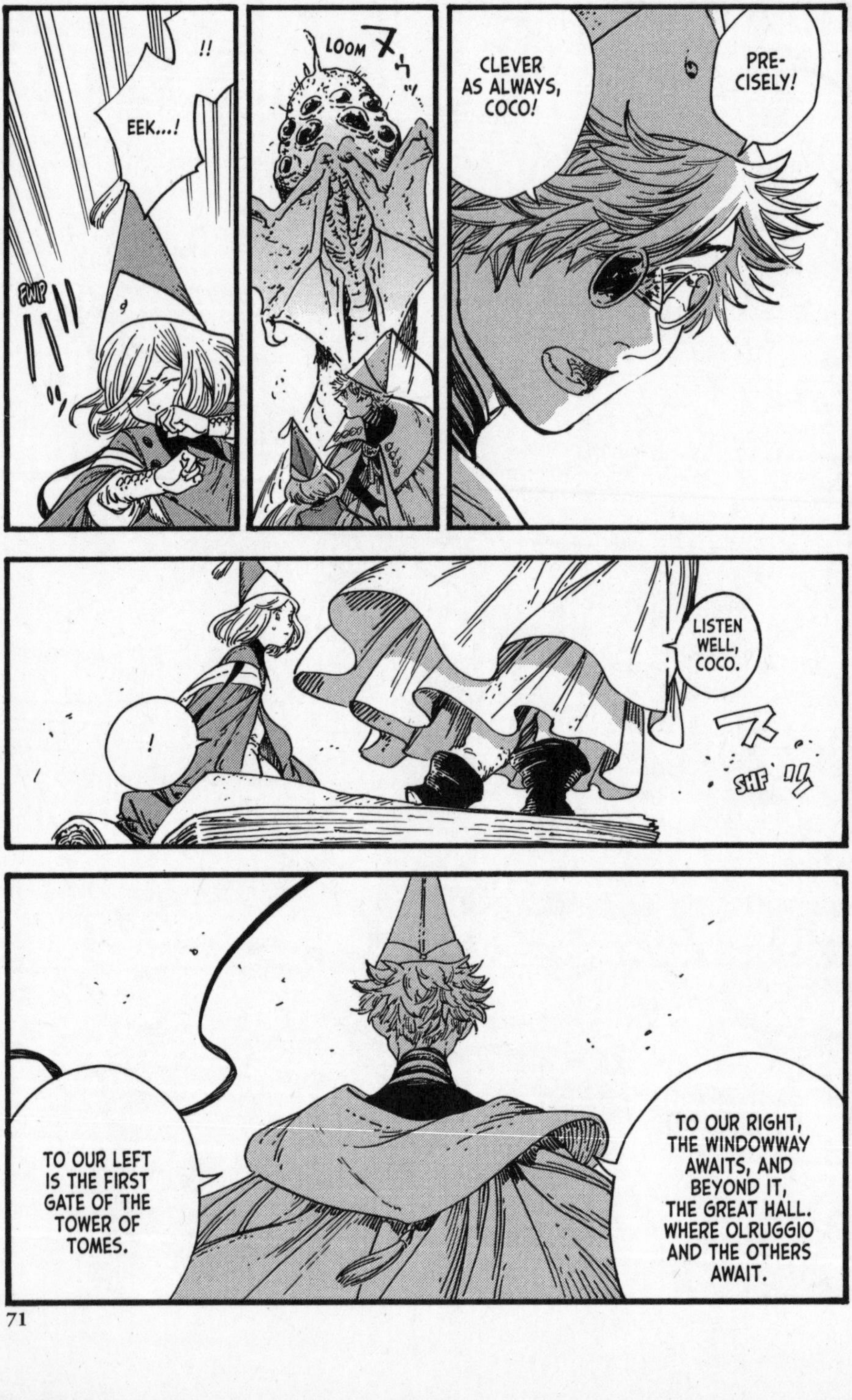
PRE-CISELY!
CLEVER AS ALWAYS, COCO!
LOOM
!!
EEK...!
FWIP
LISTEN WELL, COCO.
SHF
!
TO OUR RIGHT, THE WINDOWWAY AWAITS, AND BEYOND IT, THE GREAT HALL. WHERE OLRUGGIO AND THE OTHERS AWAIT.
TO OUR LEFT IS THE FIRST GATE OF THE TOWER OF TOMES.

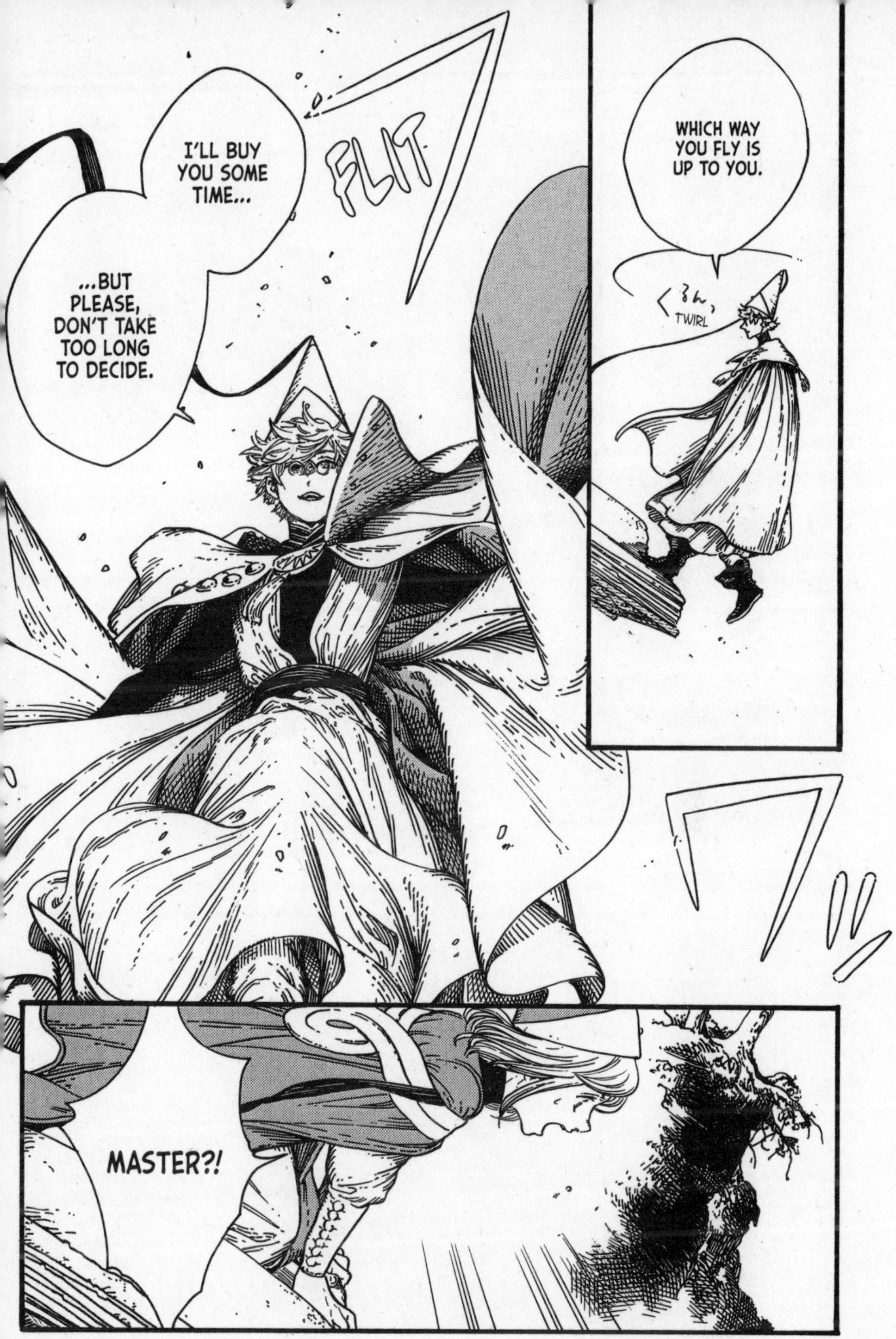
WHICH WAY YOU FLY IS UP TO YOU.
TWIRL
I'LL BUY YOU SOME TIME...
FLIT
...BUT PLEASE, DON'T TAKE TOO LONG TO DECIDE.
MASTER?!

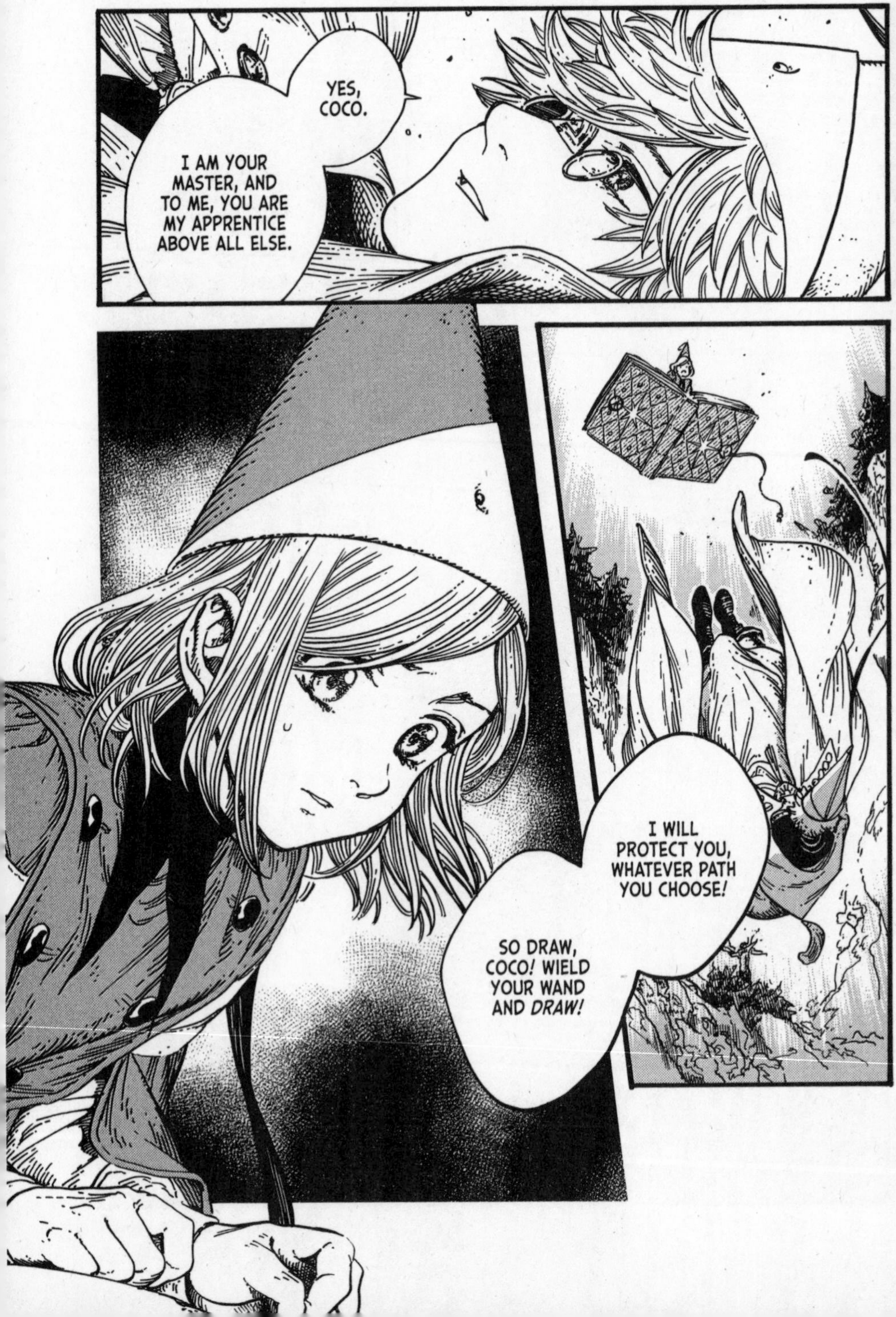
YES, COCO.
I AM YOUR MASTER, AND TO ME, YOU ARE MY APPRENTICE ABOVE ALL ELSE.
I WILL PROTECT YOU, WHATEVER PATH YOU CHOOSE!
SO DRAW, COCO! WIELD YOUR WAND AND *DRAW!*

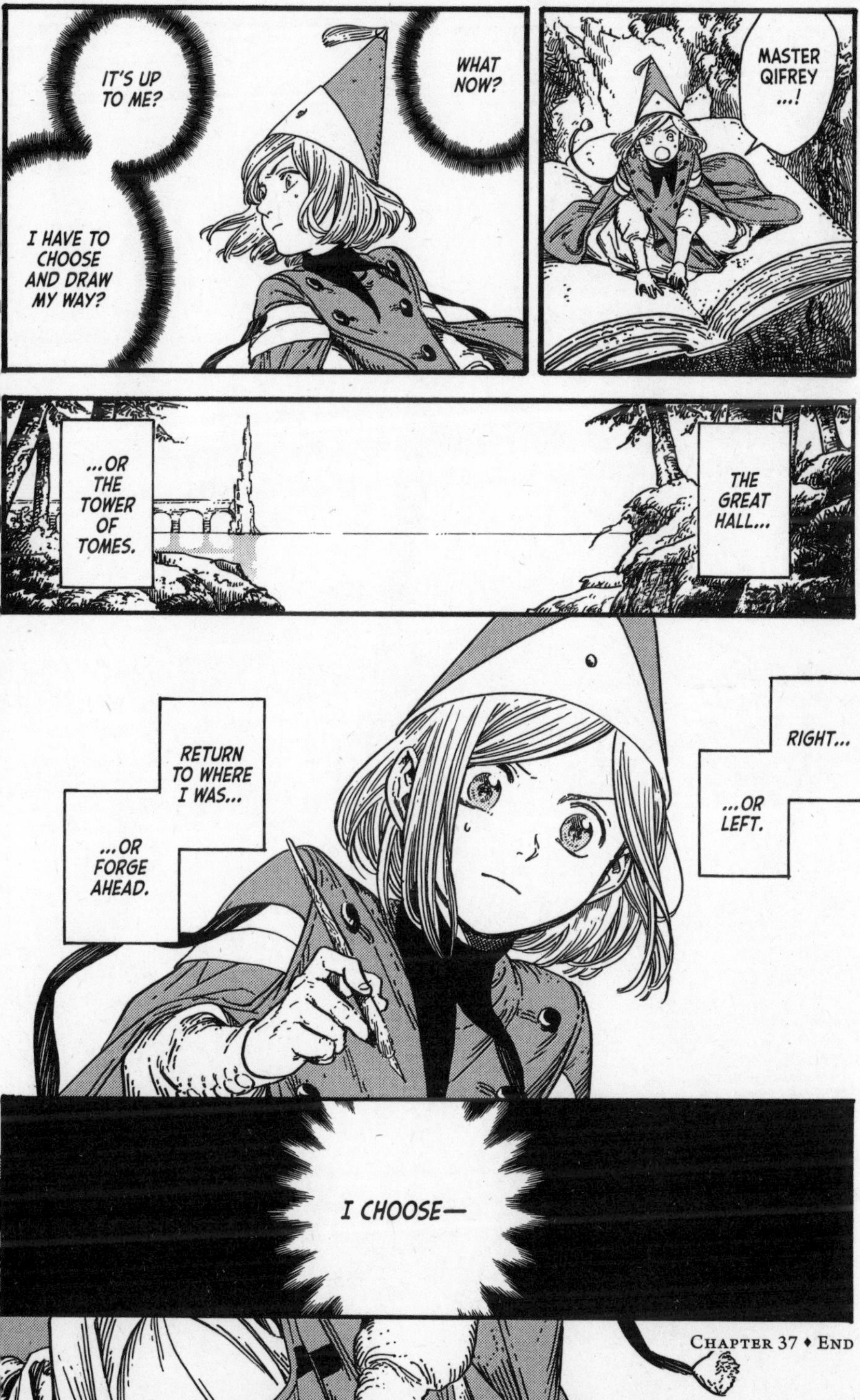
MASTER QIFREY ...!
WHAT NOW?
IT'S UP TO ME?
I HAVE TO CHOOSE AND DRAW MY WAY?
THE GREAT HALL...
...OR THE TOWER OF TOMES.
RIGHT...
...OR LEFT.
RETURN TO WHERE I WAS...
...OR FORGE AHEAD.
I CHOOSE—

CHAPTER 37 ♦ END

Witch Hat Atelier

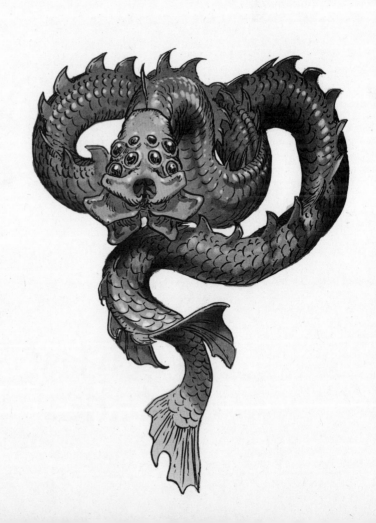

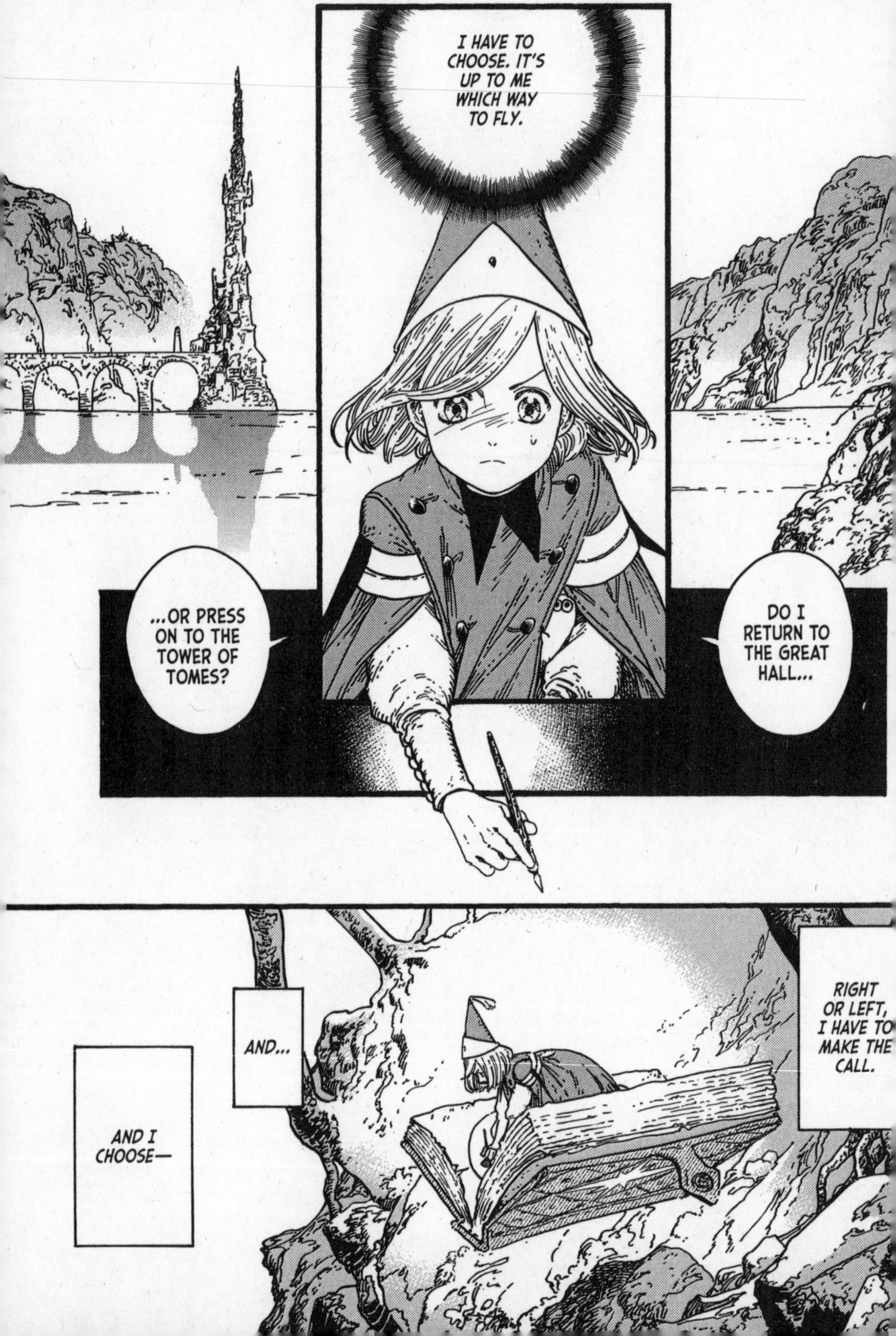
I HAVE TO CHOOSE. IT'S UP TO ME WHICH WAY TO FLY.
DO I RETURN TO THE GREAT HALL...
...OR PRESS ON TO THE TOWER OF TOMES?
RIGHT OR LEFT, I HAVE TO MAKE THE CALL.
AND...
AND I CHOOSE—

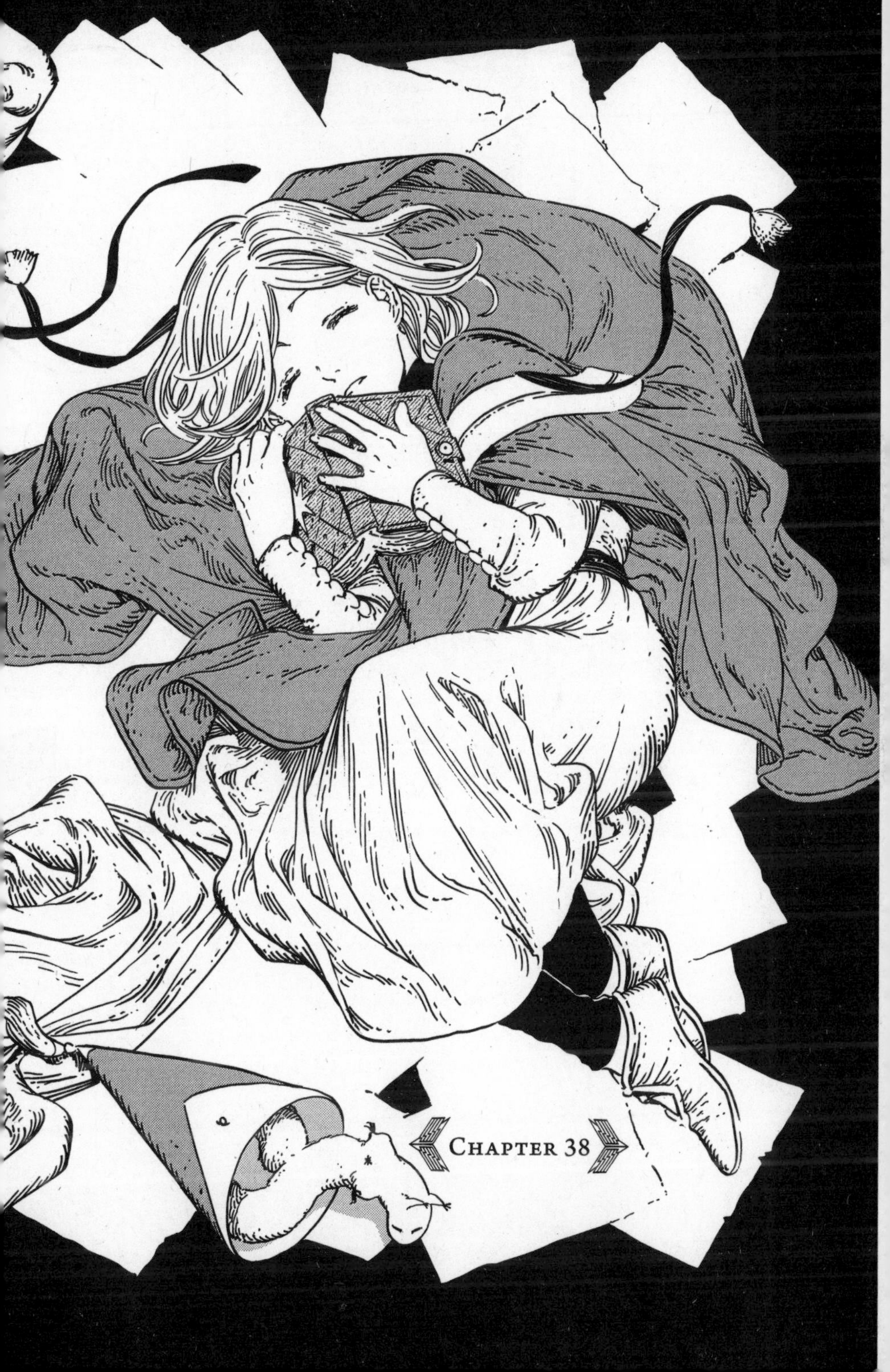

Chapter 38

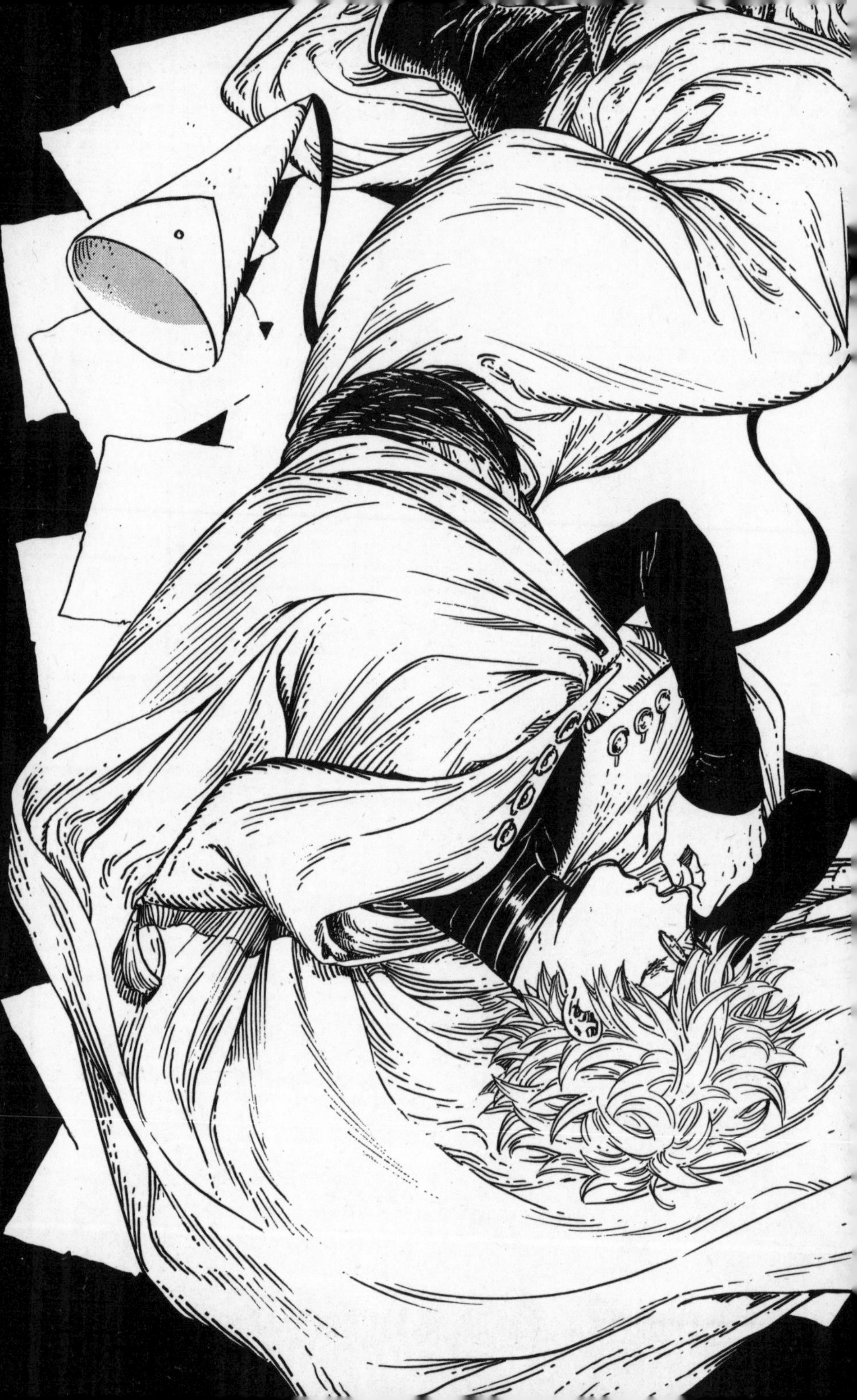

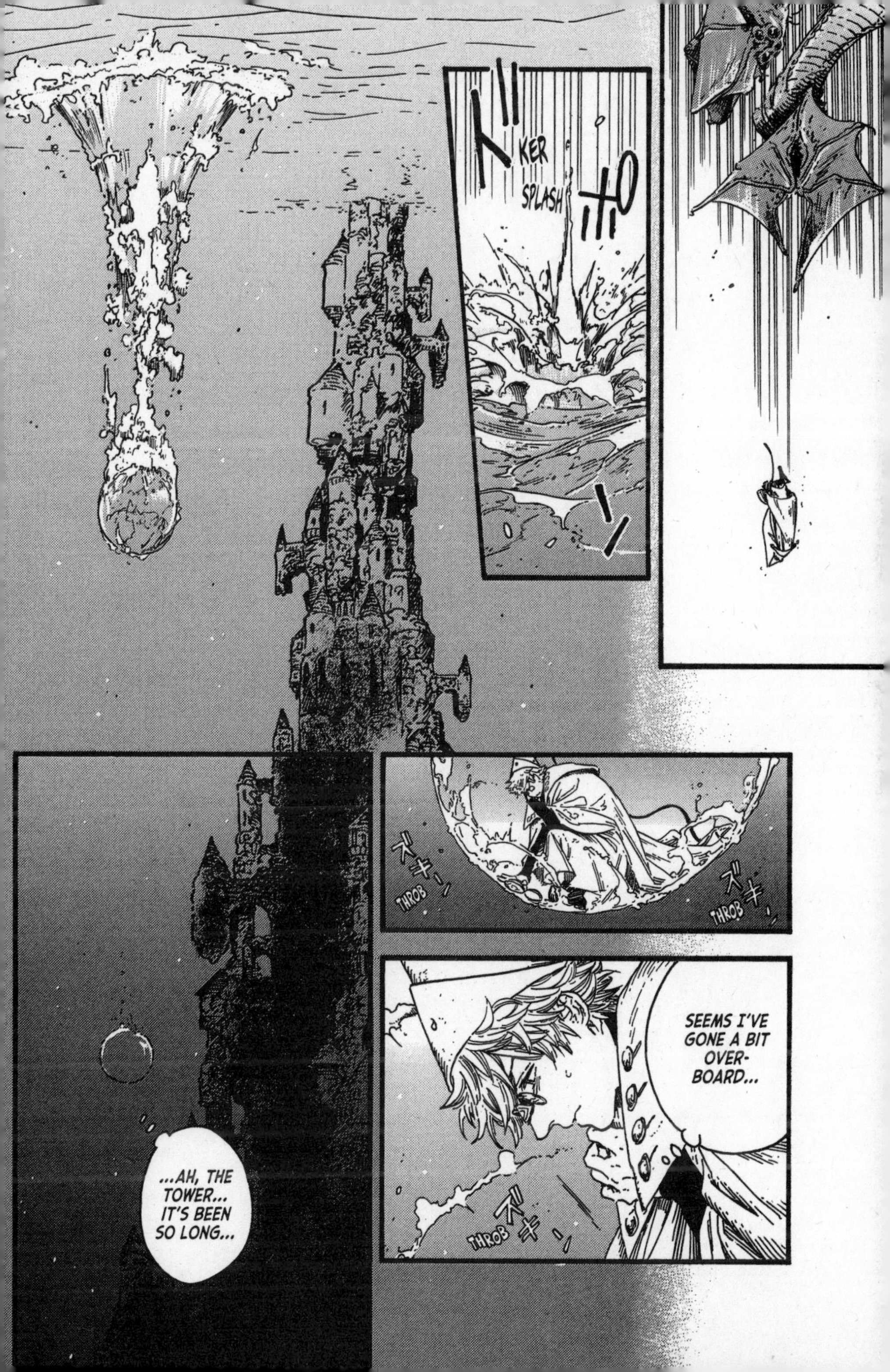
KER SPLASH
THROB
THROB
SEEMS I'VE GONE A BIT OVER-BOARD...
THROB
...AH, THE TOWER... IT'S BEEN SO LONG...

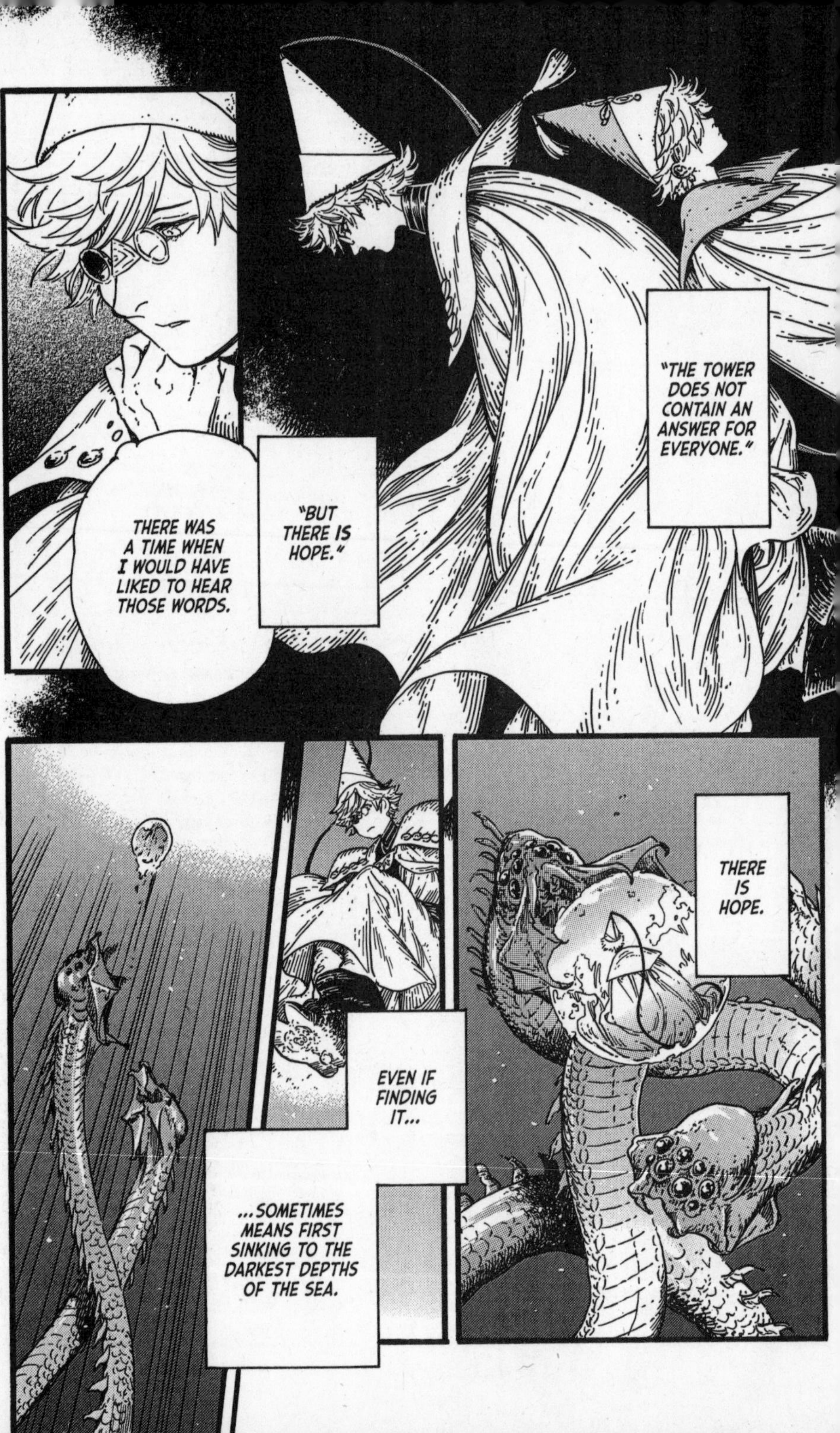
"THE TOWER DOES NOT CONTAIN AN ANSWER FOR EVERYONE."
"BUT THERE IS HOPE."
THERE WAS A TIME WHEN I WOULD HAVE LIKED TO HEAR THOSE WORDS.
THERE IS HOPE.
EVEN IF FINDING IT...
...SOMETIMES MEANS FIRST SINKING TO THE DARKEST DEPTHS OF THE SEA.

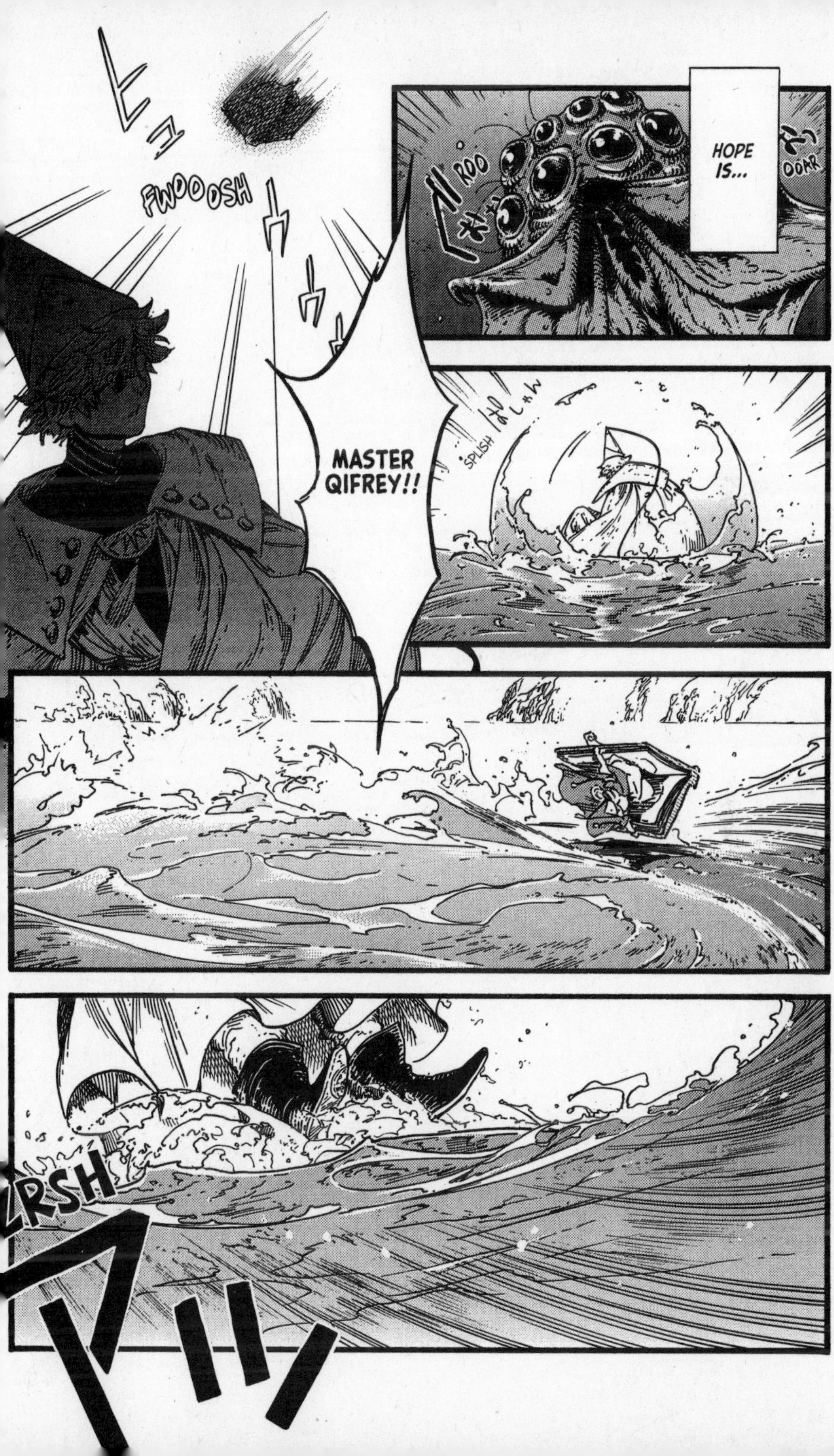
HOPE IS...
DOAR
ROO
FWOOOSH
MASTER QIFREY!!
SPLISH
ZRSH

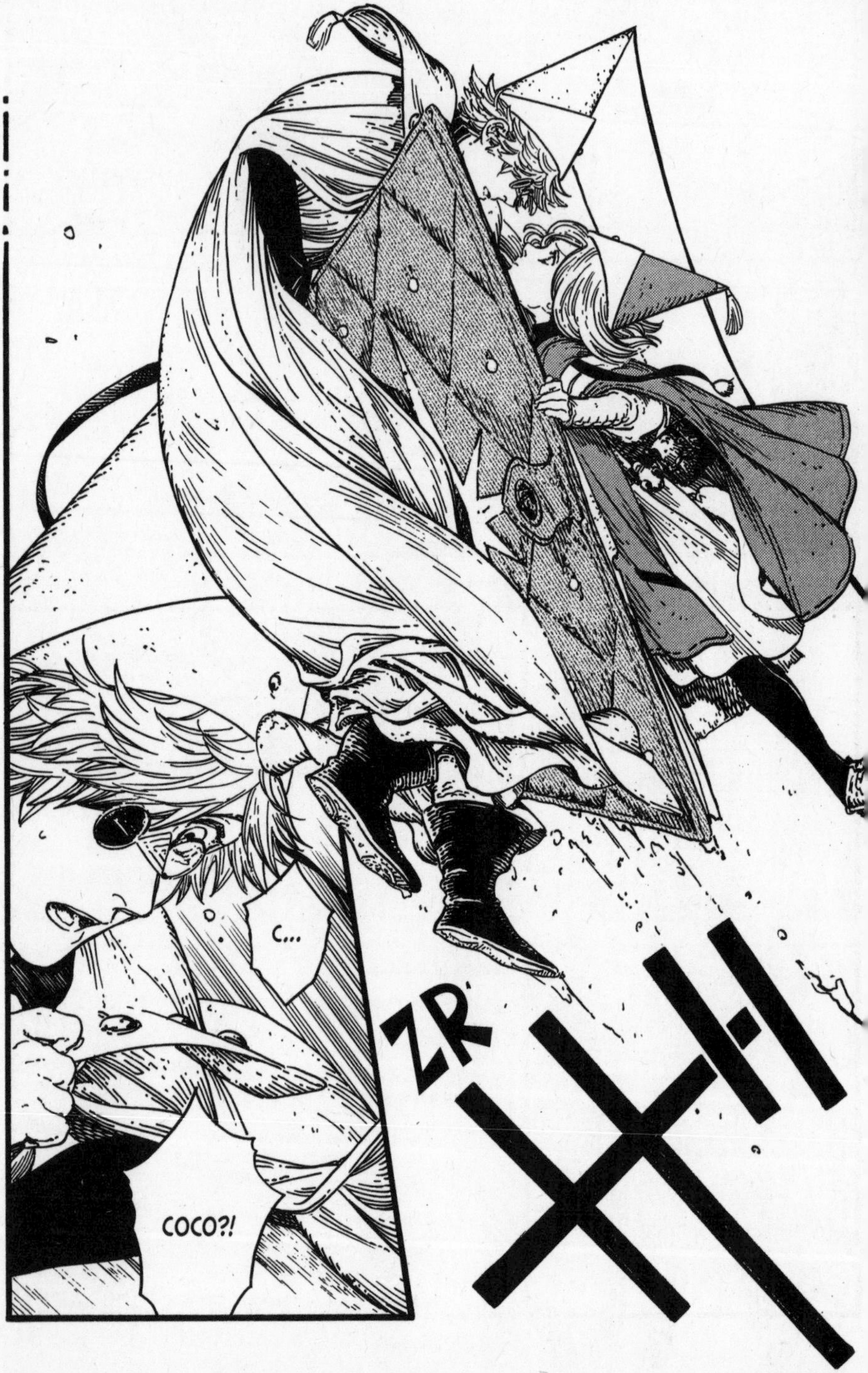
ZR
C...
COCO?!

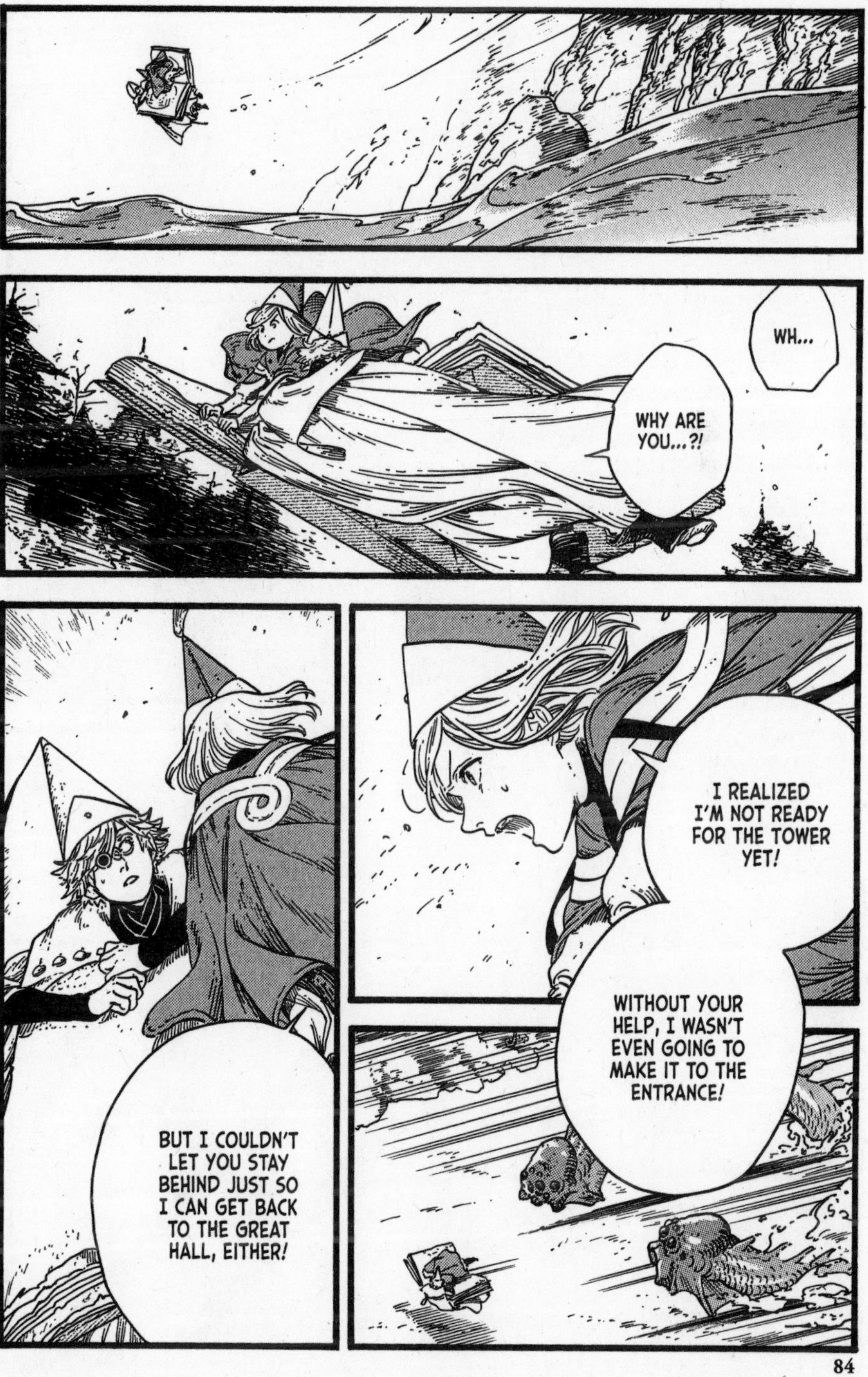
WH...
WHY ARE YOU...?!
I REALIZED I'M NOT READY FOR THE TOWER YET!
WITHOUT YOUR HELP, I WASN'T EVEN GOING TO MAKE IT TO THE ENTRANCE!
BUT I COULDN'T LET YOU STAY BEHIND JUST SO I CAN GET BACK TO THE GREAT HALL, EITHER!

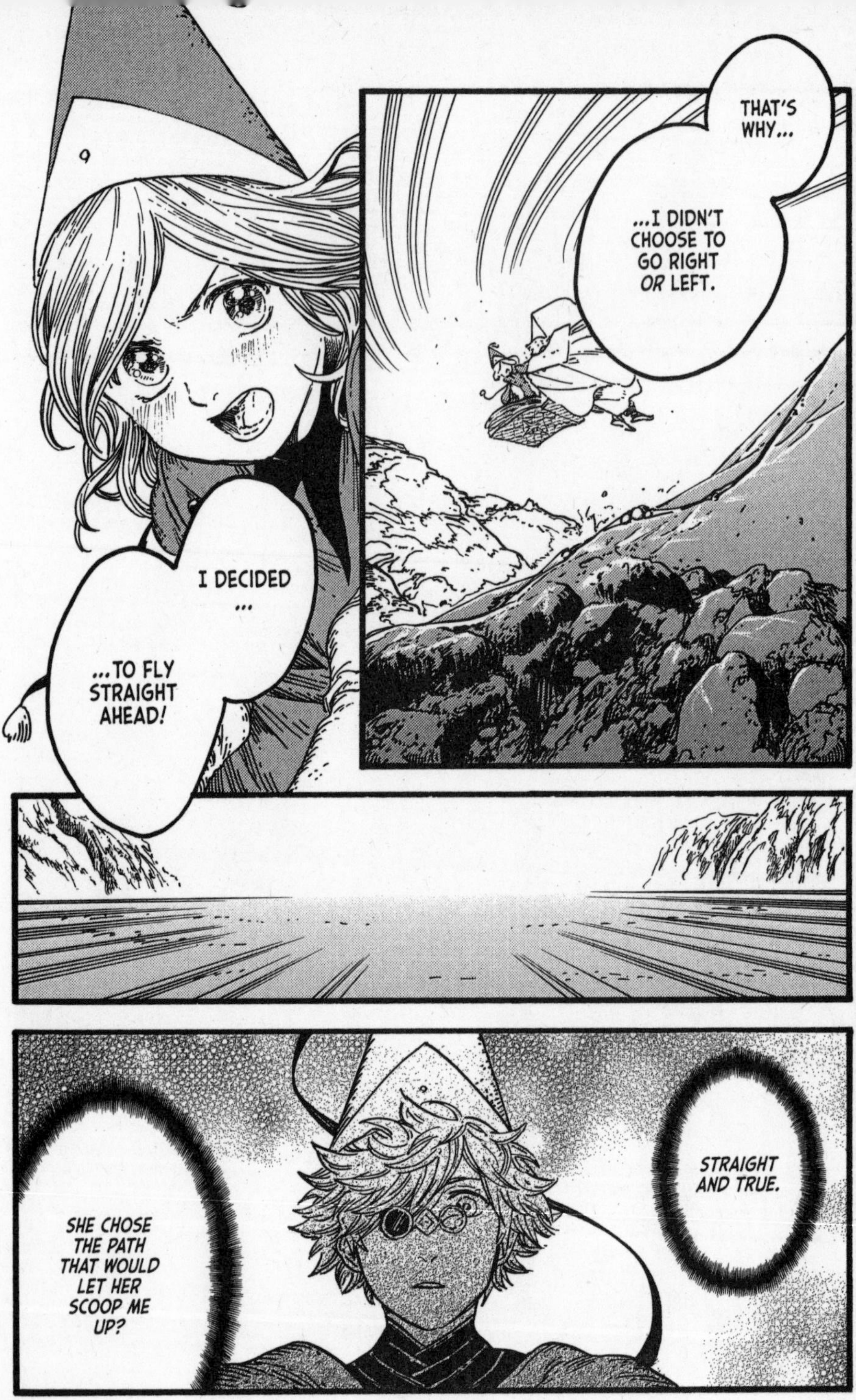
THAT'S WHY...
...I DIDN'T CHOOSE TO GO RIGHT *OR* LEFT.
I DECIDED ...
...TO FLY STRAIGHT AHEAD!
STRAIGHT AND TRUE.
SHE CHOSE THE PATH THAT WOULD LET HER SCOOP ME UP?

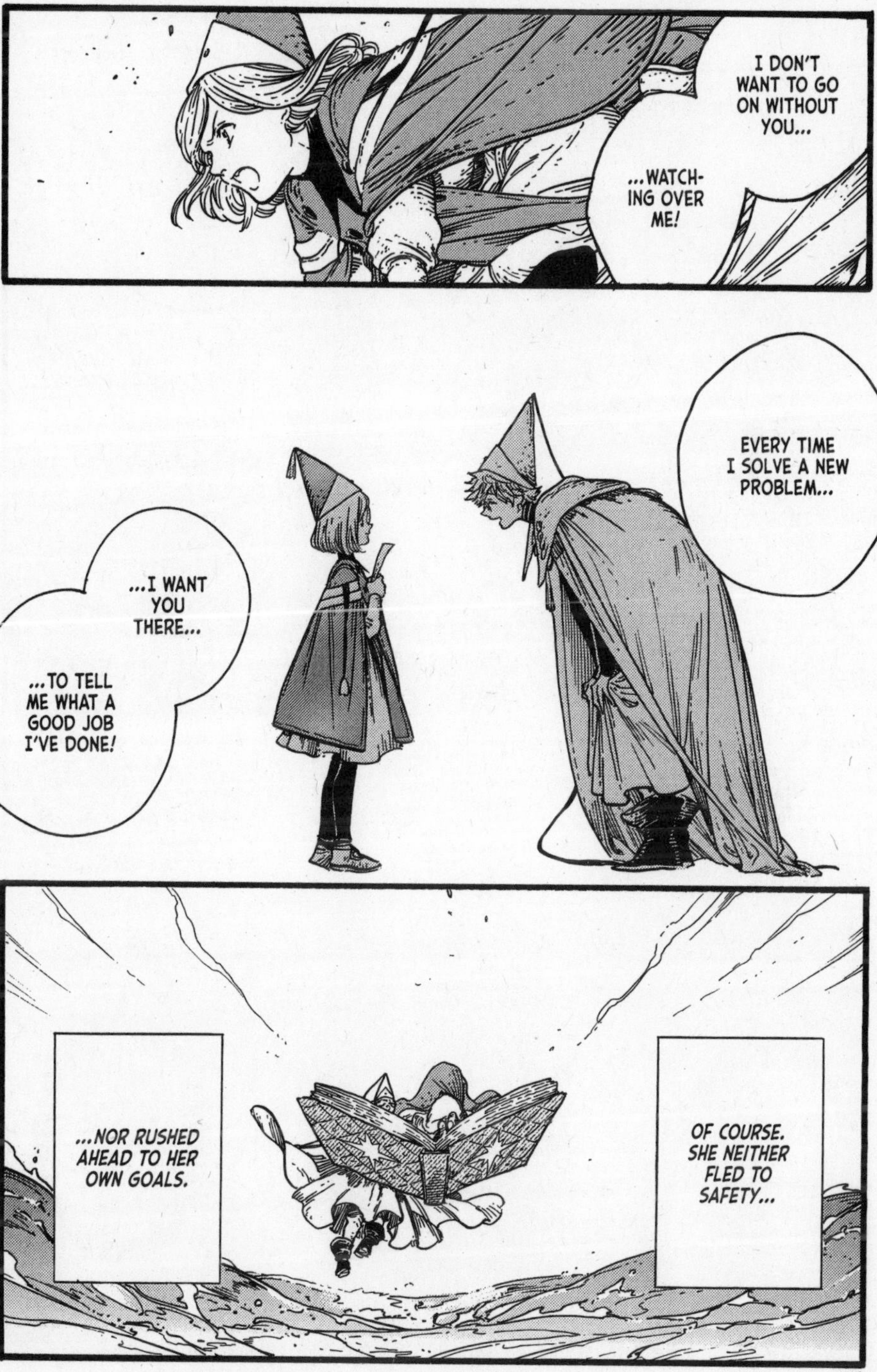
I DON'T WANT TO GO ON WITHOUT YOU...
...WATCHING OVER ME!
EVERY TIME I SOLVE A NEW PROBLEM...
...I WANT YOU THERE...
...TO TELL ME WHAT A GOOD JOB I'VE DONE!
OF COURSE. SHE NEITHER FLED TO SAFETY...
...NOR RUSHED AHEAD TO HER OWN GOALS.

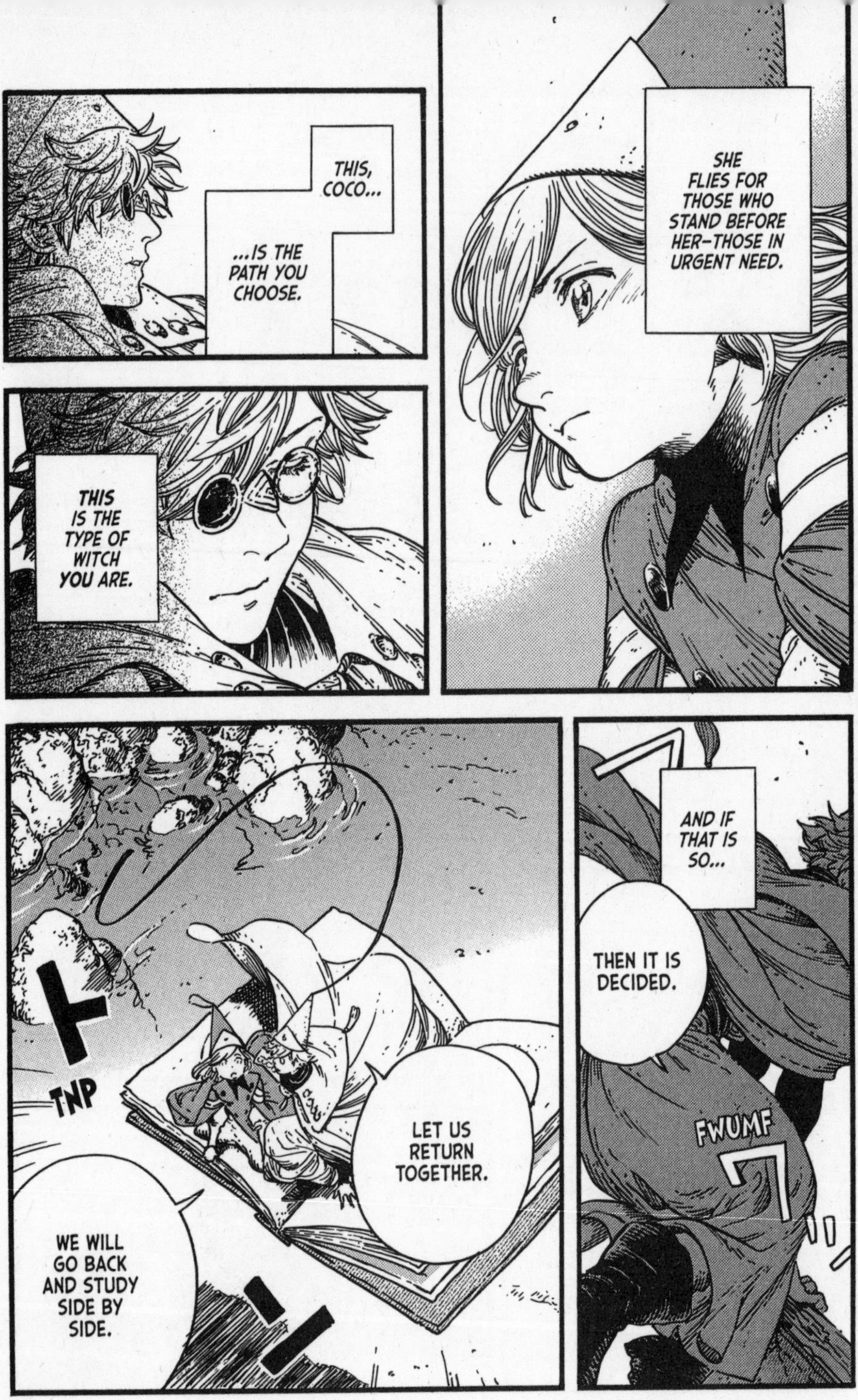
SHE FLIES FOR THOSE WHO STAND BEFORE HER–THOSE IN URGENT NEED.
THIS, COCO...
...IS THE PATH YOU CHOOSE.
THIS IS THE TYPE OF WITCH YOU ARE.
AND IF THAT IS SO...
THEN IT IS DECIDED.
FWUMF
TNP
LET US RETURN TOGETHER.
WE WILL GO BACK AND STUDY SIDE BY SIDE.

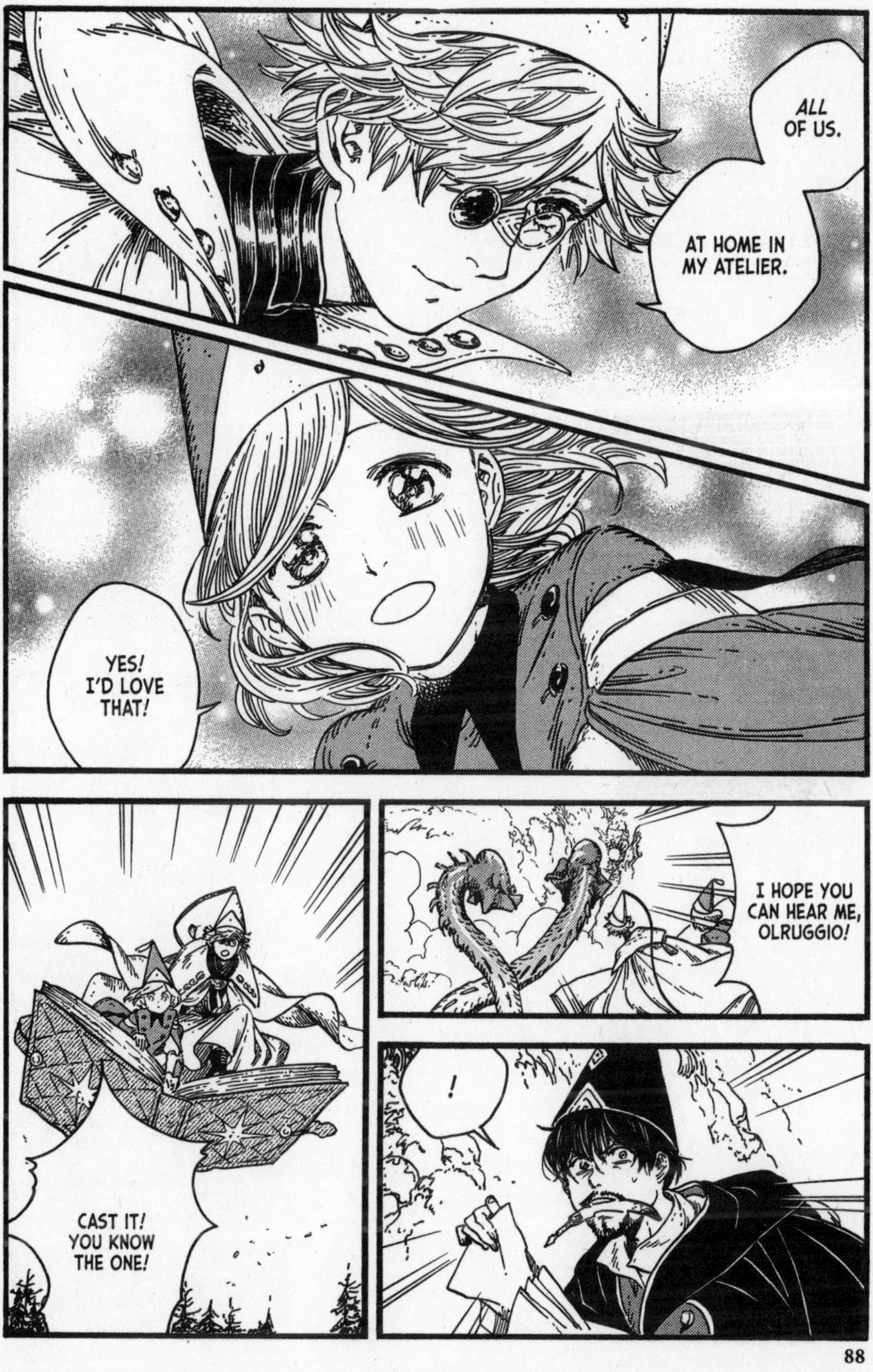
ALL OF US.
AT HOME IN MY ATELIER.
YES! I'D LOVE THAT!
I HOPE YOU CAN HEAR ME, OLRUGGIO!
!
CAST IT! YOU KNOW THE ONE!

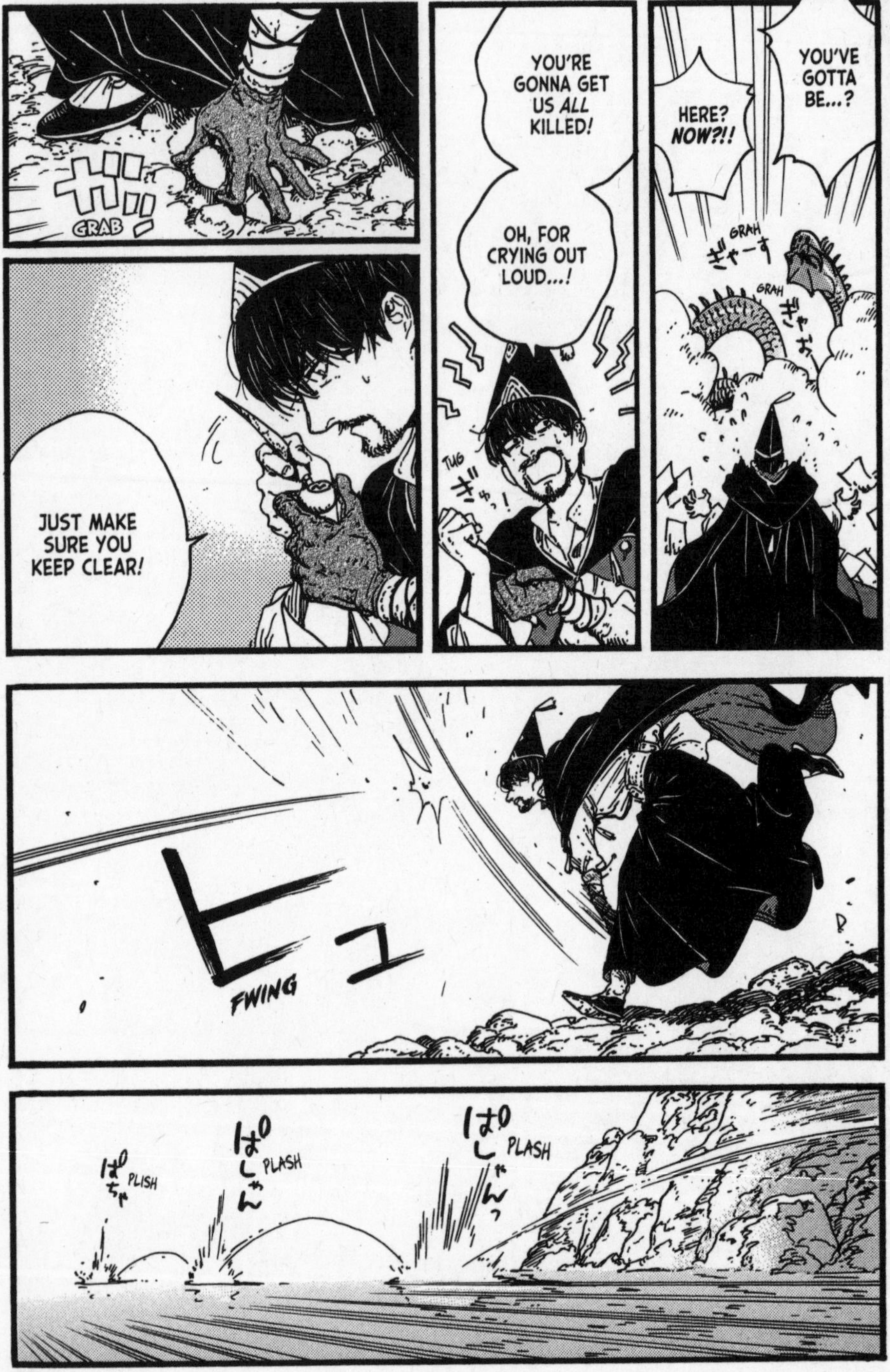
YOU'VE GOTTA BE...?
HERE? *NOW?!!*
ぎゃーす GRAH
ぎゃお GRAH
YOU'RE GONNA GET US *ALL* KILLED!
OH, FOR CRYING OUT LOUD...!
ぎゅっ TUG
ガッ GRAB
JUST MAKE SURE YOU KEEP CLEAR!
ヒュ FWING
ぱしゃんっ PLASH
ぱしゃん PLASH
ぱちゃ PLISH

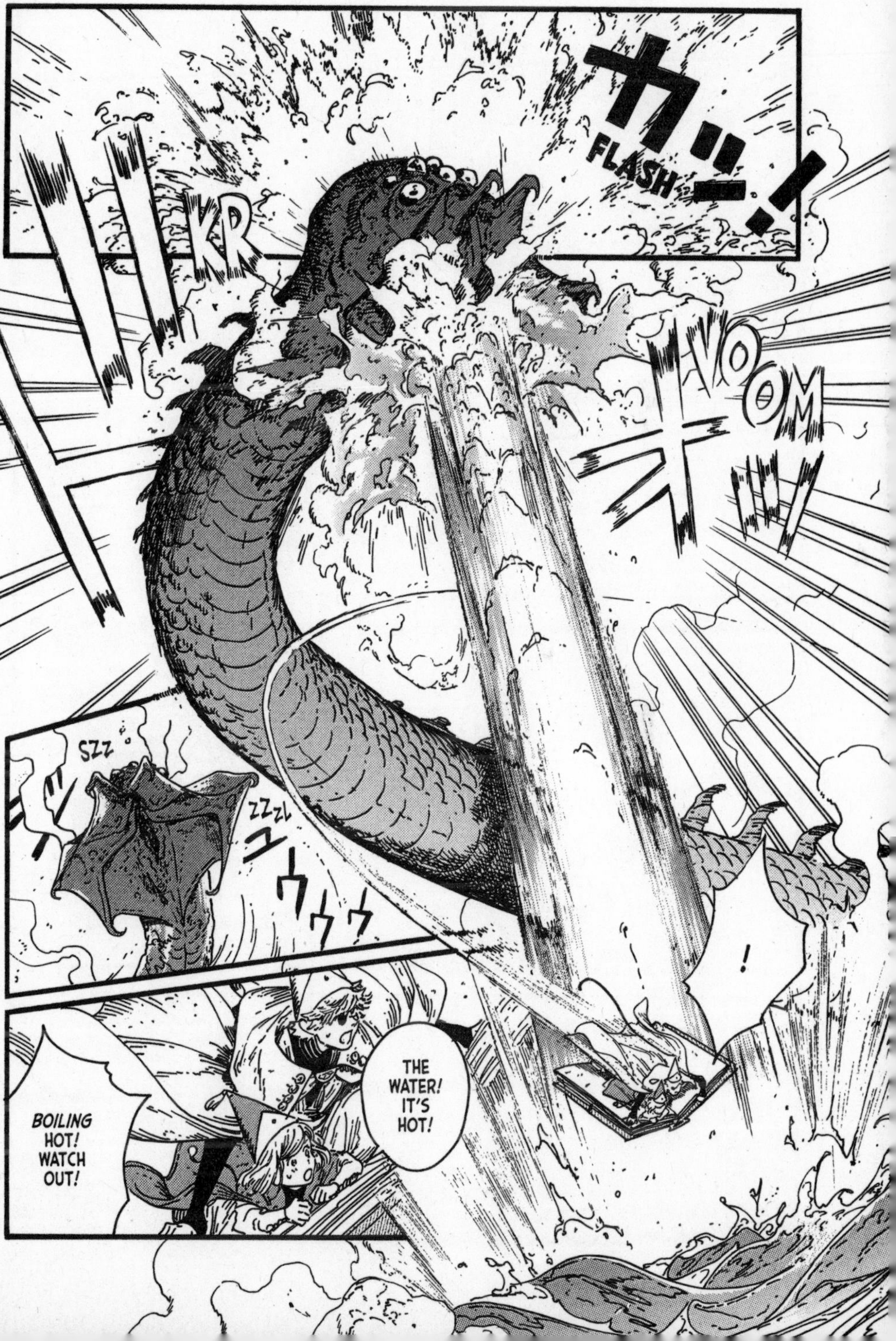
カッ!
FLASH
VOOM
KR
SZZ
ZZZL
ユウウウ
!
THE WATER! IT'S HOT!
BOILING HOT! WATCH OUT!

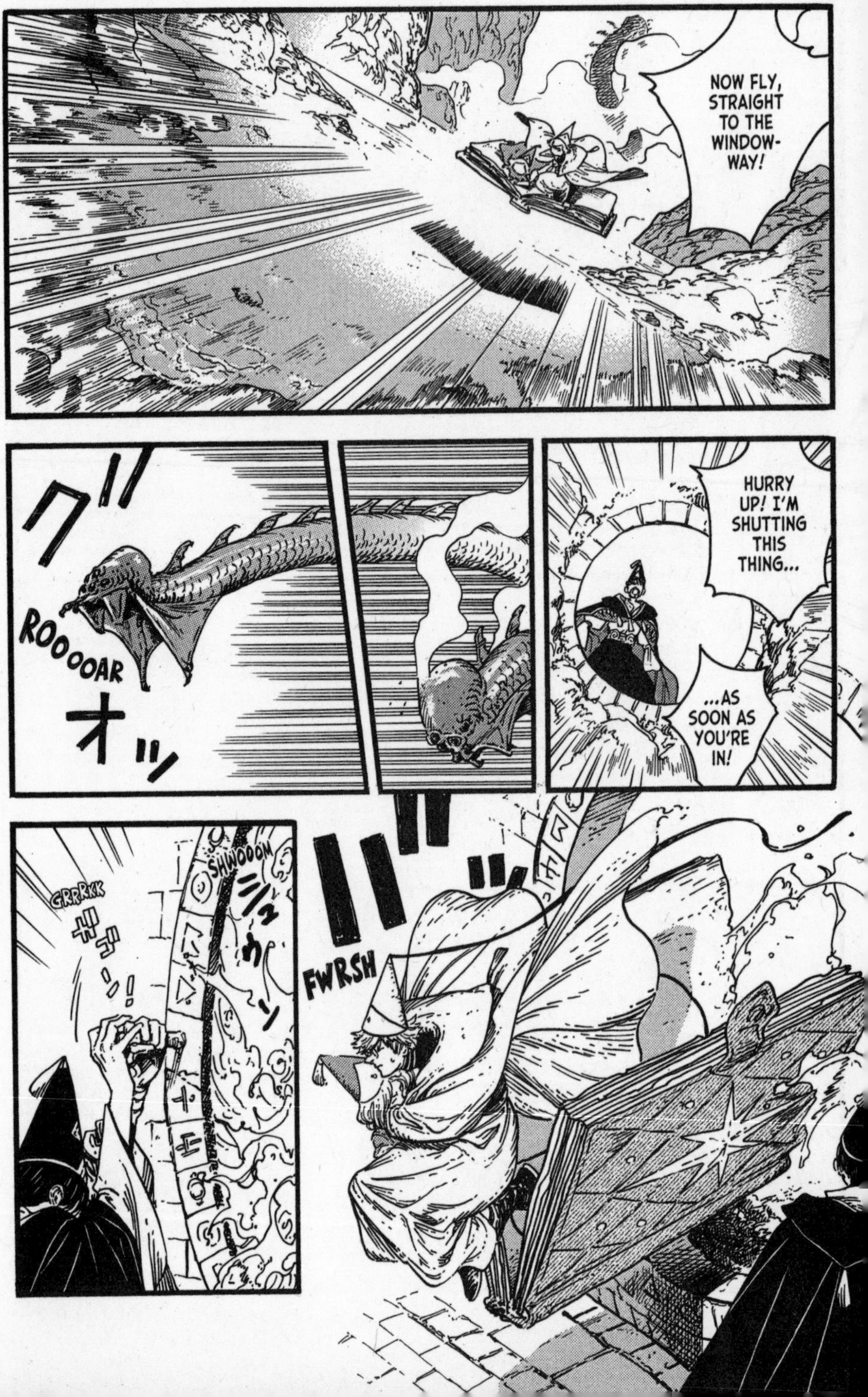

NOW FLY, STRAIGHT TO THE WINDOW-WAY!
HURRY UP! I'M SHUTTING THIS THING...
...AS SOON AS YOU'RE IN!
ROOOOAR
FWRSH
SHWOOOM
GRRRKK

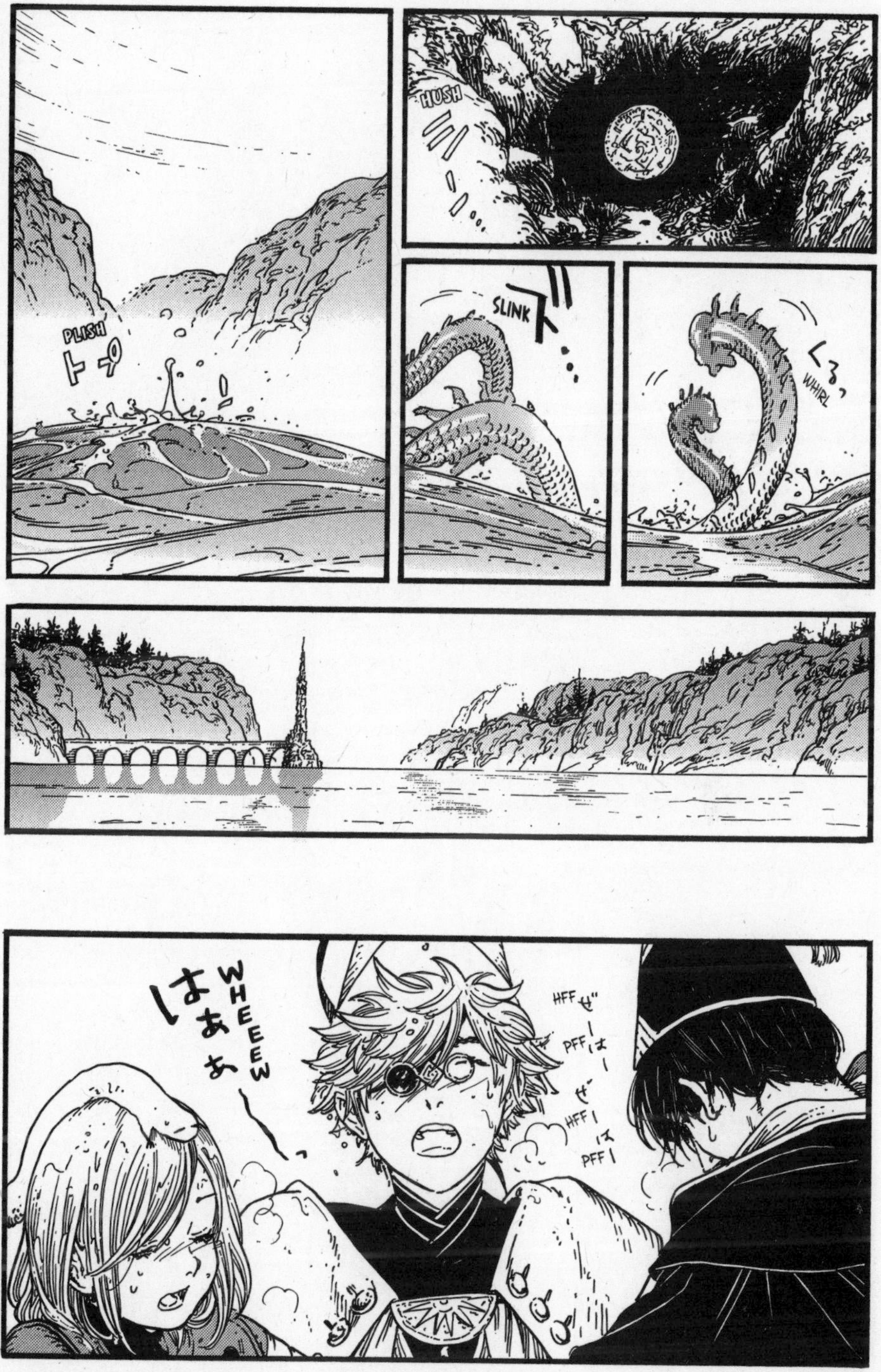
HUSH
WHIRL
SLINK
PLISH
HFF
PFF
HFF
PFF
WHEEEW

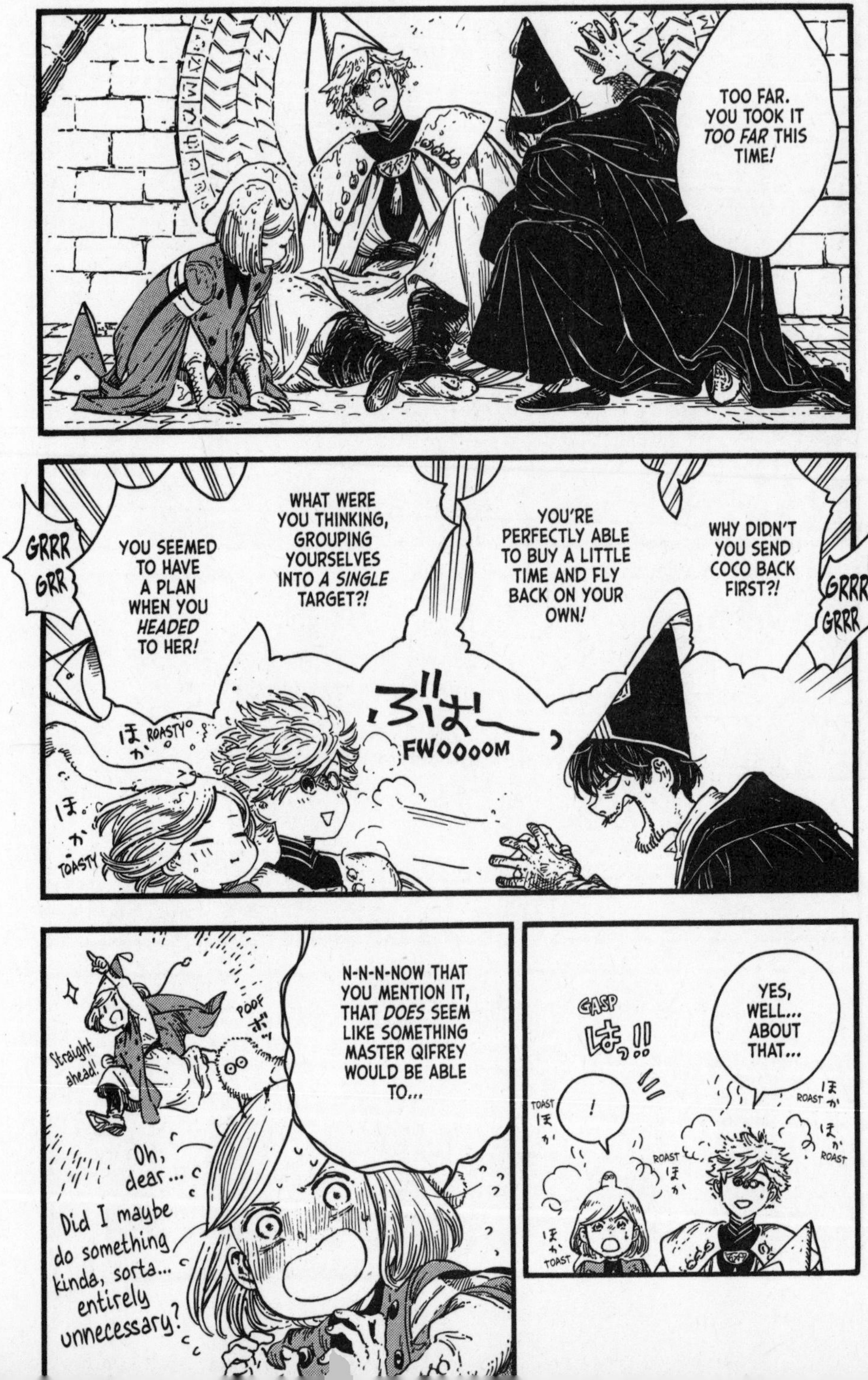
TOO FAR. YOU TOOK IT *TOO FAR* THIS TIME!
GRRR GRRR
WHY DIDN'T YOU SEND COCO BACK FIRST?!
YOU'RE PERFECTLY ABLE TO BUY A LITTLE TIME AND FLY BACK ON YOUR OWN!
WHAT WERE YOU THINKING, GROUPING YOURSELVES INTO *A SINGLE* TARGET?!
YOU SEEMED TO HAVE A PLAN WHEN YOU *HEADED* TO HER!
GRRR GRR
ぶはー
FWOOOOM
ほか ROASTY
ほか TOASTY
YES, WELL... ABOUT THAT...
ほか ROAST
ほか ROAST
ほか ROAST
GASP
はっ!!
!
TOAST ほか
ほか TOAST
N-N-N-NOW THAT YOU MENTION IT, THAT *DOES* SEEM LIKE SOMETHING MASTER QIFREY WOULD BE ABLE TO...
POOF ボッ
Straight ahead!
Oh, dear... Did I maybe do something kinda, sorta... entirely unnecessary?

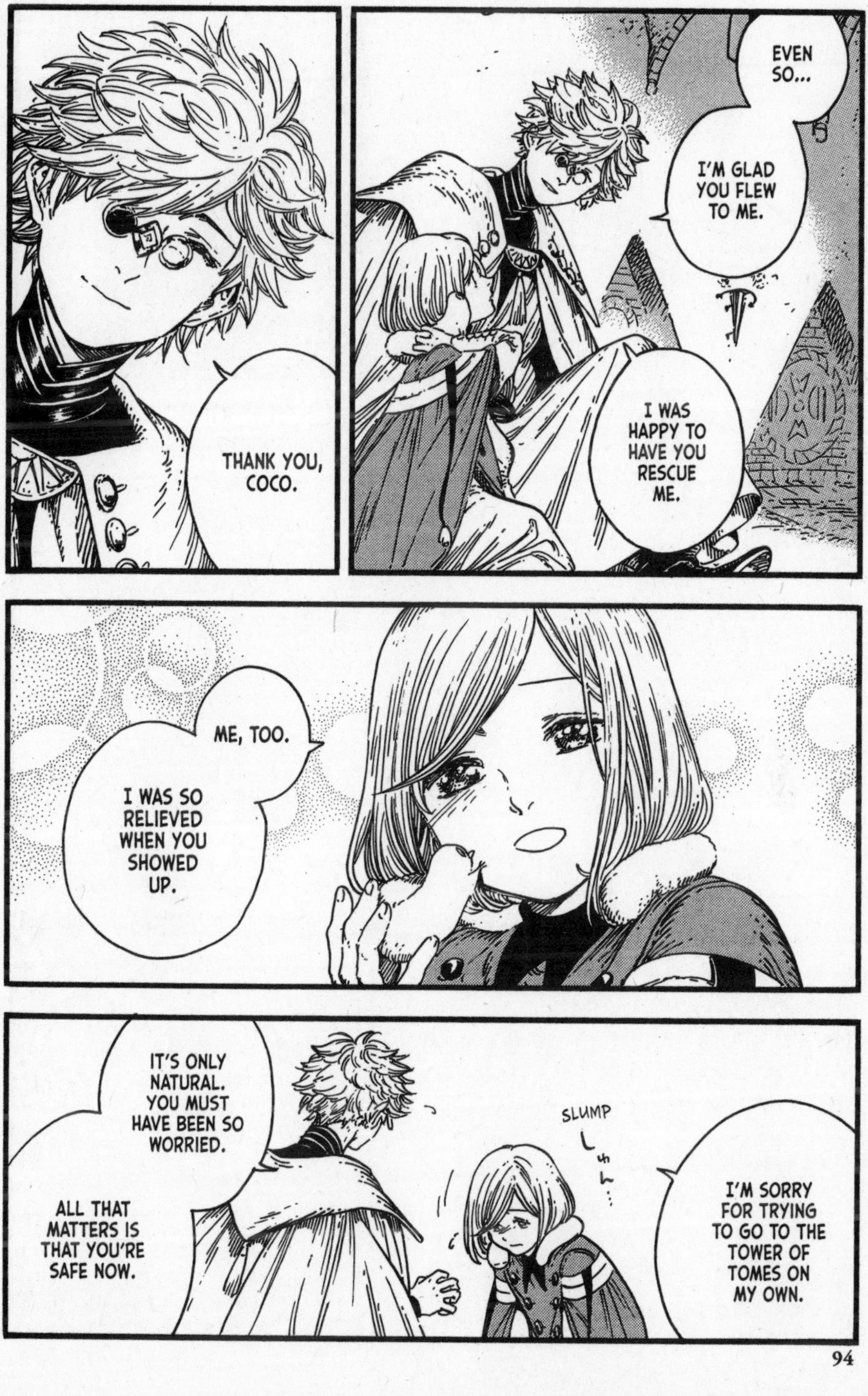
EVEN SO...
I'M GLAD YOU FLEW TO ME.
I WAS HAPPY TO HAVE YOU RESCUE ME.
THANK YOU, COCO.
ME, TOO.
I WAS SO RELIEVED WHEN YOU SHOWED UP.
I'M SORRY FOR TRYING TO GO TO THE TOWER OF TOMES ON MY OWN.
SLUMP
しゅん…
IT'S ONLY NATURAL. YOU MUST HAVE BEEN SO WORRIED.
ALL THAT MATTERS IS THAT YOU'RE SAFE NOW.

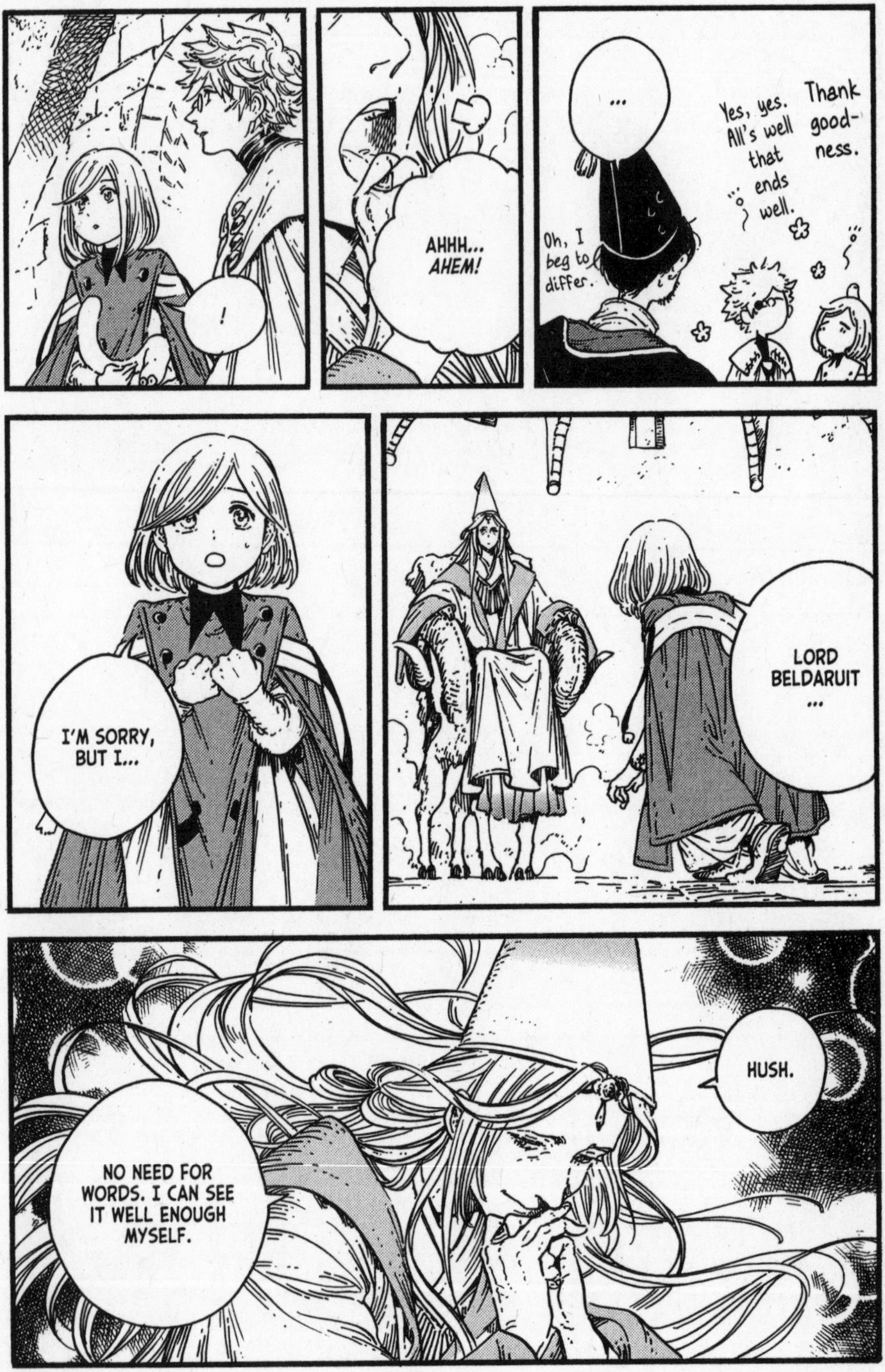
Thank goodness.
Yes, yes. All's well that ends well.
...
Oh, I beg to differ.
AHHH... AHEM!
!
LORD BELDARUIT ...
I'M SORRY, BUT I...
HUSH.
NO NEED FOR WORDS. I CAN SEE IT WELL ENOUGH MYSELF.

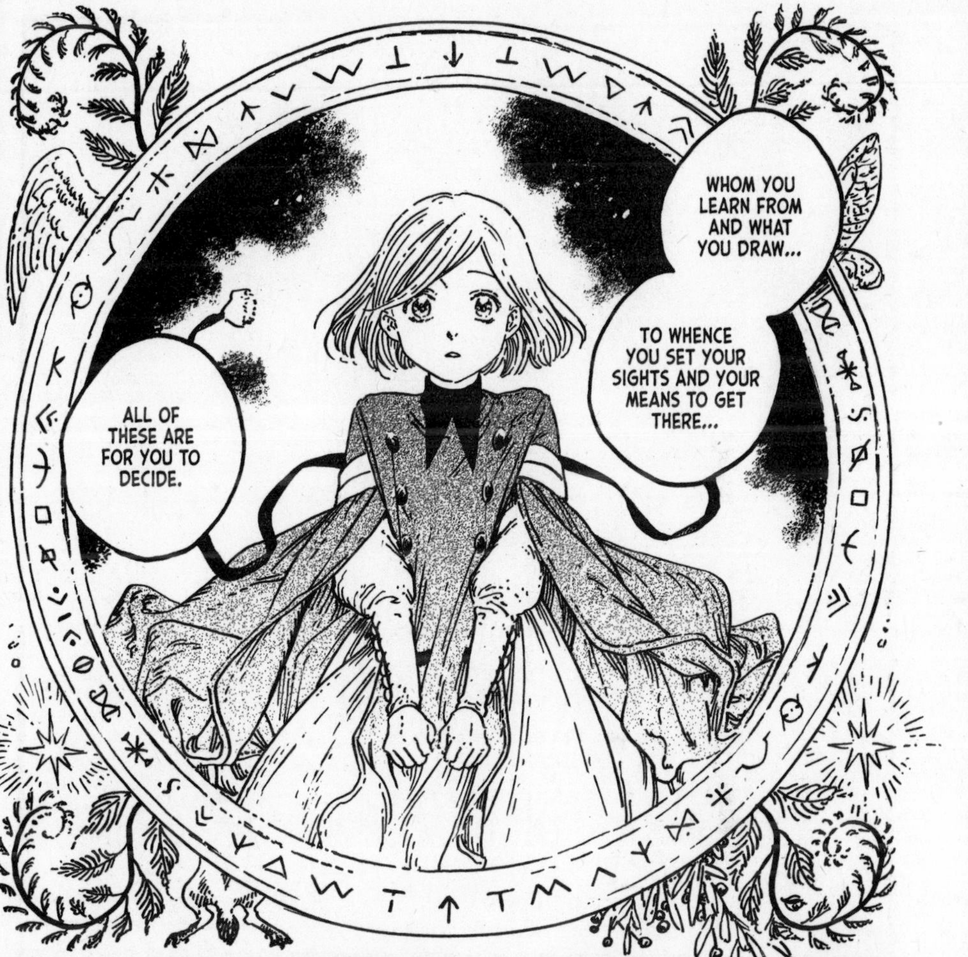
WHOM YOU LEARN FROM AND WHAT YOU DRAW...
TO WHENCE YOU SET YOUR SIGHTS AND YOUR MEANS TO GET THERE...
ALL OF THESE ARE FOR YOU TO DECIDE.

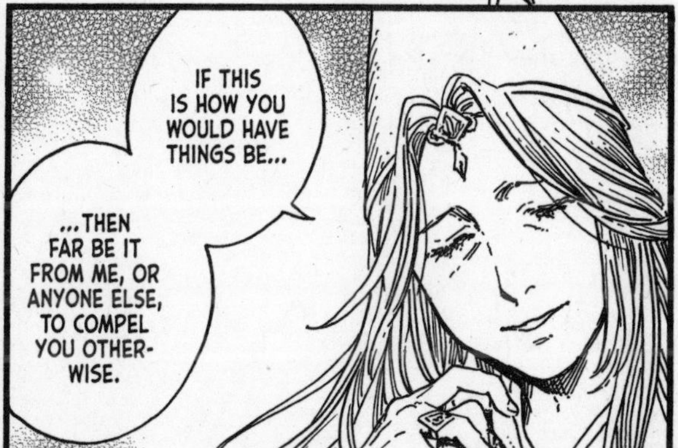
IF THIS IS HOW YOU WOULD HAVE THINGS BE...
...THEN FAR BE IT FROM ME, OR ANYONE ELSE, TO COMPEL YOU OTHER-WISE.

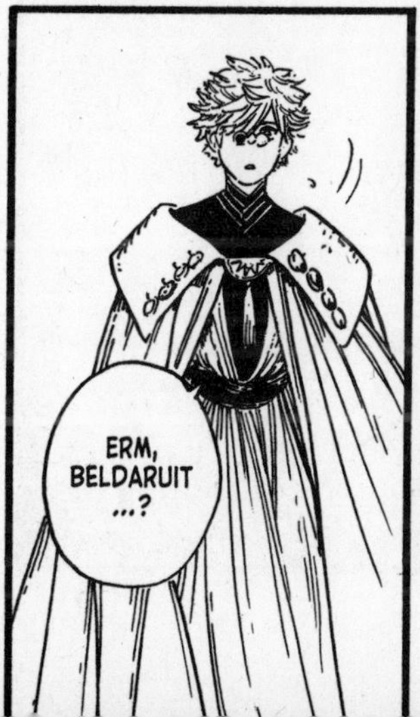
ERM, BELDARUIT ...?

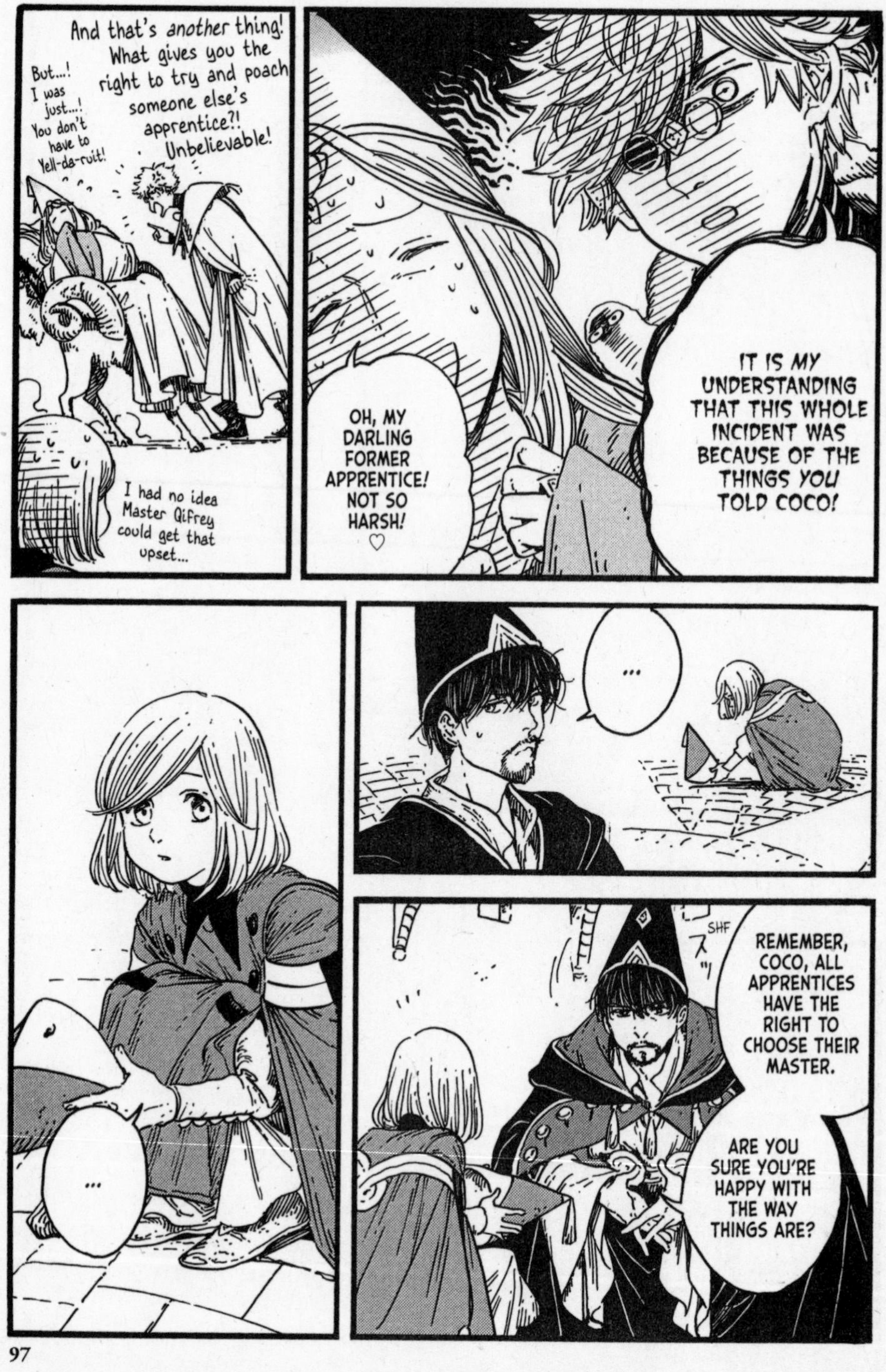
IT IS MY UNDERSTANDING THAT THIS WHOLE INCIDENT WAS BECAUSE OF THE THINGS YOU TOLD COCO!
OH, MY DARLING FORMER APPRENTICE! NOT SO HARSH! ♡
And that's another thing! What gives you the right to try and poach someone else's apprentice?! Unbelievable!
But...! I was just...! You don't have to Yell-da-ruit!
I had no idea Master Qifrey could get that upset...
...
SHF
REMEMBER, COCO, ALL APPRENTICES HAVE THE RIGHT TO CHOOSE THEIR MASTER.
ARE YOU SURE YOU'RE HAPPY WITH THE WAY THINGS ARE?
...

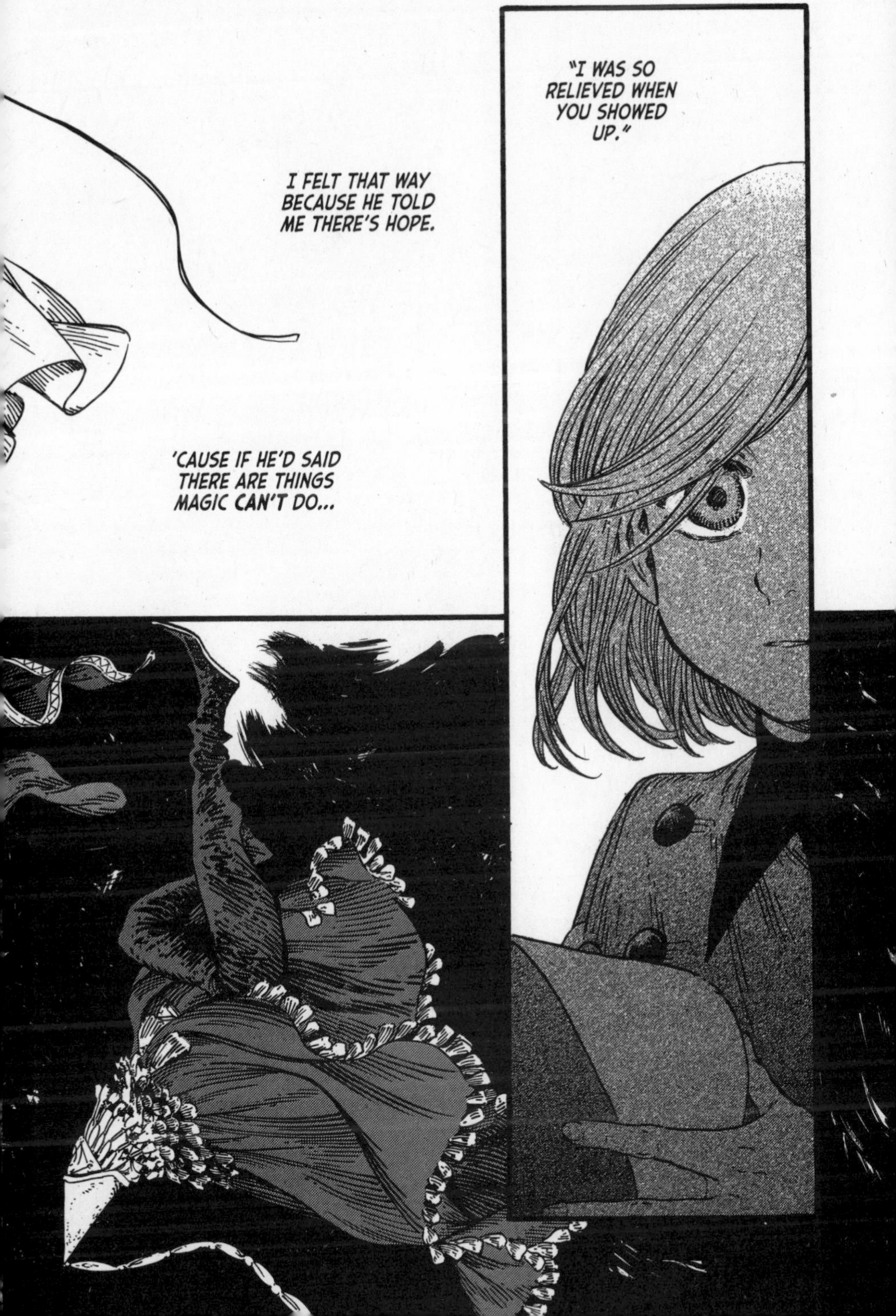
"I WAS SO RELIEVED WHEN YOU SHOWED UP."
I FELT THAT WAY BECAUSE HE TOLD ME THERE'S HOPE.
'CAUSE IF HE'D SAID THERE ARE THINGS MAGIC **CAN'T** DO...

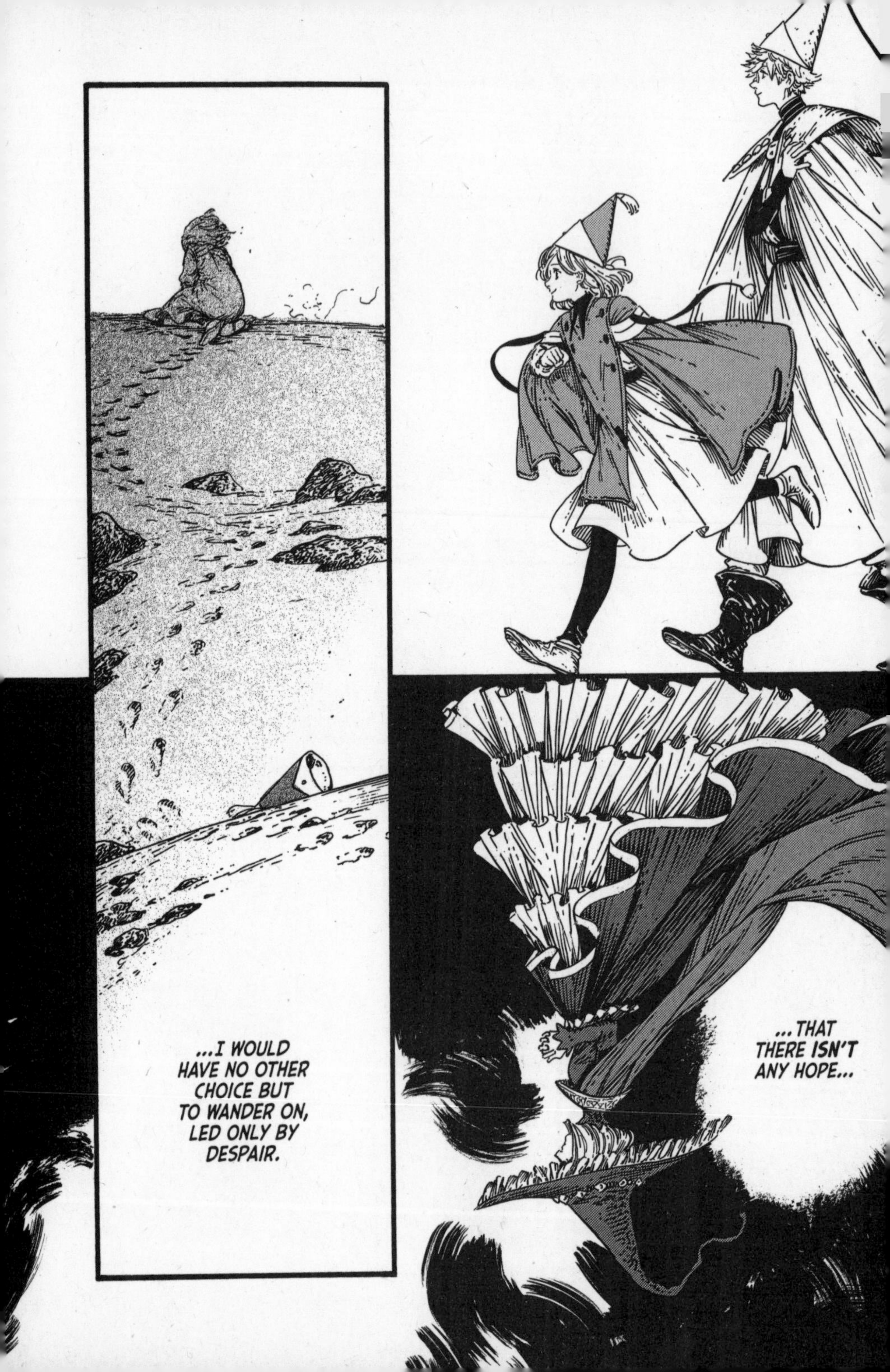
...THAT THERE ISN'T ANY HOPE...
...I WOULD HAVE NO OTHER CHOICE BUT TO WANDER ON, LED ONLY BY DESPAIR.

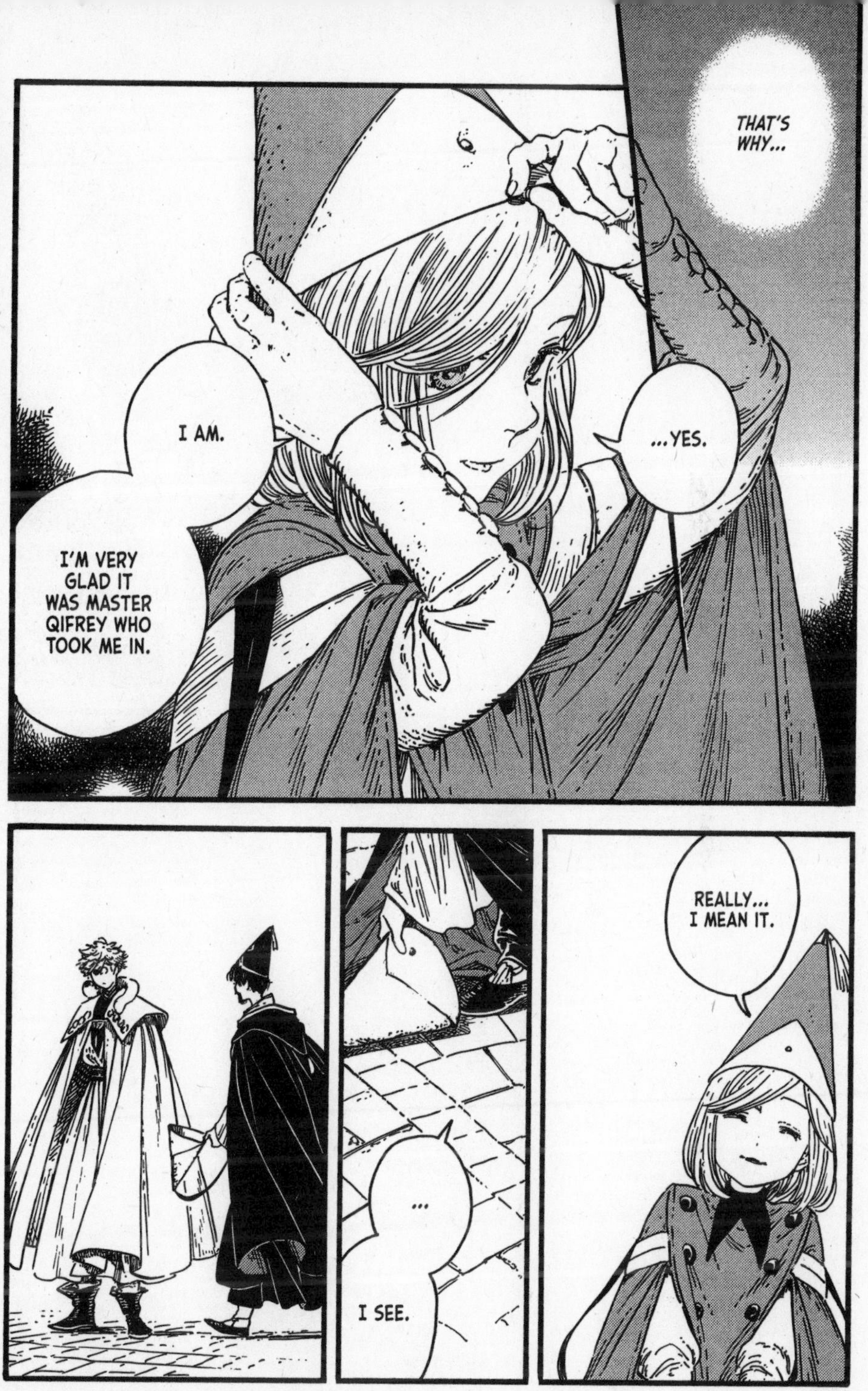
THAT'S WHY...
...YES.
I AM.
I'M VERY GLAD IT WAS MASTER QIFREY WHO TOOK ME IN.
REALLY... I MEAN IT.
...
I SEE.

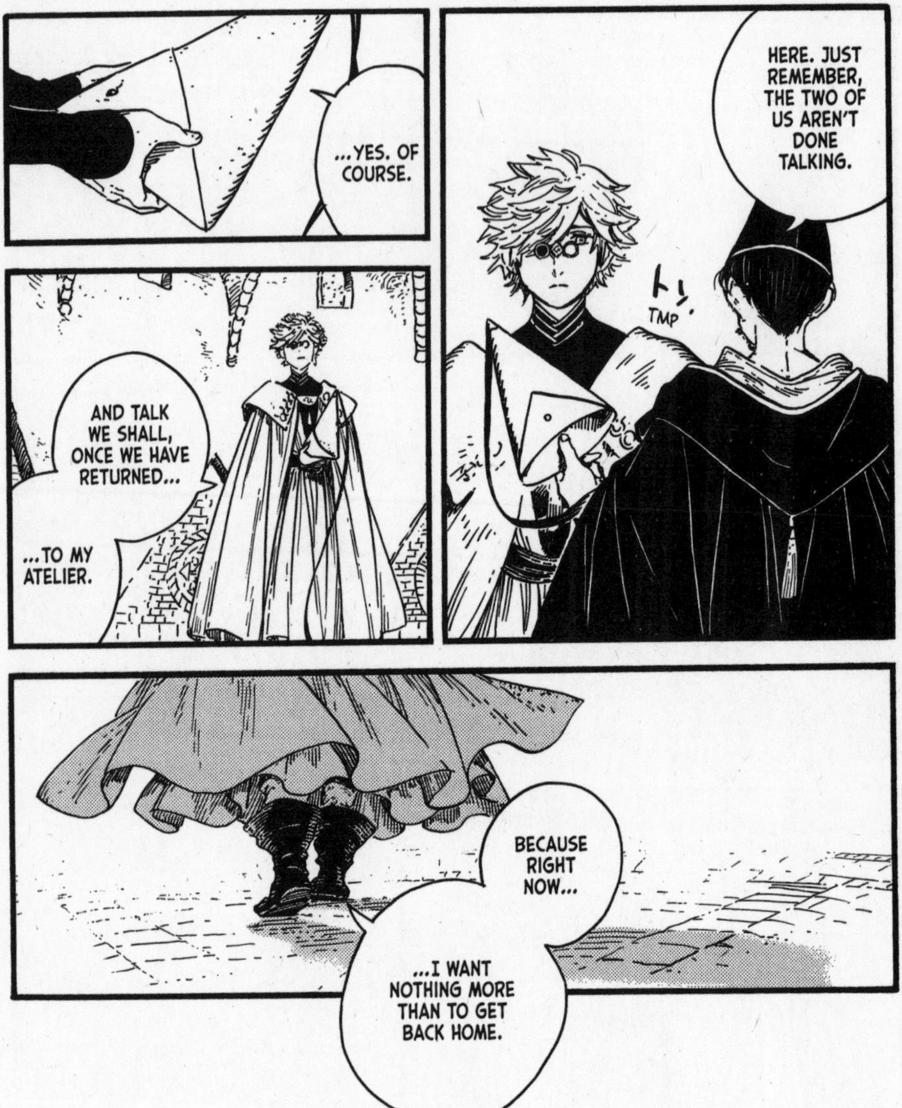
HERE. JUST REMEMBER, THE TWO OF US AREN'T DONE TALKING.
TMP
...YES. OF COURSE.
AND TALK WE SHALL, ONCE WE HAVE RETURNED...
...TO MY ATELIER.
BECAUSE RIGHT NOW...
...I WANT NOTHING MORE THAN TO GET BACK HOME.

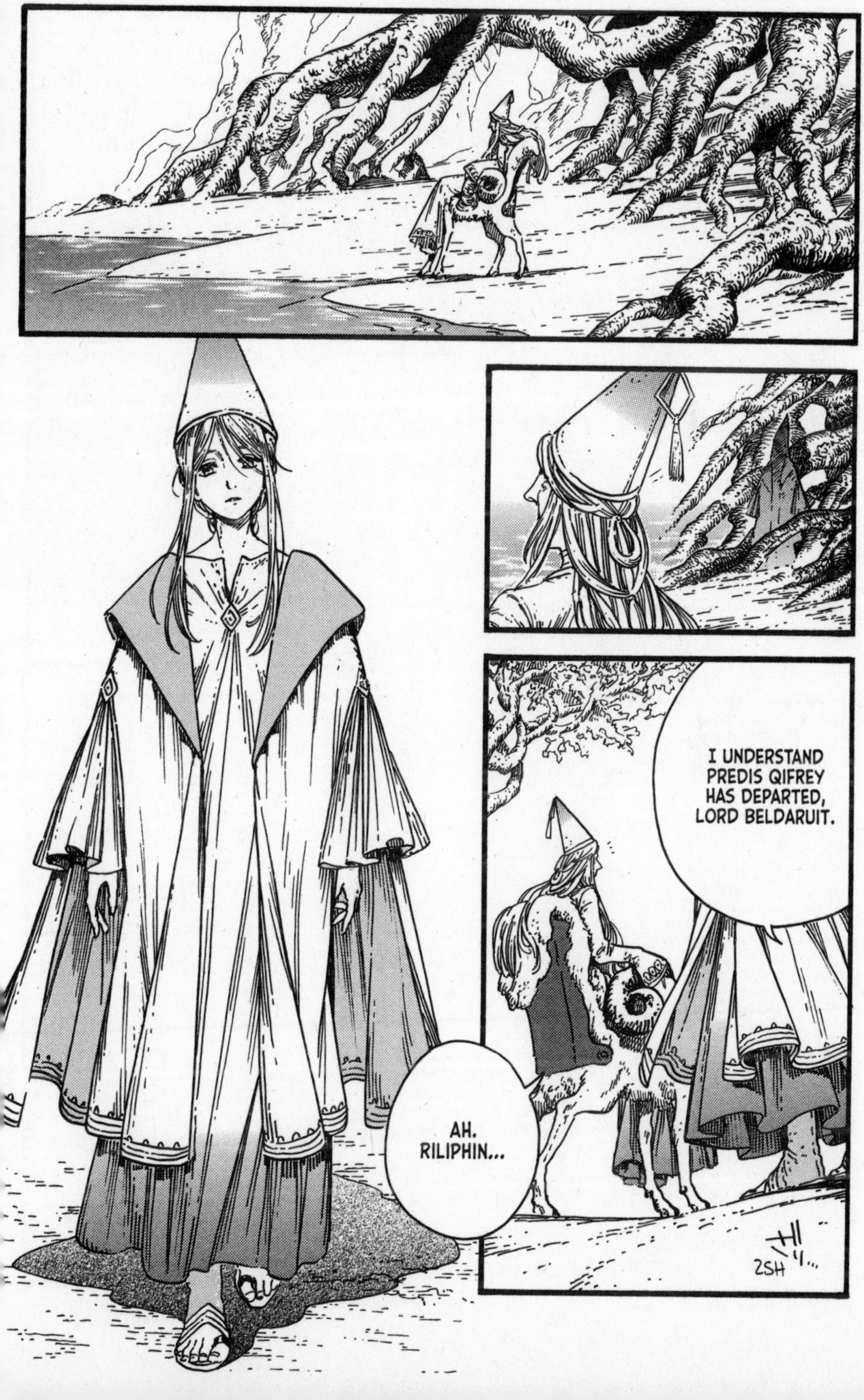
I UNDERSTAND PREDIS QIFREY HAS DEPARTED, LORD BELDARUIT.
ZSH
AH. RILIPHIN...

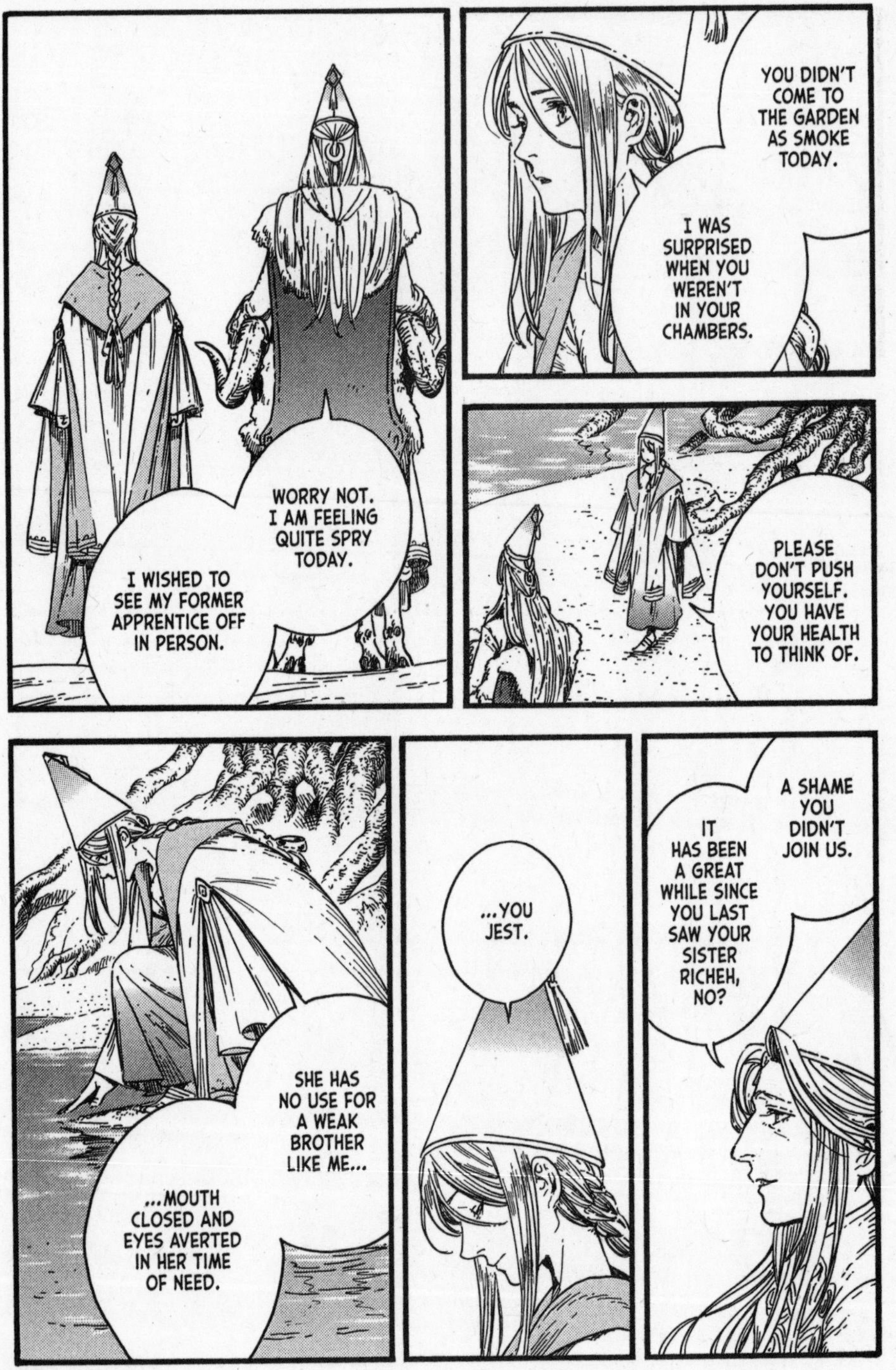
YOU DIDN'T COME TO THE GARDEN AS SMOKE TODAY.
I WAS SURPRISED WHEN YOU WEREN'T IN YOUR CHAMBERS.
PLEASE DON'T PUSH YOURSELF. YOU HAVE YOUR HEALTH TO THINK OF.
WORRY NOT. I AM FEELING QUITE SPRY TODAY.
I WISHED TO SEE MY FORMER APPRENTICE OFF IN PERSON.
A SHAME YOU DIDN'T JOIN US.
IT HAS BEEN A GREAT WHILE SINCE YOU LAST SAW YOUR SISTER RICHEH, NO?
...YOU JEST.
SHE HAS NO USE FOR A WEAK BROTHER LIKE ME...
...MOUTH CLOSED AND EYES AVERTED IN HER TIME OF NEED.

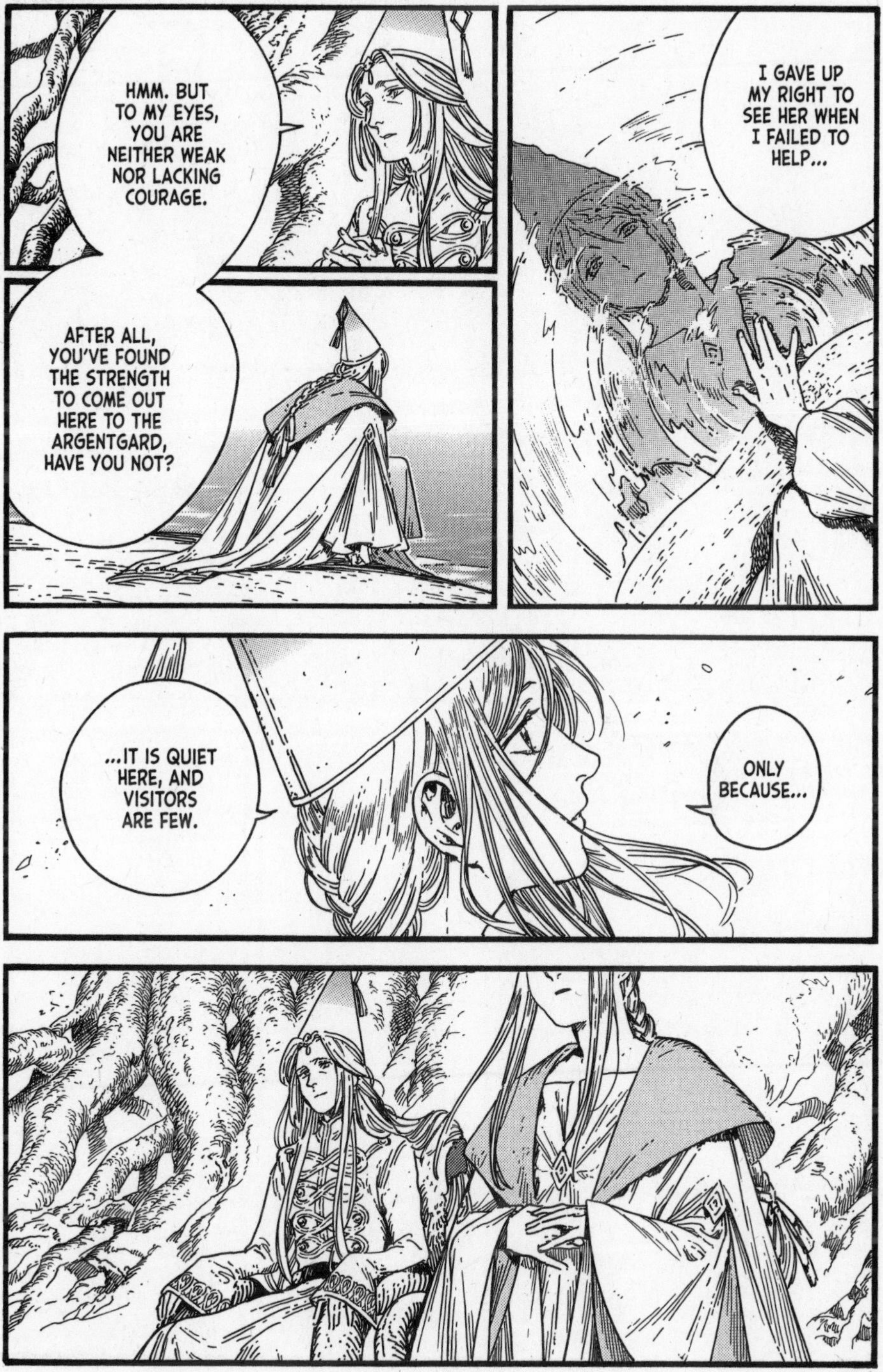
I GAVE UP MY RIGHT TO SEE HER WHEN I FAILED TO HELP...
HMM. BUT TO MY EYES, YOU ARE NEITHER WEAK NOR LACKING COURAGE.
AFTER ALL, YOU'VE FOUND THE STRENGTH TO COME OUT HERE TO THE ARGENTGARD, HAVE YOU NOT?
ONLY BECAUSE...
...IT IS QUIET HERE, AND VISITORS ARE FEW.

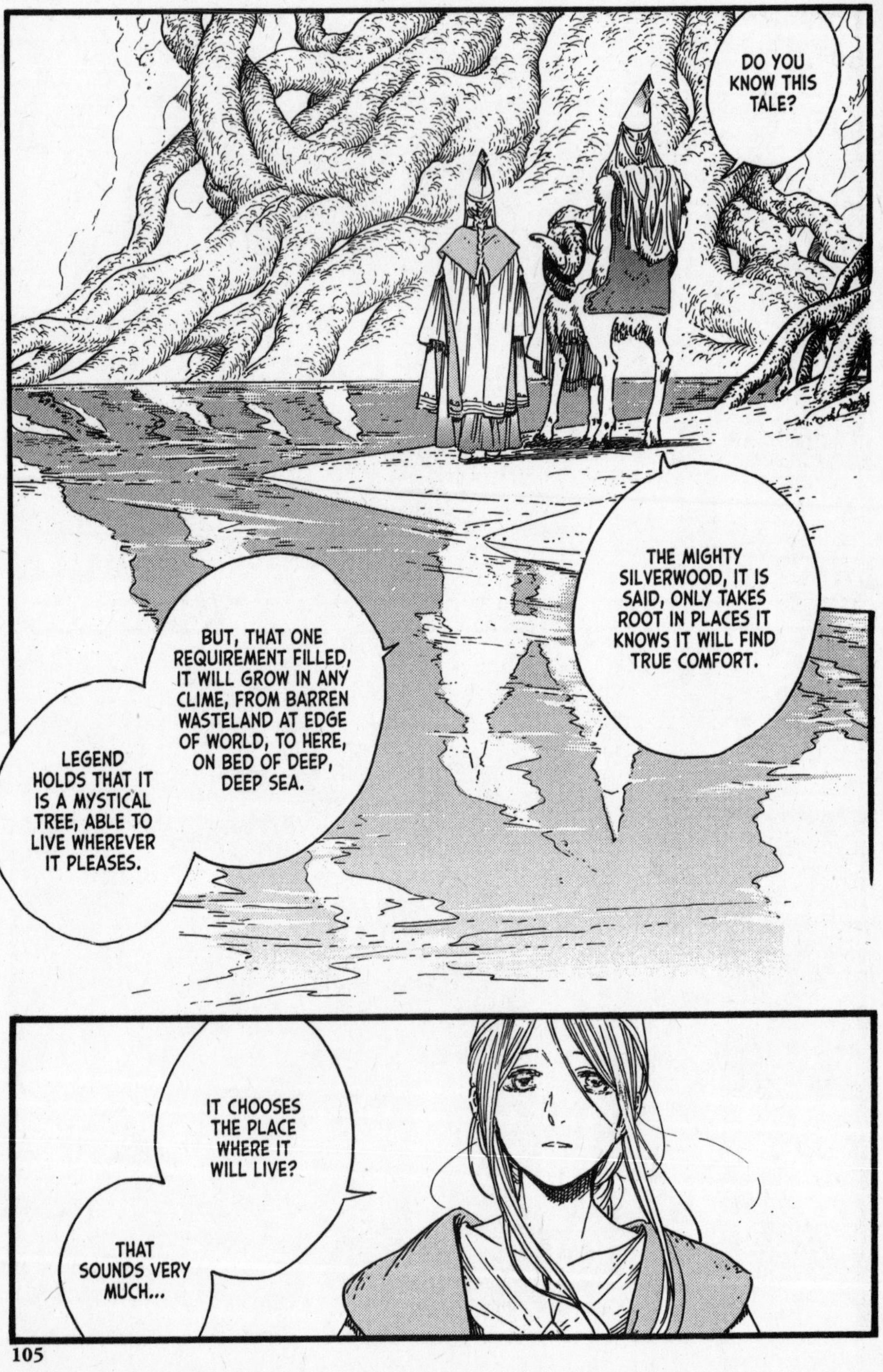
DO YOU KNOW THIS TALE?
THE MIGHTY SILVERWOOD, IT IS SAID, ONLY TAKES ROOT IN PLACES IT KNOWS IT WILL FIND TRUE COMFORT.
BUT, THAT ONE REQUIREMENT FILLED, IT WILL GROW IN ANY CLIME, FROM BARREN WASTELAND AT EDGE OF WORLD, TO HERE, ON BED OF DEEP, DEEP SEA.
LEGEND HOLDS THAT IT IS A MYSTICAL TREE, ABLE TO LIVE WHEREVER IT PLEASES.
IT CHOOSES THE PLACE WHERE IT WILL LIVE?
THAT SOUNDS VERY MUCH...

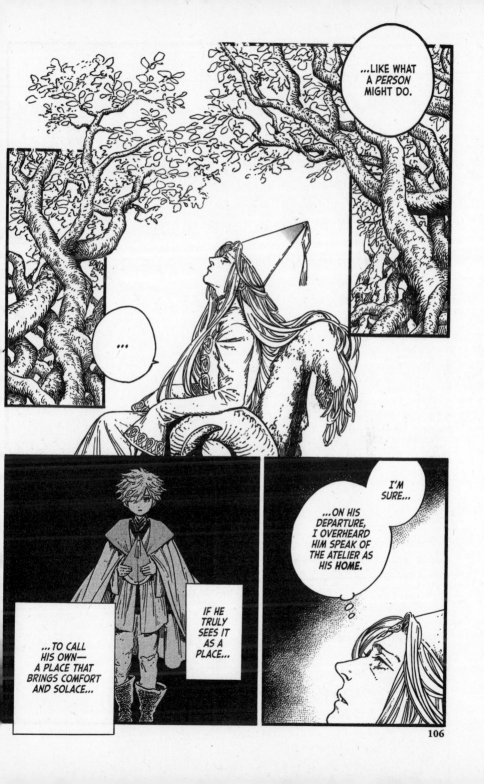

...LIKE WHAT A *PERSON* MIGHT DO.

...

I'M SURE...

...ON HIS DEPARTURE, I OVERHEARD HIM SPEAK OF THE ATELIER AS HIS **HOME**.

IF HE TRULY SEES IT AS A PLACE...

...TO CALL HIS OWN— A PLACE THAT BRINGS COMFORT AND SOLACE...

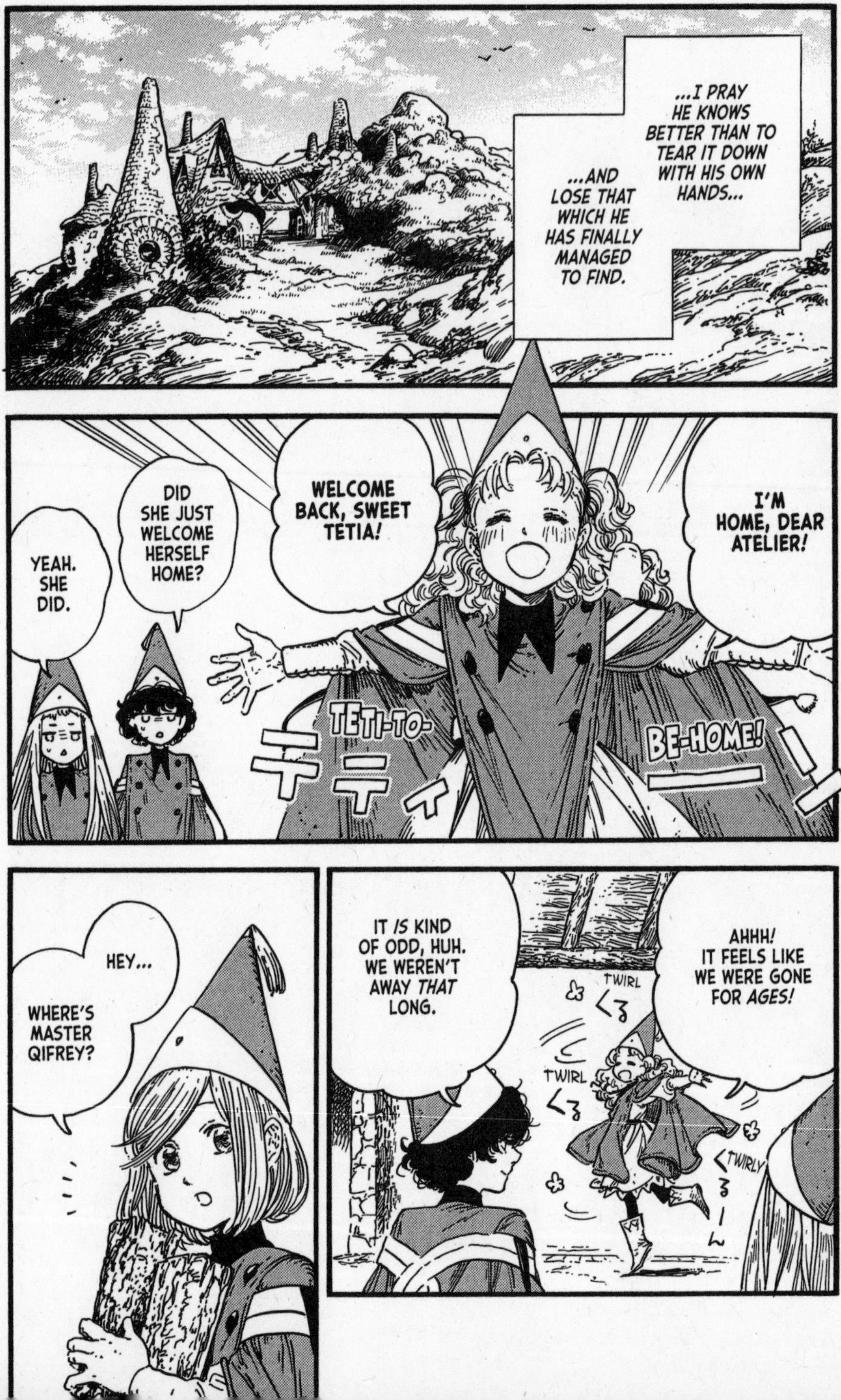
...I PRAY HE KNOWS BETTER THAN TO TEAR IT DOWN WITH HIS OWN HANDS...
...AND LOSE THAT WHICH HE HAS FINALLY MANAGED TO FIND.
I'M HOME, DEAR ATELIER!
BE-HOME!
WELCOME BACK, SWEET TETIA!
TETI-TO-
DID SHE JUST WELCOME HERSELF HOME?
YEAH. SHE DID.
AHHH! IT FEELS LIKE WE WERE GONE FOR AGES!
TWIRLY
TWIRL
TWIRL
IT IS KIND OF ODD, HUH. WE WEREN'T AWAY THAT LONG.
HEY...
WHERE'S MASTER QIFREY?

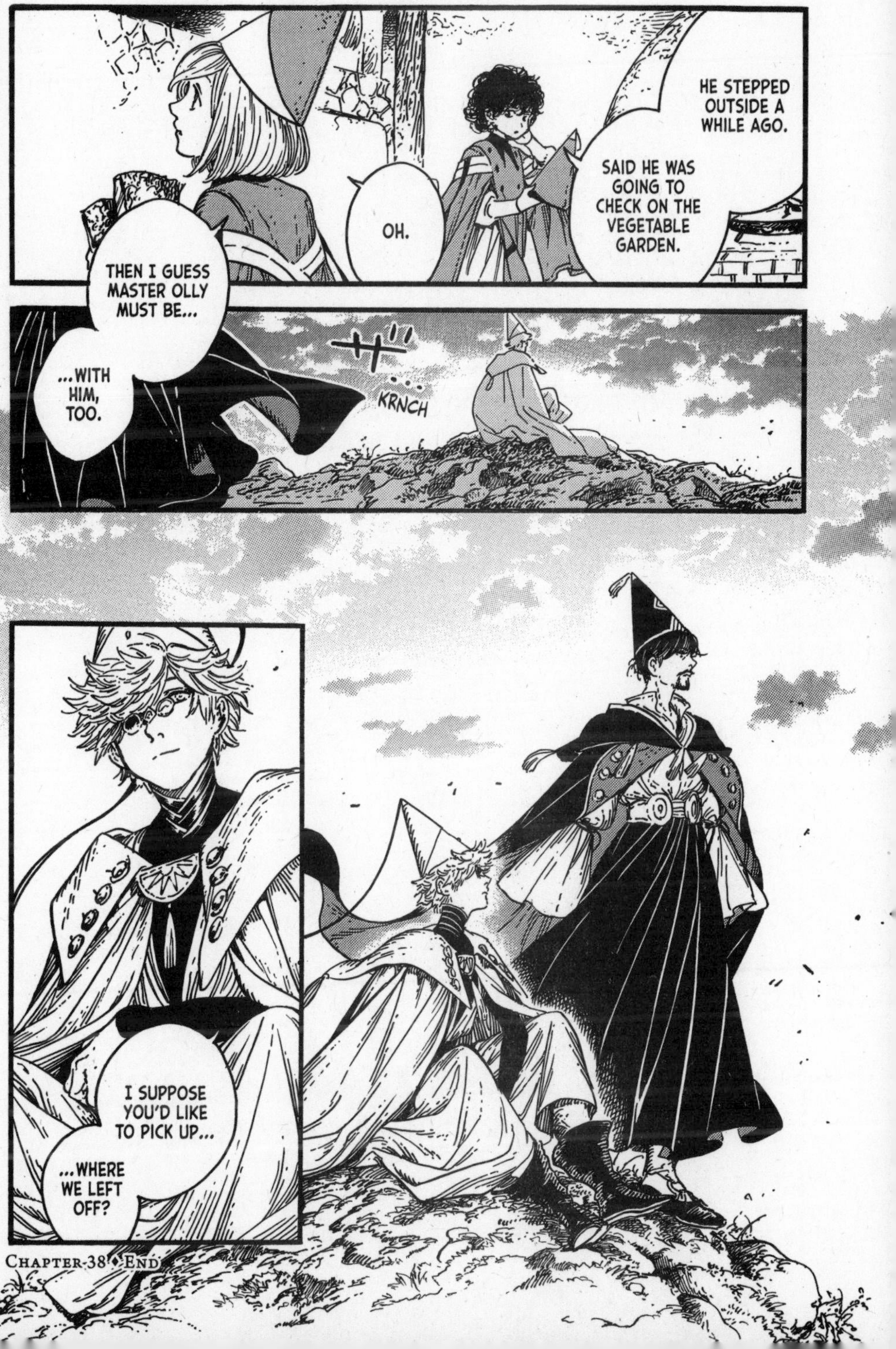
HE STEPPED OUTSIDE A WHILE AGO.
SAID HE WAS GOING TO CHECK ON THE VEGETABLE GARDEN.
OH.
THEN I GUESS MASTER OLLY MUST BE...
...WITH HIM, TOO.
KRNCH
I SUPPOSE YOU'D LIKE TO PICK UP...
...WHERE WE LEFT OFF?
CHAPTER 38 ◆ END

Witch Hat Atelier

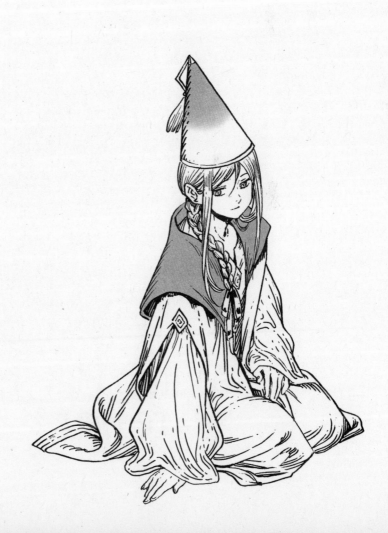

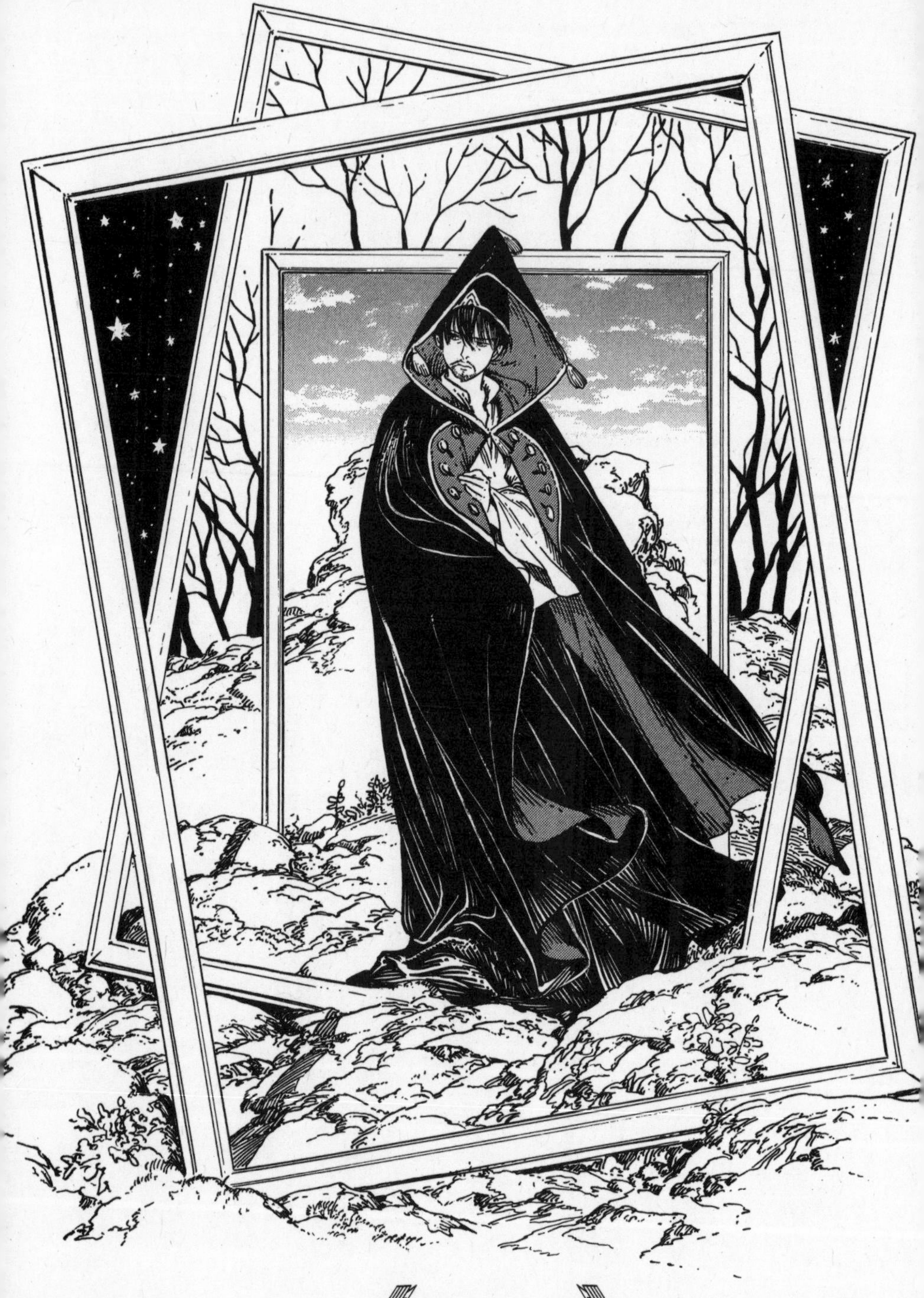

Chapter 39

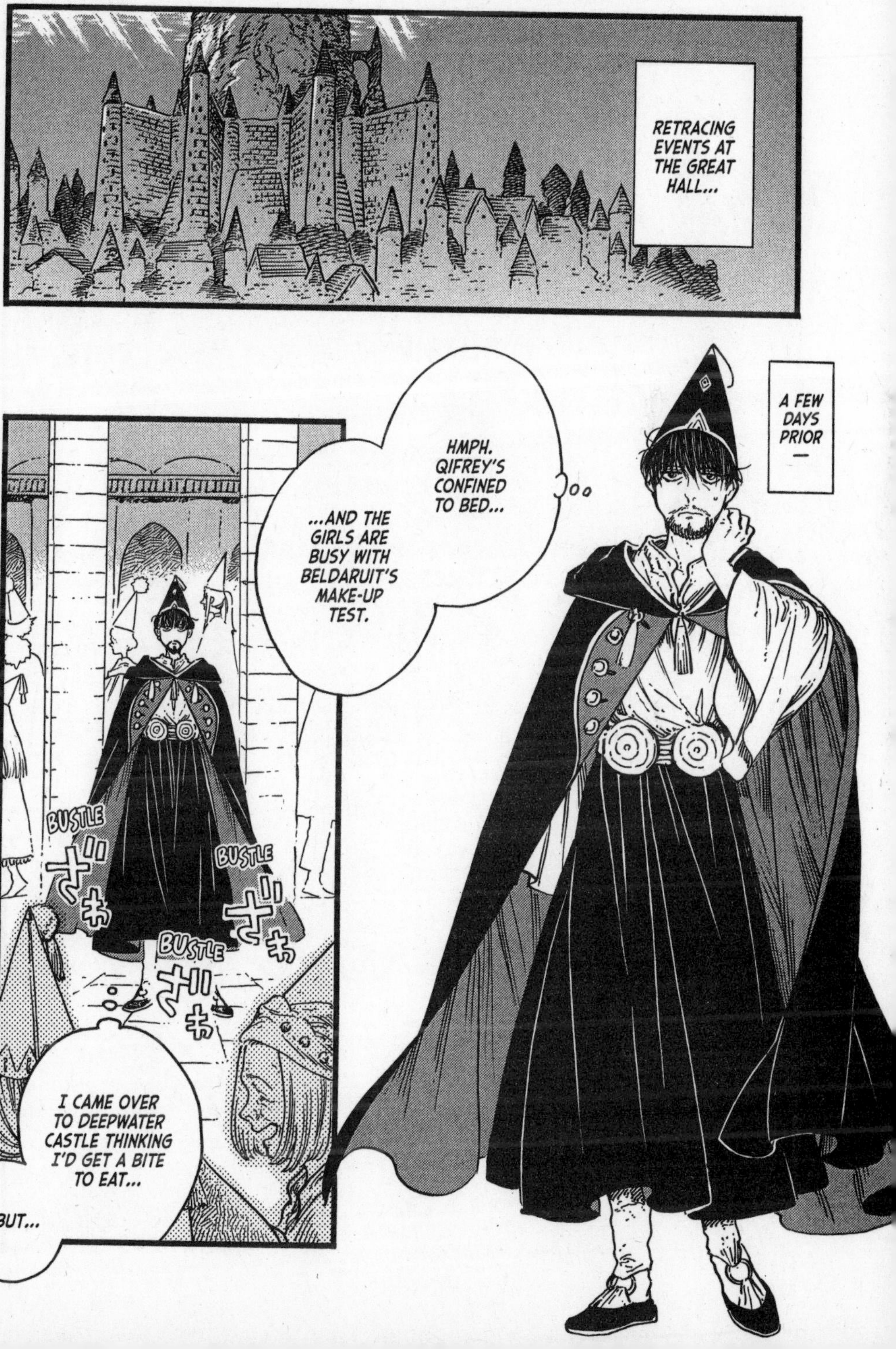
RETRACING EVENTS AT THE GREAT HALL...
A FEW DAYS PRIOR —
HMPH. QIFREY'S CONFINED TO BED...
...AND THE GIRLS ARE BUSY WITH BELDARUIT'S MAKE-UP TEST.
BUSTLE
ざわ
BUSTLE
ざわ
BUSTLE
ざわ
I CAME OVER TO DEEPWATER CASTLE THINKING I'D GET A BITE TO EAT...
...BUT...

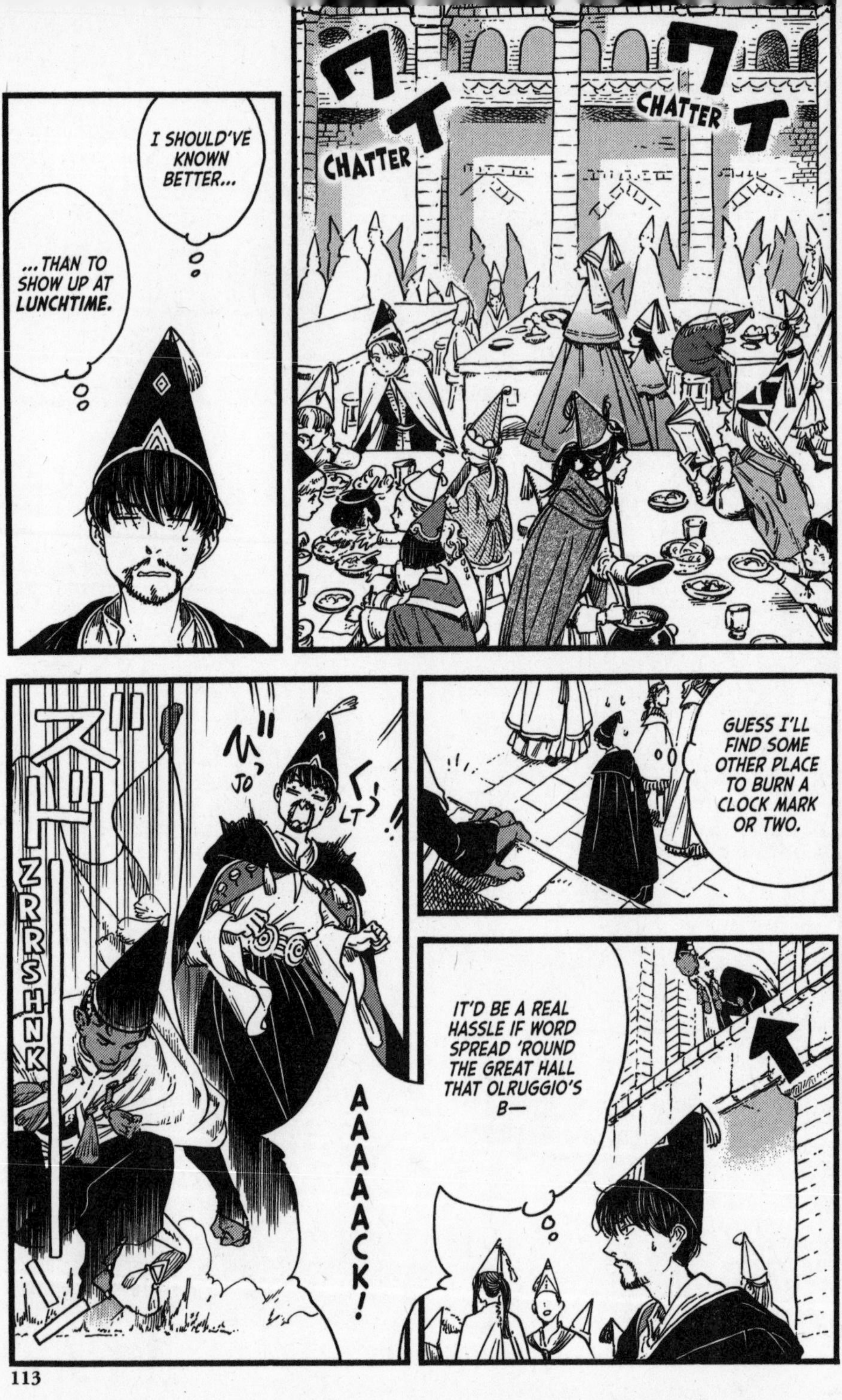
ワイ
CHATTER
ワイ
CHATTER
I SHOULD'VE KNOWN BETTER...
...THAN TO SHOW UP AT LUNCHTIME.
GUESS I'LL FIND SOME OTHER PLACE TO BURN A CLOCK MARK OR TWO.
IT'D BE A REAL HASSLE IF WORD SPREAD 'ROUND THE GREAT HALL THAT OLRUGGIO'S B—
ZRRSHNK
JO
LT
AAAAACK!

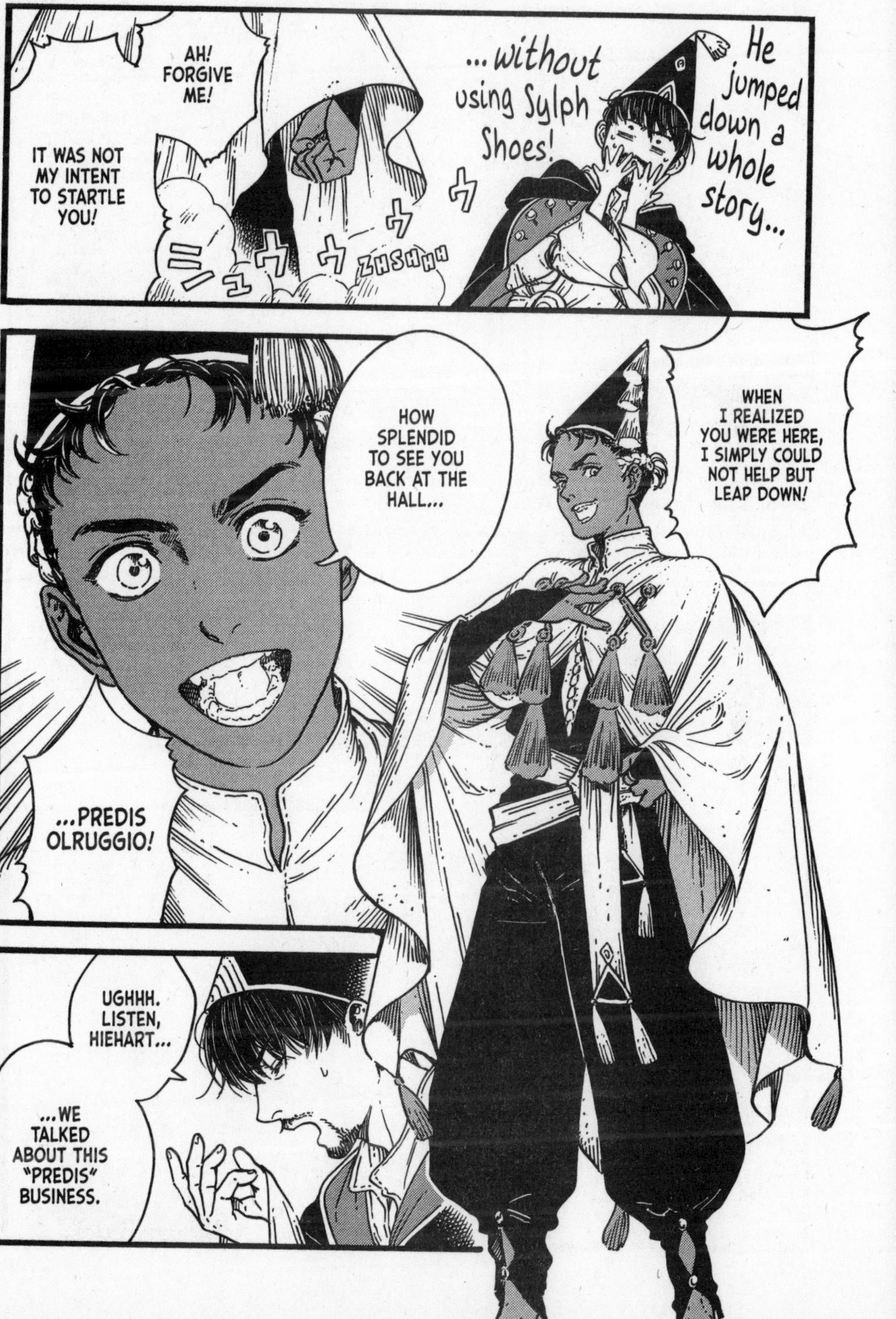
He jumped down a whole story...
...without using Sylph Shoes!
AH! FORGIVE ME!
IT WAS NOT MY INTENT TO STARTLE YOU!
ニュウウウウ
ZHSHHH
WHEN I REALIZED YOU WERE HERE, I SIMPLY COULD NOT HELP BUT LEAP DOWN!
HOW SPLENDID TO SEE YOU BACK AT THE HALL...
...PREDIS OLRUGGIO!
UGHHH. LISTEN, HIEHART...
...WE TALKED ABOUT THIS "PREDIS" BUSINESS.

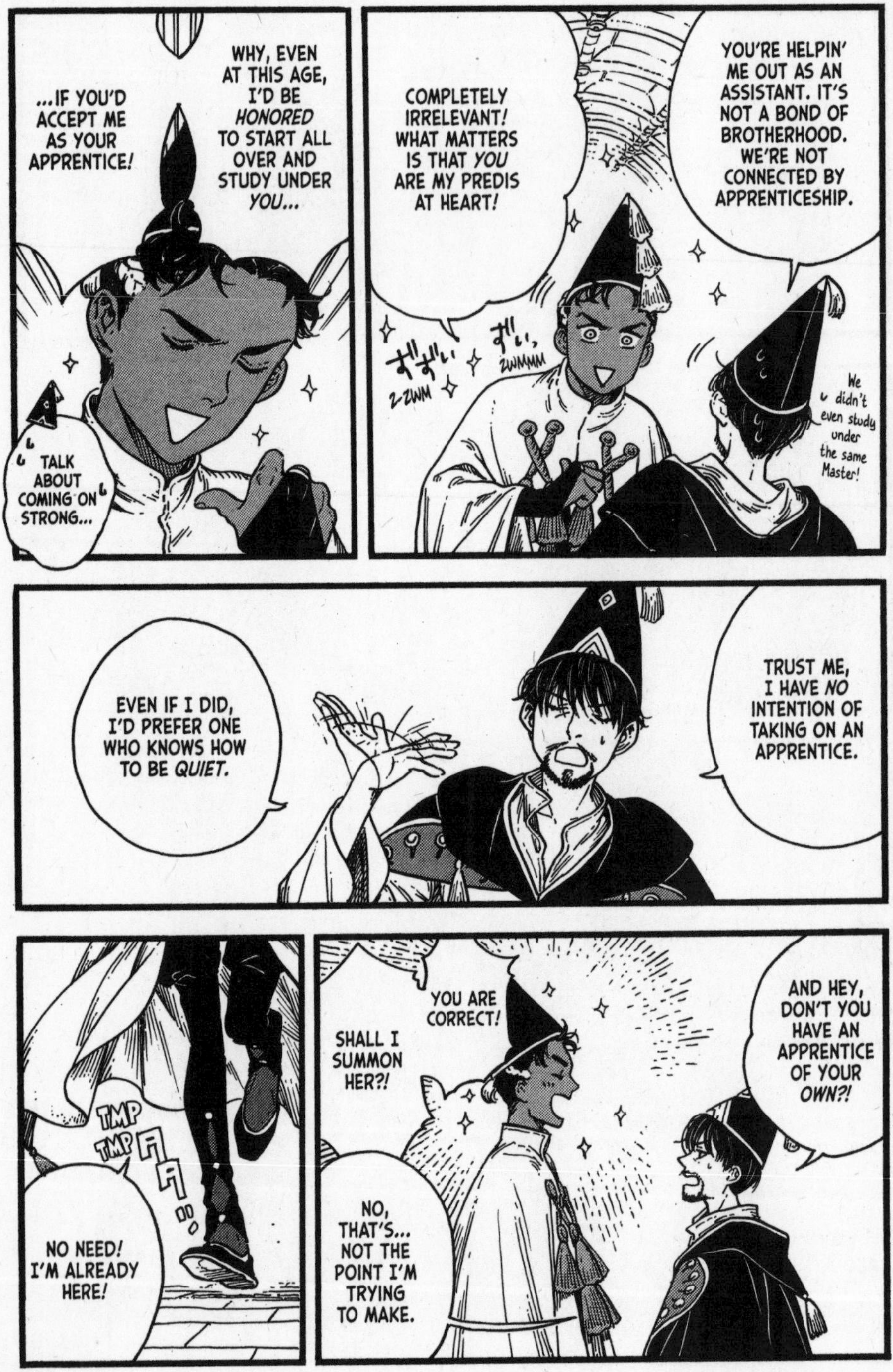

YOU'RE HELPIN' ME OUT AS AN ASSISTANT. IT'S NOT A BOND OF BROTHERHOOD. WE'RE NOT CONNECTED BY APPRENTICESHIP.
COMPLETELY IRRELEVANT! WHAT MATTERS IS THAT *YOU* ARE MY PREDIS AT HEART!
ずい, ZWMMM
ずずい ZZWM
We didn't even study under the same Master!
WHY, EVEN AT THIS AGE, I'D BE *HONORED* TO START ALL OVER AND STUDY UNDER *YOU*...
...IF YOU'D ACCEPT ME AS YOUR APPRENTICE!
TALK ABOUT COMING ON STRONG...
TRUST ME, I HAVE *NO* INTENTION OF TAKING ON AN APPRENTICE.
EVEN IF I DID, I'D PREFER ONE WHO KNOWS HOW TO BE *QUIET*.
AND HEY, DON'T YOU HAVE AN APPRENTICE OF YOUR *OWN?!*
YOU ARE CORRECT!
SHALL I SUMMON HER?!
NO, THAT'S... NOT THE POINT I'M TRYING TO MAKE.
TMP TMP
NO NEED! I'M ALREADY HERE!

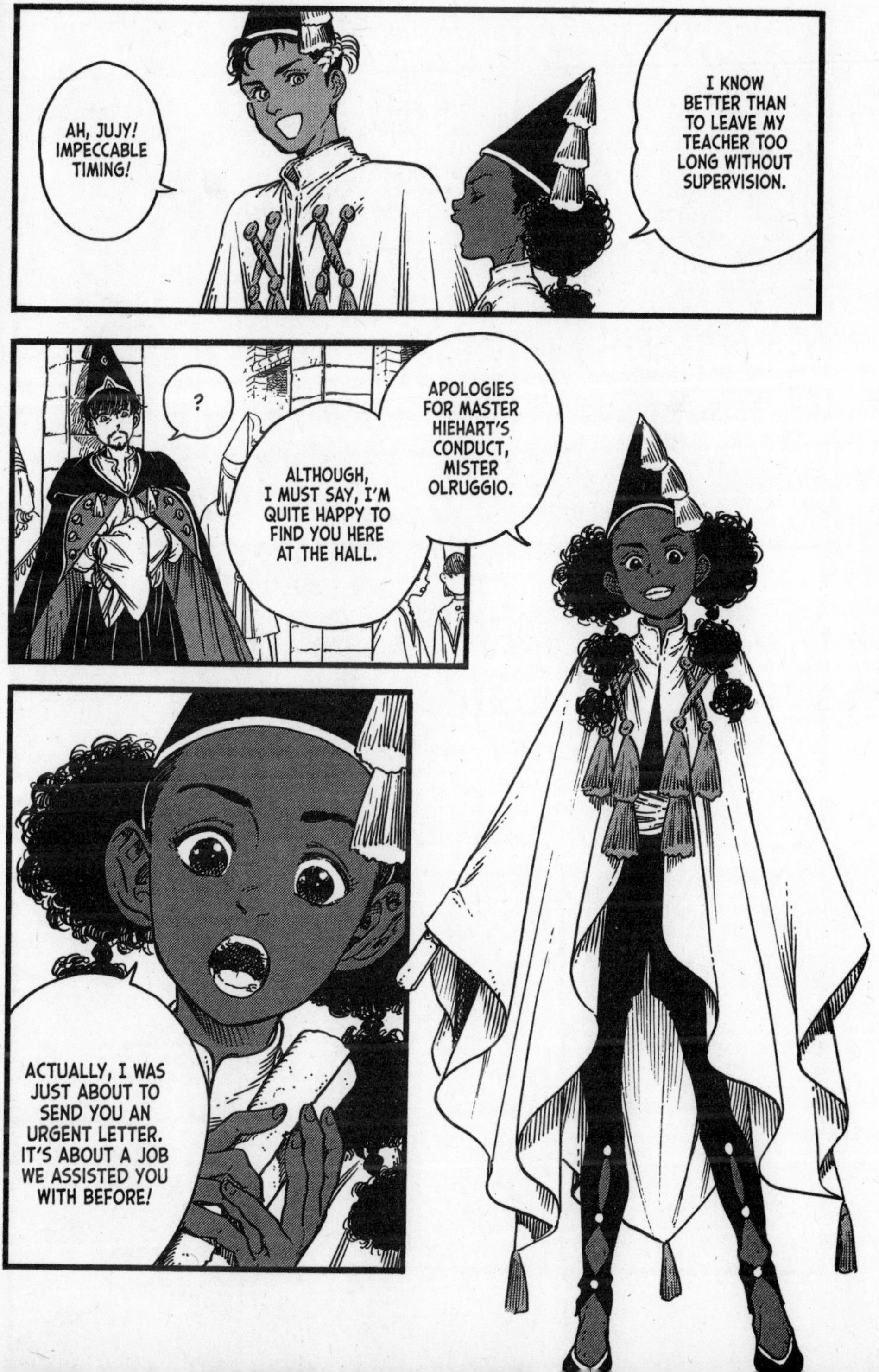
I KNOW BETTER THAN TO LEAVE MY TEACHER TOO LONG WITHOUT SUPERVISION.
AH, JUJY! IMPECCABLE TIMING!
APOLOGIES FOR MASTER HIEHART'S CONDUCT, MISTER OLRUGGIO.
ALTHOUGH, I MUST SAY, I'M QUITE HAPPY TO FIND YOU HERE AT THE HALL.
?
ACTUALLY, I WAS JUST ABOUT TO SEND YOU AN URGENT LETTER. IT'S ABOUT A JOB WE ASSISTED YOU WITH BEFORE!

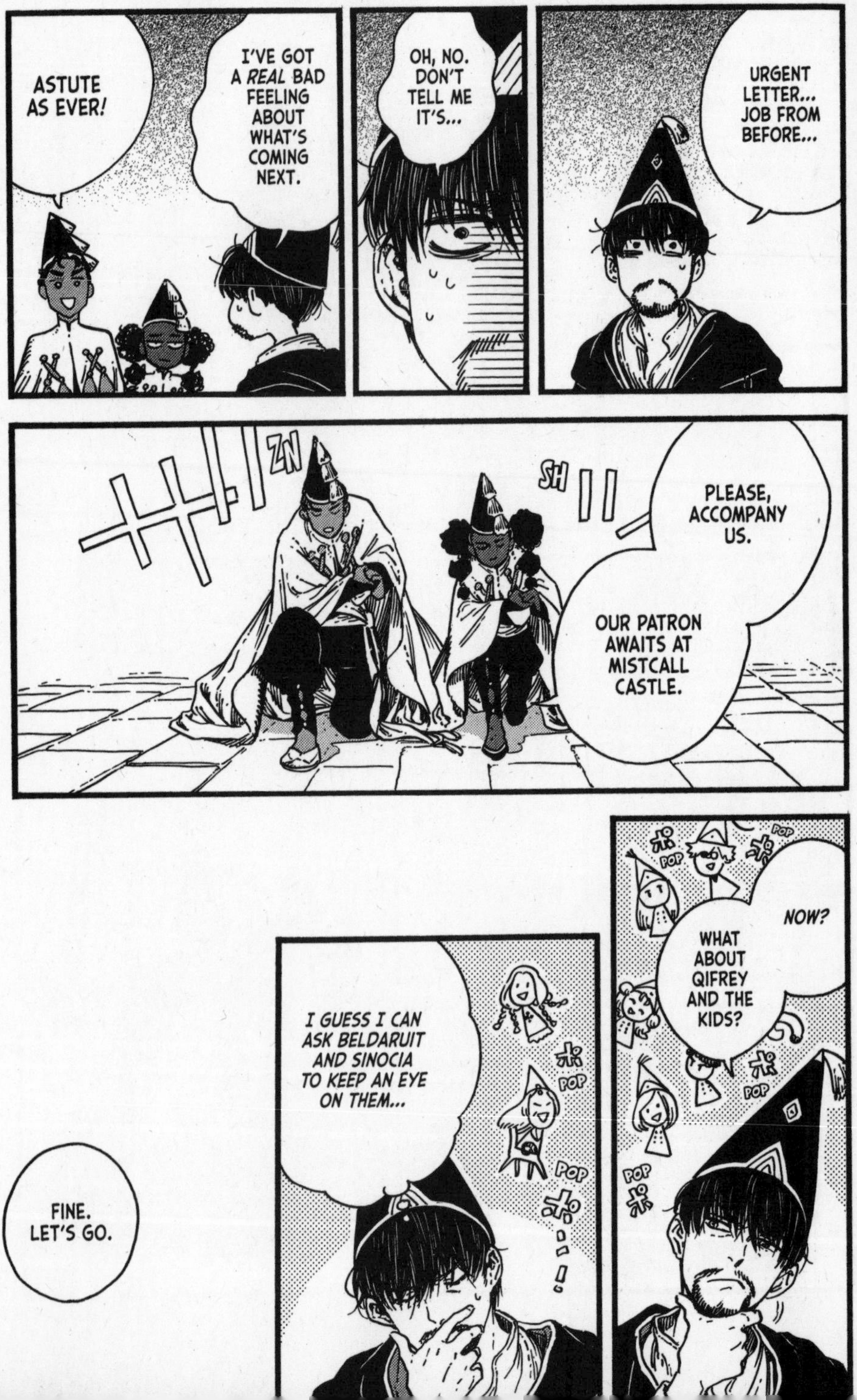
URGENT LETTER... JOB FROM BEFORE...
OH, NO. DON'T TELL ME IT'S...
I'VE GOT A *REAL* BAD FEELING ABOUT WHAT'S COMING NEXT.
ASTUTE AS EVER!
PLEASE, ACCOMPANY US.
OUR PATRON AWAITS AT MISTCALL CASTLE.
SH
ZN
POP
POP
NOW?
WHAT ABOUT QIFREY AND THE KIDS?
POP
POP
I GUESS I CAN ASK BELDARUIT AND SINOCIA TO KEEP AN EYE ON THEM...
POP
POP
FINE. LET'S GO.

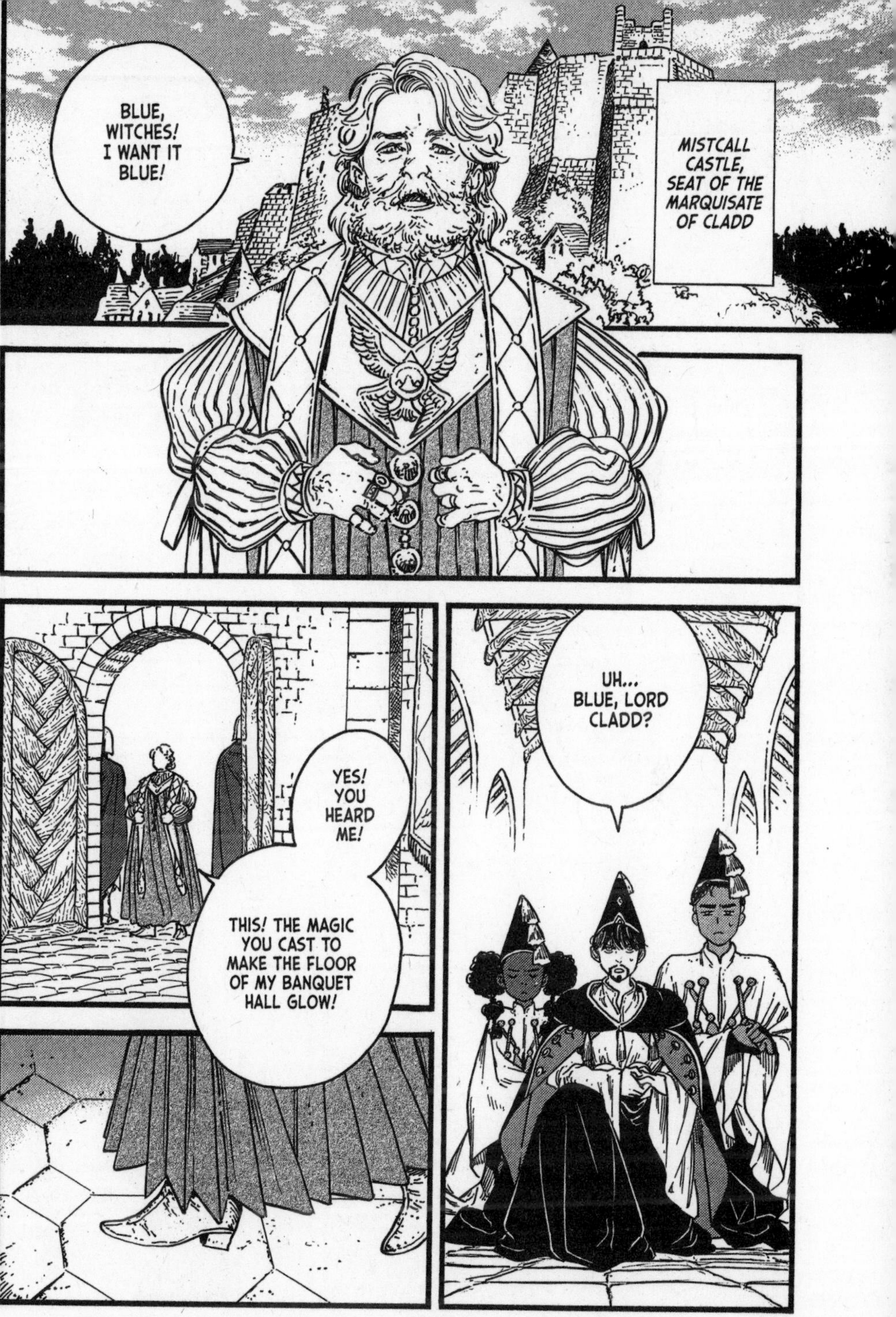
MISTCALL CASTLE, SEAT OF THE MARQUISATE OF CLADD
BLUE, WITCHES! I WANT IT BLUE!
UH... BLUE, LORD CLADD?
YES! YOU HEARD ME!
THIS! THE MAGIC YOU CAST TO MAKE THE FLOOR OF MY BANQUET HALL GLOW!

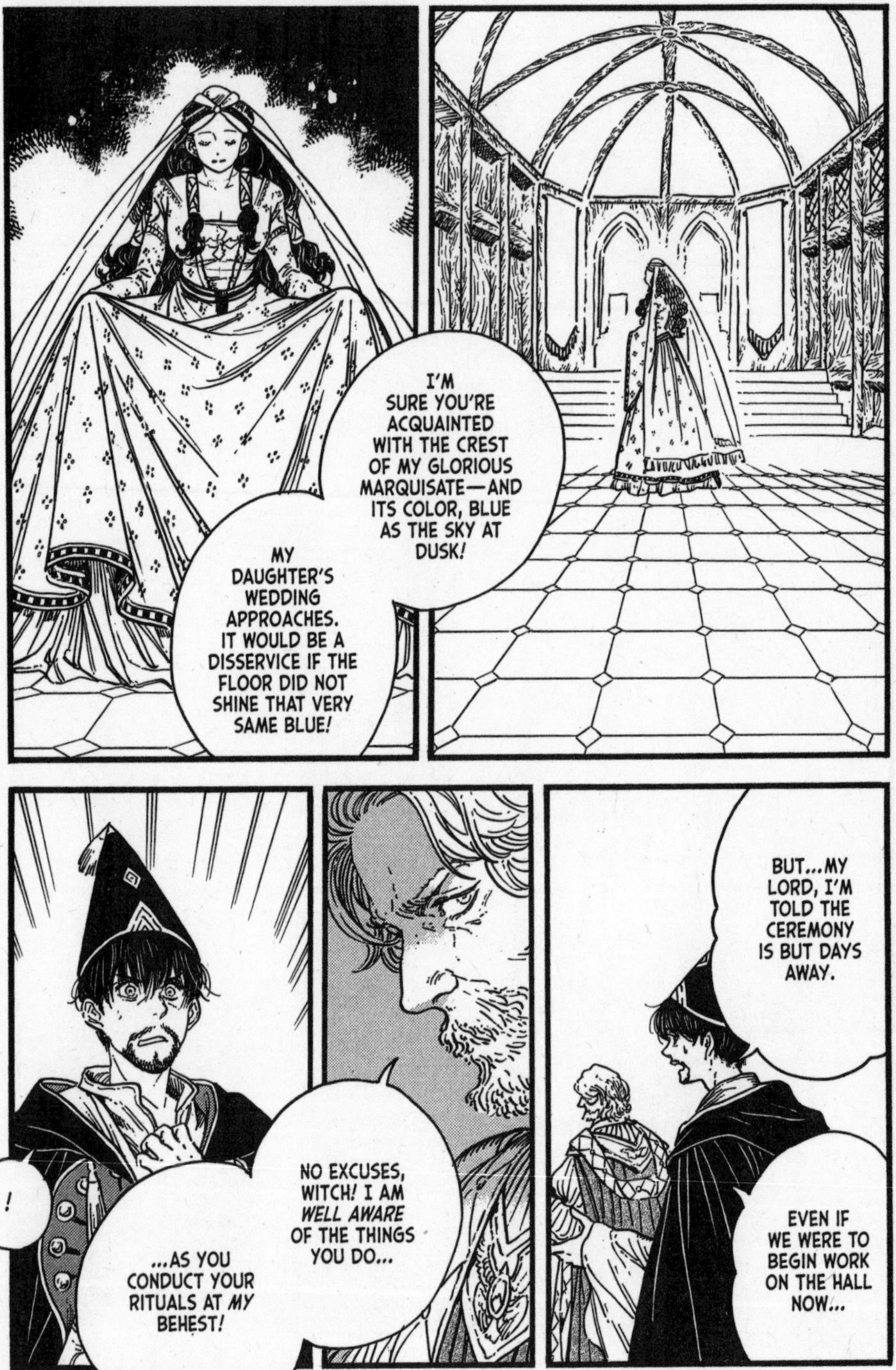
I'M SURE YOU'RE ACQUAINTED WITH THE CREST OF MY GLORIOUS MARQUISATE—AND ITS COLOR, BLUE AS THE SKY AT DUSK!
MY DAUGHTER'S WEDDING APPROACHES. IT WOULD BE A DISSERVICE IF THE FLOOR DID NOT SHINE THAT VERY SAME BLUE!
BUT...MY LORD, I'M TOLD THE CEREMONY IS BUT DAYS AWAY.
EVEN IF WE WERE TO BEGIN WORK ON THE HALL NOW...
NO EXCUSES, WITCH! I AM *WELL AWARE* OF THE THINGS YOU DO...
!
...AS YOU CONDUCT YOUR RITUALS AT *MY* BEHEST!

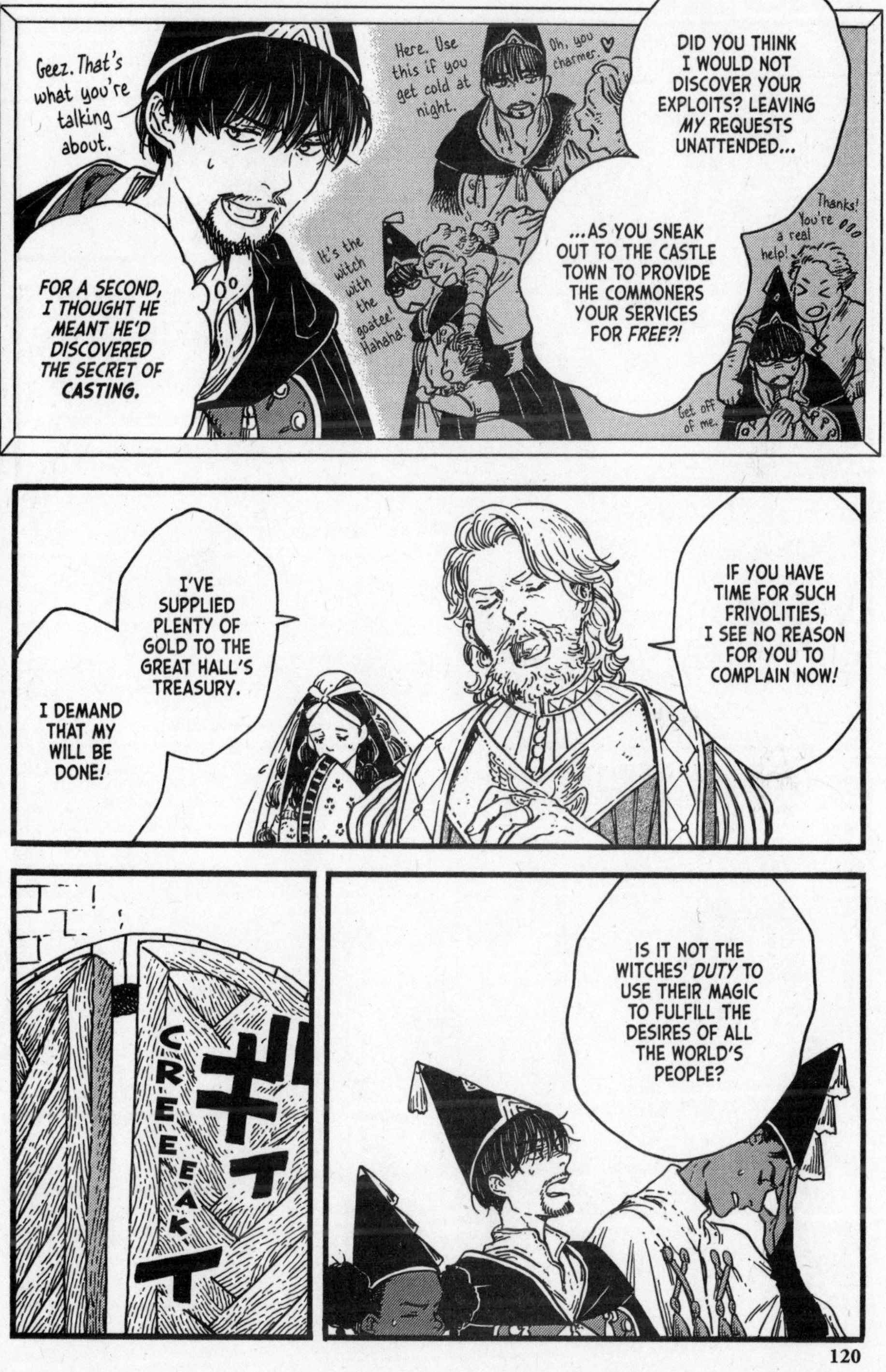
DID YOU THINK I WOULD NOT DISCOVER YOUR EXPLOITS? LEAVING *MY* REQUESTS UNATTENDED...
...AS YOU SNEAK OUT TO THE CASTLE TOWN TO PROVIDE THE COMMONERS YOUR SERVICES FOR *FREE?!*
Thanks! You're a real help!
Get off of me.
Oh, you charmer. ♥
Here. Use this if you get cold at night.
It's the witch with the goatee! Hahaha!
Geez. That's what you're talking about.
FOR A SECOND, I THOUGHT HE MEANT HE'D DISCOVERED THE SECRET OF **CASTING.**
IF YOU HAVE TIME FOR SUCH FRIVOLITIES, I SEE NO REASON FOR YOU TO COMPLAIN NOW!
I'VE SUPPLIED PLENTY OF GOLD TO THE GREAT HALL'S TREASURY.
I DEMAND THAT MY WILL BE DONE!
IS IT NOT THE WITCHES' *DUTY* TO USE THEIR MAGIC TO FULFILL THE DESIRES OF ALL THE WORLD'S PEOPLE?
CREEEAK

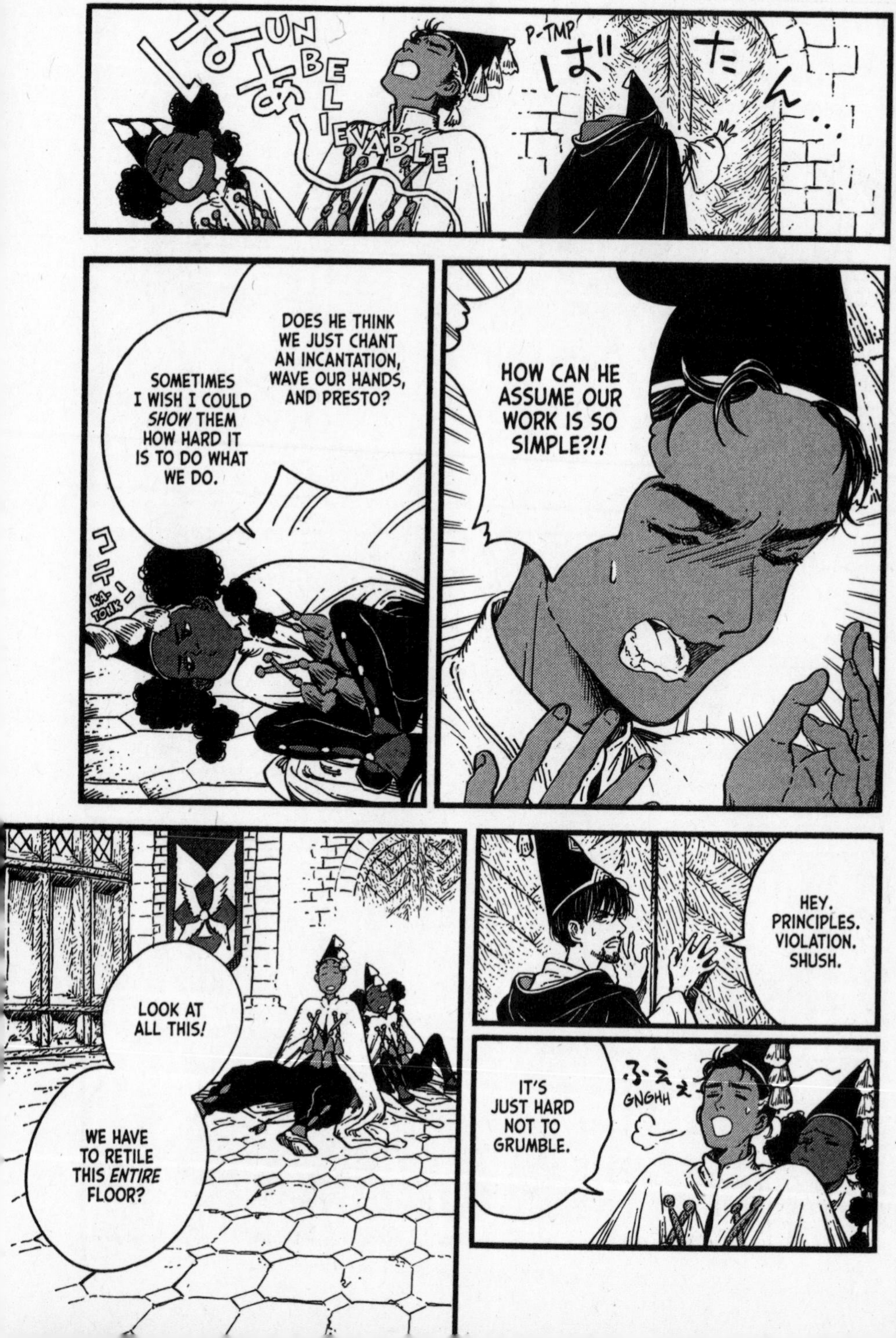
P-TMP
ばたん…
UNBELIEVABLE
HOW CAN HE ASSUME OUR WORK IS SO SIMPLE?!!
DOES HE THINK WE JUST CHANT AN INCANTATION, WAVE OUR HANDS, AND PRESTO?
SOMETIMES I WISH I COULD *SHOW* THEM HOW HARD IT IS TO DO WHAT WE DO.
KA-TONK
HEY. PRINCIPLES. VIOLATION. SHUSH.
IT'S JUST HARD NOT TO GRUMBLE.
GNGHH
LOOK AT ALL THIS!
WE HAVE TO RETILE THIS *ENTIRE* FLOOR?

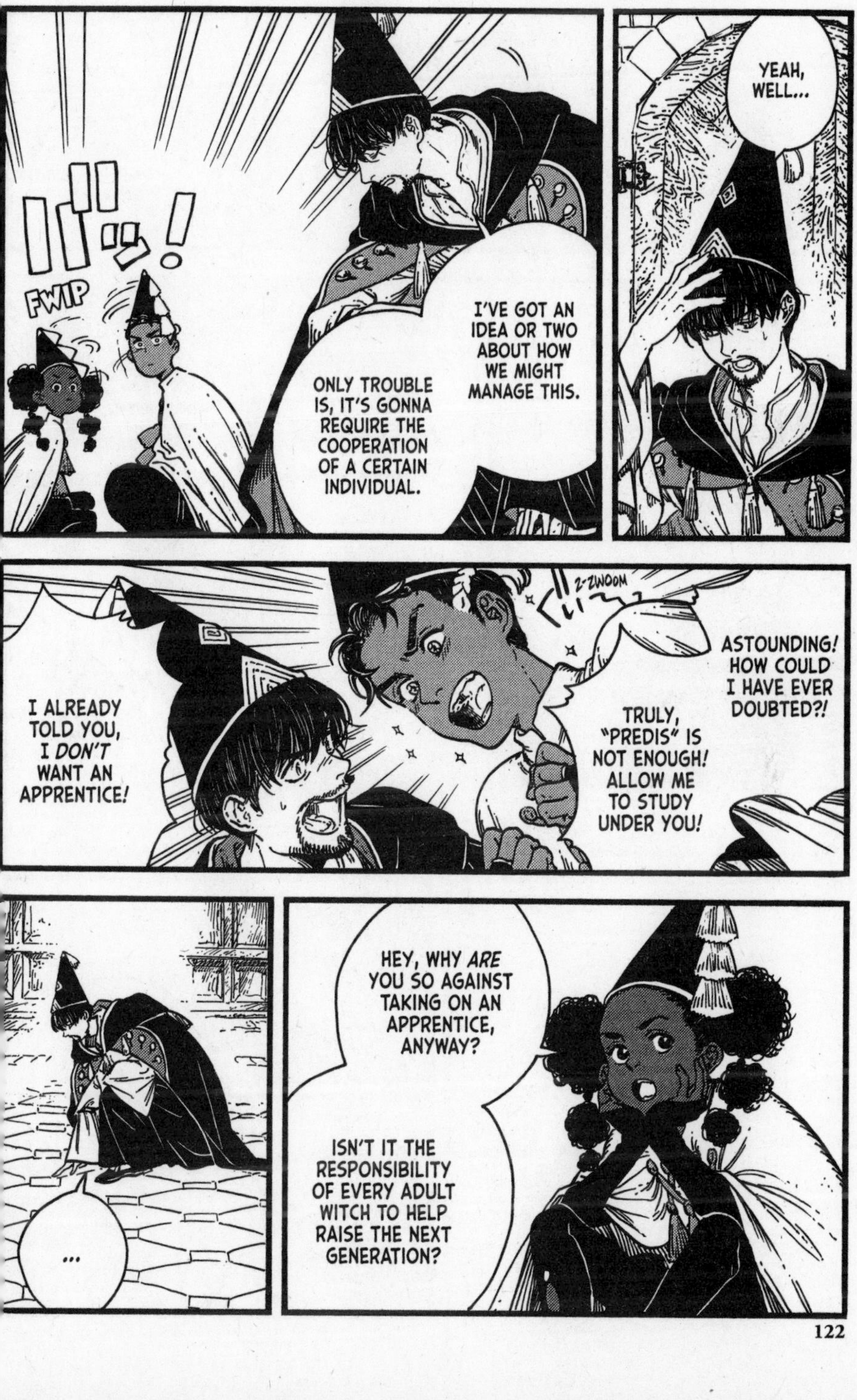
YEAH, WELL...
I'VE GOT AN IDEA OR TWO ABOUT HOW WE MIGHT MANAGE THIS.
ONLY TROUBLE IS, IT'S GONNA REQUIRE THE COOPERATION OF A CERTAIN INDIVIDUAL.
FWIP
Z-ZWOOM
ASTOUNDING! HOW COULD I HAVE EVER DOUBTED?!
TRULY, "PREDIS" IS NOT ENOUGH! ALLOW ME TO STUDY UNDER YOU!
I ALREADY TOLD YOU, I *DON'T* WANT AN APPRENTICE!
HEY, WHY *ARE* YOU SO AGAINST TAKING ON AN APPRENTICE, ANYWAY?
ISN'T IT THE RESPONSIBILITY OF EVERY ADULT WITCH TO HELP RAISE THE NEXT GENERATION?
...

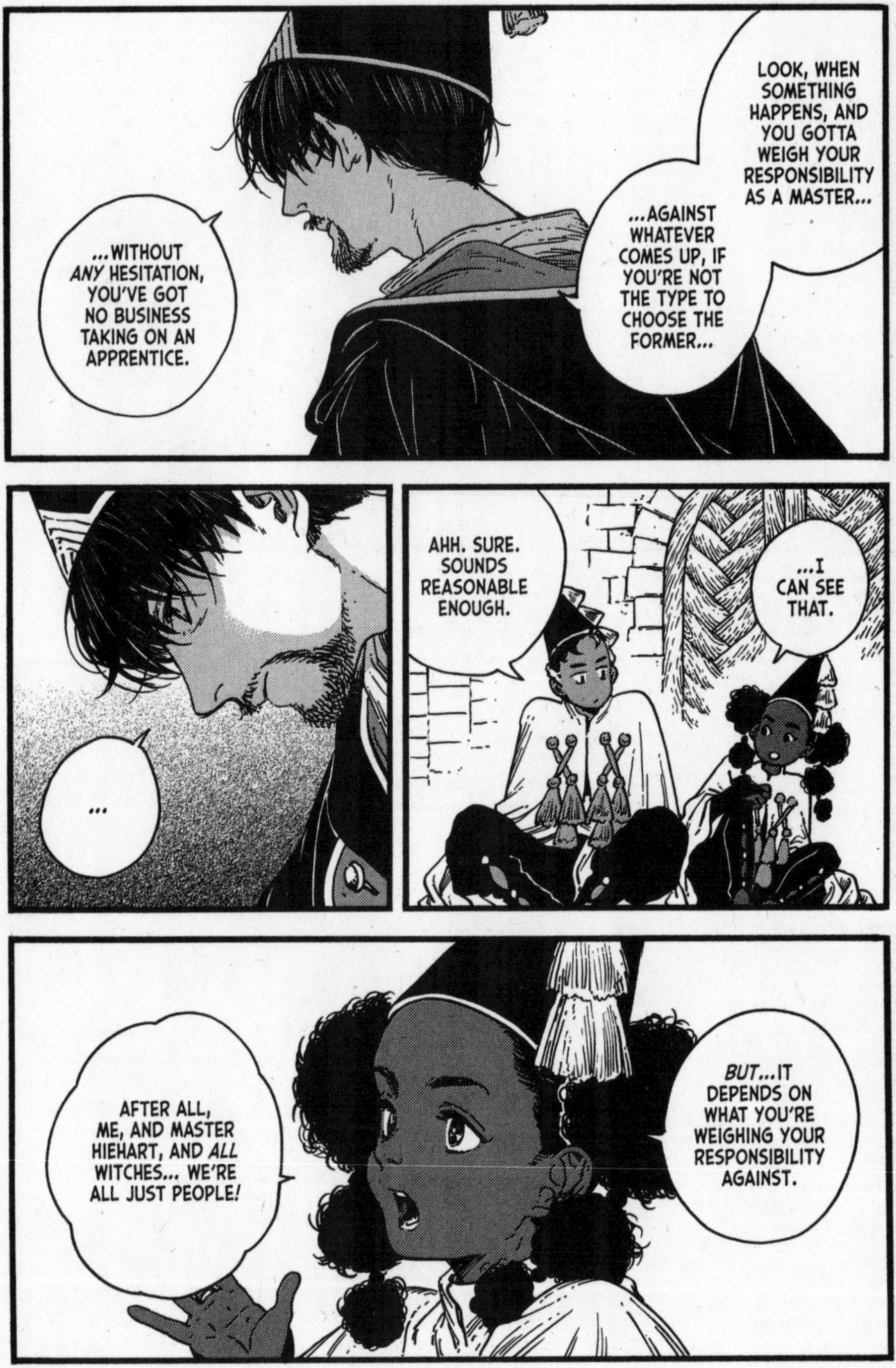
LOOK, WHEN SOMETHING HAPPENS, AND YOU GOTTA WEIGH YOUR RESPONSIBILITY AS A MASTER...
...AGAINST WHATEVER COMES UP, IF YOU'RE NOT THE TYPE TO CHOOSE THE FORMER...
...WITHOUT *ANY* HESITATION, YOU'VE GOT NO BUSINESS TAKING ON AN APPRENTICE.
...I CAN SEE THAT.
AHH. SURE. SOUNDS REASONABLE ENOUGH.
...
BUT...IT DEPENDS ON WHAT YOU'RE WEIGHING YOUR RESPONSIBILITY AGAINST.
AFTER ALL, ME, AND MASTER HIEHART, AND *ALL* WITCHES... WE'RE ALL JUST PEOPLE!

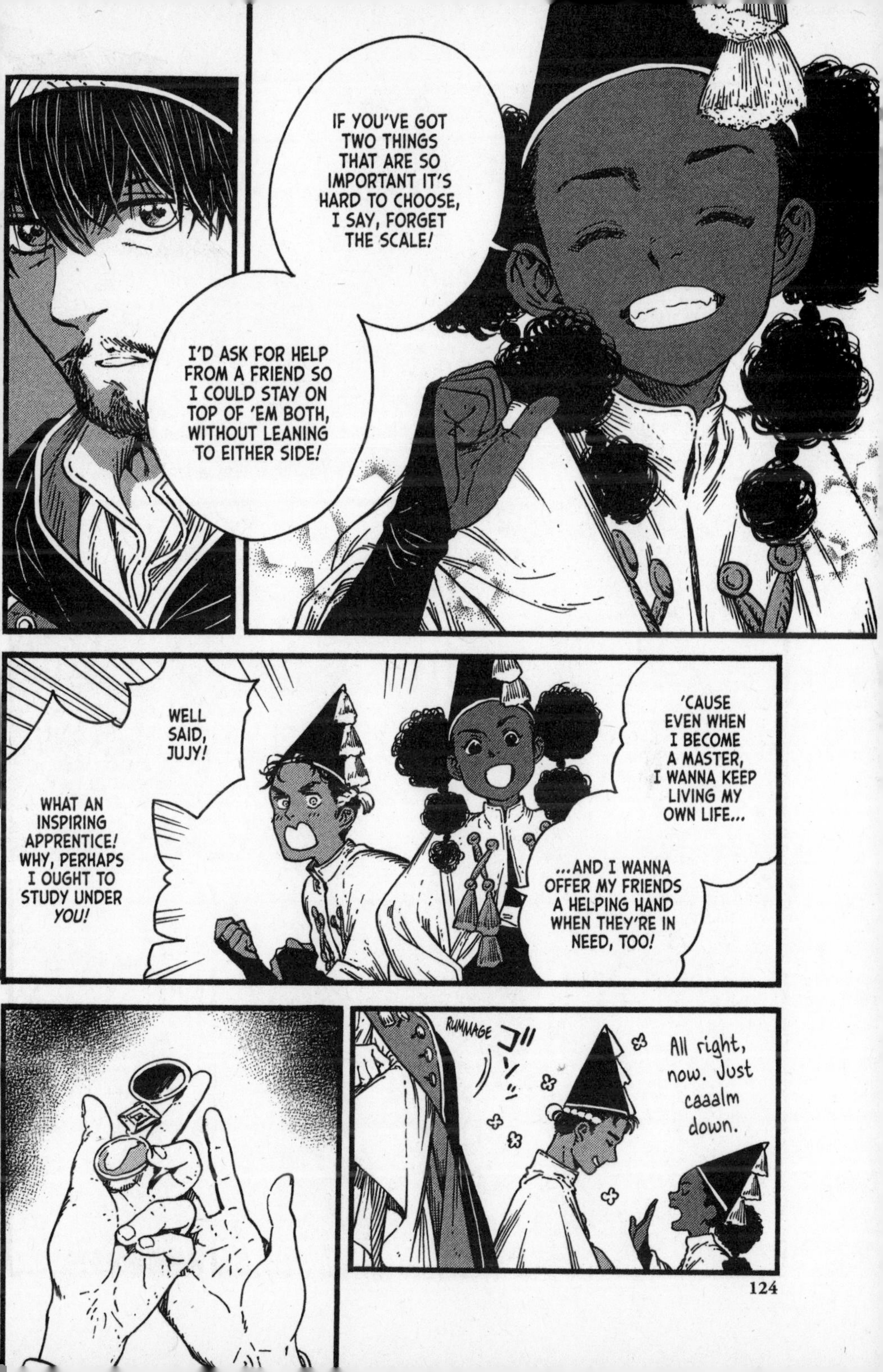
IF YOU'VE GOT TWO THINGS THAT ARE SO IMPORTANT IT'S HARD TO CHOOSE, I SAY, FORGET THE SCALE!
I'D ASK FOR HELP FROM A FRIEND SO I COULD STAY ON TOP OF 'EM BOTH, WITHOUT LEANING TO EITHER SIDE!
'CAUSE EVEN WHEN I BECOME A MASTER, I WANNA KEEP LIVING MY OWN LIFE...
...AND I WANNA OFFER MY FRIENDS A HELPING HAND WHEN THEY'RE IN NEED, TOO!
WELL SAID, JUJY!
WHAT AN INSPIRING APPRENTICE! WHY, PERHAPS I OUGHT TO STUDY UNDER *YOU*!
RUMMAGE
All right, now. Just caaalm down.

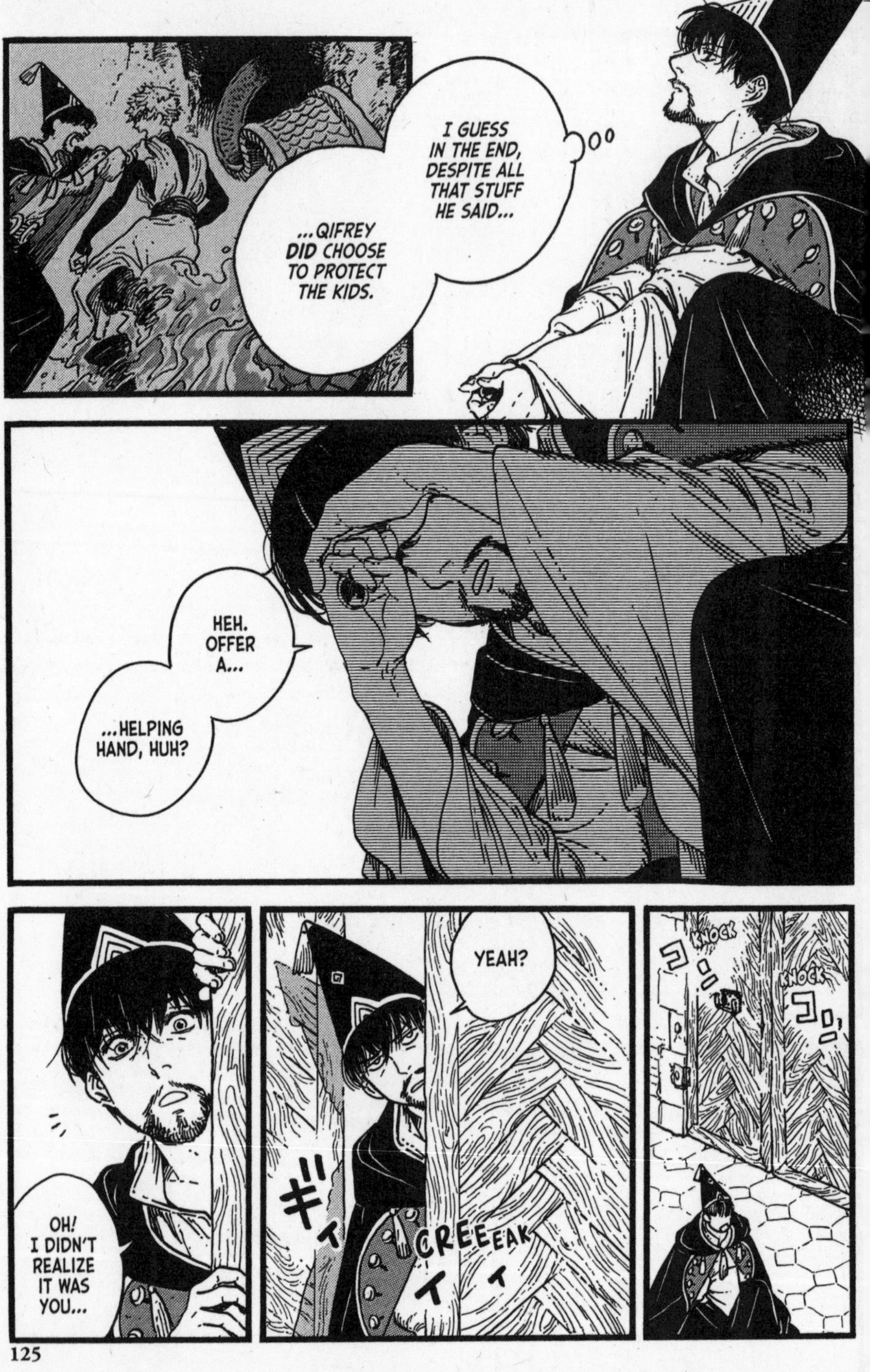
I GUESS IN THE END, DESPITE ALL THAT STUFF HE SAID...
...QIFREY DID CHOOSE TO PROTECT THE KIDS.
HEH. OFFER A...
...HELPING HAND, HUH?
KNOCK
KNOCK
YEAH?
ギィィ
CREEEAK
OH! I DIDN'T REALIZE IT WAS YOU...

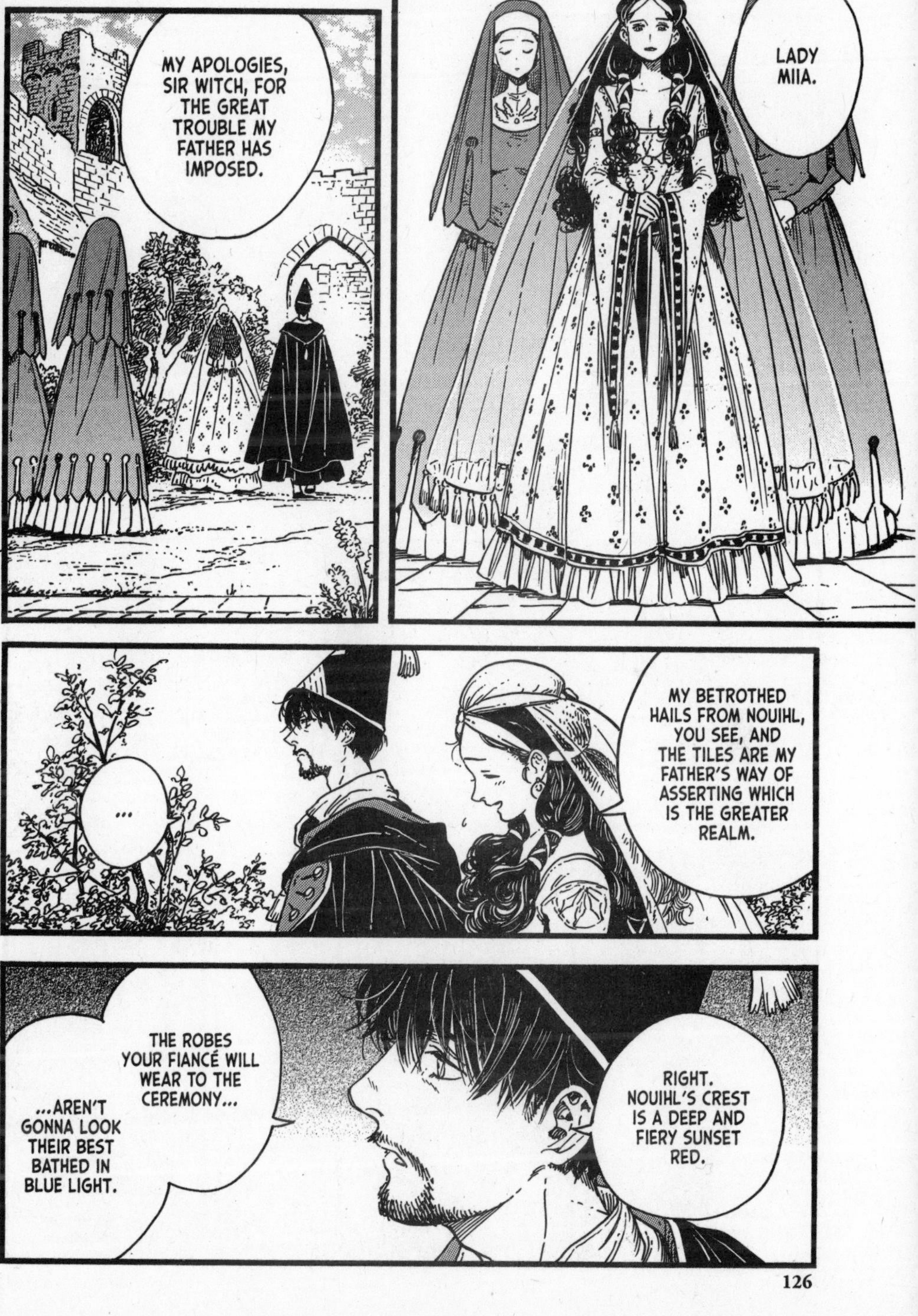
LADY MIIA.
MY APOLOGIES, SIR WITCH, FOR THE GREAT TROUBLE MY FATHER HAS IMPOSED.
MY BETROTHED HAILS FROM NOUIHL, YOU SEE, AND THE TILES ARE MY FATHER'S WAY OF ASSERTING WHICH IS THE GREATER REALM.
...
RIGHT. NOUIHL'S CREST IS A DEEP AND FIERY SUNSET RED.
THE ROBES YOUR FIANCÉ WILL WEAR TO THE CEREMONY...
...AREN'T GONNA LOOK THEIR BEST BATHED IN BLUE LIGHT.

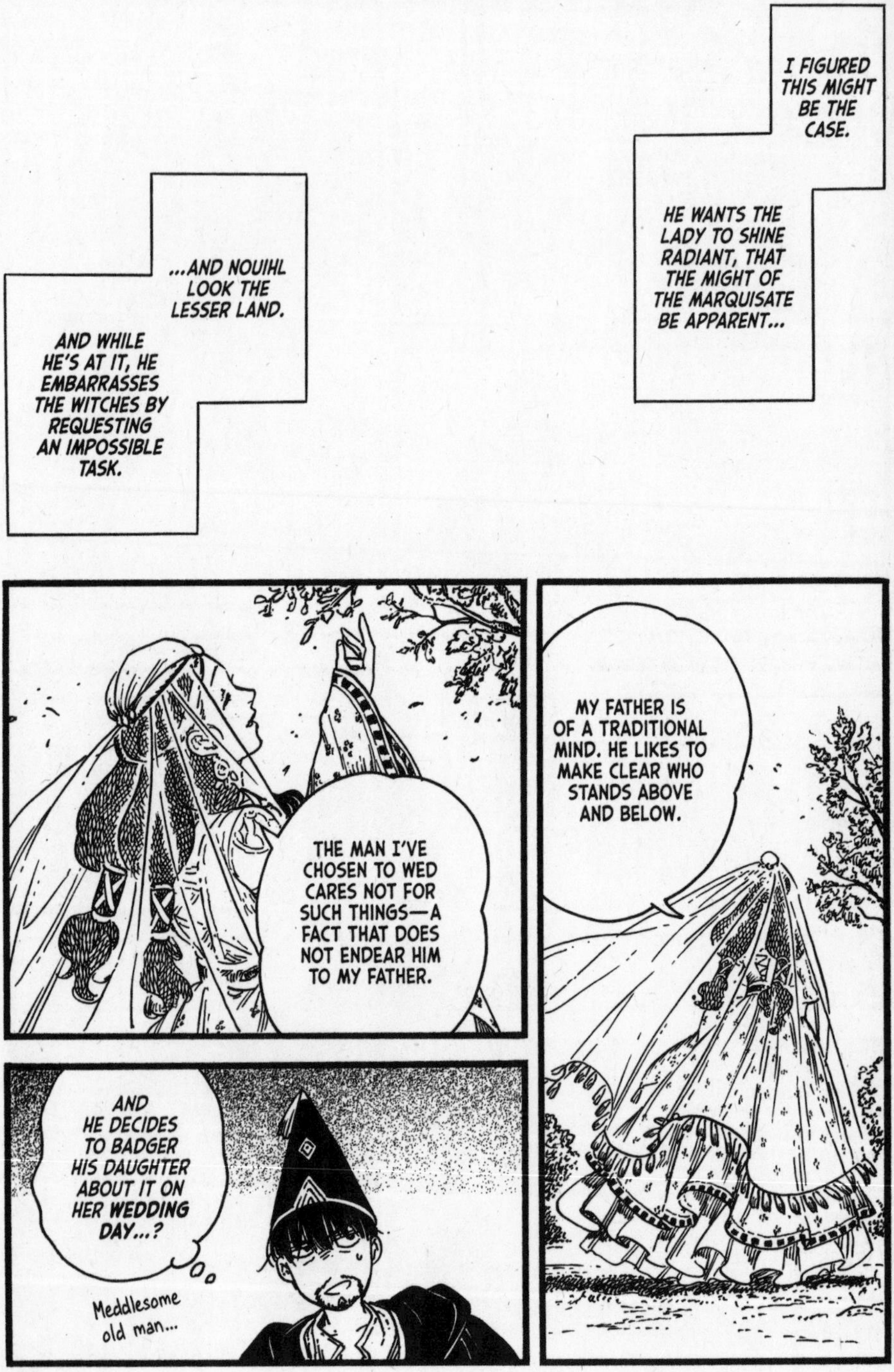
I FIGURED THIS MIGHT BE THE CASE.
HE WANTS THE LADY TO SHINE RADIANT, THAT THE MIGHT OF THE MARQUISATE BE APPARENT...
...AND NOUIHL LOOK THE LESSER LAND.
AND WHILE HE'S AT IT, HE EMBARRASSES THE WITCHES BY REQUESTING AN IMPOSSIBLE TASK.
MY FATHER IS OF A TRADITIONAL MIND. HE LIKES TO MAKE CLEAR WHO STANDS ABOVE AND BELOW.
THE MAN I'VE CHOSEN TO WED CARES NOT FOR SUCH THINGS—A FACT THAT DOES NOT ENDEAR HIM TO MY FATHER.
AND HE DECIDES TO BADGER HIS DAUGHTER ABOUT IT ON HER WEDDING DAY...?
Meddlesome old man...

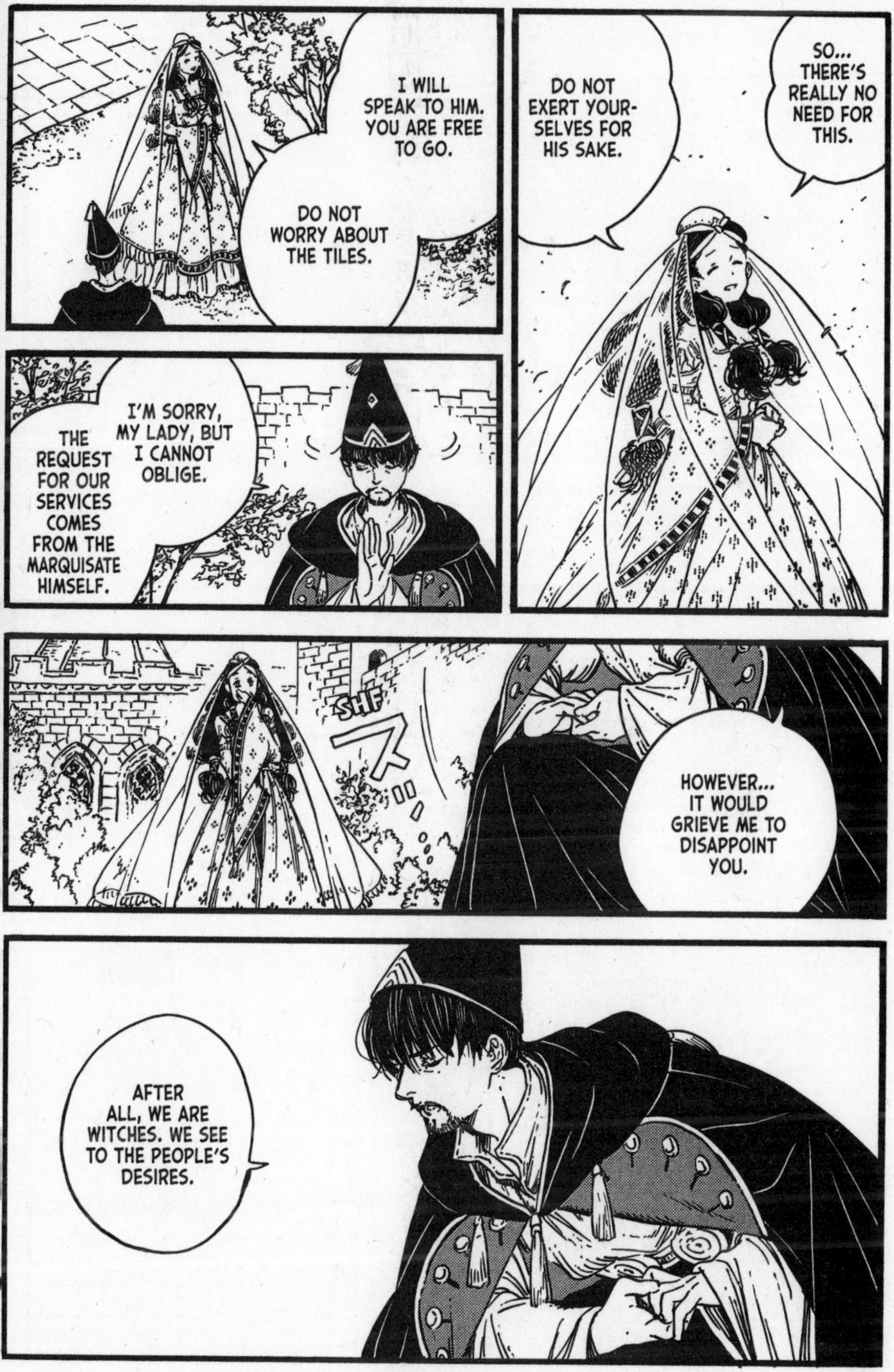
SO... THERE'S REALLY NO NEED FOR THIS.
DO NOT EXERT YOUR-SELVES FOR HIS SAKE.
I WILL SPEAK TO HIM. YOU ARE FREE TO GO.
DO NOT WORRY ABOUT THE TILES.
I'M SORRY, MY LADY, BUT I CANNOT OBLIGE.
THE REQUEST FOR OUR SERVICES COMES FROM THE MARQUISATE HIMSELF.
HOWEVER... IT WOULD GRIEVE ME TO DISAPPOINT YOU.
SHF
AFTER ALL, WE ARE WITCHES. WE SEE TO THE PEOPLE'S DESIRES.

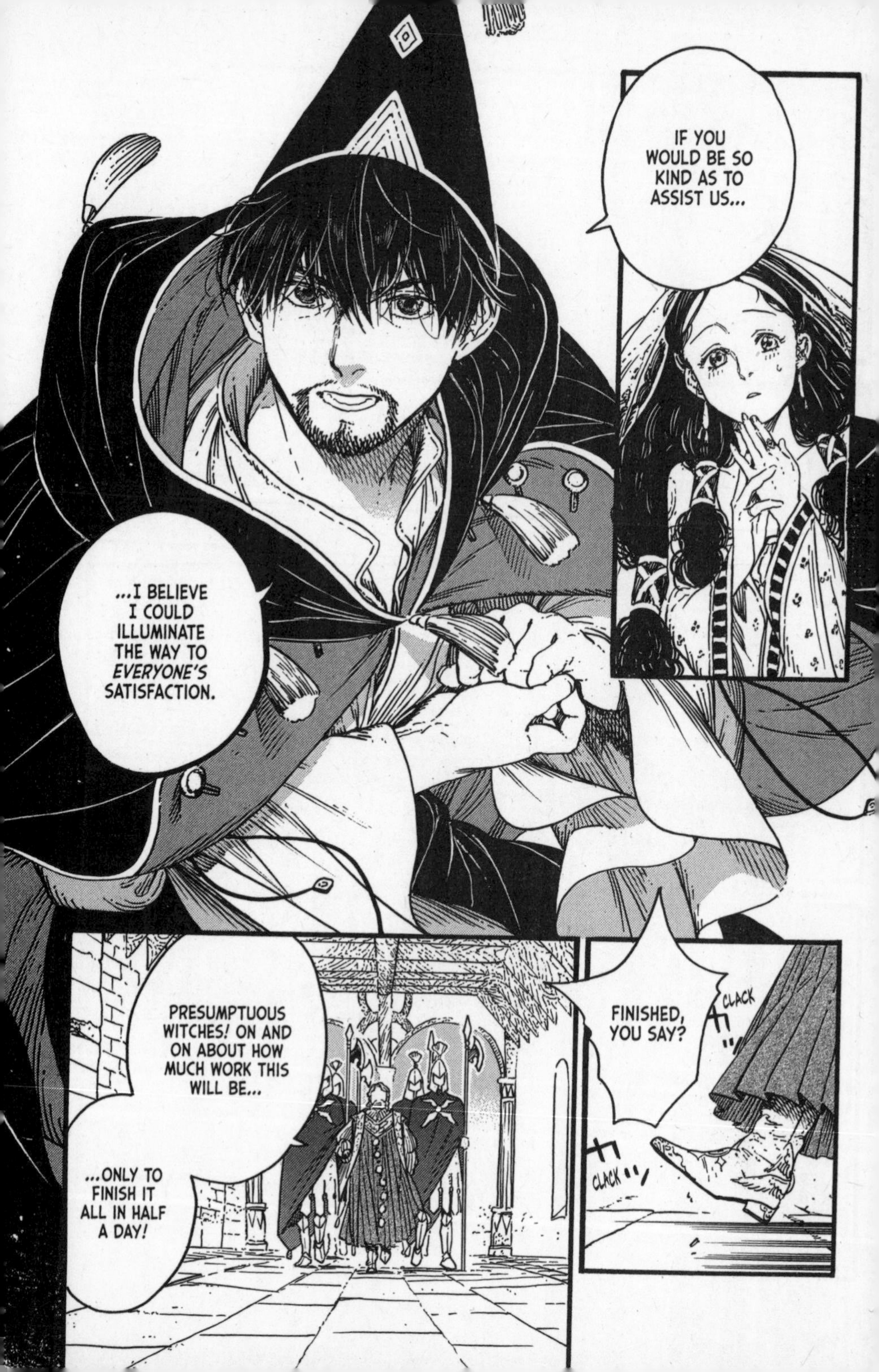
IF YOU WOULD BE SO KIND AS TO ASSIST US...
...I BELIEVE I COULD ILLUMINATE THE WAY TO *EVERYONE'S* SATISFACTION.
FINISHED, YOU SAY?
CLACK
CLACK
PRESUMPTUOUS WITCHES! ON AND ON ABOUT HOW MUCH WORK THIS WILL BE...
...ONLY TO FINISH IT ALL IN HALF A DAY!

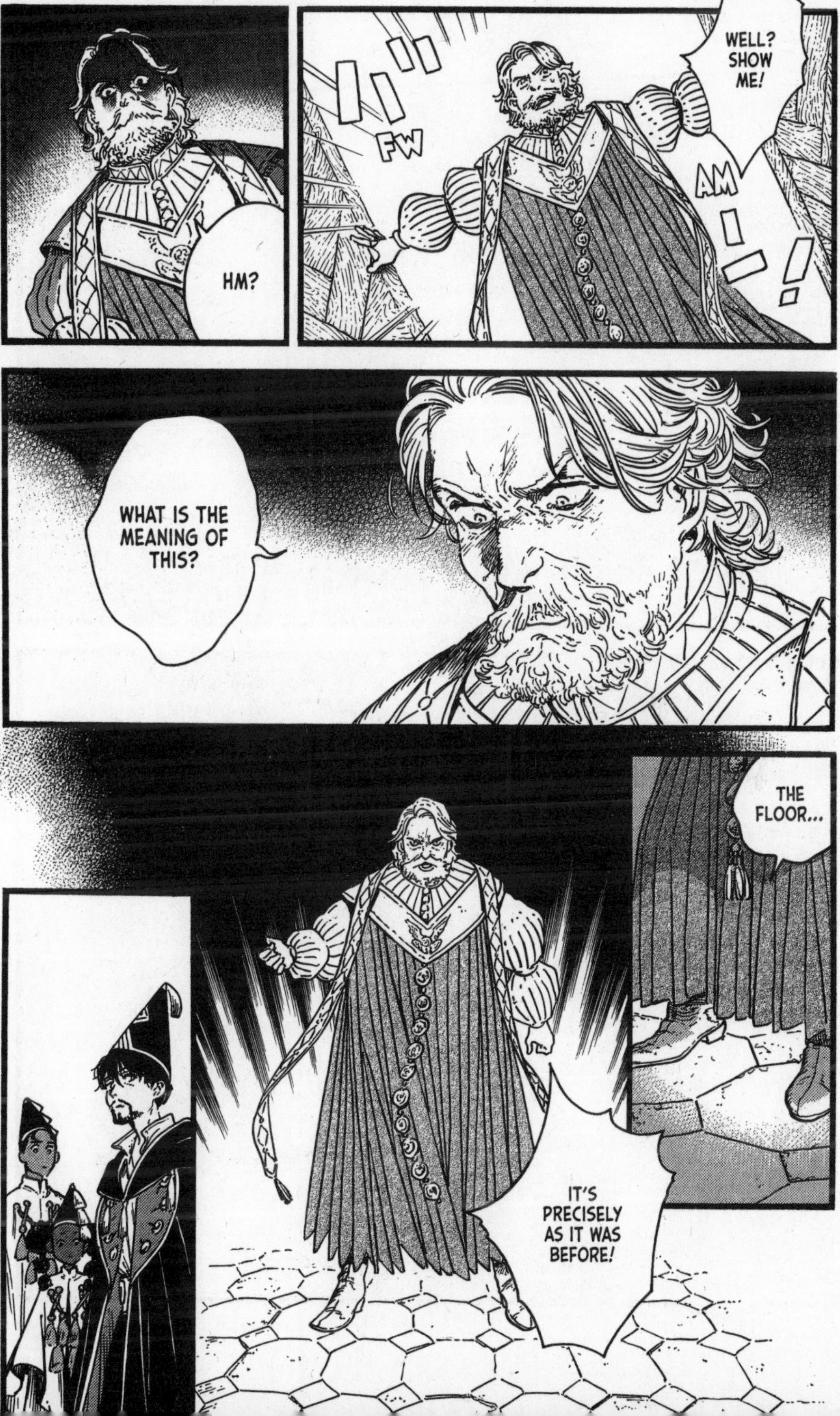
WELL? SHOW ME!
FWAM!!
HM?
WHAT IS THE MEANING OF THIS?
THE FLOOR...
IT'S PRECISELY AS IT WAS BEFORE!

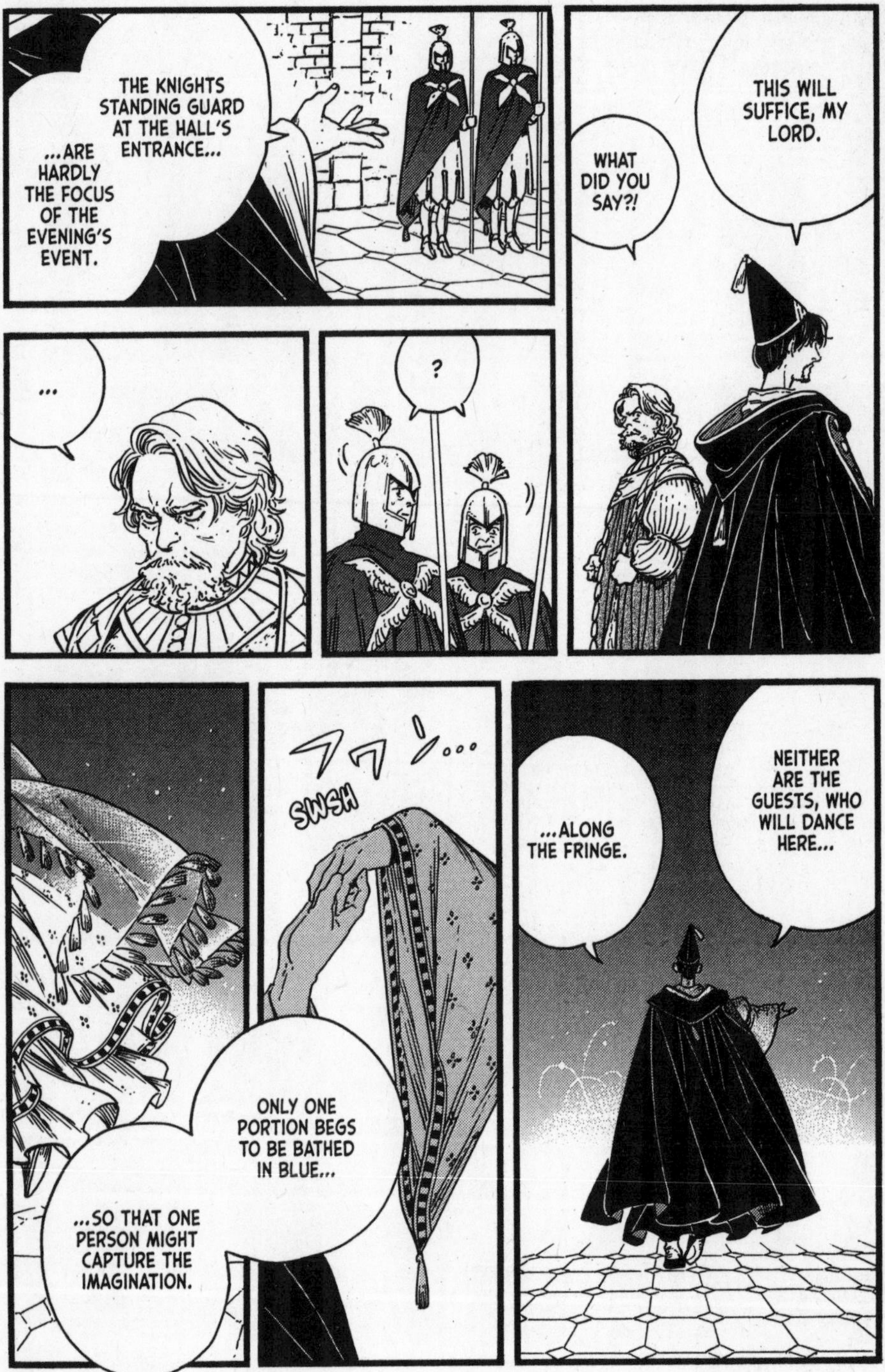
THIS WILL SUFFICE, MY LORD.
WHAT DID YOU SAY?!
THE KNIGHTS STANDING GUARD AT THE HALL'S ENTRANCE...
...ARE HARDLY THE FOCUS OF THE EVENING'S EVENT.
?
...
NEITHER ARE THE GUESTS, WHO WILL DANCE HERE...
...ALONG THE FRINGE.
SWSH
ONLY ONE PORTION BEGS TO BE BATHED IN BLUE...
...SO THAT ONE PERSON MIGHT CAPTURE THE IMAGINATION.

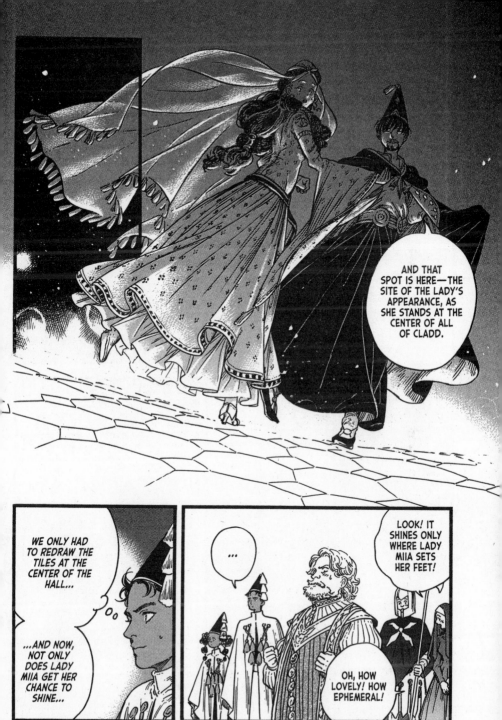

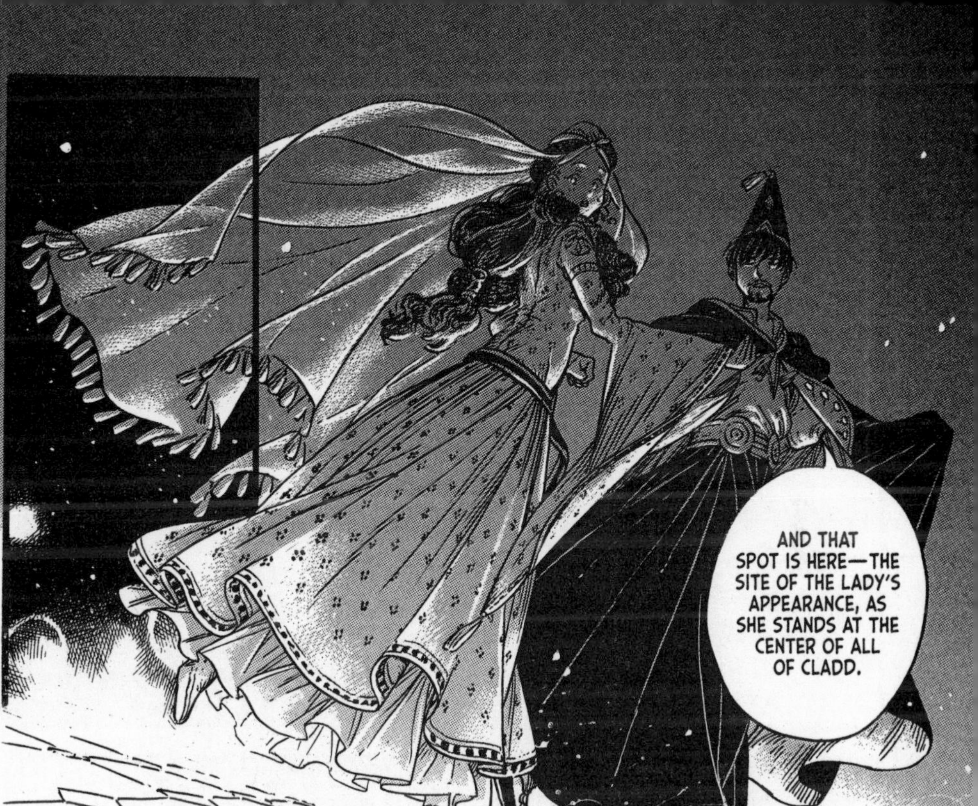
AND THAT SPOT IS HERE—THE SITE OF THE LADY'S APPEARANCE, AS SHE STANDS AT THE CENTER OF ALL OF CLADD.
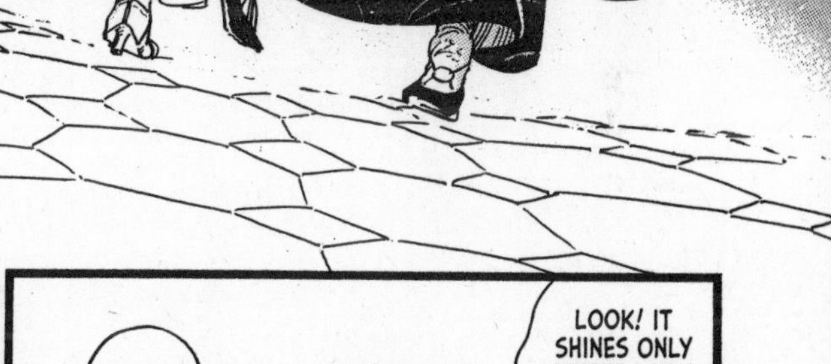
LOOK! IT SHINES ONLY WHERE LADY MIIA SETS HER FEET!
...
OH, HOW LOVELY! HOW EPHEMERAL!
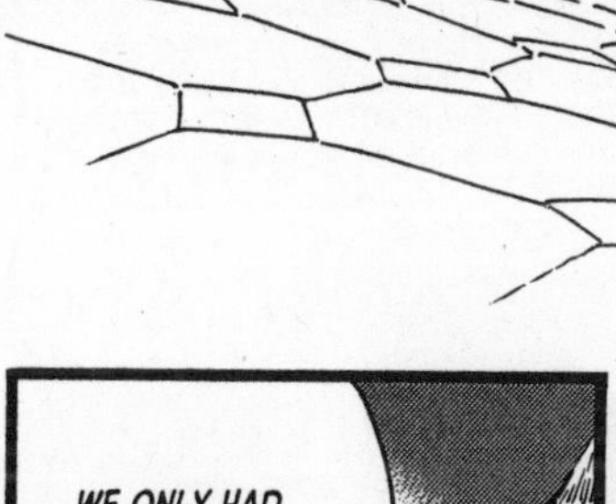
WE ONLY HAD TO REDRAW THE TILES AT THE CENTER OF THE HALL...
...AND NOW, NOT ONLY DOES LADY MIIA GET HER CHANCE TO SHINE...

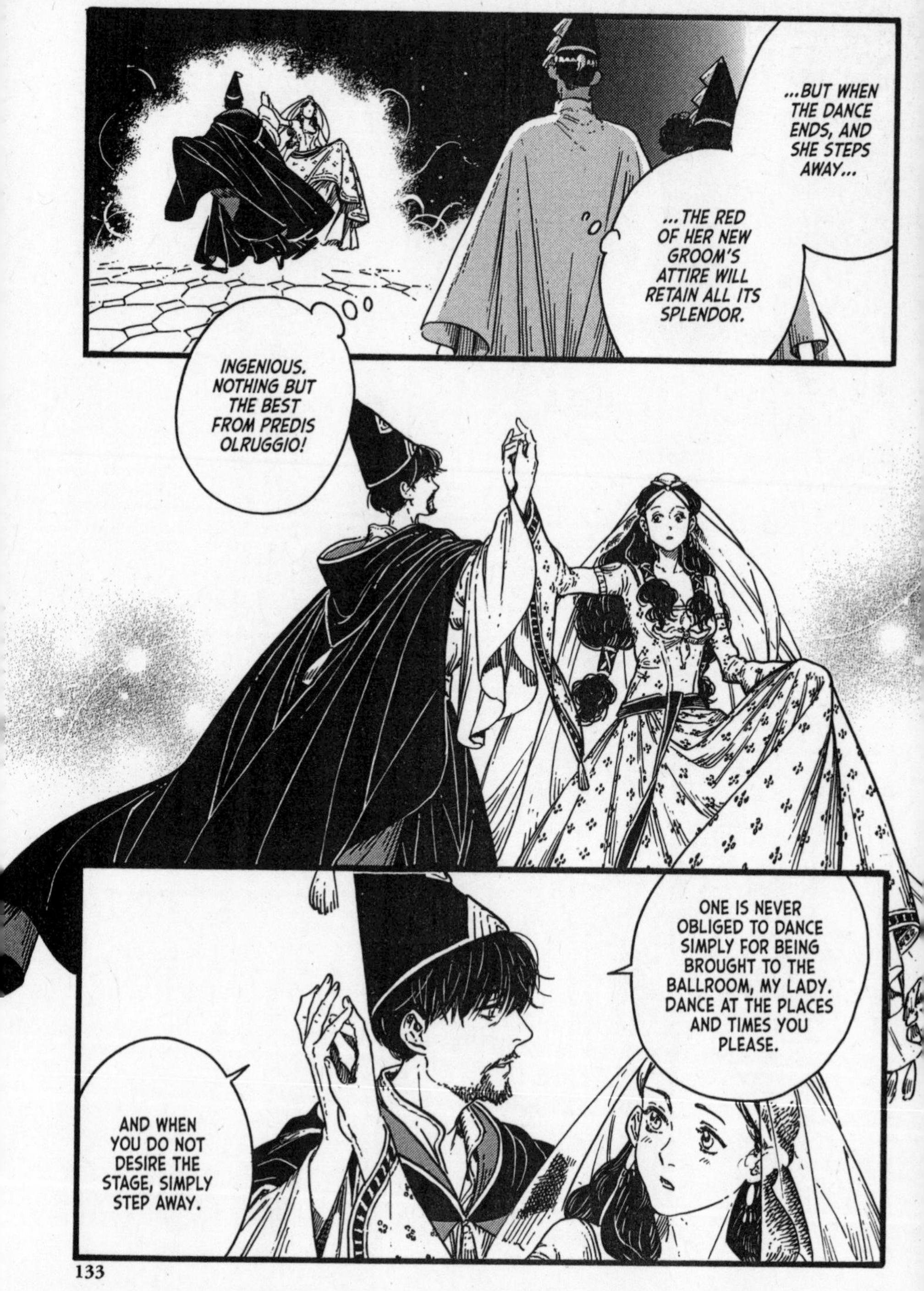
...BUT WHEN THE DANCE ENDS, AND SHE STEPS AWAY...
...THE RED OF HER NEW GROOM'S ATTIRE WILL RETAIN ALL ITS SPLENDOR.
INGENIOUS. NOTHING BUT THE BEST FROM PREDIS OLRUGGIO!
ONE IS NEVER OBLIGED TO DANCE SIMPLY FOR BEING BROUGHT TO THE BALLROOM, MY LADY. DANCE AT THE PLACES AND TIMES YOU PLEASE.
AND WHEN YOU DO NOT DESIRE THE STAGE, SIMPLY STEP AWAY.

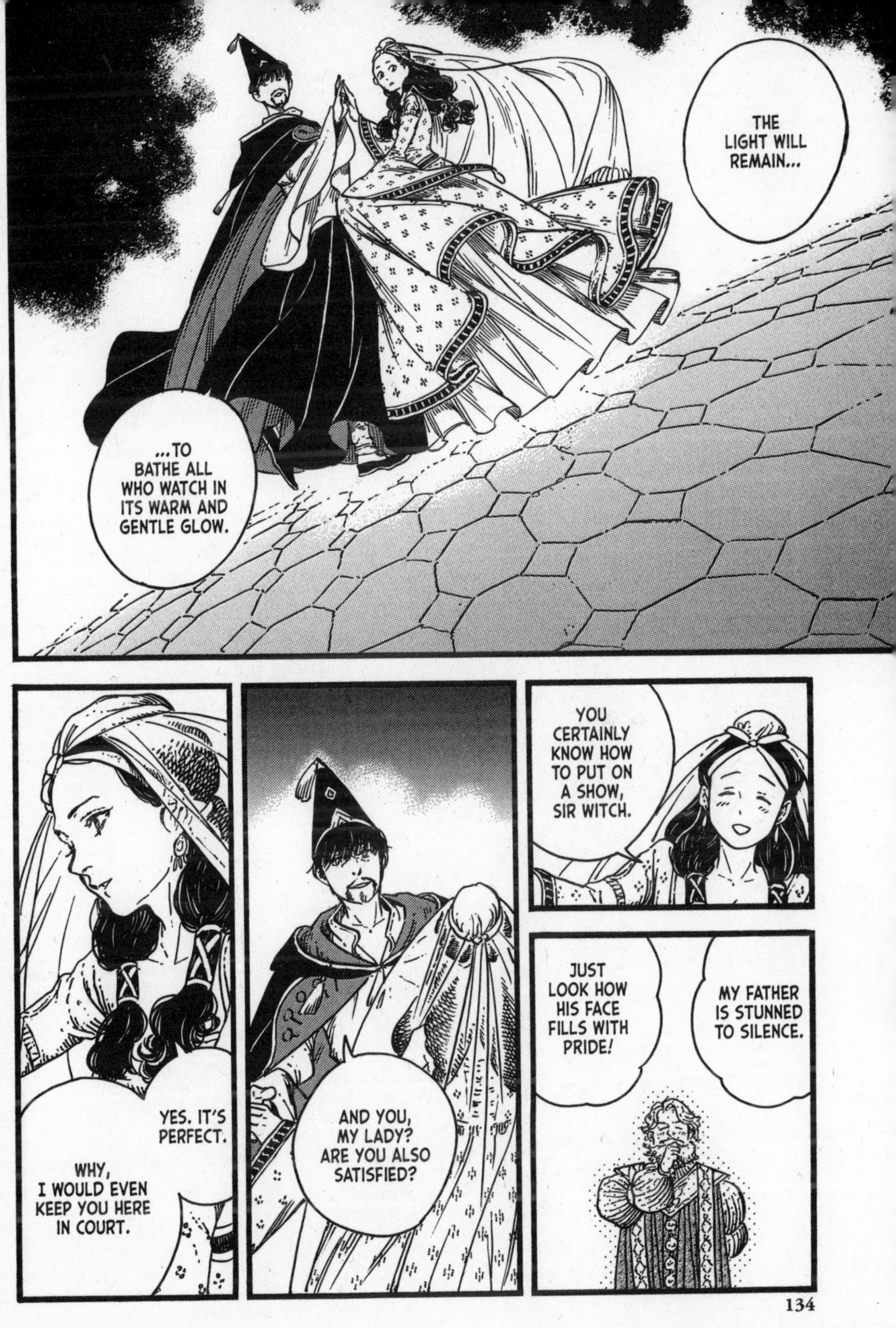
THE LIGHT WILL REMAIN...
...TO BATHE ALL WHO WATCH IN ITS WARM AND GENTLE GLOW.
YOU CERTAINLY KNOW HOW TO PUT ON A SHOW, SIR WITCH.
MY FATHER IS STUNNED TO SILENCE.
JUST LOOK HOW HIS FACE FILLS WITH PRIDE!
AND YOU, MY LADY? ARE YOU ALSO SATISFIED?
YES. IT'S PERFECT.
WHY, I WOULD EVEN KEEP YOU HERE IN COURT.

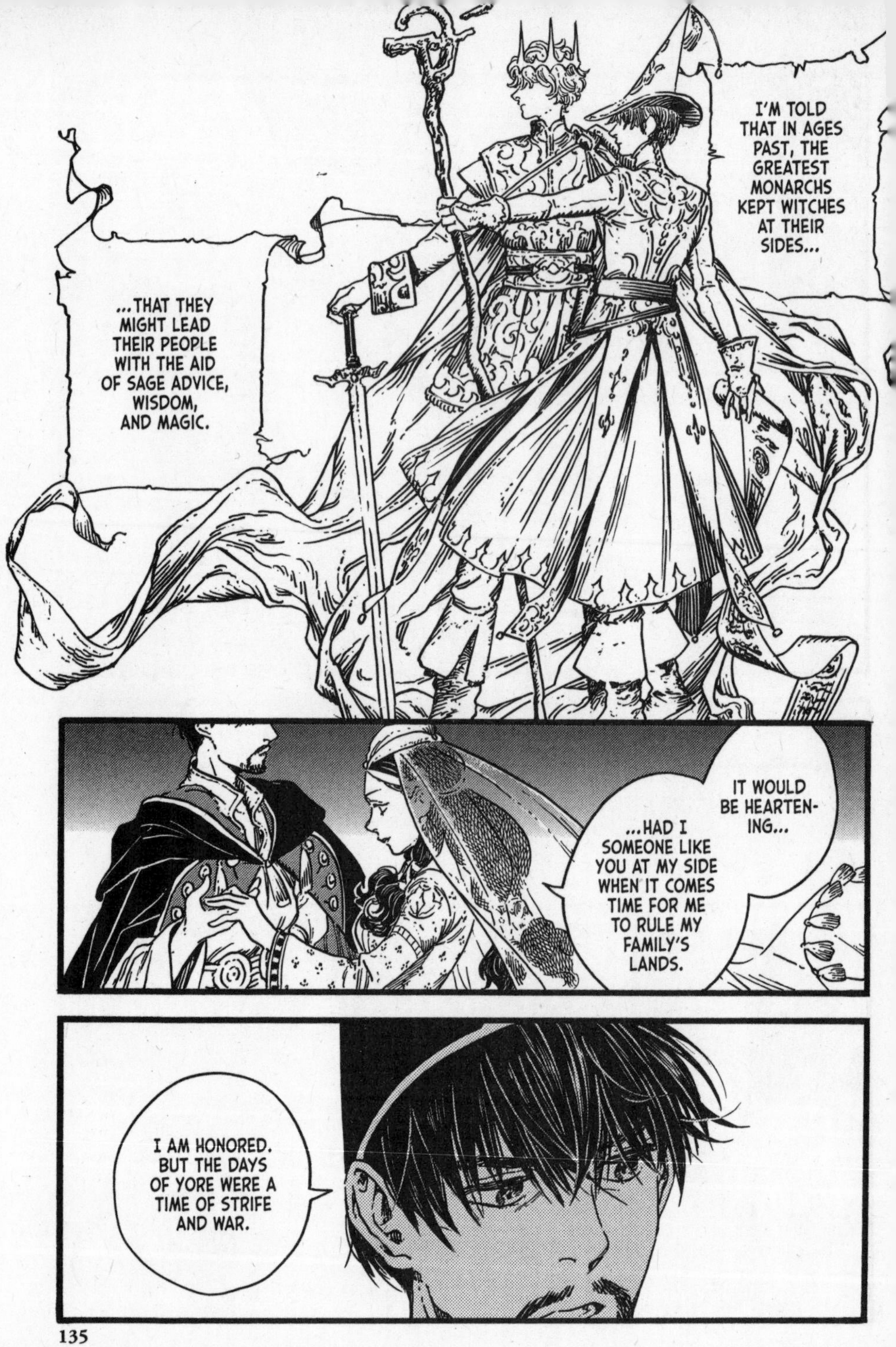
I'M TOLD THAT IN AGES PAST, THE GREATEST MONARCHS KEPT WITCHES AT THEIR SIDES...
...THAT THEY MIGHT LEAD THEIR PEOPLE WITH THE AID OF SAGE ADVICE, WISDOM, AND MAGIC.
IT WOULD BE HEARTEN-ING...
...HAD I SOMEONE LIKE YOU AT MY SIDE WHEN IT COMES TIME FOR ME TO RULE MY FAMILY'S LANDS.
I AM HONORED. BUT THE DAYS OF YORE WERE A TIME OF STRIFE AND WAR.

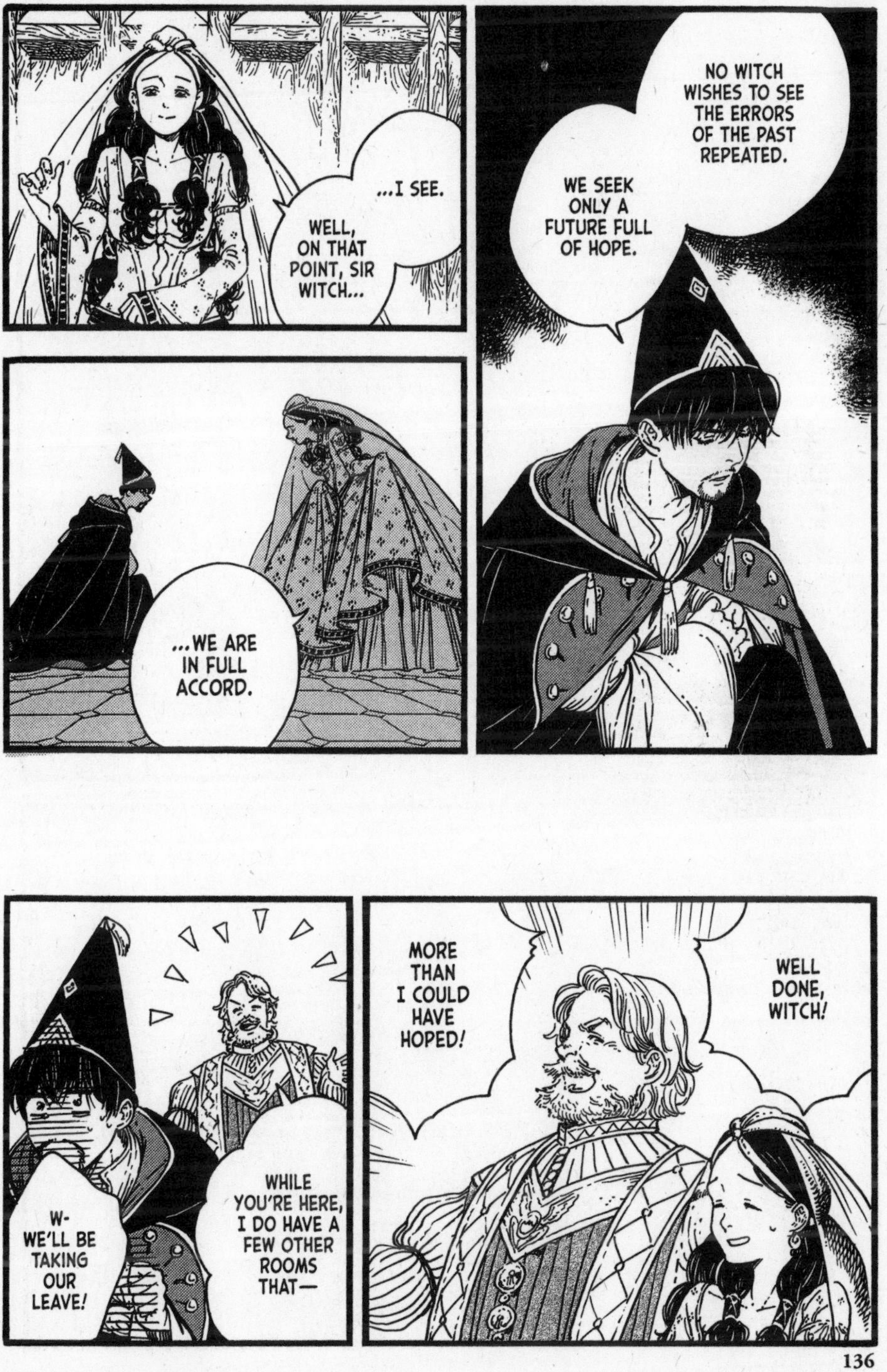
NO WITCH WISHES TO SEE THE ERRORS OF THE PAST REPEATED.
WE SEEK ONLY A FUTURE FULL OF HOPE.
...I SEE.
WELL, ON THAT POINT, SIR WITCH...
...WE ARE IN FULL ACCORD.
WELL DONE, WITCH!
MORE THAN I COULD HAVE HOPED!
WHILE YOU'RE HERE, I DO HAVE A FEW OTHER ROOMS THAT—
W- WE'LL BE TAKING OUR LEAVE!

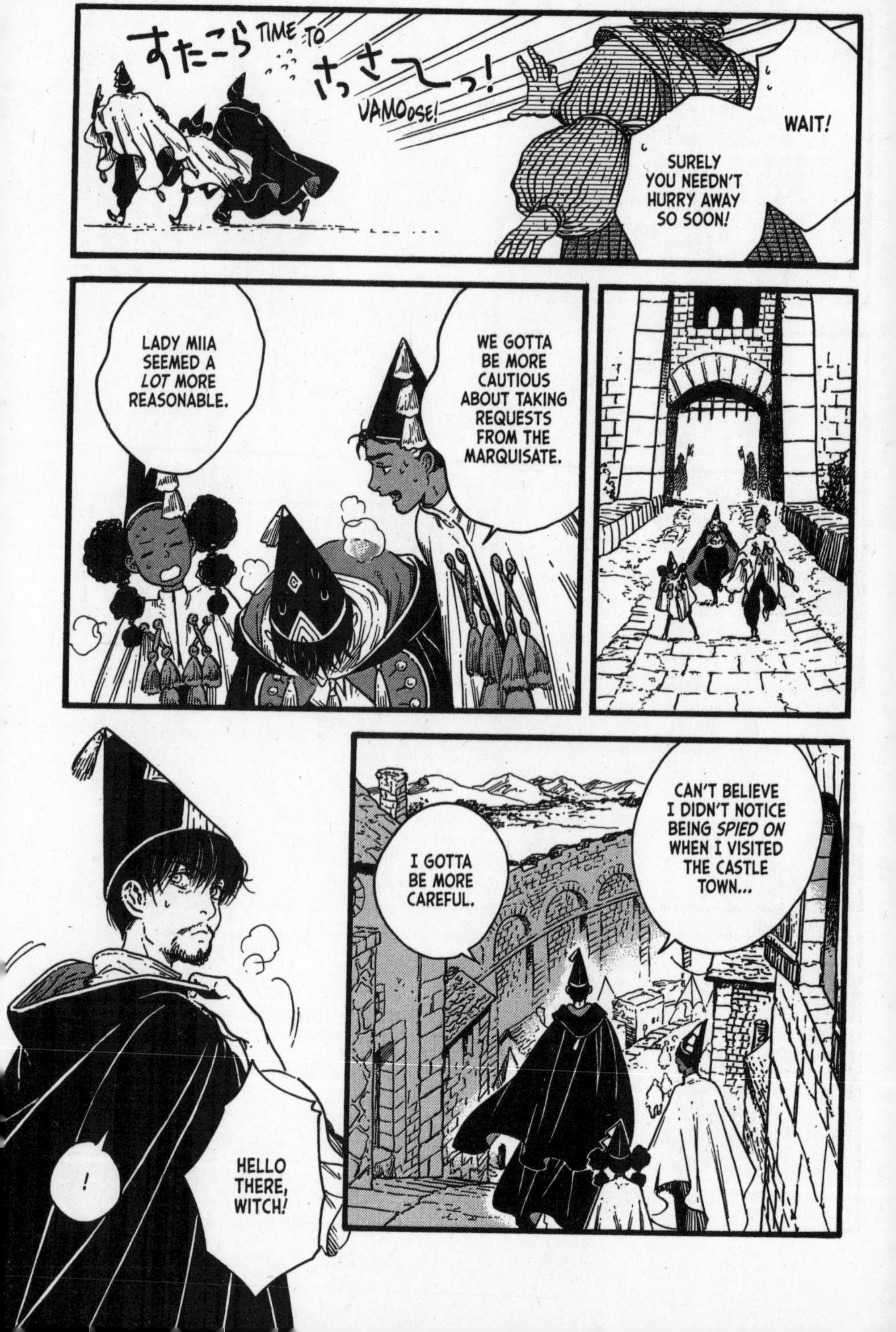
WAIT!
SURELY YOU NEEDN'T HURRY AWAY SO SOON!
すたこら
TIME TO
さっさ〜っ!
VAMOOSE!
WE GOTTA BE MORE CAUTIOUS ABOUT TAKING REQUESTS FROM THE MARQUISATE.
LADY MIIA SEEMED A *LOT* MORE REASONABLE.
CAN'T BELIEVE I DIDN'T NOTICE BEING *SPIED ON* WHEN I VISITED THE CASTLE TOWN...
I GOTTA BE MORE CAREFUL.
HELLO THERE, WITCH!
!

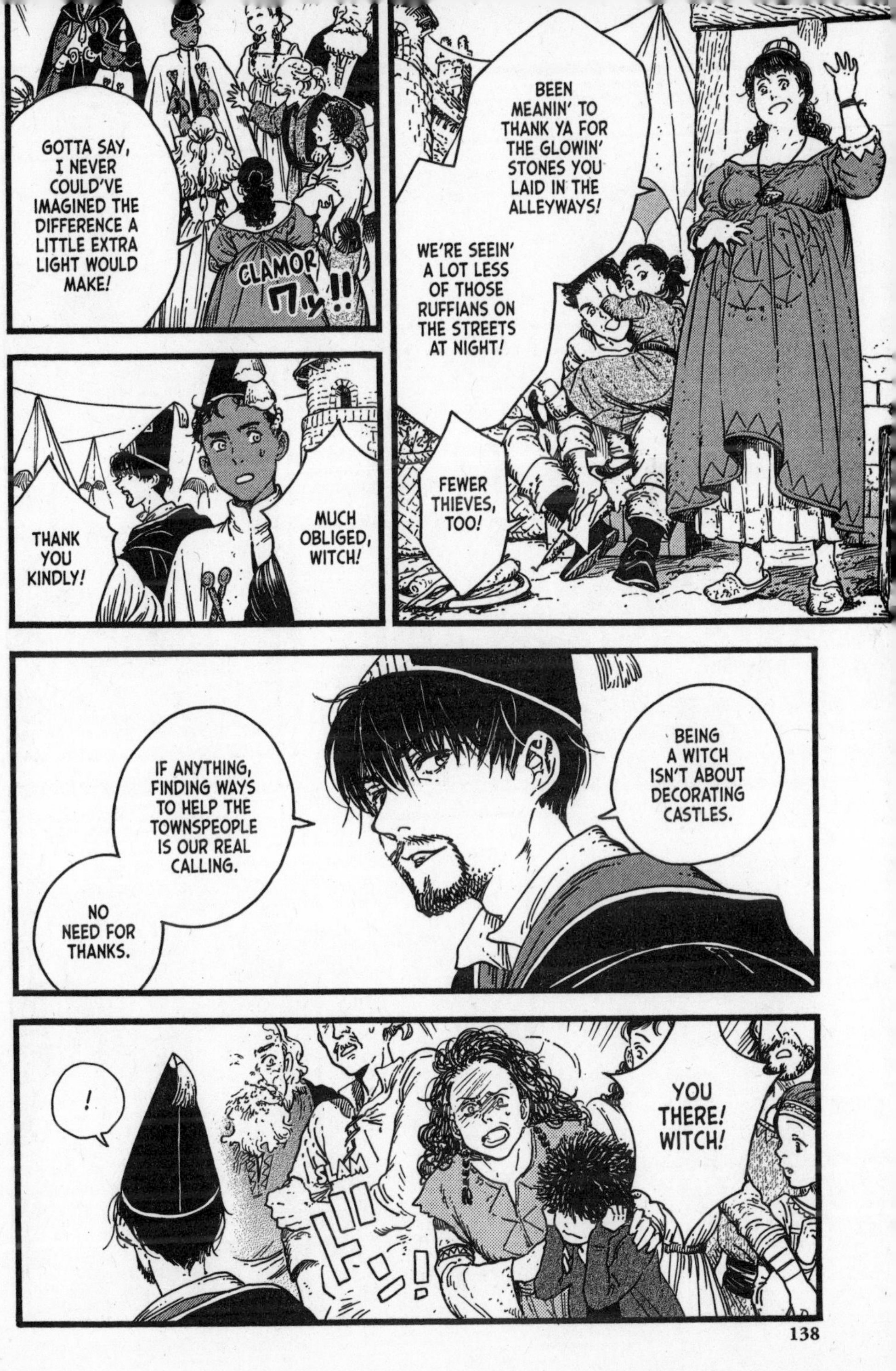
BEEN MEANIN' TO THANK YA FOR THE GLOWIN' STONES YOU LAID IN THE ALLEYWAYS!
WE'RE SEEIN' A LOT LESS OF THOSE RUFFIANS ON THE STREETS AT NIGHT!
FEWER THIEVES, TOO!
GOTTA SAY, I NEVER COULD'VE IMAGINED THE DIFFERENCE A LITTLE EXTRA LIGHT WOULD MAKE!
CLAMOR
ワッ!!
MUCH OBLIGED, WITCH!
THANK YOU KINDLY!
BEING A WITCH ISN'T ABOUT DECORATING CASTLES.
IF ANYTHING, FINDING WAYS TO HELP THE TOWNSPEOPLE IS OUR REAL CALLING.
NO NEED FOR THANKS.
YOU THERE! WITCH!
SLAM
ドン!
!

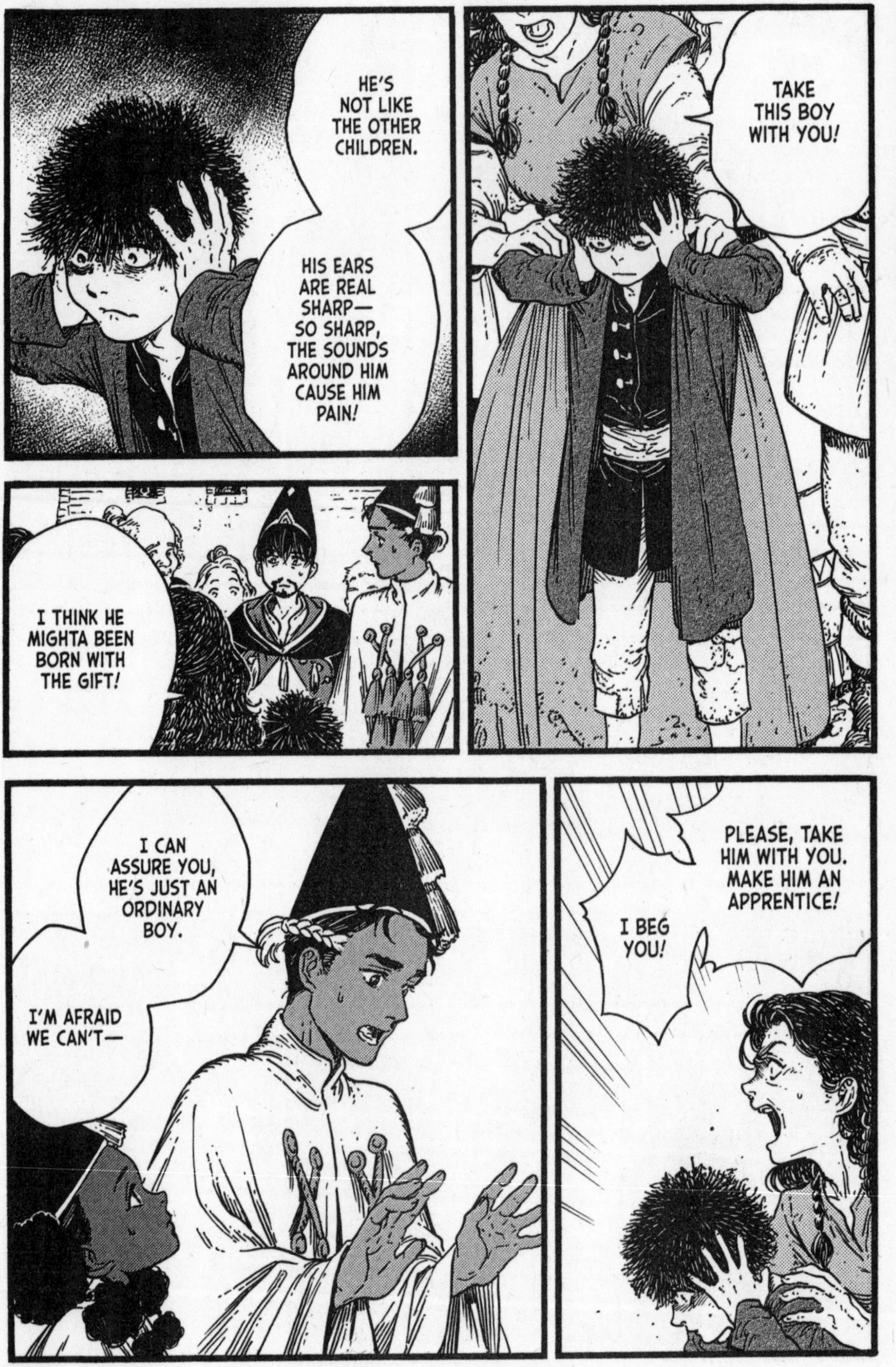
TAKE THIS BOY WITH YOU!
HE'S NOT LIKE THE OTHER CHILDREN.
HIS EARS ARE REAL SHARP— SO SHARP, THE SOUNDS AROUND HIM CAUSE HIM PAIN!
I THINK HE MIGHTA BEEN BORN WITH THE GIFT!
PLEASE, TAKE HIM WITH YOU. MAKE HIM AN APPRENTICE!
I BEG YOU!
I CAN ASSURE YOU, HE'S JUST AN ORDINARY BOY.
I'M AFRAID WE CAN'T—

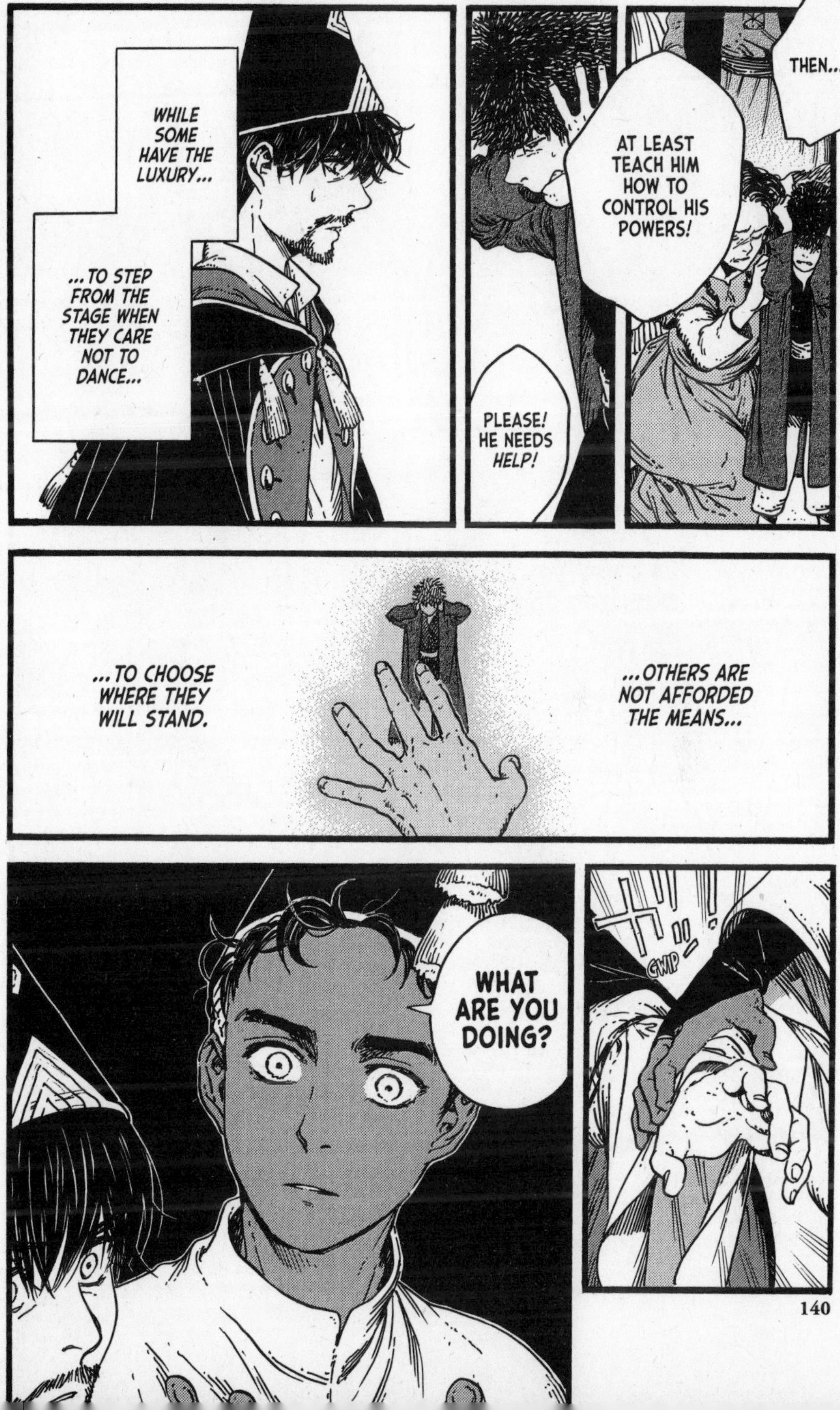
THEN...
AT LEAST TEACH HIM HOW TO CONTROL HIS POWERS!
PLEASE! HE NEEDS HELP!
WHILE SOME HAVE THE LUXURY...
...TO STEP FROM THE STAGE WHEN THEY CARE NOT TO DANCE...
...OTHERS ARE NOT AFFORDED THE MEANS...
...TO CHOOSE WHERE THEY WILL STAND.
GWIP
WHAT ARE YOU DOING?

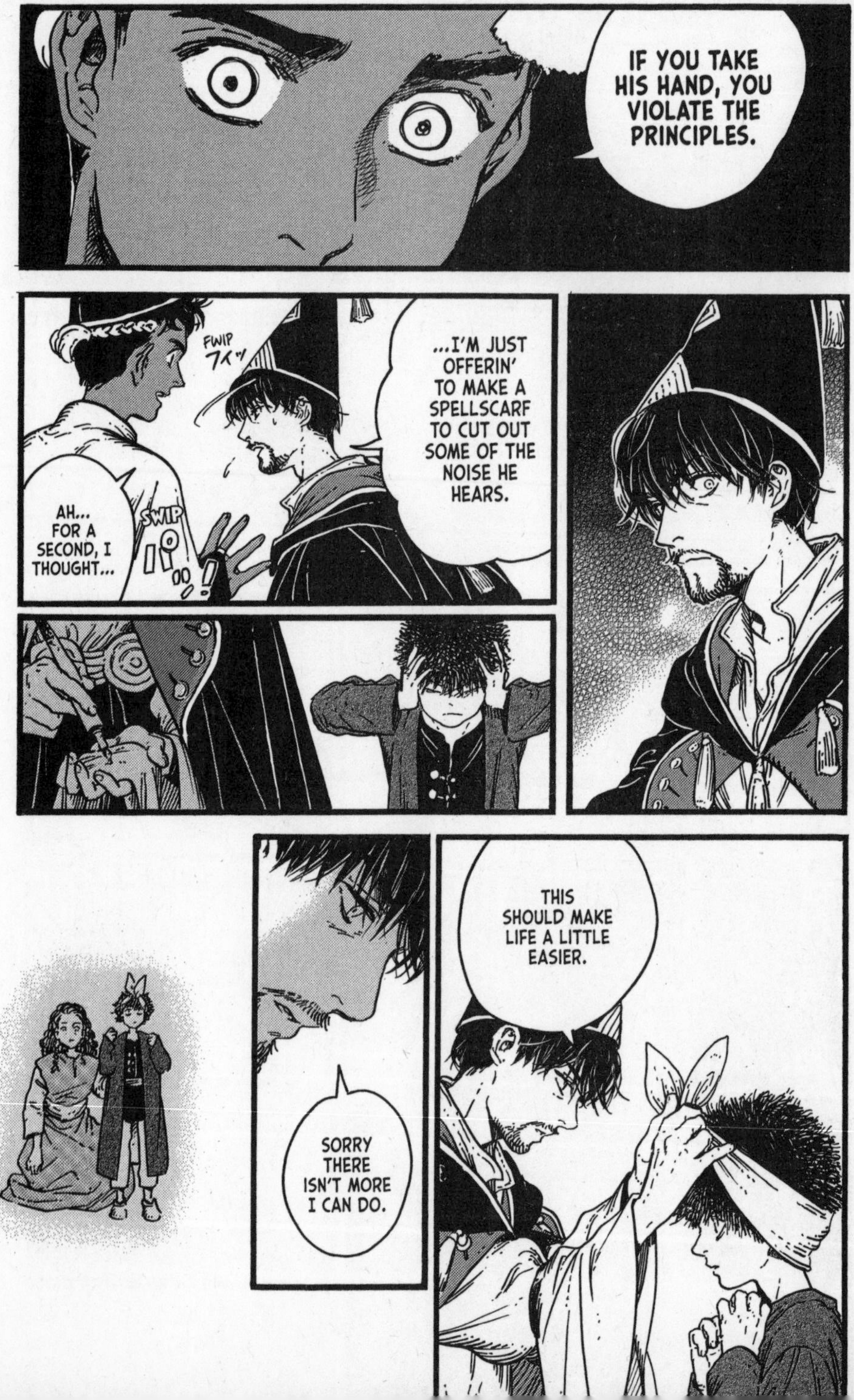
IF YOU TAKE HIS HAND, YOU VIOLATE THE PRINCIPLES.
...I'M JUST OFFERIN' TO MAKE A SPELLSCARF TO CUT OUT SOME OF THE NOISE HE HEARS.
FWIP
フィッ
AH... FOR A SECOND, I THOUGHT...
SWIP
THIS SHOULD MAKE LIFE A LITTLE EASIER.
SORRY THERE ISN'T MORE I CAN DO.

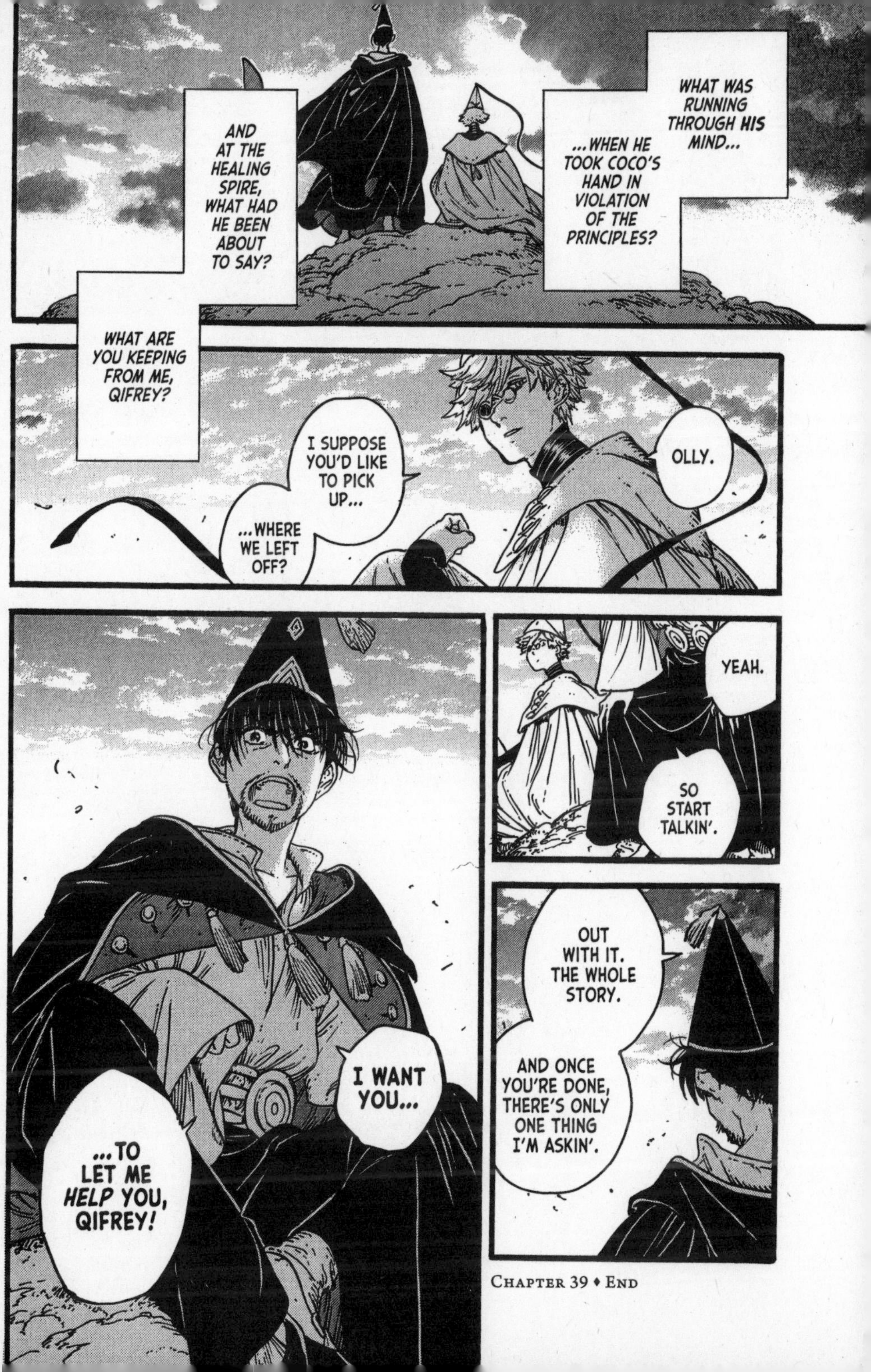
WHAT WAS RUNNING THROUGH *HIS* MIND...
...WHEN HE TOOK COCO'S HAND IN VIOLATION OF THE PRINCIPLES?
AND AT THE HEALING SPIRE, WHAT HAD HE BEEN ABOUT TO SAY?
WHAT ARE YOU KEEPING FROM ME, QIFREY?
OLLY.
I SUPPOSE YOU'D LIKE TO PICK UP...
...WHERE WE LEFT OFF?
YEAH.
SO START TALKIN'.
OUT WITH IT. THE WHOLE STORY.
AND ONCE YOU'RE DONE, THERE'S ONLY ONE THING I'M ASKIN'.
I WANT YOU...
...TO LET ME *HELP* YOU, QIFREY!

Chapter 39 ♦ End

Witch Hat Atelier

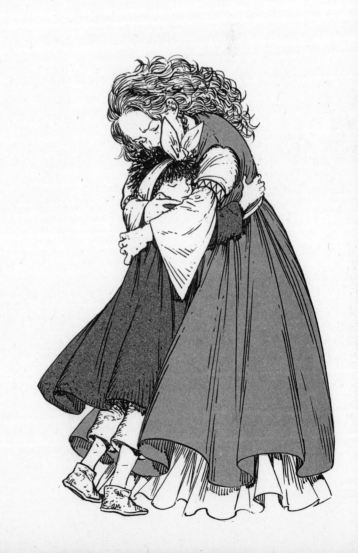

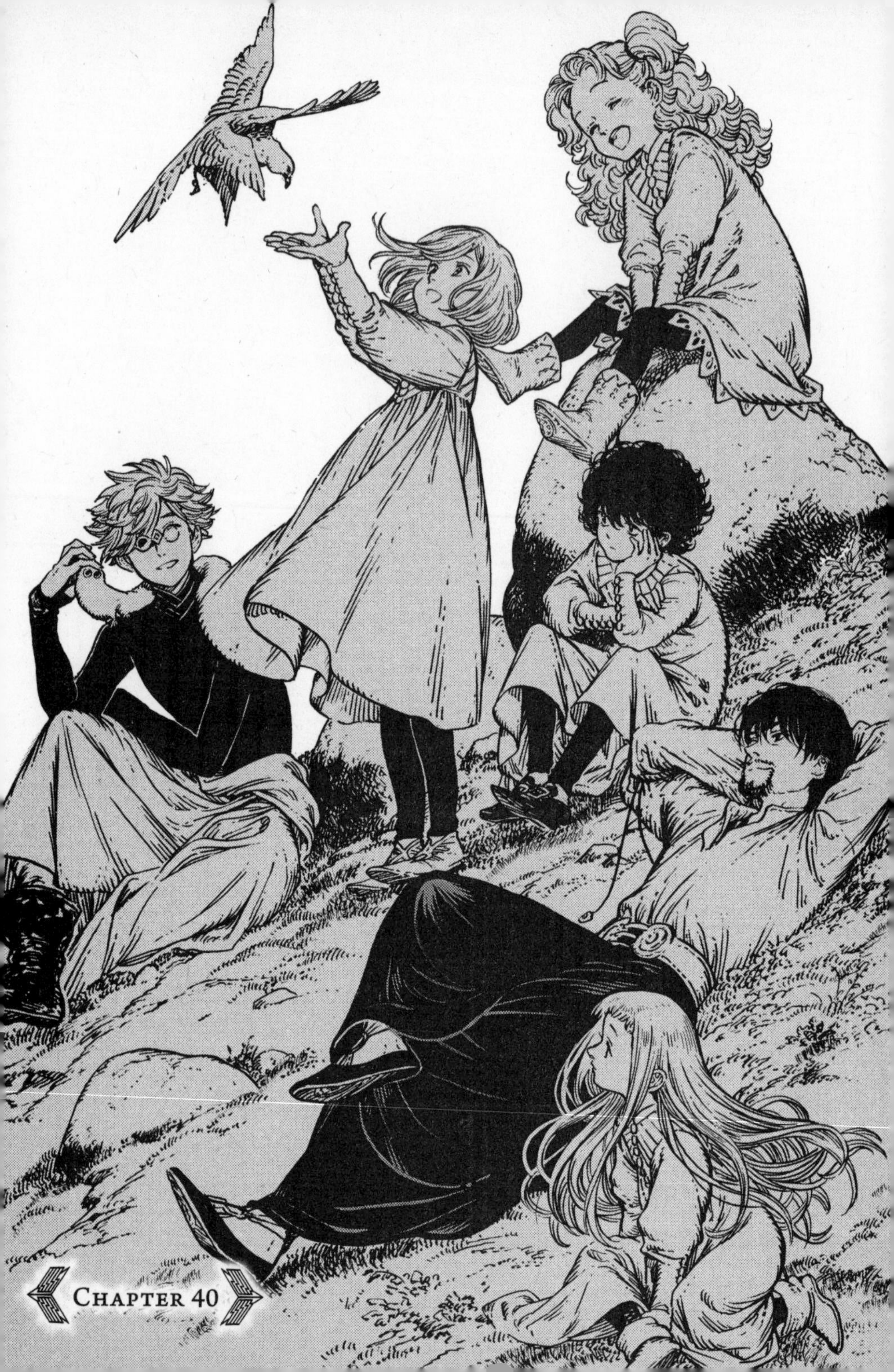
Chapter 40

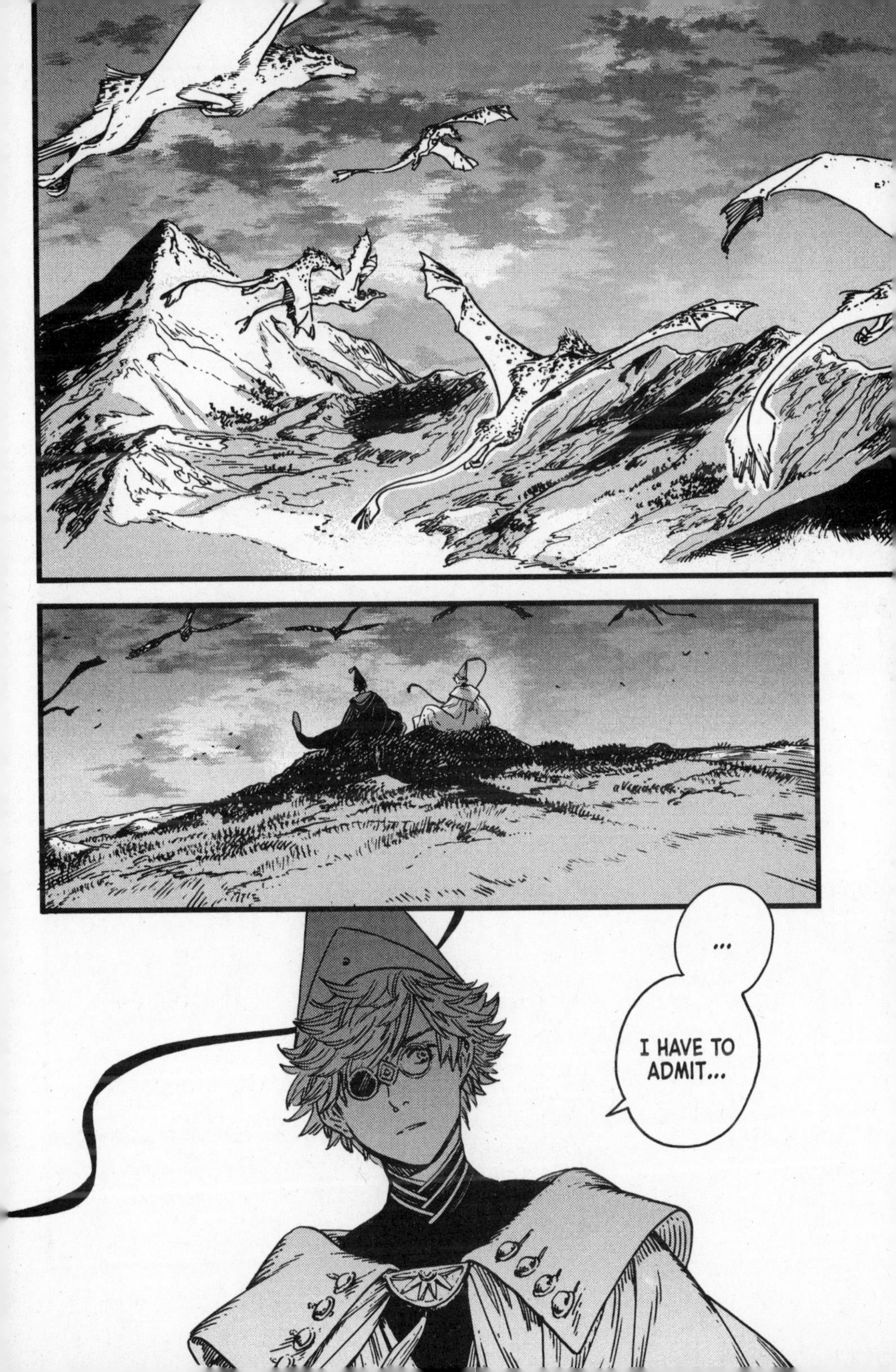
...
I HAVE TO ADMIT...

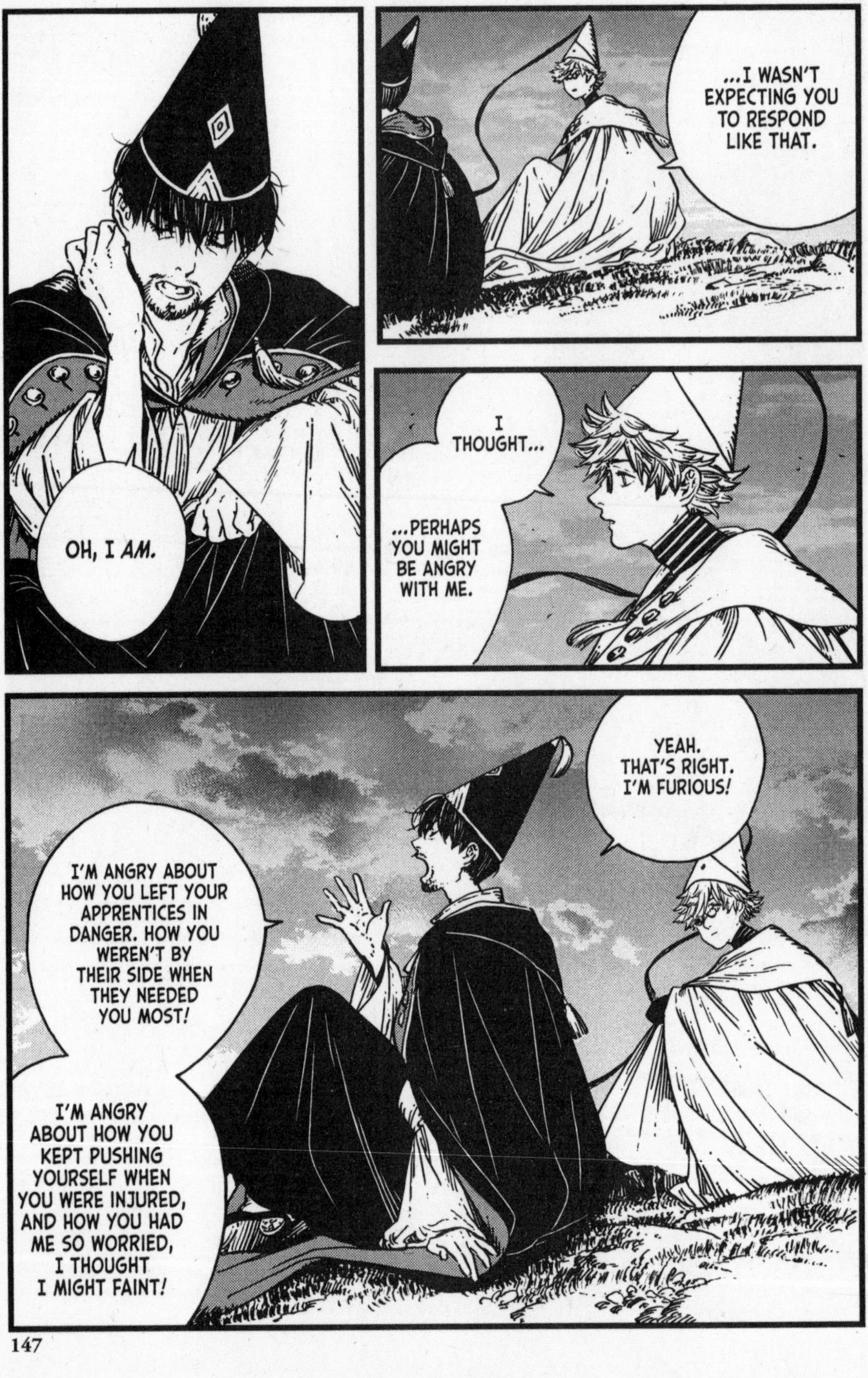
...I WASN'T EXPECTING YOU TO RESPOND LIKE THAT.
I THOUGHT...
...PERHAPS YOU MIGHT BE ANGRY WITH ME.
OH, I *AM.*
YEAH. THAT'S RIGHT. I'M FURIOUS!
I'M ANGRY ABOUT HOW YOU LEFT YOUR APPRENTICES IN DANGER. HOW YOU WEREN'T BY THEIR SIDE WHEN THEY NEEDED YOU MOST!
I'M ANGRY ABOUT HOW YOU KEPT PUSHING YOURSELF WHEN YOU WERE INJURED, AND HOW YOU HAD ME SO WORRIED, I THOUGHT I MIGHT FAINT!

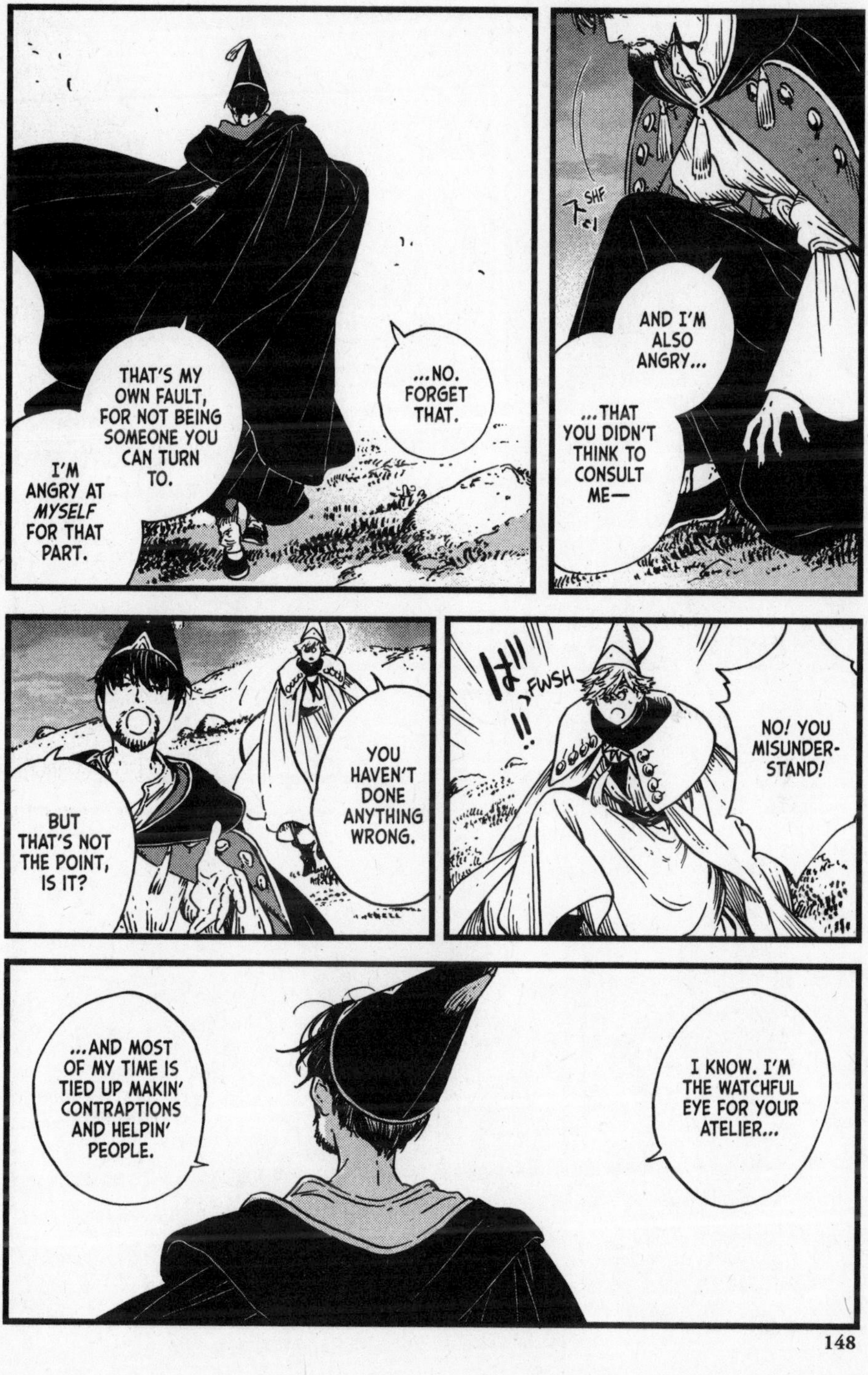
SHF
AND I'M ALSO ANGRY...
...THAT YOU DIDN'T THINK TO CONSULT ME—
...NO. FORGET THAT.
THAT'S MY OWN FAULT, FOR NOT BEING SOMEONE YOU CAN TURN TO.
I'M ANGRY AT *MYSELF* FOR THAT PART.
FWSH
NO! YOU MISUNDERSTAND!
YOU HAVEN'T DONE ANYTHING WRONG.
BUT THAT'S NOT THE POINT, IS IT?
I KNOW. I'M THE WATCHFUL EYE FOR YOUR ATELIER...
...AND MOST OF MY TIME IS TIED UP MAKIN' CONTRAPTIONS AND HELPIN' PEOPLE.

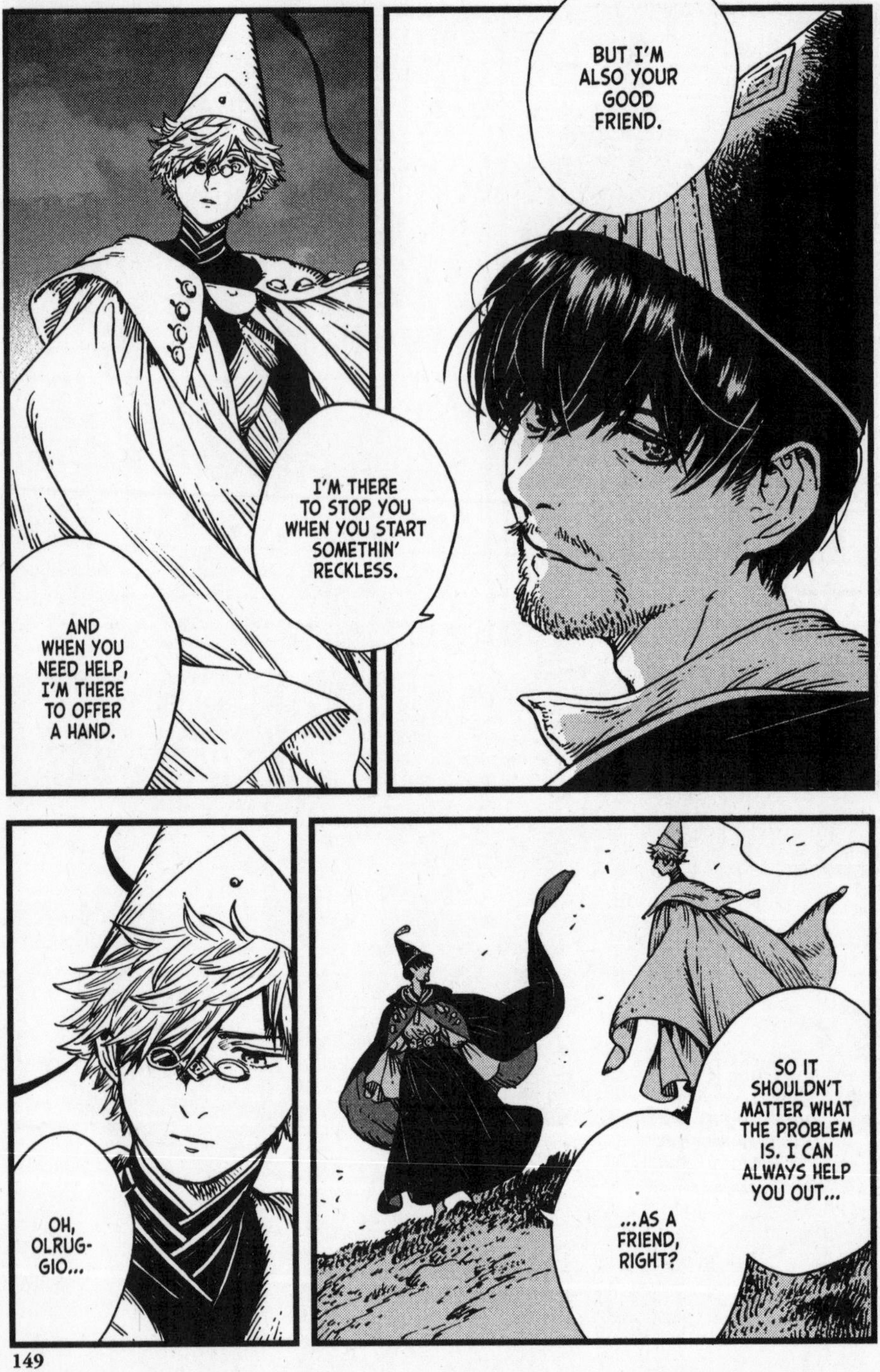
BUT I'M ALSO YOUR GOOD FRIEND.
I'M THERE TO STOP YOU WHEN YOU START SOMETHIN' RECKLESS.
AND WHEN YOU NEED HELP, I'M THERE TO OFFER A HAND.
SO IT SHOULDN'T MATTER WHAT THE PROBLEM IS. I CAN ALWAYS HELP YOU OUT...
...AS A FRIEND, RIGHT?
OH, OLRUG-GIO...

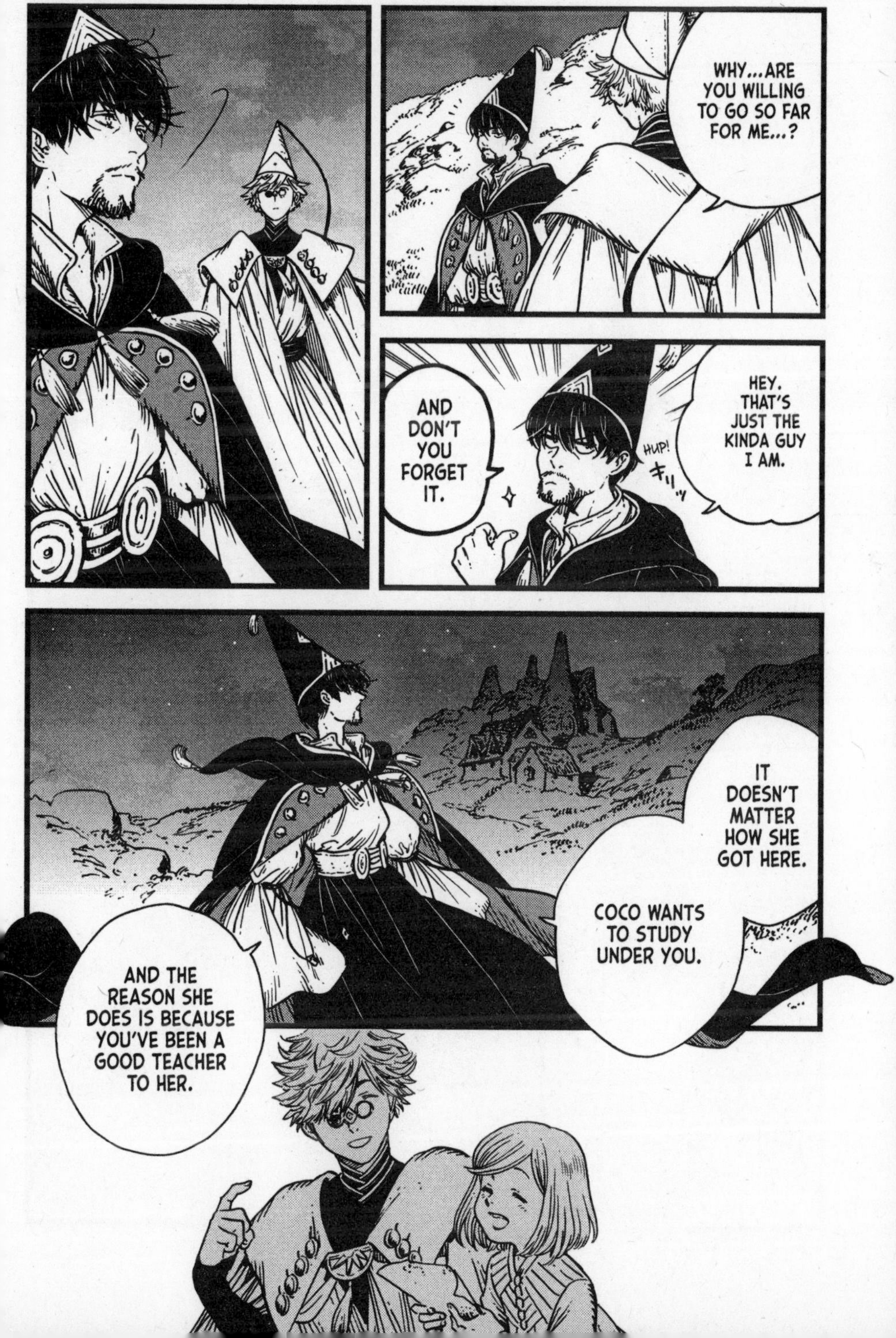
WHY...ARE YOU WILLING TO GO SO FAR FOR ME...?
HEY. THAT'S JUST THE KINDA GUY I AM.
HUP!
キリッ
AND DON'T YOU FORGET IT.
IT DOESN'T MATTER HOW SHE GOT HERE.
COCO WANTS TO STUDY UNDER YOU.
AND THE REASON SHE DOES IS BECAUSE YOU'VE BEEN A GOOD TEACHER TO HER.

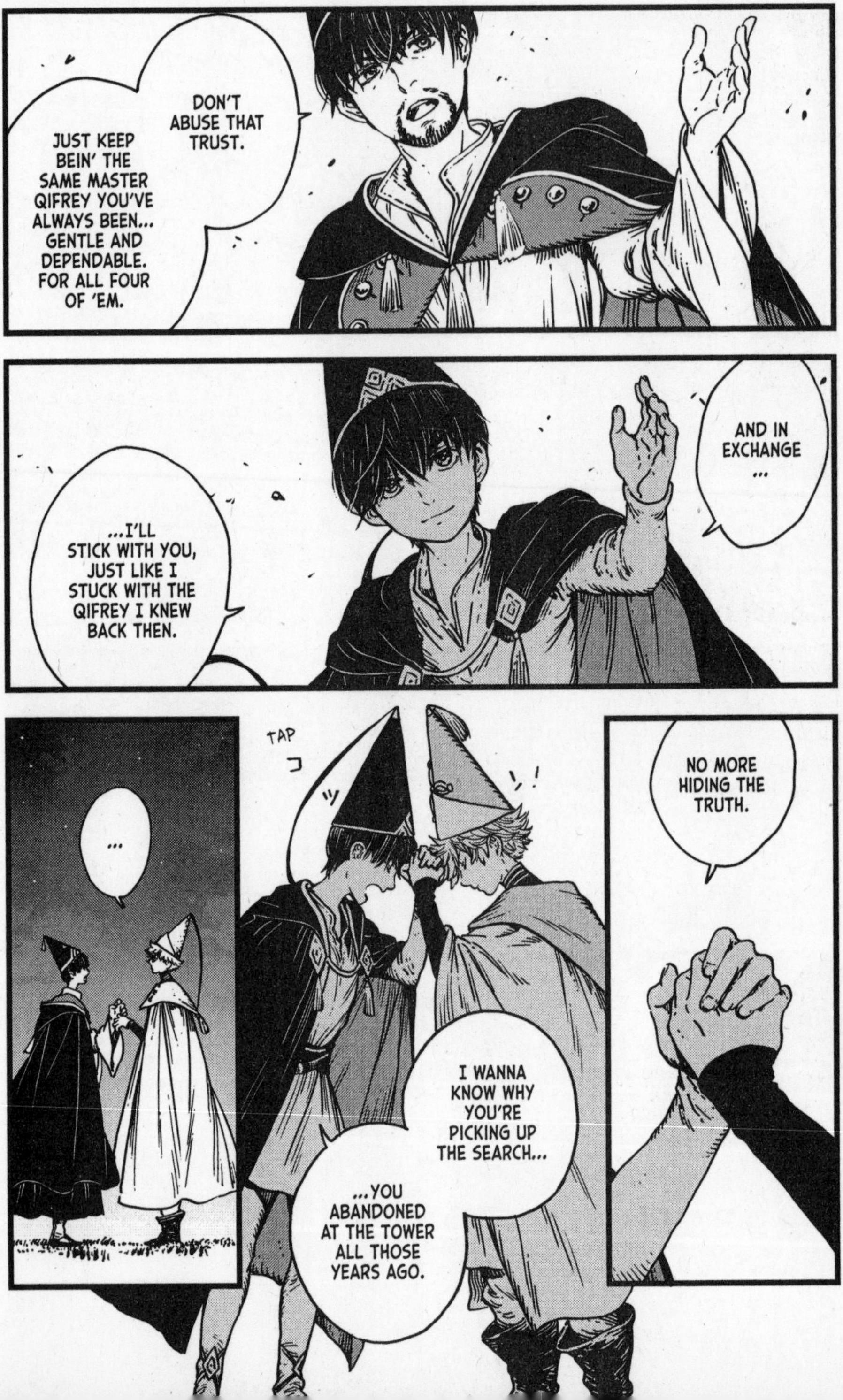
DON'T ABUSE THAT TRUST.
JUST KEEP BEIN' THE SAME MASTER QIFREY YOU'VE ALWAYS BEEN... GENTLE AND DEPENDABLE. FOR ALL FOUR OF 'EM.
AND IN EXCHANGE...
...I'LL STICK WITH YOU, JUST LIKE I STUCK WITH THE QIFREY I KNEW BACK THEN.
NO MORE HIDING THE TRUTH.
TAP
コツ
I WANNA KNOW WHY YOU'RE PICKING UP THE SEARCH...
...YOU ABANDONED AT THE TOWER ALL THOSE YEARS AGO.
...

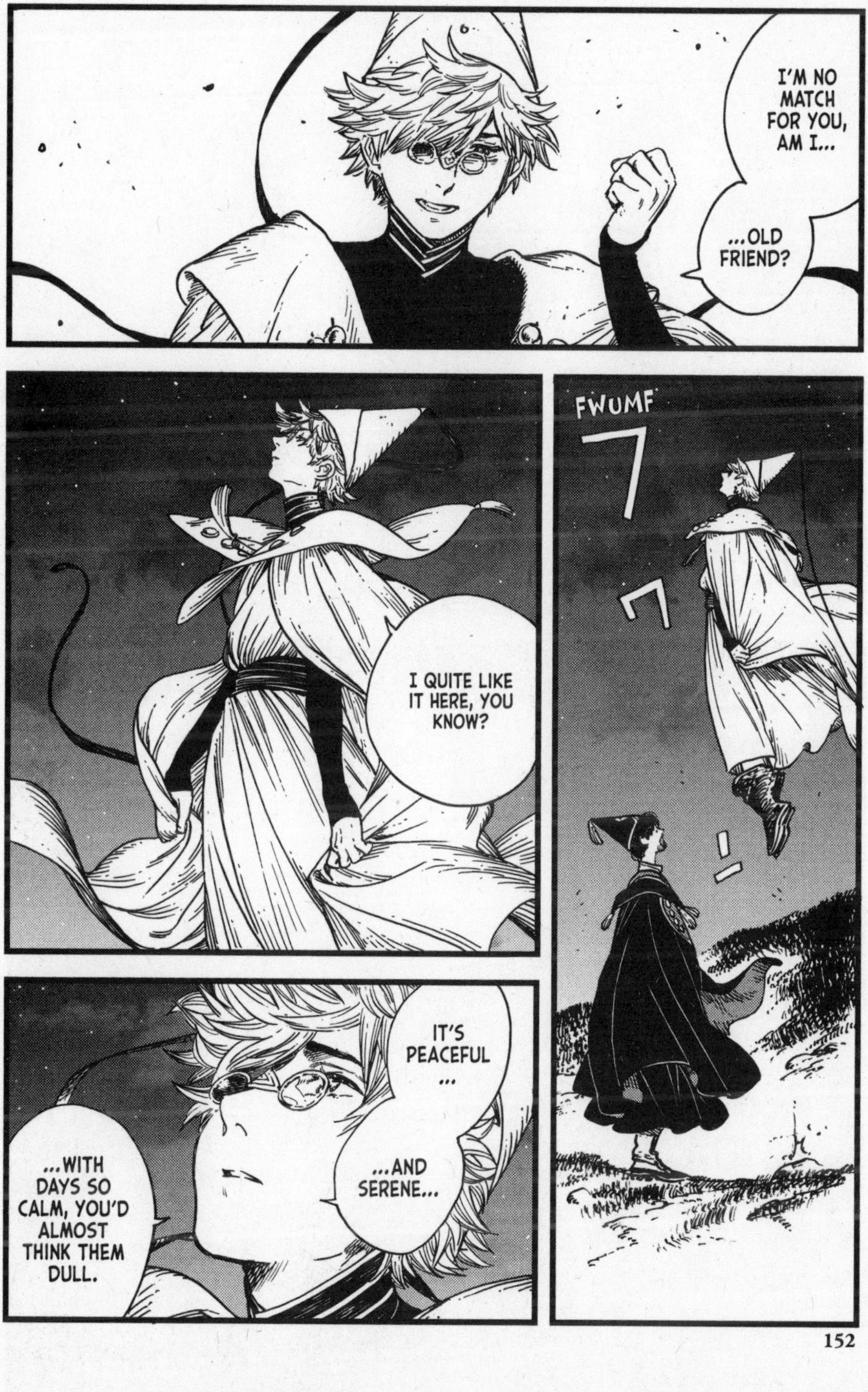
I'M NO MATCH FOR YOU, AM I...
...OLD FRIEND?
FWUMF
!
I QUITE LIKE IT HERE, YOU KNOW?
IT'S PEACEFUL ...
...AND SERENE...
...WITH DAYS SO CALM, YOU'D ALMOST THINK THEM DULL.

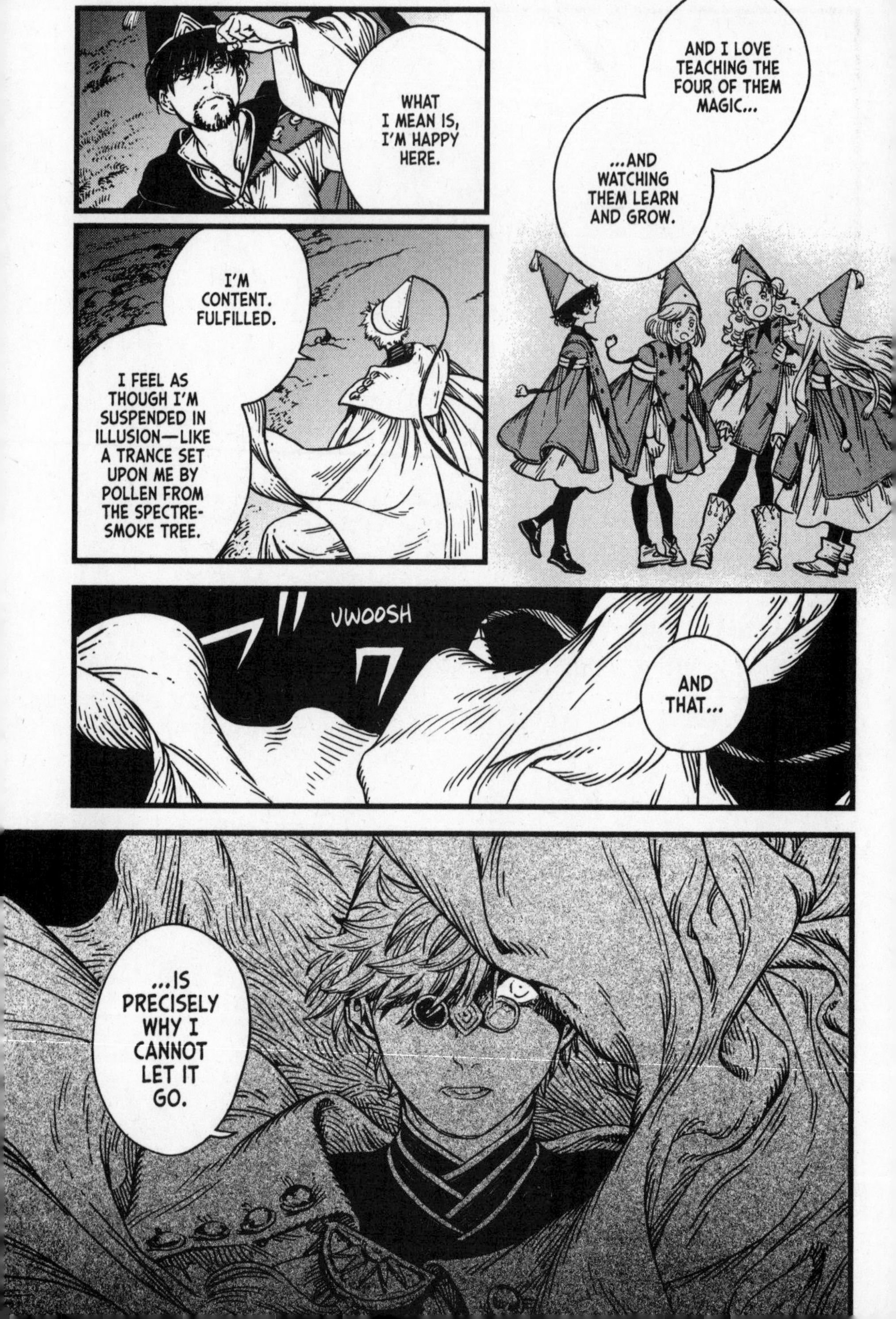
AND I LOVE TEACHING THE FOUR OF THEM MAGIC...
...AND WATCHING THEM LEARN AND GROW.
WHAT I MEAN IS, I'M HAPPY HERE.
I'M CONTENT. FULFILLED.
I FEEL AS THOUGH I'M SUSPENDED IN ILLUSION—LIKE A TRANCE SET UPON ME BY POLLEN FROM THE SPECTRE-SMOKE TREE.
AND THAT...
UWOOSH
...IS PRECISELY WHY I CANNOT LET IT GO.

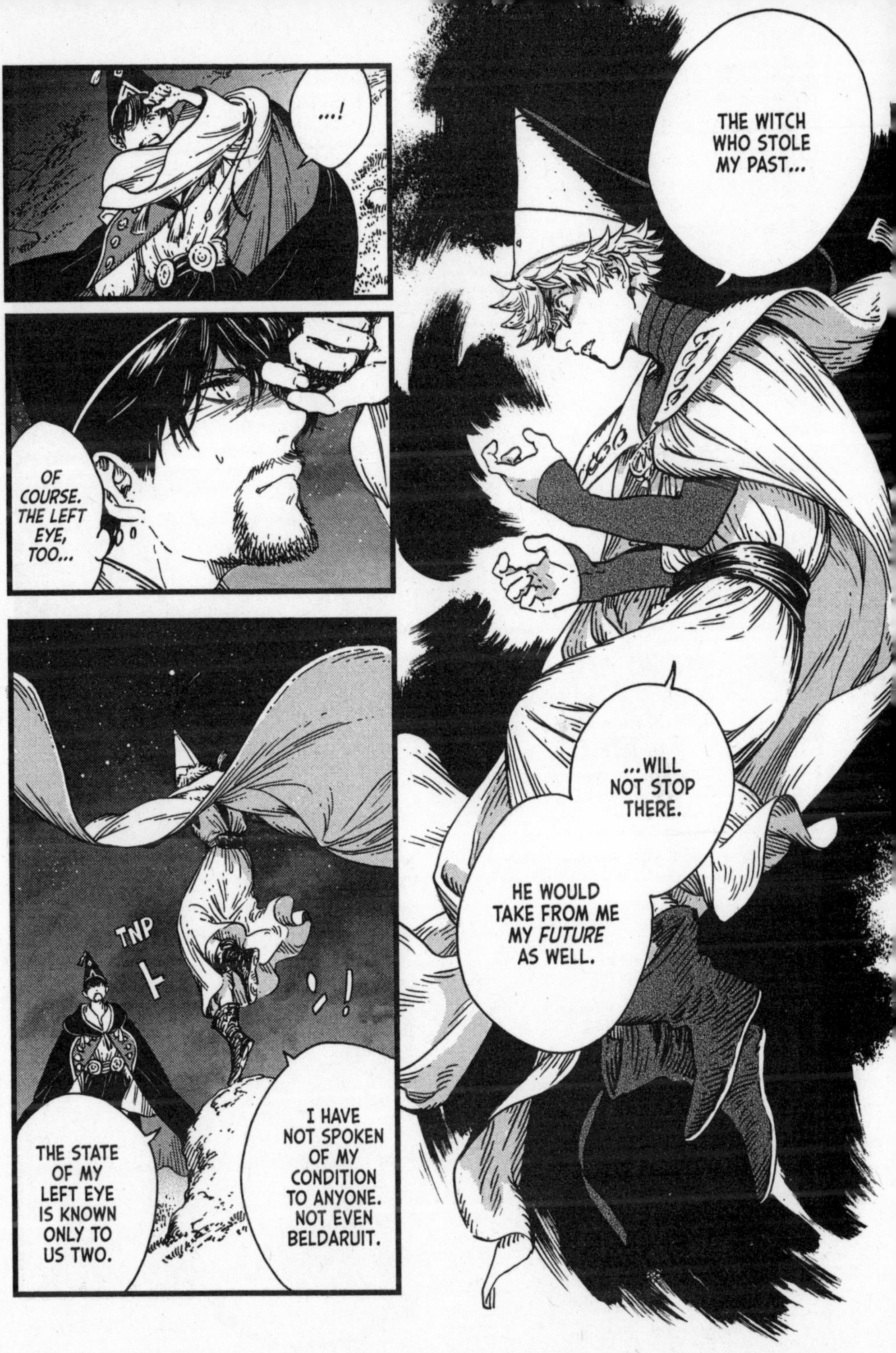
THE WITCH WHO STOLE MY PAST...
...WILL NOT STOP THERE.
HE WOULD TAKE FROM ME MY *FUTURE* AS WELL.
...!
OF COURSE. THE LEFT EYE, TOO...
TNP
!
I HAVE NOT SPOKEN OF MY CONDITION TO ANYONE. NOT EVEN BELDARUIT.
THE STATE OF MY LEFT EYE IS KNOWN ONLY TO US TWO.

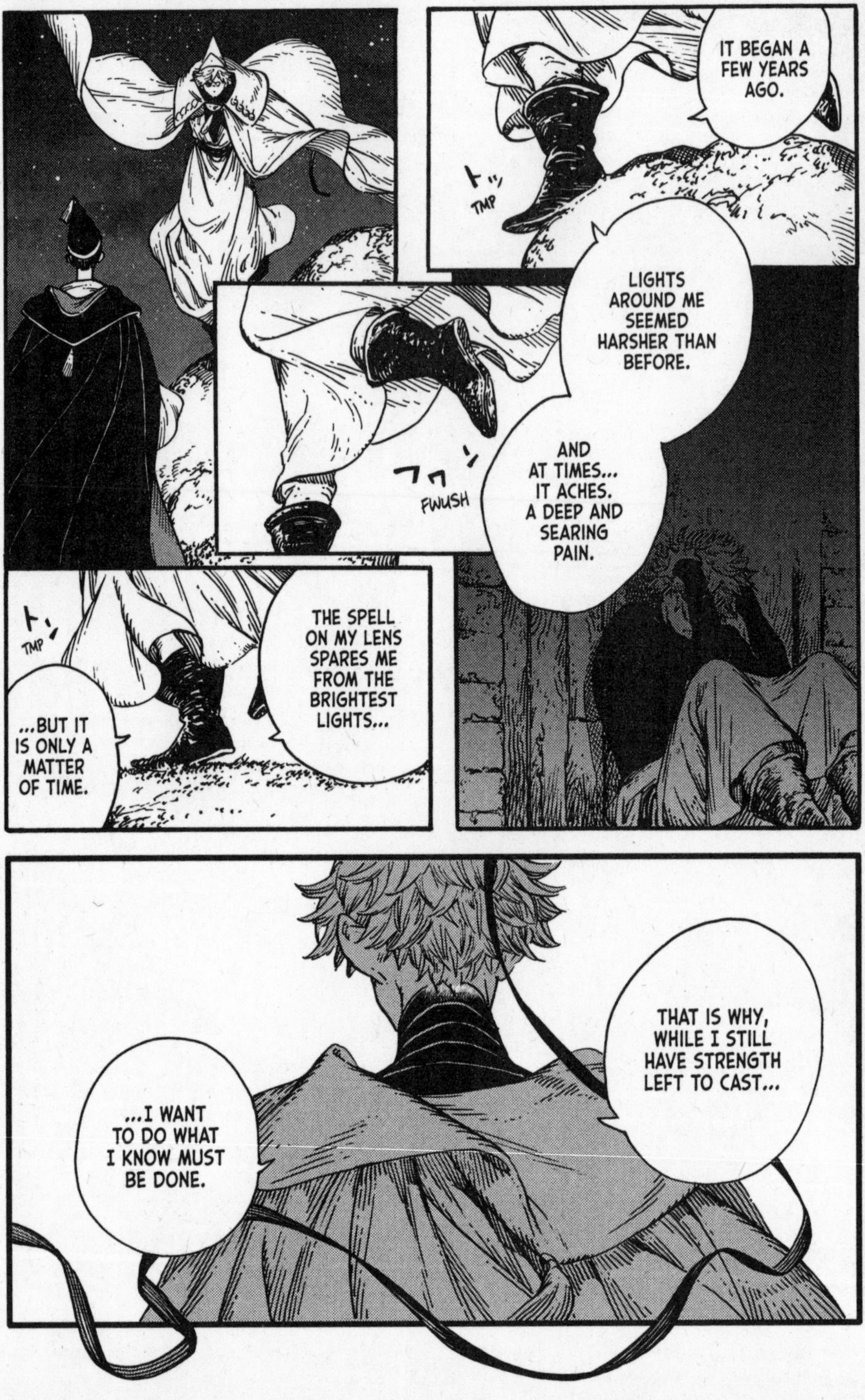
IT BEGAN A FEW YEARS AGO.
トッ
TMP
LIGHTS AROUND ME SEEMED HARSHER THAN BEFORE.
フワッ
FWUSH
AND AT TIMES... IT ACHES. A DEEP AND SEARING PAIN.
THE SPELL ON MY LENS SPARES ME FROM THE BRIGHTEST LIGHTS...
トッ
TMP
...BUT IT IS ONLY A MATTER OF TIME.
THAT IS WHY, WHILE I STILL HAVE STRENGTH LEFT TO CAST...
...I WANT TO DO WHAT I KNOW MUST BE DONE.

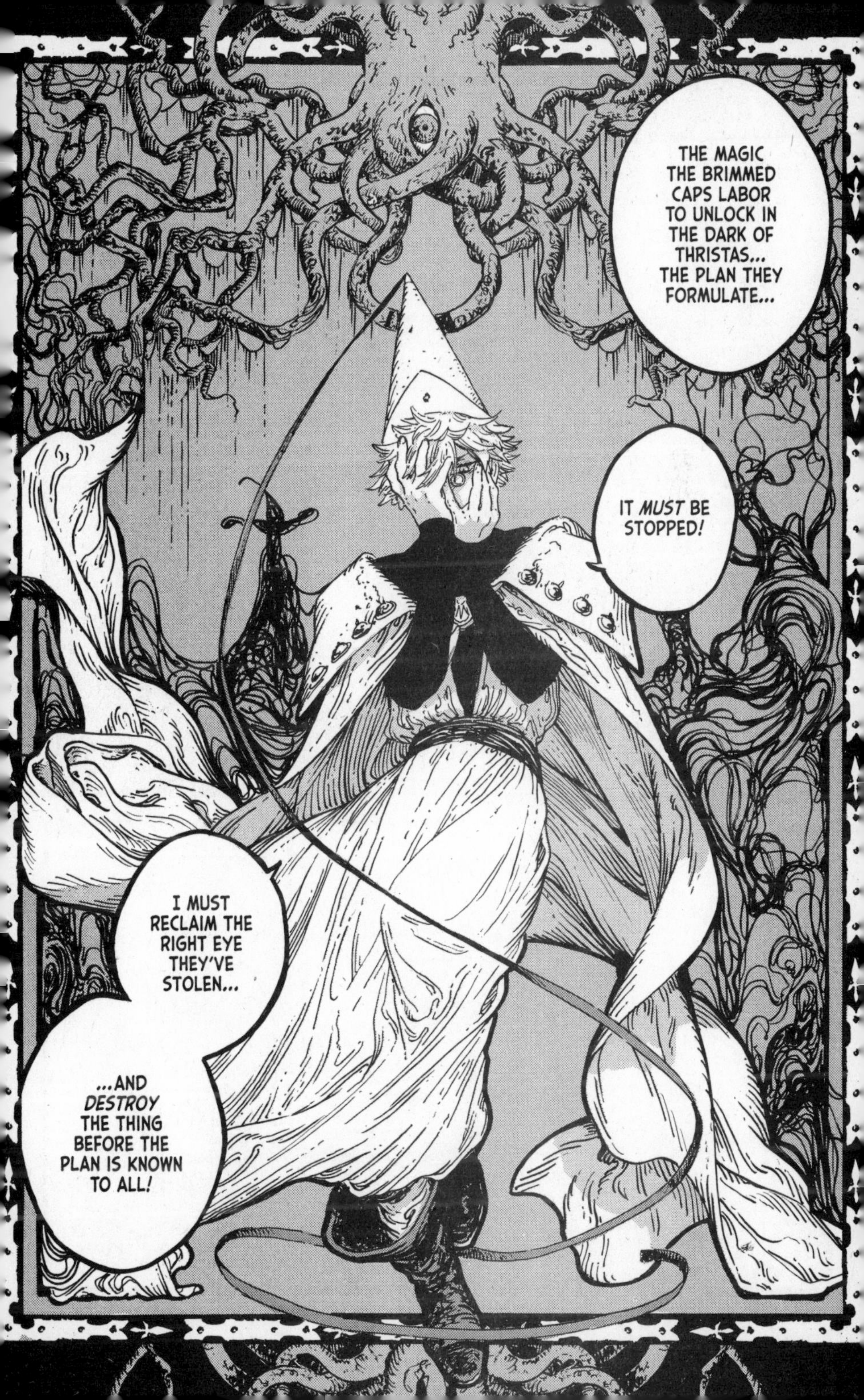
THE MAGIC THE BRIMMED CAPS LABOR TO UNLOCK IN THE DARK OF THRISTAS... THE PLAN THEY FORMULATE...
IT *MUST* BE STOPPED!
I MUST RECLAIM THE RIGHT EYE THEY'VE STOLEN...
...AND *DESTROY* THE THING BEFORE THE PLAN IS KNOWN TO ALL!

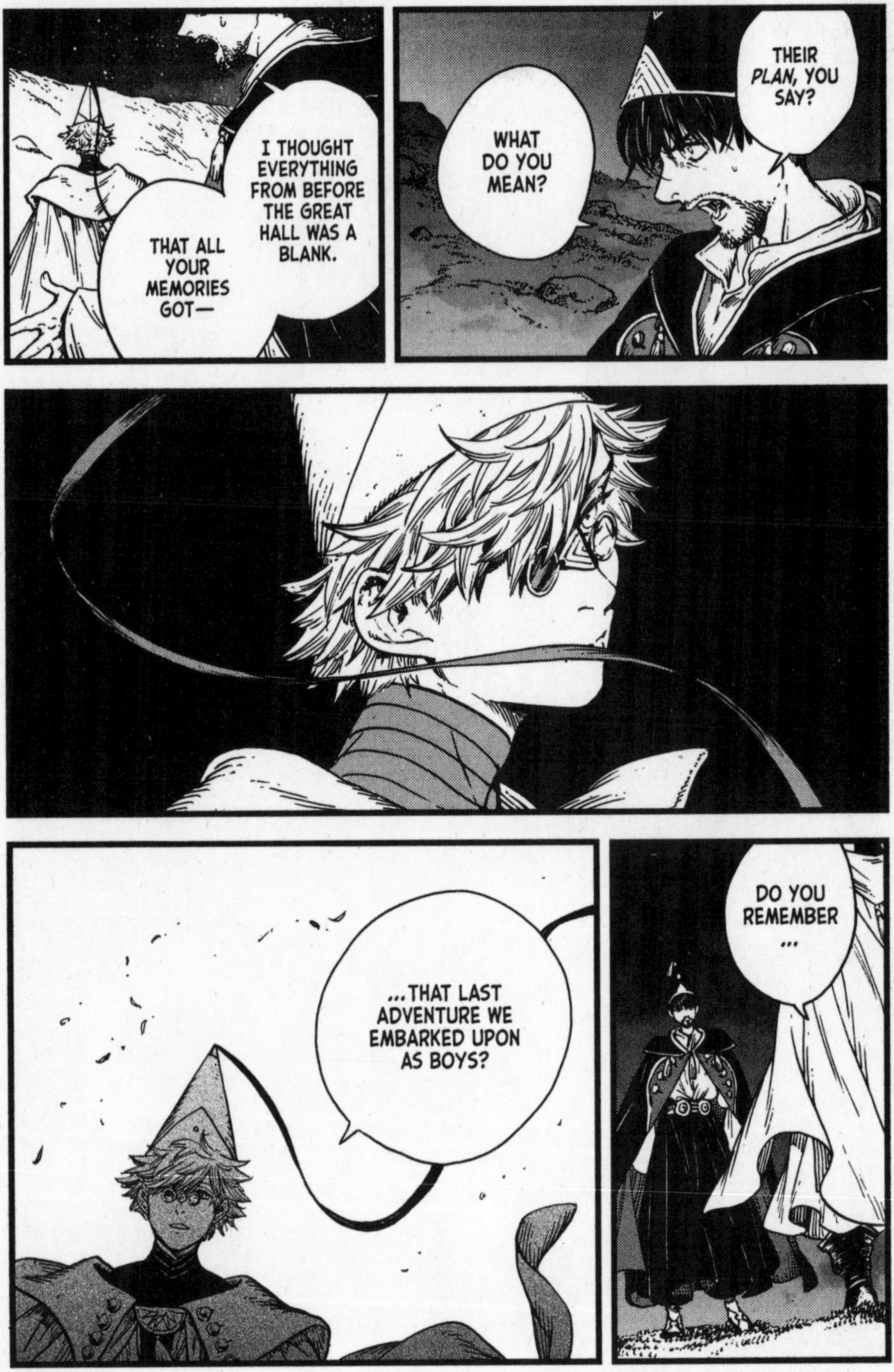
THEIR *PLAN*, YOU SAY?
WHAT DO YOU MEAN?
I THOUGHT EVERYTHING FROM BEFORE THE GREAT HALL WAS A BLANK.
THAT ALL YOUR MEMORIES GOT—
DO YOU REMEMBER ...
...THAT LAST ADVENTURE WE EMBARKED UPON AS BOYS?

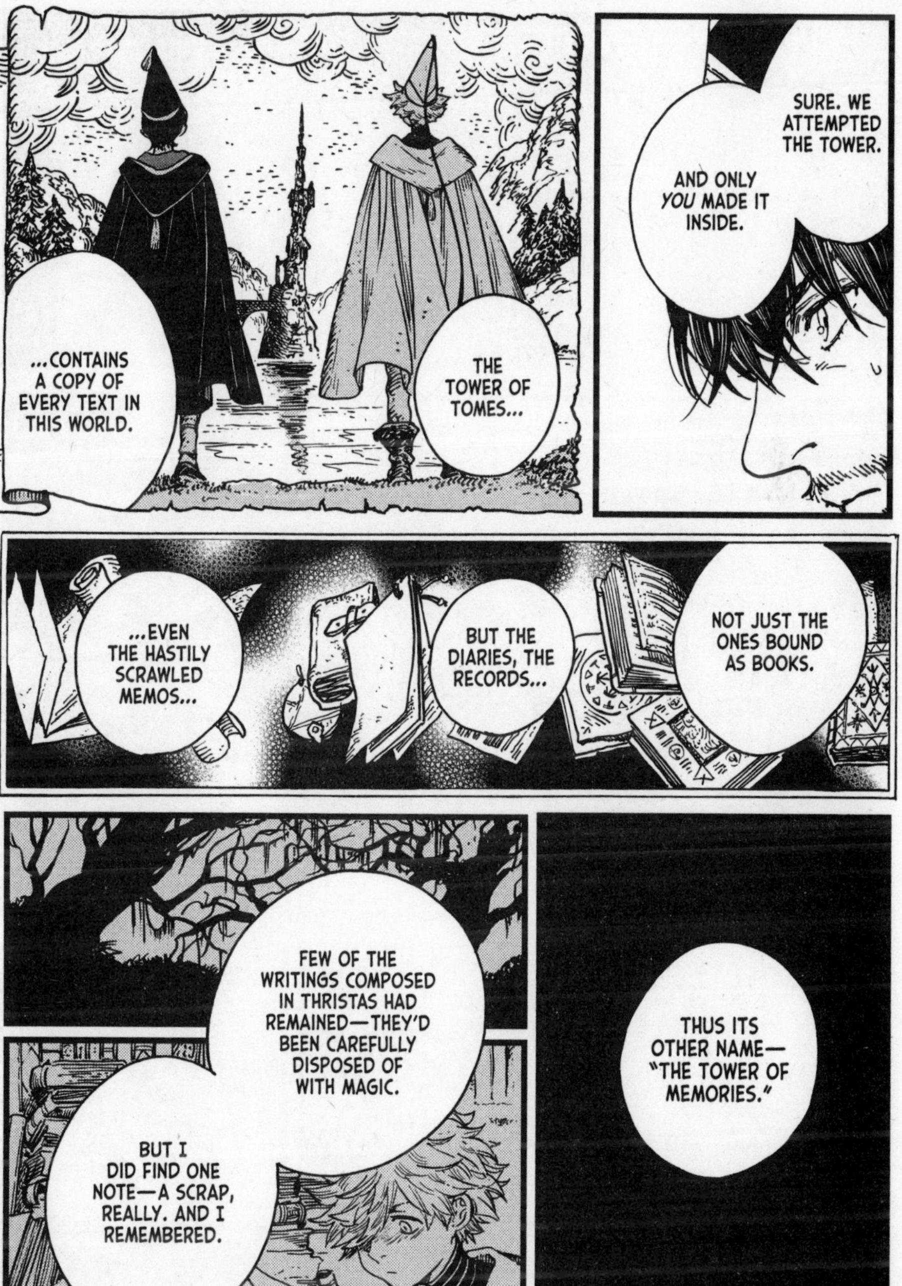
SURE. WE ATTEMPTED THE TOWER.
AND ONLY *YOU* MADE IT INSIDE.
THE TOWER OF TOMES...
...CONTAINS A COPY OF EVERY TEXT IN THIS WORLD.
NOT JUST THE ONES BOUND AS BOOKS.
BUT THE DIARIES, THE RECORDS...
...EVEN THE HASTILY SCRAWLED MEMOS...
THUS ITS OTHER NAME—"THE TOWER OF MEMORIES."
FEW OF THE WRITINGS COMPOSED IN THRISTAS HAD REMAINED—THEY'D BEEN CAREFULLY DISPOSED OF WITH MAGIC.
BUT I DID FIND ONE NOTE—A SCRAP, REALLY. AND I REMEMBERED.

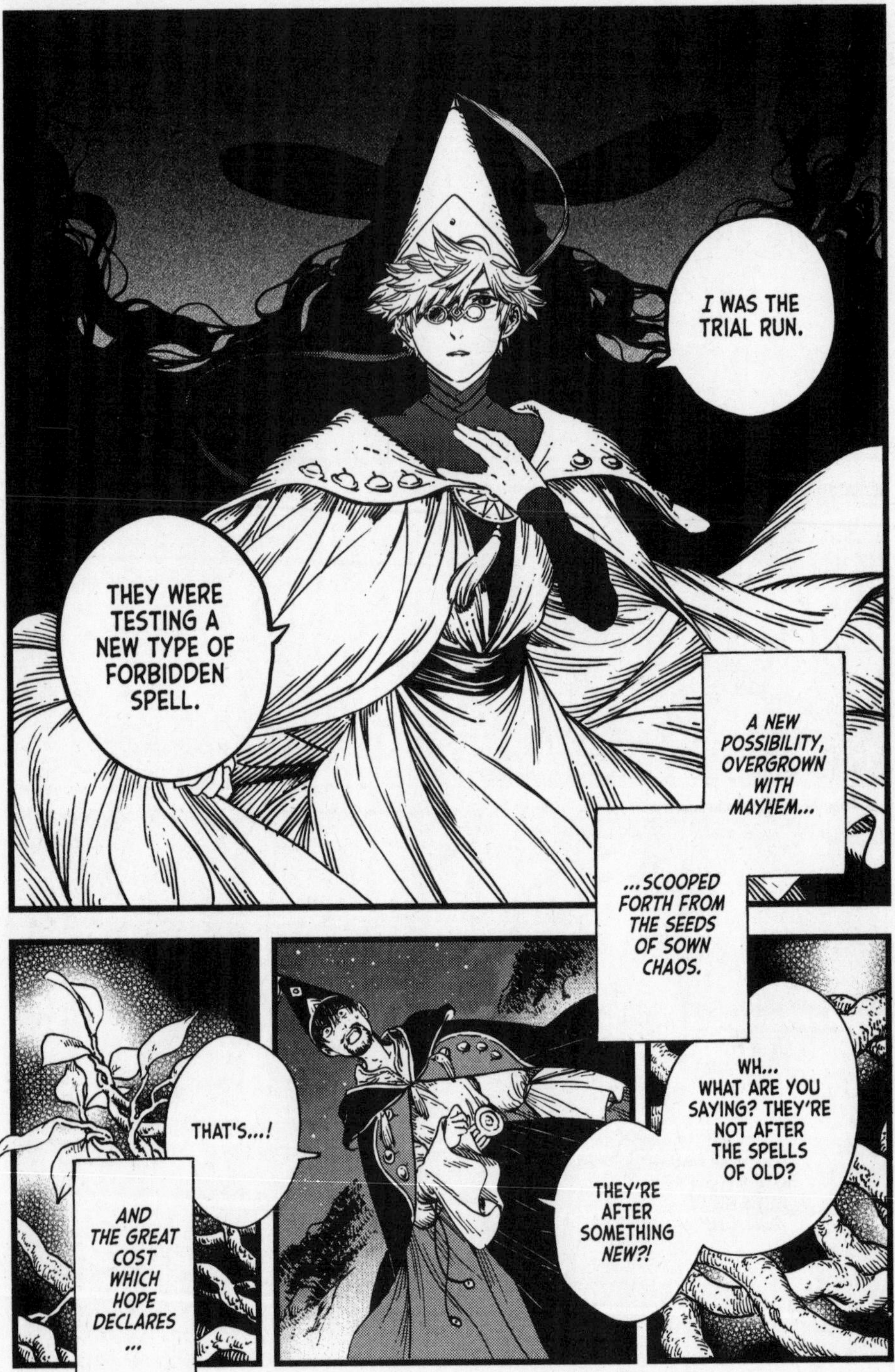

I WAS THE TRIAL RUN.
THEY WERE TESTING A NEW TYPE OF FORBIDDEN SPELL.
A NEW POSSIBILITY, OVERGROWN WITH MAYHEM...
...SCOOPED FORTH FROM THE SEEDS OF SOWN CHAOS.
WH... WHAT ARE YOU SAYING? THEY'RE NOT AFTER THE SPELLS OF OLD?
THEY'RE AFTER SOMETHING NEW?!
THAT'S...!
AND THE GREAT COST WHICH HOPE DECLARES ...

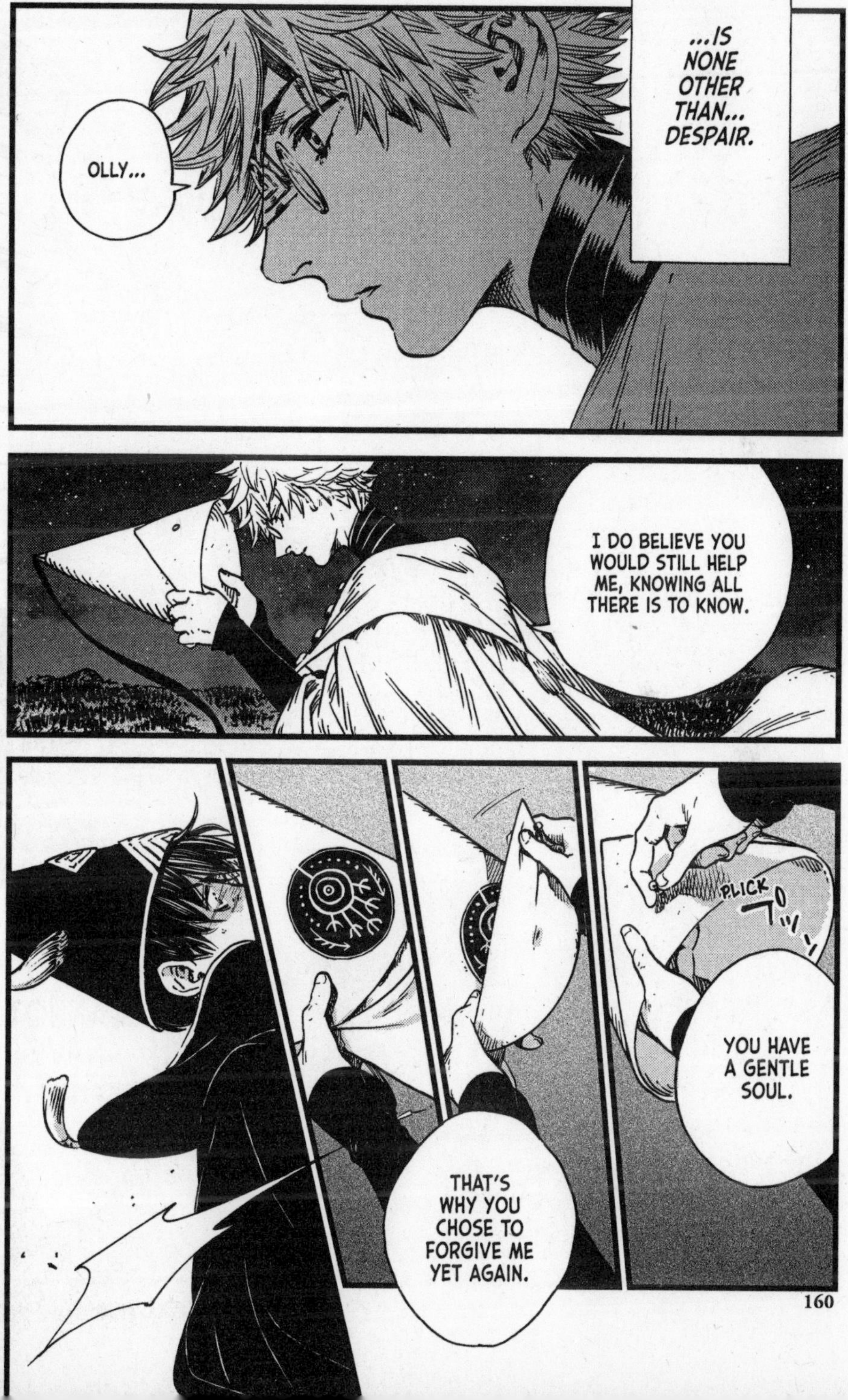
...IS NONE OTHER THAN... DESPAIR.
OLLY...
I DO BELIEVE YOU WOULD STILL HELP ME, KNOWING ALL THERE IS TO KNOW.
PLICK
YOU HAVE A GENTLE SOUL.
THAT'S WHY YOU CHOSE TO FORGIVE ME YET AGAIN.

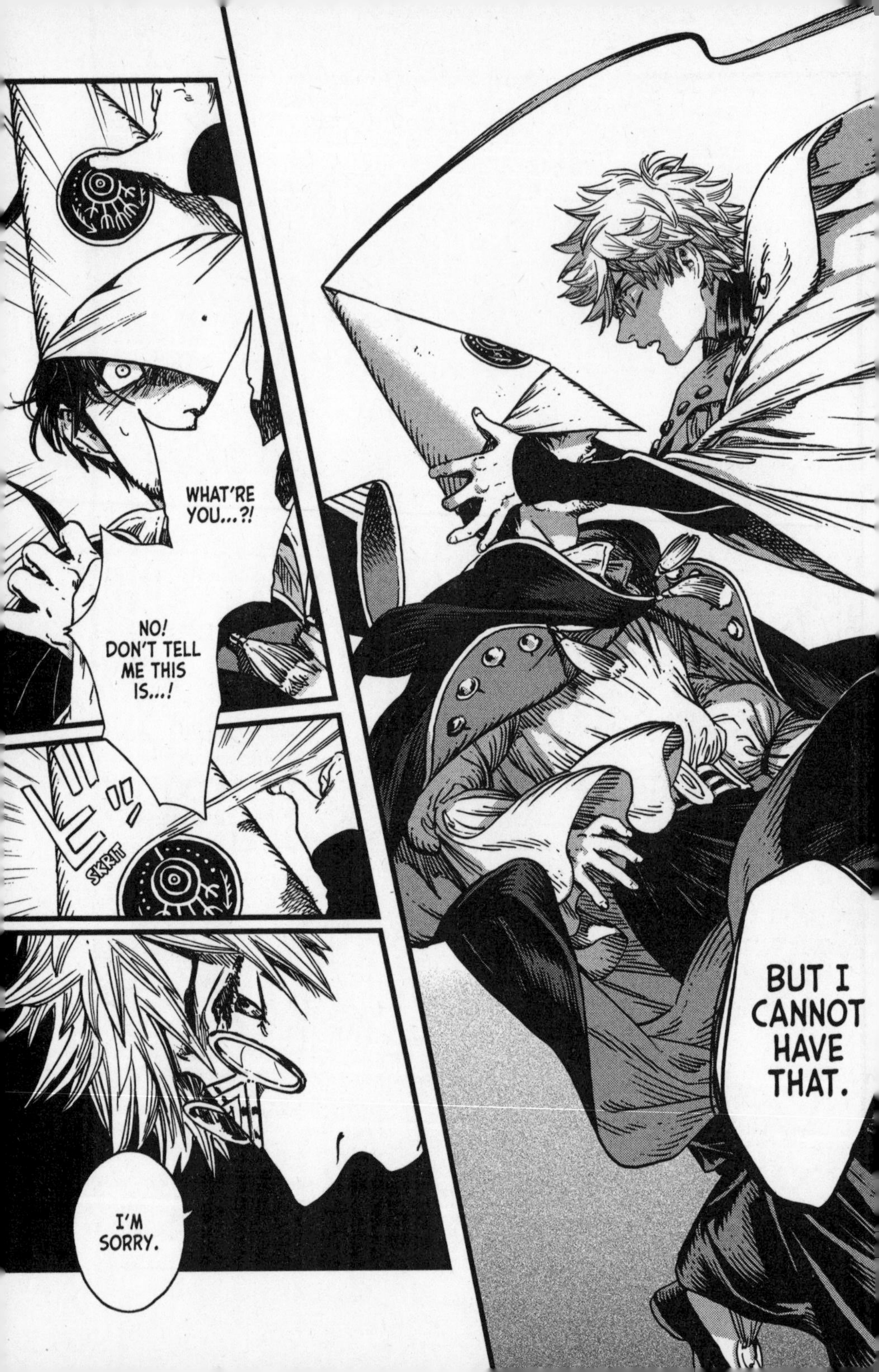
BUT I CANNOT HAVE THAT.
WHAT'RE YOU...?!
NO! DON'T TELL ME THIS IS...!
SKRIT
I'M SORRY.

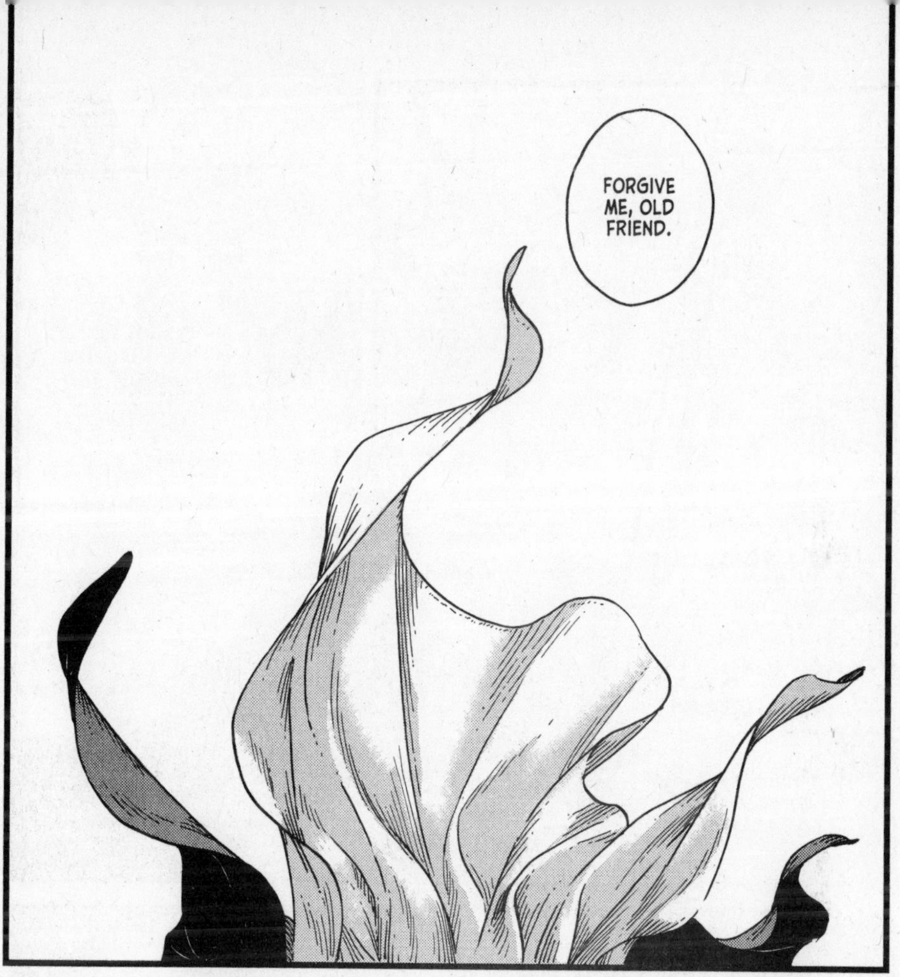
FORGIVE ME, OLD FRIEND.

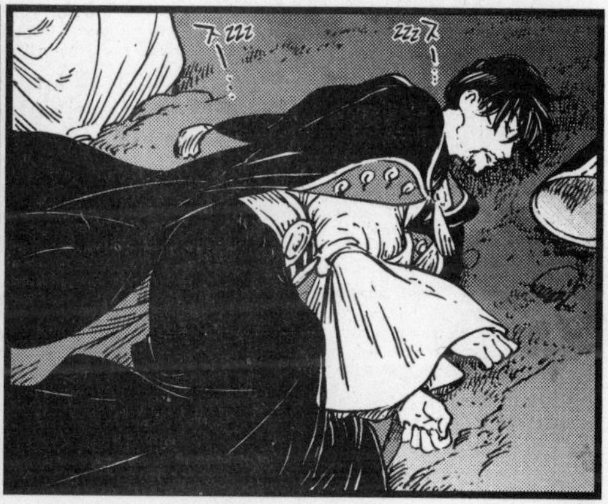
zzz
zzz

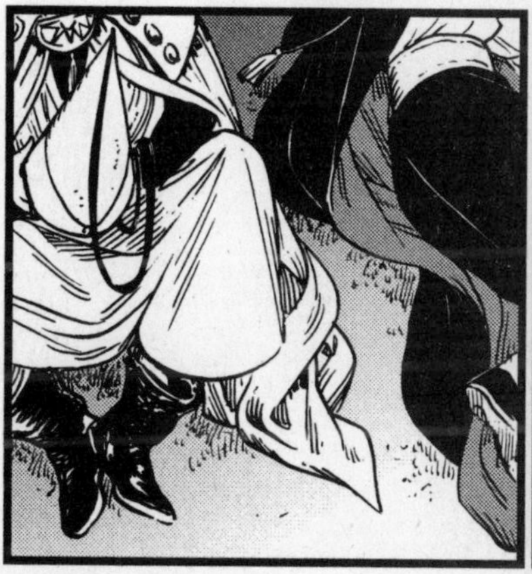

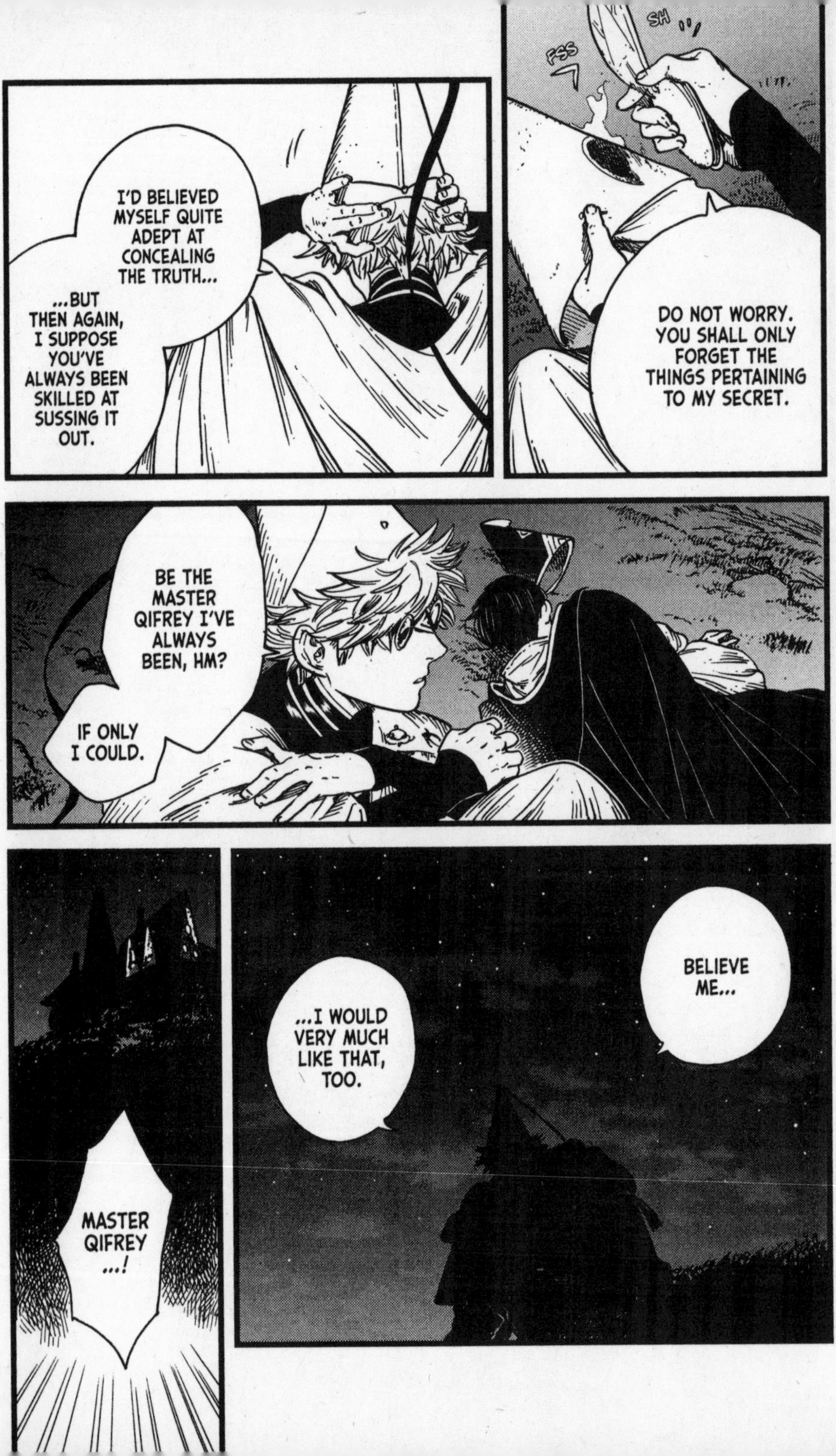
SH
FSS
DO NOT WORRY. YOU SHALL ONLY FORGET THE THINGS PERTAINING TO MY SECRET.
I'D BELIEVED MYSELF QUITE ADEPT AT CONCEALING THE TRUTH...
...BUT THEN AGAIN, I SUPPOSE YOU'VE ALWAYS BEEN SKILLED AT SUSSING IT OUT.
BE THE MASTER QIFREY I'VE ALWAYS BEEN, HM?
IF ONLY I COULD.
BELIEVE ME...
...I WOULD VERY MUCH LIKE THAT, TOO.
MASTER QIFREY ...!

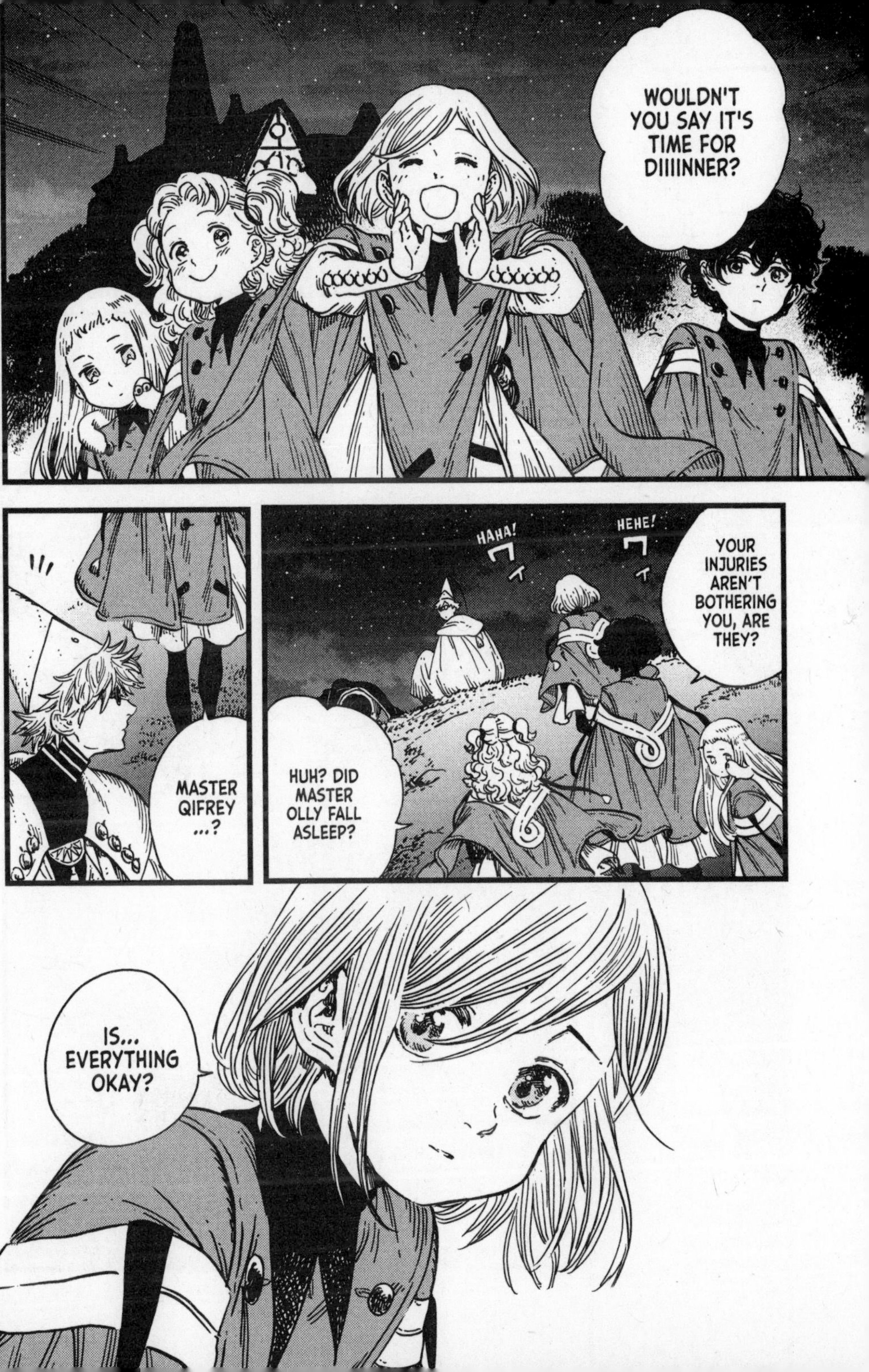
WOULDN'T YOU SAY IT'S TIME FOR DIIIINNER?
HEHE!
YOUR INJURIES AREN'T BOTHERING YOU, ARE THEY?
HAHA!
HUH? DID MASTER OLLY FALL ASLEEP?
MASTER QIFREY ...?
IS... EVERYTHING OKAY?

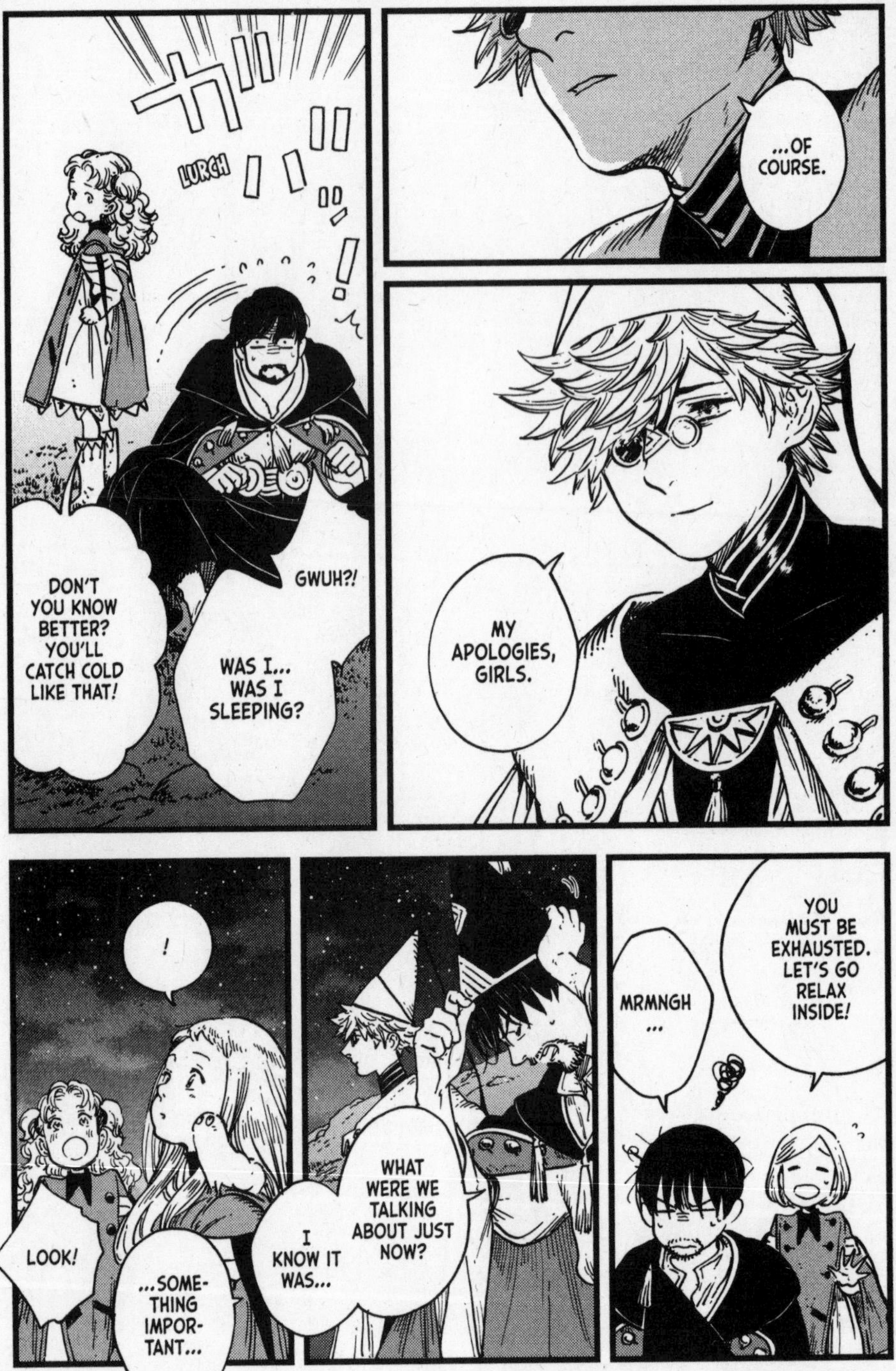
...OF COURSE.
MY APOLOGIES, GIRLS.
LURCH
GWUH?!
WAS I... WAS I SLEEPING?
DON'T YOU KNOW BETTER? YOU'LL CATCH COLD LIKE THAT!
YOU MUST BE EXHAUSTED. LET'S GO RELAX INSIDE!
MRMNGH...
WHAT WERE WE TALKING ABOUT JUST NOW?
I KNOW IT WAS...
!
...SOMETHING IMPORTANT...
LOOK!

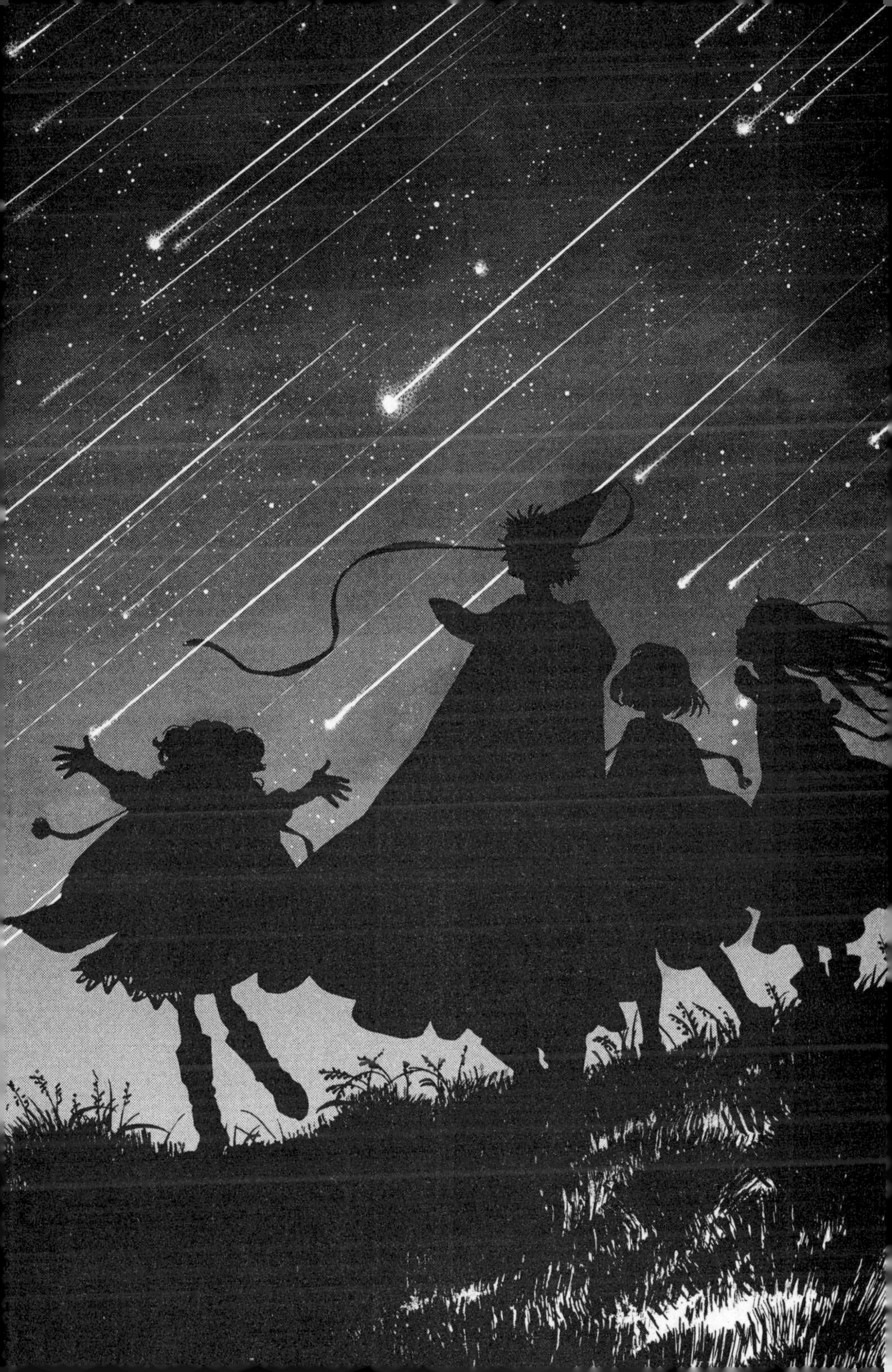

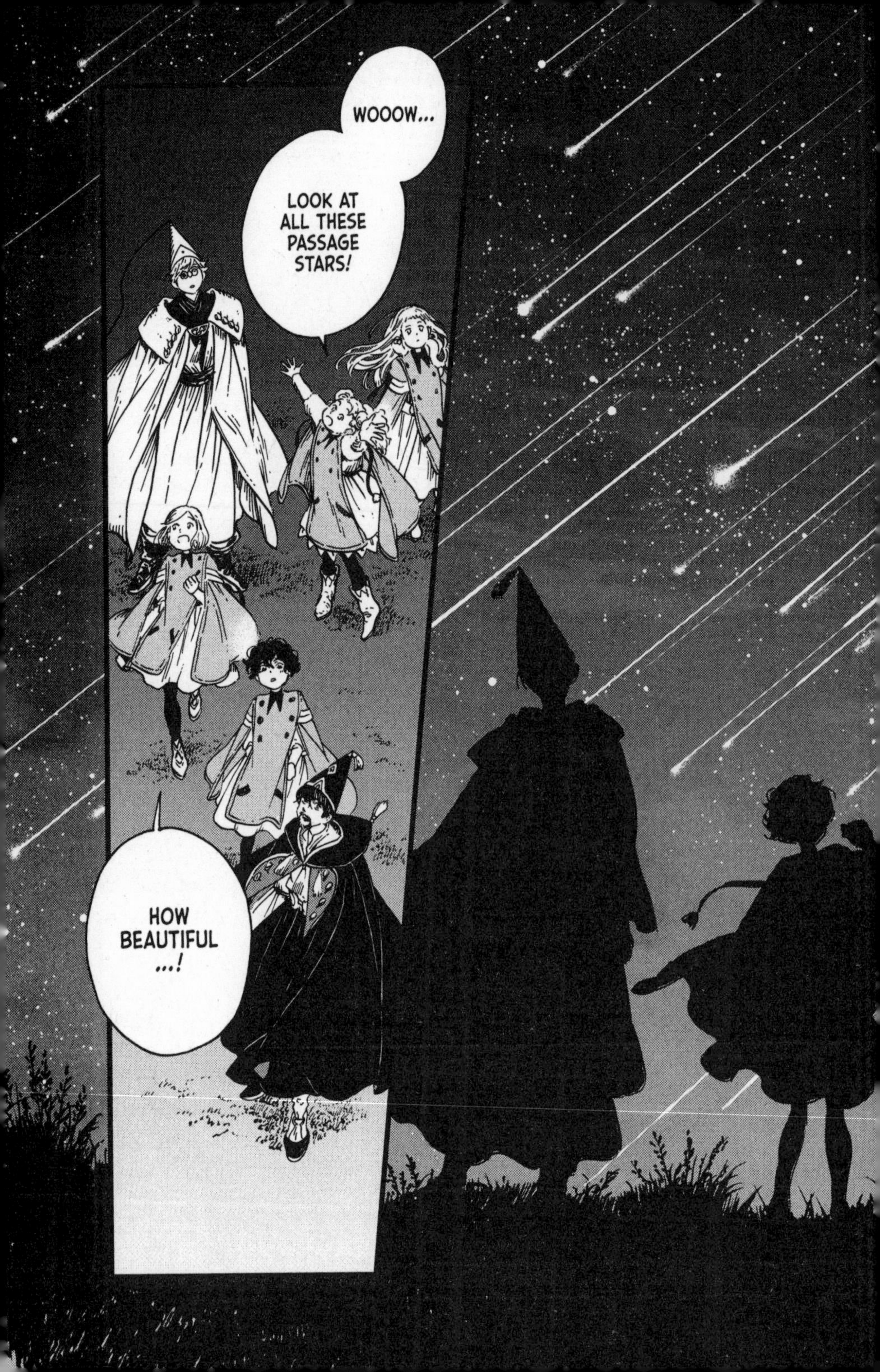
WOOOW...
LOOK AT ALL THESE PASSAGE STARS!
HOW BEAUTIFUL ...!

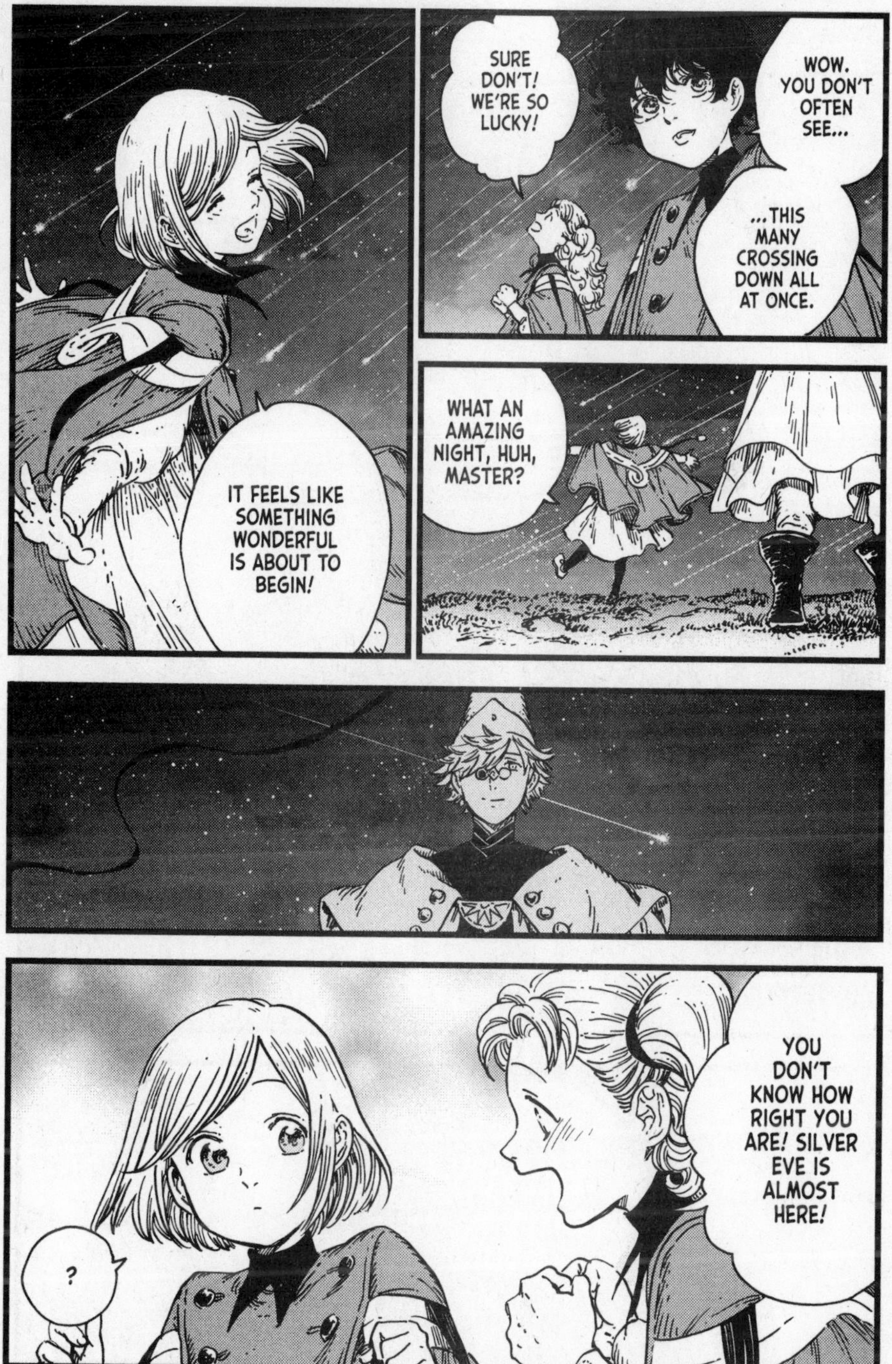
WOW. YOU DON'T OFTEN SEE...
...THIS MANY CROSSING DOWN ALL AT ONCE.
SURE DON'T! WE'RE SO LUCKY!
WHAT AN AMAZING NIGHT, HUH, MASTER?
IT FEELS LIKE SOMETHING WONDERFUL IS ABOUT TO BEGIN!
YOU DON'T KNOW HOW RIGHT YOU ARE! SILVER EVE IS ALMOST HERE!
?

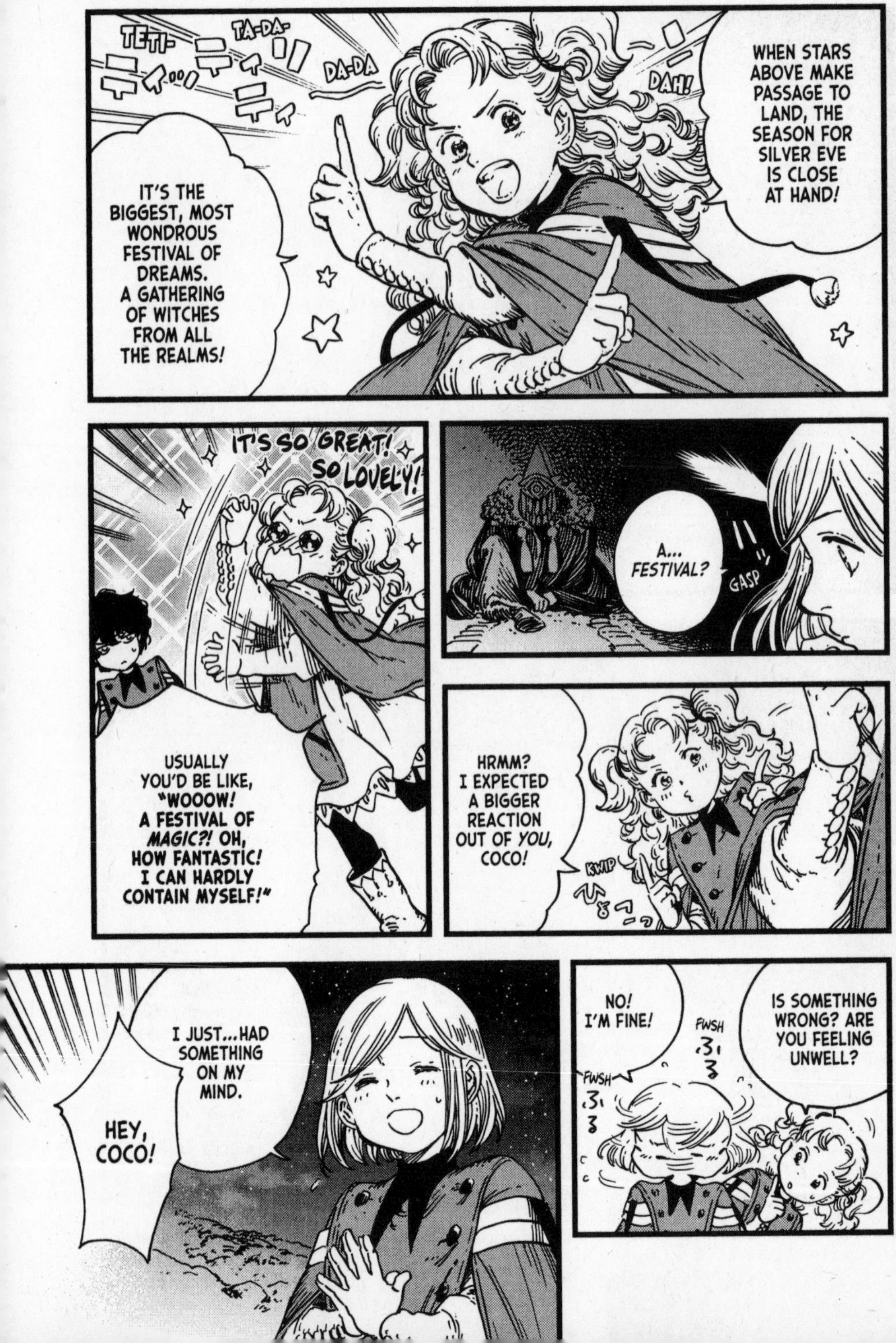
WHEN STARS ABOVE MAKE PASSAGE TO LAND, THE SEASON FOR SILVER EVE IS CLOSE AT HAND!
DAH!
DA-DA
TA-DA-
TETI-
IT'S THE BIGGEST, MOST WONDROUS FESTIVAL OF DREAMS. A GATHERING OF WITCHES FROM ALL THE REALMS!
A... FESTIVAL?
GASP
HRMM? I EXPECTED A BIGGER REACTION OUT OF *YOU*, COCO!
KWIP
IT'S SO GREAT! SO LOVELY!
USUALLY YOU'D BE LIKE, "WOOOW! A FESTIVAL OF *MAGIC?!* OH, HOW FANTASTIC! I CAN HARDLY CONTAIN MYSELF!"
IS SOMETHING WRONG? ARE YOU FEELING UNWELL?
NO! I'M FINE!
FWSH
FWSH
I JUST...HAD SOMETHING ON MY MIND.
HEY, COCO!

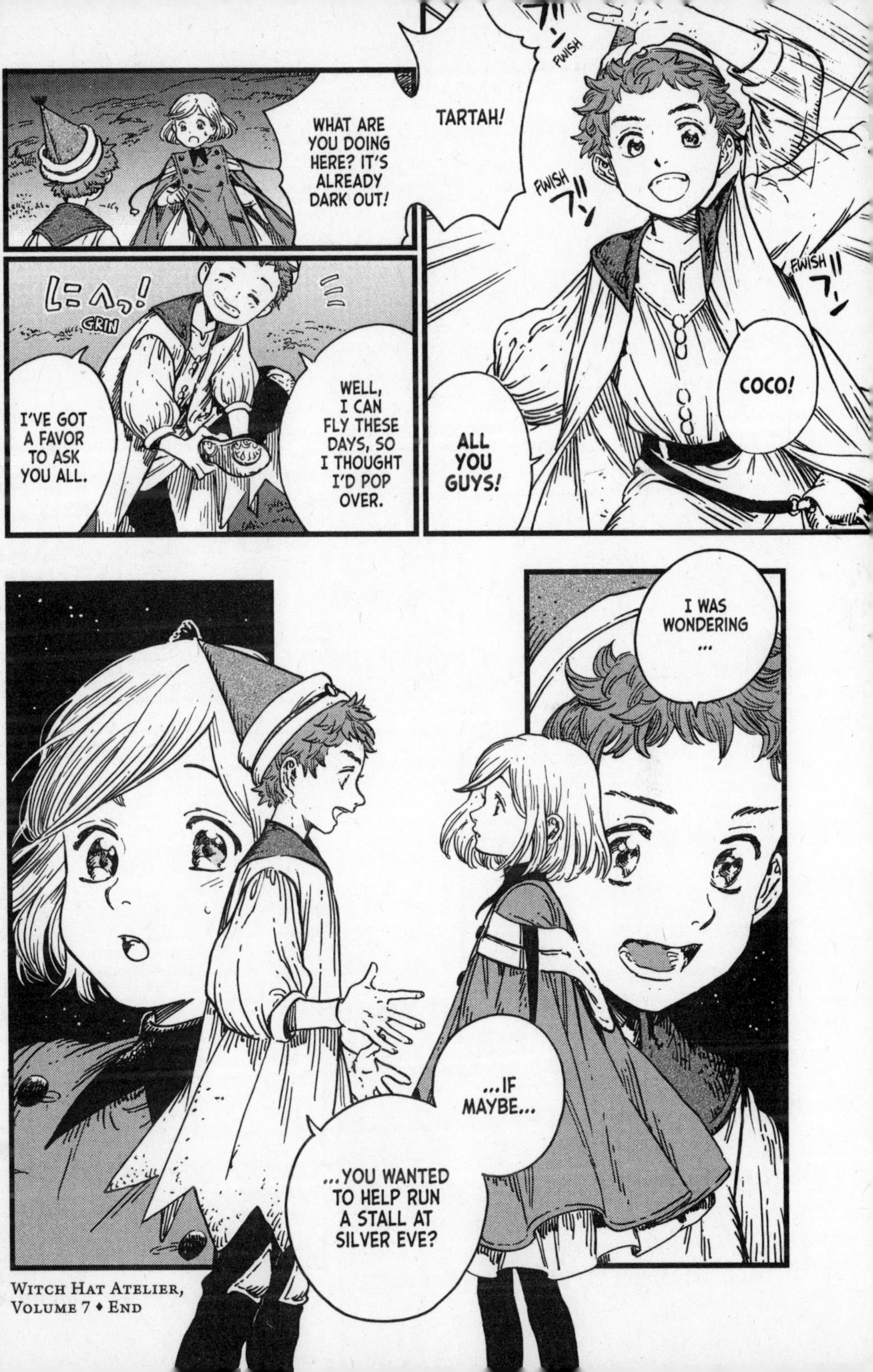
FWISH ブン
FWISH ブン
FWISH ブン
COCO!
ALL YOU GUYS!
TARTAH!
WHAT ARE YOU DOING HERE? IT'S ALREADY DARK OUT!
しにへっ!
GRIN
WELL, I CAN FLY THESE DAYS, SO I THOUGHT I'D POP OVER.
I'VE GOT A FAVOR TO ASK YOU ALL.
I WAS WONDERING ...
...IF MAYBE...
...YOU WANTED TO HELP RUN A STALL AT SILVER EVE?

Witch Hat Atelier, Volume 7 ♦ End

THE WORLD OF *WITCH HAT ATELIER*

2

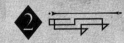

A BRIEF RECAP OF THE WORLD INHABITED BY COCO AND HER FRIENDS.

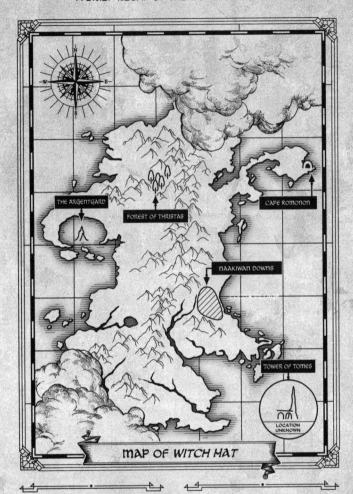

N
E
S
W
THE ARGENTGARD
FOREST OF THRISTAS
CAPE ROMONON
NAAKIWAN DOWNS
TOWER OF TOMES
LOCATION UNKNOWN
MAP OF *WITCH HAT*

CAPE ROMONON

THE SITE OF THE SECOND TEST, "THE SINCERITY OF THE SHIELD," AND THE LOCATION OF THE SERPENTBACK CAVE—A MYSTICAL RUIN FROM THE AGE OF CHAOS, NOW LEFT UNTRODDEN EXCEPT FOR THE TEST. THE NEARBY CLIFFTOPS ARE AN IMPORTANT BREEDING GROUND FOR MYRPHON.

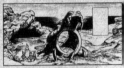

THE ARGENTGARD

A QUIET GARDEN AT THE CENTER OF DEEPWATER CASTLE. ITS CALM, SANDY BANKS SERVE AS A PLACE OF RELAXATION FOR THE MANY WITCHES WHO LIVE AT THE GREAT HALL, AS WELL AS A HOME TO SILVERWOODS, MYSTICAL TREES THAT PROVIDE WOODCRUOR, THE KEY INGREDIENT OF CONJURING INK.

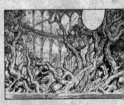

TOWER OF TOMES

A MYSTICAL TOWER IN WHICH A COPY OF EVERY BOOK APPEARS THE MOMENT IT IS CREATED. VIGILANTLY MANAGED BY WITCHES TASKED TO SERVE AS LIBRARIANS. THE MOST PROMINENT FOUR ADMINISTER TRIALS TO ALL WHO SEEK ENTRANCE; ONLY THOSE WHO PASS GAIN THE RIGHT TO STEP INSIDE.

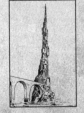

NAAKIWAN DOWNS

THE HILLY REGION HOME TO QIFREY'S ATELIER. WINDY, DOTTED WITH COUNTLESS BOULDERS AND SHRUBS, AND WELL-TRAVERSED BY WILDLIFE, INCLUDING SCALEWOLVES, TASSELMICE, AND GRAVEWATCHER FOXES. DURING THE SEASON FOR PASSAGE STARS, SCHOOLS OF ASH-MOTTLED DRAGONS SOAR THROUGH ITS SKIES.

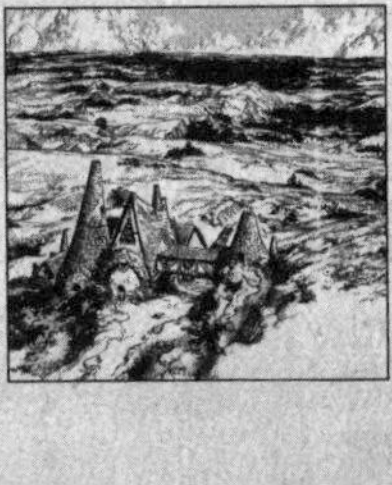

FOREST OF THRISTAS

A FOREST OF DEATH, EVERY PART OF WHICH IS DYED BLACK. ONCE A GLITTERING EXPANSE O SILVERWOODS, IT CHANGED TO A SHADOWY, MIASMA-CHOKED EXPANSE WHEN THE DARK WITC THRISTAS USED IT AS A SITE TO EXPERIMENT WITH FORBIDDEN MAGIC, SEEKING A MEANS TO RESURRECT THE DEAD.

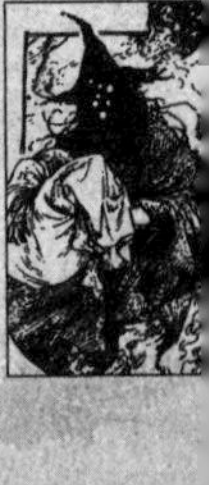

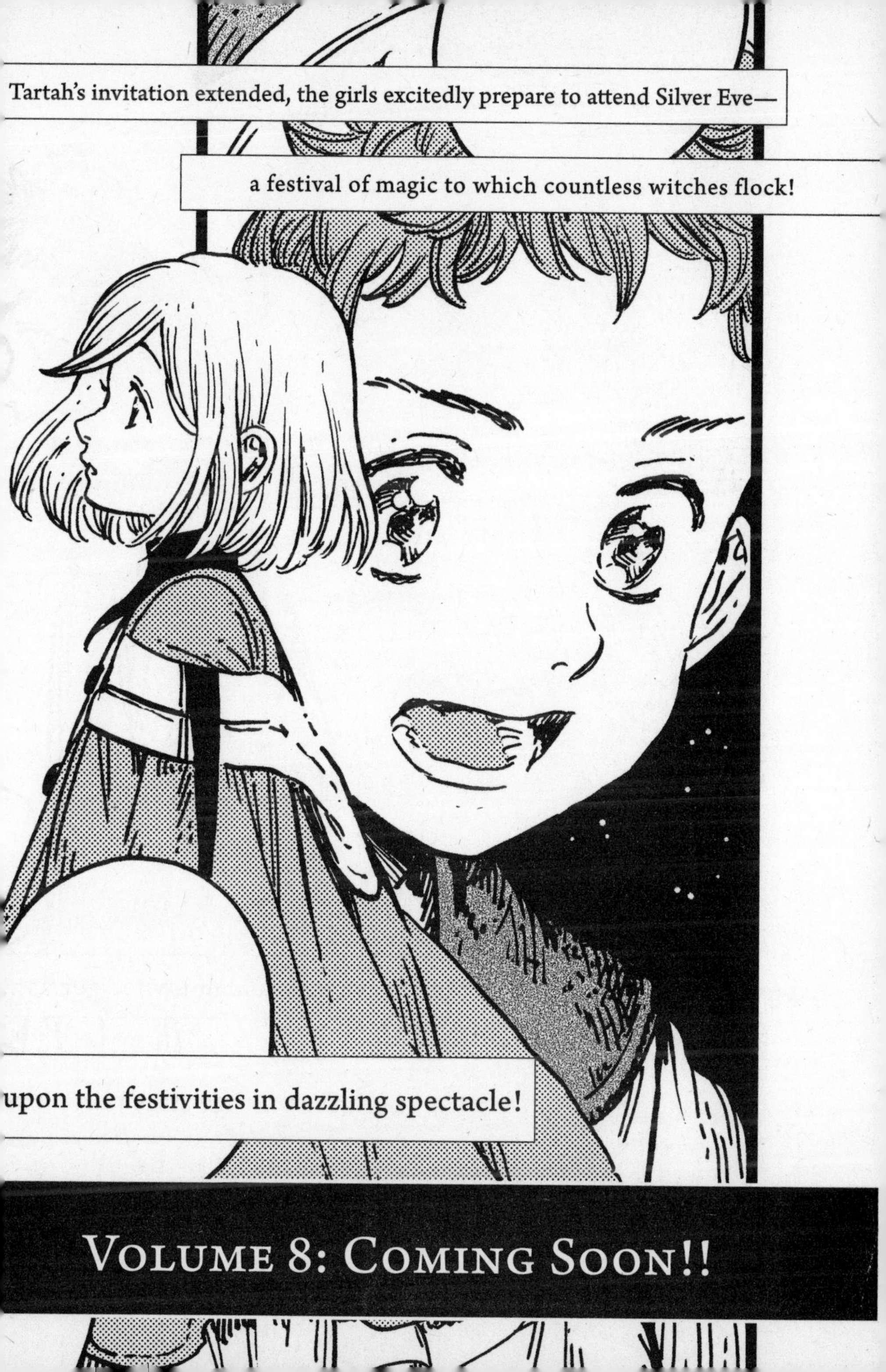
Tartah's invitation extended, the girls excitedly prepare to attend Silver Eve—
a festival of magic to which countless witches flock!
upon the festivities in dazzling spectacle!
Volume 8: Coming Soon!!

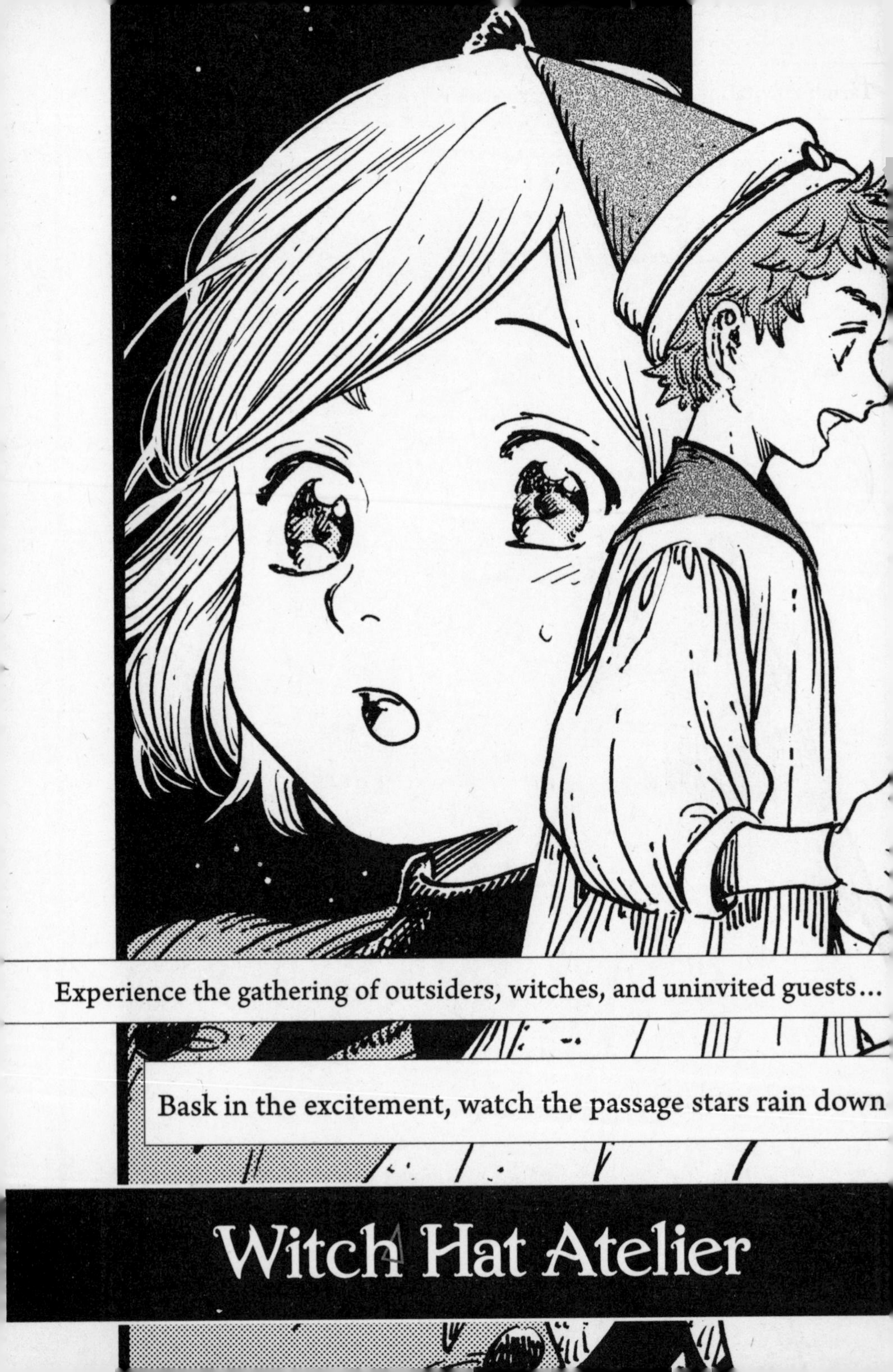
Experience the gathering of outsiders, witches, and uninvited guests...
Bask in the excitement, watch the passage stars rain down
Witch Hat Atelier

Young characters and steampunk setting, like *Howl's Moving Castle* and *Battle Angel Alita*

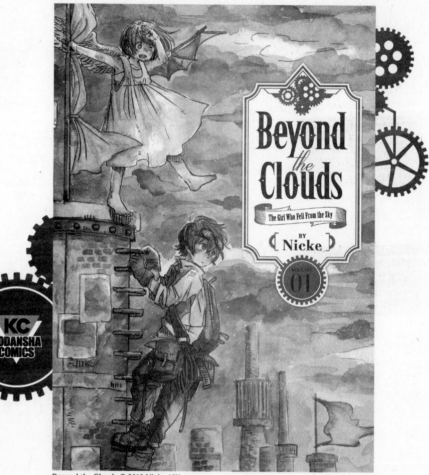

Beyond the Clouds © 2018 Nicke / Ki-oon

A boy with a talent for machines and a mysterious girl whose wings he's fixed will take you beyond the clouds! In the tradition of the high-flying, resonant adventure stories of Studio Ghibli comes a gorgeous tale about the longing of young hearts for adventure and friendship!

CUTE ANIMALS AND LIFE LESSONS, PERFECT FOR ASPIRING PET VETS OF ALL AGES!

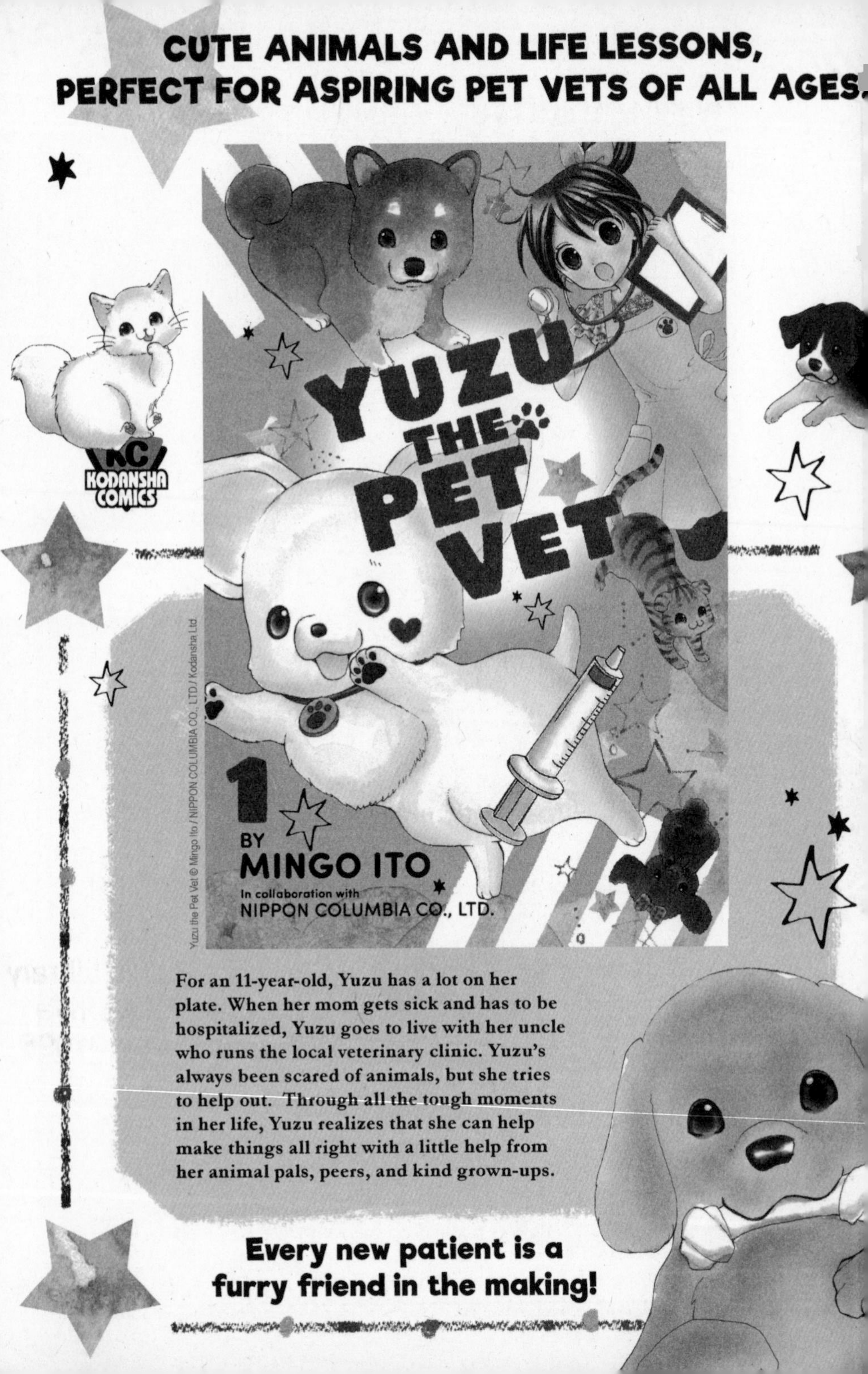
YUZU THE PET VET
1
BY
MINGO ITO
In collaboration with
NIPPON COLUMBIA CO., LTD.

For an 11-year-old, Yuzu has a lot on her plate. When her mom gets sick and has to be hospitalized, Yuzu goes to live with her uncle who runs the local veterinary clinic. Yuzu's always been scared of animals, but she tries to help out. Through all the tough moments in her life, Yuzu realizes that she can help make things all right with a little help from her animal pals, peers, and kind grown-ups.

Every new patient is a furry friend in the making!

Witch Hat Atelier 7 is a work of fiction. Names, characters, places, and incidents are the products of the author's imagination or are used fictitiously. Any resemblance to actual events, locales, or persons, living or dead, is entirely coincidental.

A Kodansha Comics Trade Paperback Original

Published in the United States by Kodansha Comics, an imprint of Kodansha USA Publishing, LLC, New York.

Publication rights for this English edition arranged through Kodansha Ltd., Tokyo.

First published in Japan in 2020 by Kodansha Ltd., Tokyo as *Tongari Boshi no Atorie*, volume 7

ISBN 978-1-64651-078-8

Original cover design by SAVA DESIGN

Printed in the United States of America.

www.kodansha.us

9 8 7 6
Translation: Stephen Kohler
Lettering: Lys Blakeslee
Editing: Haruko Hashimoto
Kodansha Comics edition cover design by Phil Balsman

KC KODANSHA COMICS

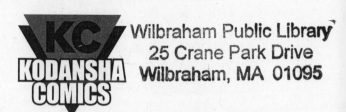

Publisher: Kiichiro Sugawara
Vice president of marketing & publicity: Naho Yamada

Director of publishing services: Ben Applegate
Associate director of operations: Stephen Pakula
Publishing services managing editor: Noelle Webster
Assistant production manager: Emi Lotto, Angela Zurlo